THE MYTH OF RIGHTS

THE MYTH OF RIGHTS

THE PURPOSES AND LIMITS OF

CONSTITUTIONAL RIGHTS

ASHUTOSH BHAGWAT

OXFORD
UNIVERSITY PRESS

Oxford University Press, Inc., publishes works that further Oxford University's objective of excellence in research, scholarship, and education.

Oxford   New York
Auckland   Cape Town   Dar es Salaam   Hong Kong   Karachi   Kuala Lumpur   Madrid
Melbourne   Mexico City   Nairobi   New Delhi   Shanghai   Taipei   Toronto

With offices in
Argentina   Austria   Brazil   Chile   Czech Republic   France   Greece   Guatemala   Hungary
Italy   Japan   Poland   Portugal   Singapore   South Korea   Switzerland   Thailand
Turkey   Ukraine   Vietnam

Published by Oxford University Press, Inc.
198 Madison Avenue, New York, New York 10016

Oxford is a registered trademark of Oxford University Press
Oxford University Press is a registered trademark of Oxford University Press, Inc.

First printing in paperback, 2012   ISBN 978-0-19-989774-2 (paperback : alk. paper)
The Library of Congress has catalogued the hardcover edition as follows:

Library of Congress Cataloging-in-Publication Data

Bhagwat, Ashutosh A.
  The myth of rights : the purposes and limits of constitutional
  rights / Ashutosh Bhagwat.
      p. cm.
  Includes bibliographical references and index.
  ISBN 978-0-19-537778-1 (hardback : alk. paper)
  1. Civil rights—United States. I. Title.
  KF4749.B48 2010
  342.7308'5—dc22   2009038185

Printed in the United States of America on acid-free paper

Note to Readers
This publication is designed to provide accurate and authoritative information in regard to the subject matter covered. It is based upon sources believed to be accurate and reliable and is intended to be current as of the time it was written. It is sold with the understanding that the publisher is not engaged in rendering legal, accounting, or other professional services. If legal advice or other expert assistance is required, the services of a competent professional person should be sought. Also, to confirm that the information has not been affected or changed by recent developments, traditional legal research techniques should be used, including checking primary sources where appropriate.

(Based on the Declaration of Principles jointly adopted by a Committee of the American Bar Association and a Committee of Publishers and Associations.)

You may order this or any other Oxford University Press publication by
visiting the Oxford University Press website at www.oup.com

For Uma and Declan, who know they have no rights

CONTENTS

ACKNOWLEDGMENTS

I first started thinking about this book during a sabbatical in the fall of 2001. In the midst of that semester came the attacks of September 11, which profoundly changed the way I and most Americans view the world and our nation's place in it. The ensuing years brought the War on Terror, the Second Iraq War, the election of President Barack Obama, and a panoply of political and constitutional conflicts. On a personal level, the intervening years saw the birth of my son, two years working on the administrative side of legal education, and a host of other changes in my life. The book that has emerged at the end of these experiences is profoundly different from the book I first envisioned. This is not a book about the War on Terror; it is a book about government, and the role for government in our society that the Constitution of the United States envisions. But, while my fundamental views on that subject have not changed, events of the past decade have highlighted particular problems and concerns which receive detailed attention here.

This book could never have happened without support from my friends, family, and colleagues. Special thanks to Aditya Bhagwat, Mike Dorf, Evan Lee, and John McManus for providing very helpful comments, and extra special thanks to Bill Dodge for careful, detailed, substantive comments that went well beyond the demands of friendship. This book would have been a far lesser thing without their help. Thanks also to the Board of Directors and to Deans Mary Kay Kane, Nell Newton, and Shauna Marshall of the University of California, Hastings College of the Law for supporting this research in a myriad ways, including an appointment to the Harry H. and Lillian H. Hastings Research Chair which permitted me the necessary time away from teaching, in order to complete my writing.

Finally, and above all, thanks to my wife, Shannon Gaffney. It is a cliché to acknowledge the support of one's family, but in this case I can testify without hesitation that without Shannon's support, love, encouragement, and a critically timed (metaphorical) kick in the pants, I would never have written this book. Hopefully it was all worth it.

1. THE MYTH OF RIGHTS
Of Aliens, Corporations, and Guns

From the time the American Republic was founded, the idea that we are a People with *rights* has been an essential element of our understanding of ourselves as a nation. We may disagree about what those right are, or what their source is, but that Americans have rights has been accepted as a truth beyond dispute. Furthermore, this distinctly American notion of rights has long been closely associated with our Constitution, and in particular with the first ten amendments to the Constitution, the Bill of Rights, as well as the Fourteenth Amendment (which was added in 1868, in the wake of the Civil War, to protect newly emancipated African Americans from racist state governments). This particular view of rights, as personal, legally binding, inalienable, and written into our founding document, has been and continues to be an essential component of the American experience of self-government. Indeed, arguably our self-definition as a People with constitutional rights is what marks us as different from the rest of the world, what makes the United States special and unique. Nonetheless, it is the thesis of this book that whatever they may believe, American citizens have no constitutional rights as that word is generally understood, and indeed, that the very notion of constitutional rights is a myth. Furthermore, the Bill of Rights, despite its name and language, does not even purport to create individual rights as they are today understood. It is not that the Bill of Rights is not important—indeed, its provisions form an essential part of the structure of our government—but its provisions do not create individual rights. The idea that the Constitution does create rights is based on a misunderstanding founded in changes in political thinking and language usage in the two hundred plus years since the Constitution was ratified. Thus the entire modern edifice of theory, belief, and romance that has been built around the existence of constitutional rights is hollow, a structure without a foundation.

The primary focus of this book will be on the provisions and amendments of the Constitution that are generally understood to grant the most important individual rights: the First Amendment, which is said to create the rights of free speech, freedom of assembly, free exercise of religion, and separation of church and state (i.e., no establishment of religion); the Second Amendment, which speaks of a right to keep and bear arms; and the Fifth and Fourteenth Amendments, which are said to give rights to due process of law and to the equal protection of the laws.[1] Despite the fact that all of these provisions have long

---

1. I will not focus closely on the "criminal procedure" provisions of the Bill of Rights, such as the search-and-seizure limitations of the Fourth Amendment and the provisions

been understood to create individual rights, and indeed some of them even *speak* of rights, it is the contention of this book that in fact none of them create true, individual rights. Americans have no right to speak that shields them from all governmental interference when they speak. People are stopped from speaking, or punished for their speech all the time, completely in accordance with the Constitution. Even flag-burners, those famously protected speakers, may be punished by the government under any number of laws. Similarly, there is no right to free exercise of religion, as countless Americans from Mormons to members of the Native American Church have discovered over the years. There is also no right to bear arms, no right not to be discriminated against, and so on with all the other rights purportedly created in the Constitution.

To understand why this is so, why the primary "rights-creating" provisions of the Constitution do not in fact create individual rights, it is necessary to first understand what in modern American parlance it means to possess a "constitutional right."[2] As we understand the term "right" today, it is inevitably understood as an *individual* entitlement, a license to engage in (or refuse to engage in) some behavior free from interference from others, most notably the government (or more accurately, from governments, whether state or federal). In other words, possessing a right grants an individual the power to create a sphere of autonomy in her personal life. Constitutional rights in particular identify certain "fundamental" types of activities such as speech or (more controversially) choosing an abortion, and shield them from *governmental* interference. Probably the best expression of this idea is one Ronald Dworkin has popularized, that a right is a trump held by an individual against the government, entitling the individual to stop the government from interfering with her actions or freedom even when the common good would seem to be advanced by such interference.[3] There are thus two essential components to a constitutional right: first, it provides a powerful shield for particular kinds of conduct against governmental interference; and second that it is possessed by *individuals*, by people who are empowered to invoke a right when the government tries to stop them from doing something they want to do. If either component is missing there is no *right*, as commonly understood.

Under this understanding of what it means to have a right, which I will argue is the only possible one, the Constitution and the Bill of Rights do not create rights at all, for two different reasons. First, those provisions do not provide true

---

of the Fifth and Sixth Amendments, because they raise somewhat distinct questions. The basic approach presented in this book, however, applies fully to those provisions, as is briefly discussed in Chapter 2.

2. I should emphasize at the outset that this is a book about American constitutional rights. It is not a book about the theory of rights generally, and it does not seek to address or answer the vast jurisprudential literature regarding the abstract nature of rights.

3. *See* RONALD DWORKIN, TAKING RIGHTS SERIOUSLY xi (1977).

shields for any particular kind of conduct. Thus despite the First Amendment, the government retains the practical power to punish speech or religious exercise, and despite the Fourteenth Amendment the government remains able to distinguish among citizens based on their race or gender (or any number of other criteria). Second, and even more importantly, the Constitution does not grant, indeed does not even claim to grant, *individuals* any particular license, entitlement, or "right" (using the term in its modern sense) to engage in particular behavior. The Constitution and the Bill of Rights generally do not speak in terms of individuals at all, they speak in terms of "the People" and the rights of the People,[4] but those terms were understood during the framing period in *collective* terms, as powers and prerogatives retained by the population as a whole as against the State,[5] not as individual entitlements. It was only during the late nineteenth and twentieth centuries that rights came to be understood, in popular and legal parlance, in individualistic terms. This understanding has undoubtedly entered the *language* of constitutional law and the decisions of judges, but as I will demonstrate in this book, it hides and distorts the reality of constitutional practice, which continues to reflect an absence of meaningful individual rights.

One might ask, if the Bill of Rights and the Fourteenth Amendment do not create individual rights, then what if anything do they do? The answer is that these parts of the Constitution place specific, limited constraints on the government's exercise of power, on the scope of governmental authority. In other words, rather than granting individual rights, the Constitution limits governmental actions, it says what the government may not do. Thus the First Amendment does not grant individuals a "right" to free speech, it says instead that the government may not act *in particular ways* to restrain or punish speech. Similarly, the Equal Protection Clause of the Fourteenth Amendment does not grant individuals a right not to be discriminated against, it prevents the government from treating similarly situated people differently for specific reasons or in specific ways.

But does this distinction matter? What difference does it make if the Constitution is said to grant rights, or to limit power? In fact, it makes a great deal of difference. At the most basic level, shifting from a fruitless and empty

---

4. The statement requires some qualification. While the most important of the Bill of Rights, including notably the First, Second, Fourth, and Ninth Amendments, speak of "the People" generally, it is true that certain provisions, including notably the criminal procedure provisions of the Fifth and Sixth Amendments, including the Due Process Clause, do seem to focus on individuals, providing protections to "persons" and "the accused." However, for reasons that will be elucidated briefly in Chapter 2, these provisions also do not truly create individual rights, as commonly understood.

5. The term "the State," as used throughout this book, refers generally to government, at any particular level—i.e., federal, state, or local. When it is necessary to distinguish between different levels of government, especially between the federal government and the governments of the fifty states, that distinction will be drawn explicitly.

debate about what kinds of "rights" individuals have and when they are violated to a more productive discussion of what kinds of things we believe the government should not do would be an enormous improvement, both for the law and for American political debate more generally. If our primary concern is about the government, as the Constitution suggests it should be, we should be talking about the government, and not about nonexistent individual rights. This shift in focus from individual rights to limits on state power in turn provides invaluable insights regarding a number of foundational issues in modern constitutional law. For example, most of modern constitutional law regarding individual rights is oriented around purported conflicts between individual rights and the government's right or power to pursue particular policies. Thus the courts often resolve constitutional disputes by asking whether the government has a good enough reason to infringe on a particular person's rights. Once one recognizes that individual constitutional rights are in fact a myth, it becomes clear that this focus on conflicts between rights and governmental power is entirely false.

The true question in *every* constitutional case is whether what the government is doing violates the limits on its power imposed by the Constitution, and the proper analysis of that question turns on determining the nature and contours of those limits, not on "weighing" individual rights and societal interests, as modern law seems to require. Balancing is in any event problematic because presumably the very *reason* the framers inserted certain provisions such as the First Amendment into the Constitution was because they had decided that the values protected by those provisions outweigh normal societal objectives. Furthermore, a focus on the limits of state power also makes it clear that it should matter profoundly for constitutional analysis *why* the government is acting as it is, what the government's purposes are, because it seems obvious that restrictions on state power will be violated by particular governmental motives. On the other hand, the actual impact of governmental conduct on a particular individual is of only peripheral importance in an analysis of limits on state power (in complete contrast to an analysis based on individual rights), because the same governmental action might have very different impacts on individuals depending on coincidental details about the affected individuals. Thus the government's decision to close a particular park for refurbishing cannot be unconstitutional just because I happen to use the park every week to make political speeches, even though the government's action has a severe impact on my "right" to speak. On the other hand, if the government closes the park *because* it dislikes the speeches being given in the park (by me or others), that seems obviously unconstitutional regardless of the actual impact on individuals (who might just move to another park).

As the discussion of park closings suggests, moving our thinking from a sterile debate about rights to a grounded debate about limits on state power helps in resolving not only broad, theoretical questions, but also very specific constitutional disputes. Indeed, one of the objectives of this book is to demonstrate how such a shift in analysis clarifies a number of specific, seemingly intractable constitutional issues such as whether governmental affirmative action violates the Equal Protection Clause, why corporations and not merely individuals may invoke the Constitution, why the Constitution does not grant "affirmative" rights to assistance from the government, and whether and to what extent the First Amendment permits state regulation of media giants and modern communications facilities such as the Internet. Those and many other important constitutional issues today simply do not lend themselves to an analysis of "rights," because the rights purportedly at issue seem either nonexistent or in conflict. But when we begin to think instead about whether it is consistent with constitutional principles for the government to do what it wants to do, some clearer answers emerge, or at the least it becomes clear what the crucial disagreements are, and should be, about.

The rest of this book fills out the above ideas in more detail. In the first part of the book (Chapters 2 through 4), I explain in more detail what individual rights *are*, what makes them distinctive and important, and why the Constitution does not create individual rights as we generally understand them. I then explain what the provisions of the Constitution and the Bill of Rights that are generally understood to create individual rights actually *do* create, which are specific, limited but important restraints on governmental power. In the second part of the book, Chapters 5 onwards, I take the general lessons derived in the first part of the book, and apply them to specific areas of constitutional law, focusing in particular on some issues that are great sources of controversy today. Before turning to these matters, however, there is some value in examining some specific examples of important, modern constitutional controversies, which are illuminated by analyzing them in terms of appropriate limits on governmental power, rather than in terms of individual rights.

STATE ACTION AND POSITIVE RIGHTS

One of the simplest illustrations of why the Constitution is best understood as limiting official power rather than creating individual rights is the fact that with one exception,[6] the key allegedly rights-granting provisions of the Constitution protect individuals *only* against governmental action, not private action. This principle, known as the "state action doctrine," is a bedrock of modern constitutional law, and is largely uncontroversial within the legal community. And yet, the impact and implications of the state action doctrine are immense. Most fundamentally,

---

6. The exception is the Thirteenth Amendment, which flatly bans slavery and involuntary servitude within the United States. It is unique because through it, the Constitution fundamentally altered a fundamental institution of private society, and its reach and ambitiousness are explained by the context in which it was adopted, which was of course the Civil War and its aftermath.

the state action limitation on constitutional rights largely eviscerates the idea that constitutional rights create any true zone of liberty, or autonomy, for individuals. The reason is, simply, that in people's daily lives, many if not most of the restrictions they face on their conduct are a product not of governmental laws, but of private action. Consider, for example, the "right" to speak protected by the First Amendment. In a democracy, surely at a minimum the First Amendment means that citizens may not be punished for speaking their mind on political issues, including criticizing their leaders. And in fact, the First Amendment probably does prevent the *government* from punishing an individual for, say, criticizing the president (though as we shall see in Chapter 5, even this principle has its limits). What if, however, you are employed, and your boss fires you when she hears you criticize the president, whom she supports? The state action doctrine means that unless your employer is the government, that firing does *not* in any way violate the First Amendment, or any other constitutional provision.[7] As another example, consider the Equal Protection Clause of the Fourteenth Amendment, which has been interpreted to prohibit racial discrimination. Because of the state action doctrine, if individuals are discriminated against in their jobs, in searching for housing, or in any number of other ways by a *private* individual, such discrimination again normally does not implicate the Constitution.[8] Admittedly, in the modern world private discrimination is likely to violate any number of statutes such as Title VII of the Civil Rights Act of 1964, which ban employment discrimination, or any number of fair housing laws; but such statutory antidiscrimination laws are *not* required by the Constitution and can be repealed at any time by legislatures. Given these uncontroversial legal rules, what does it mean to say that the Constitution guarantees an individual "right" to free speech, or a "right" to be free from racial discrimination? After all, in practice the restrictions, or discrimination, that individuals face are far more likely to come from private sources, from employers, landlords, business owners, and the like, than from the government. As a consequence, it is clearly incorrect to say that the Constitution meaningfully preserves individual liberty, or freedom from discrimination. At most, rather, it protects individuals from governmental interference, which is a very different thing.

In addition to the state action limitation, another well accepted but highly significant aspect of constitutional rights is that generally, the Constitution

---

7. Indeed, as we will discuss in Chapter 5, even government employees can sometimes be disciplined or fired for their speech.

8. *See The Civil Rights Cases*, 109 U.S. 3 (1883). The one qualification that is necessary here is that under some circumstances, the Supreme Court has held that private racial discrimination against African Americans *does* violate the Thirteenth Amendment, because such discrimination can constitute "badges and incidents of slavery," Jones v. Alfred H. Meyer Co., 392 U.S. 409 (1968), and as noted in footnote 6 above, the Thirteenth Amendment is not limited by the state action doctrine.

imposes only negative, not positive obligations on government. In other words, the provisions of the Bill of Rights and the Fourteenth Amendment do not generally require the government to *act*, they merely specify certain ways in which the government may not act. Most fundamentally, this means that, as the Supreme Court has clearly held, the Constitution does *not* require the government to provide its citizens even minimum necessities such as welfare[9] or education,[10] and also imposes almost no limitations on government when it does choose, voluntarily, to provide its citizens with such services. Similarly, even though the Court has famously held that the Due Process clauses of the Fifth and Fourteenth Amendment protect a women's "right" to choose an abortion,[11] it has also said that the government has absolutely no obligation to provide funding for medical services so that poor women can afford abortions, even if the government does choose to fund the expenses of childbirth for these women.[12] In yet another case, the Court held that minor political candidates have no First Amendment right to participate in a candidates' debate sponsored by a public television station (though it should be noted that if the government excluded a candidate because of his or her substantive views, that would, as the Court recognized, violate the Constitution).[13] More generally, it is why the Court has consistently rejected the idea that the Constitution creates "positive" rights, in the sense of an entitlement to governmental services. The strength of this principle is demonstrated by a particularly famous case called *DeShaney v. Winnebago County Department of Social Services.* Joshua DeShaney was a young child who, after his parents were divorced, was placed in his father's custody. Government social workers in the county in which he resided received repeated reports (confirmed by suspicious injuries) that his father was physically abusing him, but they took no action. Ultimately, his father beat Joshua so severely that he suffered permanent brain damage. Joshua and his mother brought a lawsuit against the county government claiming damages for his injuries, but the U.S. Supreme Court rejected the claim, holding that the Constitution did not impose any obligation on the government to protect citizens against private violence, even when the government was or should have been aware of the violence.[14] As Justice William Rehnquist put it, the Constitution "is phrased as a limitation on the State's power to act, not as a guarantee of certain minimal levels of safety and security." And in fact, despite its troubling and brutal facts, the result reached by the Court in the *DeShaney* was almost certainly correct.

---

9. Dandridge v. Williams, 397 U.S. 471 (1970).

10. San Antonio Independent School District v. Rodriguez, 411 U.S. 1 (1973).

11. *See* Roe v. Wade, 410 U.S. 113 (1973).

12. *See* Maher v. Roe, 432 U.S. 464 (1977); Harris v. McRae, 448 U.S. 297 (1980).

13. Arkansas Educational Television Commission v. Forbes, 523 U.S. 666 (1998).

14. 489 U.S. 189 (1989).

The state action doctrine and the lack of positive constitutional rights, in combination, not only refute the idea that constitutional rights generally create
spheres of autonomy for individuals, they also impose important limitations on
the scope of whatever protections the Bill of Rights does provide. In particular,
they clarify that the Constitution does not create any individual entitlement to
effective or *meaningful* independence or autonomy. At the broadest level, this is
illustrated by the fact that the Constitution does nothing to alleviate the effects of
poverty, since it provides no right to public support or services. The impact of
this reality on individual autonomy, however, is devastating. After all, in what
meaningful sense does someone who is homeless or starving have a right to
speak, a right to exercise his or her religion, or even a right to bear arms? Surely
extreme poverty is a thorough barrier to any meaningful liberty or autonomy; yet
the Constitution clearly does not speak to the issue. Abortion funding provides a
more specific example of this principle. It is true that *Roe v. Wade* protects a
"right" to an abortion; but abortion is, after all, a medical procedure that typically
involves not insignificant expense. For poor women, therefore, lack of public
funding for abortion means that it is often completely out of reach (unless they
are lucky enough to have access to a charitable, private clinic), making the *Roe*
"right" largely illusory. Finally, consider an example from the free speech area.
As we will discuss further in Chapter 5, the Supreme Court has long interpreted
the First Amendment to require the government to permit individuals to speak,
free of unreasonable interference, on streets and in parks owned by the government. In the modern world, however, access to such property has little practical
significance, because most important political dialogue and communication
occurs through the mass media, primarily through the medium of television
(though the Internet is beginning to change this). Television stations and networks are generally private entities that are not subject to constitutional constraints because of the state action doctrine. Over the years a number of activists
and commentators have made the argument that the First Amendment should
be interpreted to *require* television broadcasters to sell space to private speakers,
or otherwise provide private speakers access to the airwaves.[15] The Supreme
Court, however, firmly rejected that claim, in part because the broadcasters'
behavior did not constitute state action constrained by the Constitution.[16] In a
similar vein, the Supreme Court has also held that private shopping center
owners have no constitutional obligation to permit individuals to speak on their
property.[17] Logical as they are given the state action doctrine, the practical impact

---

15. *See, e.g.*, Owen Fiss, *Free Speech and Social Structure*, 71 Iowa L. Rev. 1405 (1986);
Cass Sunstein, *Free Speech Now*, 59 U. Chi. L. Rev. 255 (1992); J. M. Balkin, *Some Realism
About Pluralism: Legal Realist Approaches to the First Amendment*, 1990 Duke L. J. 375.

16. Columbia Broadcasting System v. Democratic National Committee, 412 U.S. 94
(1973).

17. Hudgens v. NLRB, 424 U.S. 507 (1976).

of these rulings is to reject an effective or meaningful constitutional right of free speech, which would empower individuals to actually reach significant audiences.

Indeed, at the most basic level, the critical implication of the state action doctrine and the negative nature of constitutional rights is that the Bill of Rights and the Fourteenth Amendment do not in fact require any particular organization for society, or any other particular social outcome. Instead, they are designed, as discussed earlier, only to restrict the role of government in our society. This point is vividly illustrated by a debate that arose in the context of a constitutional challenge to campaign finance reform (a topic discussed in more detail in Chapter 5). In the Supreme Court's most important modern decision on whether campaign finance reform violates the Free Speech Clause of the First Amendment, defenders of campaign regulation argued to the Court that restricting how much money individuals may spend on election advertising was consistent with the First Amendment because absent such restrictions, the wealthy would dominate political debate, and therefore restrictions were necessary to "equalize" debate, and ensure that political discussion was fair and unbiased. The Court firmly rejected this argument, responding that "the concept that government may restrict the speech of some . . . to enhance the relative voice of others is wholly foreign to the First Amendment."[18] Yale Law Professor Jack Balkin describes the Court's argument as "incoherent,"[19] and leading constitutional scholar (later Dean of the Harvard Law School and then, under President Barack Obama, Solicitor General of the United States) Elena Kagan describes this sentence as "the most castigated passage in modern First Amendment case law."[20] Nonetheless, as Kagan recognizes, the Court's comment *is* defensible (and indeed, probably correct). This is because, even if one agrees (as I do) that absent expenditure limits, political dialog tends to be dominated by the powerful, the First Amendment does not in fact ensure any particular outcome, including even the seemingly neutral and desirable outcome of unbiased and open dialog. What the First Amendment does instead is limit governmental power to interfere with speech, because of a basic distrust of government—which in the context of campaign finance reform, translates to a concern that any such "reform" will be designed to favor incumbent politicians. Given that constitutional structure, it is dubious to argue that the First Amendment requires or even permits the government to design or control the market for political speech, because the argument is based on a faith in government that is antithetical to the very design of the First Amendment, and indeed, of the Constitution generally. Of course,

---

18. Buckley v. Valeo, 424 U.S. 1, 48–49 (1976).

19. Jack Balkin, *Some Realism About Pluralism: Legal Realist Approaches to the First Amendment*, 1990 DUKE L. J. 375, 410–412.

20. Elena Kagan, *Private Speech, Public Purpose: The Role of Governmental Motive in First Amendment Doctrine*, 63 U. CHI. L. REV. 415, 467 (1996).

governmental inaction leads to the maintenance of the status quo, including the continuing exclusion of poor candidates; but that is the predictable consequence of a Constitution founded upon distrust of government.

A broader point follows from this. One might ask, why is it that the Bill of Rights has always been read only to limit government, and not to limit private actors, or to require the government to act? Given the shape of our society and the realities of inequality of power and resources, both in the framing era and today, how does this make any sense? The short answer is that if we view the Bill of Rights as protecting individual freedom or autonomy, these limitations do *not* make any sense. Once one recognizes, however, that the true function of the Bill of Rights is not to protect individuals, but to constrain government, then these limitations make perfect sense. In the next several chapters, we will explore in more detail how and why this is the best reading of the Constitution, and what specific implications follow for constitutional law.

THE RIGHTS OF CORPORATIONS AND ALIENS

As our discussion of the state action doctrine indicates, viewing constitutional rights as limitations on power, rather than as grants of individual autonomy, sheds great light on certain otherwise difficult-to-understand features of constitutional law. Another such foundational question of constitutional law is who is entitled to claim the protections of the Constitution, and in particular, whether artificial entities such as corporations, and individuals who are not citizens, should be entitled to those protections. We will begin with the more difficult question of corporate rights.

As a matter of constitutional text, the question of whether governmental restrictions on corporations can ever violate the Bill of Rights or the Fourteenth Amendment is a difficult one. The First Amendment, for example, forbids Congress from abridging "the freedom" of speech and the press, and later says that "the right of the people" to assemble, petition the government, etc., may not be abridged. Many of the later provisions of the Bill of Rights speak of the "right of the people" to bear arms, to be secure in their persons and property from unreasonable searches and seizures, and so forth. No explanation is given of who possesses the relevant "freedom," or who constitutes "the people." Perhaps most significantly, in its critical provisions the Fourteenth Amendment provides that no state shall deprive "any person" of either due process or the equal protection of the laws (why the Fourteenth Amendment is most significant will be discussed in Chapter 3). Again, no definition is provided for the term "person." As a practical matter, however, it seems a perfectly reasonable reading to limit these provisions to natural persons, or even only citizens (on which more later). After all, in 1791 when the Bill of Rights was ratified (or in 1789, when the amendments were proposed by Congress), corporations played an insignificant role in American life. Certainly, it is hard to imagine that the framers thought of corporations as part of the "People" who created the Constitution (as in "We the People of the United States," the first words of the Constitution). Similarly, when the Fourteenth Amendment was adopted in 1868, it again seems unlikely that corporations, which were still in their infancy, would have been thought of as "persons." Finally, given the fact that corporations are artificial entities, creatures of law rather than individuals, and so cannot exercise "freedom" or autonomy in any meaningful way, there seems to be a strong argument to make that there is no justification for granting corporations the protections of the Constitution.

Despite these arguments, as a matter of positive law it has been well established since the Supreme Court's 1886 decision in *Santa Clara County v. Southern P.R. Co.*[21] that corporations are in fact "persons" within the meaning of the Fourteenth Amendment, and so are entitled to claim the protections of the Due Process and Equal Protection clauses. Indeed, the *Santa Clara County* Court found the proposition so unexceptional, that the Court refused to even hear argument from the lawyers in the case on this point. Since that time, the Court has consistently held, without serious dissent, that corporations can claim all of the protections of the Bill of Rights and the Fourteenth Amendment, on the same terms as citizens and other natural persons. The fact that corporate rights are well accepted as a matter of law, however, does not make them uncontroversial. In fact, there is a strong movement among certain (primarily left-wing) political groups to reverse the *Santa Clara County* result.[22] Furthermore, for the reasons noted above, on its face the textual and practical arguments made by these groups seem convincing. Nonetheless, the arguments are incorrect, and the Supreme Court is quite right to permit corporations to bring claims under the Constitution.

The fundamental flaw in the arguments raised against granting corporations the protections of the Constitution is that they are founded on a mistaken understanding of the nature of the Bill of Rights and the Fourteenth Amendment. The basic argument against corporate rights is that the Bill of Rights and the Fourteenth Amendment are intended to protect *individual* autonomy and freedom; and since corporations are artificial entitles, not individuals (i.e., not "persons" or part of "the People"), they have no claim to the protections of the Constitution. Once one accepts the true nature of the Bill of Rights and Fourteenth Amendment, however, as limits on governmental power rather than assurances of individual autonomy, the fallacy of this argument becomes clear. The truth is that granting the government carte blanche to impose any limits it wanted on corporations, free of any constitutional restraint, would constitute an *enormous*

---

21. 118 U.S. 394 (1886). In 2010 the Supreme Court confirmed that corporations also enjoy First Amendment rights to spend money to fund campaign speech. *See Citizens United v. Federal Election Commission,* 130 S. Ct. 876 (2010).

22. *See, e.g.,* http://www.reclaimdemocracy.org/personhood/; http://www.pbs.org/now/politics/corprightsdebate.html.

increase in the power of the State, with extremely troubling results. Most obviously, this would be true with respect to limits on nonprofit corporations and similar entities—which, remember, are no less artificial entities than for-profit corporations. Are we really comfortable saying that the Sierra Club, the National Rifle Association, and the National Organization for Women can be regulated, even silenced, without any constitutional implications? Or that the NAACP has no right to litigate antidiscrimination claims (which are often brought pursuant to the Equal Protection Clause of the Fourteenth Amendment)? Of course, these entities might always be able to raise and litigate claims on behalf of individuals, but especially with respect to speech, there are strong reasons to believe that it is essential to permit these entities to *speak* in their joint, organizational capacity.

Even with respect to for-profit corporations, the consequences of accepting the anti-corporate-rights approach are profound and deeply troubling. Corporations, are after all, the primary mechanism through which, in our society, wealth is aggregated and invested in economic activities. A very large portion of the property in the United States is held in the corporate form, and most economic activity, including job creation, investment, and production, is carried out by corporations. Of course, corporations themselves are artificial entities, legal fictions, but the activity they engage in is engaged in by individuals, on behalf of other individuals (the shareholders of the corporation) who all constitute a part of the sovereign People. To grant the federal and state governments plenary control over all of that property, and all of that economic activity, free of constitutional constraints, is effectively to give the government plenary control over the economy, and in truth over our society—because after all, to control the wealth and livelihoods of individuals is ultimately to control those individuals. It should be obvious however (as we will discuss in more detail in future chapters) that the very purpose of the constitutional structure of the United States, including especially the Bill of Rights and the Fourteenth Amendment, is to prevent government from obtaining such absolute power. Moreover, the power that such a move would grant the government is not just power over property and economic activity (which are, after all, both subject to extensive regulation in the modern era). Many other crucial aspects of our society that are protected by the Constitution from excessive governmental intrusion, such as political debate, religious activity, and even family life, are critically dependent on access to economic resources. Therefore, to control a vast proportion of private wealth, as plenary power over corporations would permit the government to do, is effectively to control much of the rest of society, including notably most political debate. Again, for reasons that should be clear already but will be explained in greater detail later, such a result contravenes the fundamental structure of our system of constitutional government.

The question of why corporations should enjoy constitutional "rights" was presented clearly to the Supreme Court in a 1978 case, *First National Bank of*

Boston v. Bellotti.[23] Massachusetts had passed a statute prohibiting corporations from spending money to influence popular votes, unless the matter "materially affected" the corporation's business interests, and specifically excluded taxation issues from those that corporations could speak on. The State defended the statute by claiming that a corporation's First Amendment rights were limited to speaking on issues materially affecting its business, but the Supreme Court rejected this argument. The Court stated that this argument "posed the wrong question. . . . The proper question . . . is not whether corporations 'have' First Amendment rights and, if so, whether they are coextensive with those of natural persons. Instead, the question must be whether [the law] abridges expression that the First Amendment was meant to protect." The Court went on to strike down the law, emphasizing along the way that critical role that *all* speech, regardless of its source, played in the democratic process, and highlighting the dangers of permitting the government to decide who may or may not speak on issues affecting the government itself.[24] In short, what the Court was saying was that the reason that corporations and other artificial entities enjoy constitutional "rights" is not because we inherently value the "liberty" or "autonomy" of such entities, but because we believe that the government's power over such entities must be restricted, if the role of government in our society is to be kept in its proper, limited place.

A related issue to the question of corporate "rights" is the question of whether aliens—i.e., non-U.S. citizens—should be entitled to claim the protections of the Constitution. We will examine this topic in more detail in Chapter 11, in the course of discussing the "War on Terror," but a preliminary examination seems in order here. As with corporations, the constitutional text here is unclear. On the one hand, as noted above the Fourteenth Amendment shields "any person" from the government, and surely aliens are "persons." On the other hand, the references to "the People" in the Constitution and Bill of Rights are probably best understood as references to citizens, since "the People" who created the Constitution are surely the citizens of this country, acting in their political capacity—after all, by definition aliens do not vote or otherwise constitute part of the polity that has the power to create law in our system of democratic, popular sovereignty.[25] Based on this reasoning, the Supreme Court has clearly held that aliens located *outside* the United States are generally not entitled to constitutional

---

23. 435 U.S. 765 (1978).

24. *Id.* at 776–777. This aspect of *Bellotti* was reaffirmed in the *Citizens United* case in 2010.

25. This raises the question of the status of citizens who were denied the right to vote, which in the framing era would have included not only women and children, but also a large fraction of adult men. This topic is examined in more detail in Chapter 11, but suffice to say that such individuals were considered to be "virtually represented" by voters during the framing era, and so were part of the body politic.

protections,[26] and some of the reasoning of that opinion (relying in particular on the identification of "the People" as entitled to protections) would seem to extend to aliens within the United States as well. Nonetheless, however, as with corporations, in recent decades the Supreme Court has consistently permitted aliens who are legally within this country to claim the protections of the Constitution (indeed, most protections are extended to undocumented aliens as well).[27] Indeed, the Supreme Court not only has granted aliens constitutional protections, it has gone so far as to hold that discrimination against legal resident aliens, at least by state governments, is presumptively unconstitutional.[28] The principle that the Constitution protects noncitizens is thus extremely well established.

As with corporate rights, as a matter of principle, granting constitutional protection to aliens is not easily explained if constitutional rights are viewed as grants of autonomy to individuals. After all, the Constitution is the creation of the People of the United States, and the natural inference from this point is that if the People, in amending the Constitution, were doling out legal rights, presumably they intended to give those rights only to themselves. This inference is further supported by the fact that one provision of the Fourteenth Amendment, the Privileges or Immunities Clause (which is discussed in more detail in Chapter 3), specifically refers to "citizens of the United States." Yet today, few people seriously argue that aliens (at least those legally present in the United States) should enjoy no constitutional protections. Why? The answer, quite simply, is that as with corporations, to grant the federal and state governments plenary power over aliens, subject to no constitutional restrictions, would be to enormously increase the power and influence of the government. Given our history as a nation of immigrants, aliens have always had an important role in our society, but in the time since the framing and Civil War, the sheer number and significance of noncitizens in our country has inevitably grown immensely because of the greatly increased scale of immigration. To say that the government can treat all aliens as it wishes, for example imprisoning them for criticizing the government, or depriving them of their property or livelihood without claim of recourse, would grant the government a means of repression that would be exceedingly dangerous, and the knock-on effects of which could not help but shape the very fabric of our society. Of course, as a matter of morality and justice

---

26. United States v. Verdugo-Urquidez, 494 U.S. 259 (1990). As discussed in Chapter 11, the Supreme Court has departed from that principle slightly with regard to detainees at Guantanamo Bay, but that departure is based on special circumstances.

27. *See* Zadvydas v. Davis, 533 U.S. 678, 693 (2001); Plyler v. Doe, 457 U.S. 202 (1982); *but see* Reno v. American-Arab Anti-discrimination Comm., 525 U.S. 471 (1999) (holding that deportable aliens may not challenge deportation on the grounds that they were singled out for deportation because of their speech or associations).

28. Graham v. Richardson, 403 U.S. 365 (1971).

I have no doubt that it is appropriate to provide noncitizens with legal protections; but that argument does not resolve the constitutional conundrum. The reason that the *Constitution* is best read to protect aliens as well as citizens is that to read it otherwise would be to empower the government in ways that are inconsistent with the kind of democratic society that our Constitution seeks to create.

THE SECOND AMENDMENT

The final topic we will consider is one that has been the source of highly visible controversy in recent years: the proper scope of the right granted by the Second Amendment "to keep and bear arms." The text of the Second Amendment, in its entirety, reads as follows: "A well-regulated Militia, being necessary to the security of a free State, the right of the people to keep and bear Arms, shall not be infringed."[29] The exact meaning of this seemingly simple language, however, has been fraught with uncertainty. Until very recently, the only significant pronouncement by the Supreme Court on the subject was a brief 1939 opinion holding that the Second Amendment did not protect the right to transport a sawed-off shotgun in interstate commerce, because possession of such a weapon had no relation to service in a well-regulated militia.[30] For the next half a century, most legal authorities believed that the Second Amendment had extremely limited scope and did not protect any *individual* right to bear arms, independent of militia service—indeed, in 1991 former Chief Justice Warren E. Burger, otherwise a well-known conservative, went so far as to describe the individual-rights view of the Second Amendment as a "fraud."[31] Beginning in the late 1980s, however, a number of legal academics, including several well-respected liberals, began to write supporting the view that the Second Amendment granted an individual right to bear arms.[32] Over the following two decades this position gained greater ground, and finally in 2008 in its landmark decision in *District of*

---

29. There is in fact some dispute about the precise, canonical text of the Second Amendment, focusing on the number of commas, and on capitalization. *See generally* William W. Van Alstyne, *A Constitutional Conundrum of Second Amendment Commas: A Short Epistolary Report*, 10 GREEN BAG 2d 469 (2007). Needless to say, the dispute has little significance for the main points made here.

30. United States v. Miller, 307 U.S. 174 (1939).

31. *See* Joan Biskupic, *Guns: A Second (Amendment) Look*, WASHINGTON POST A20, May 10, 1995 (quoting contents of interview given by Chief Justice Burger on PBS's "MacNeil/Lehrer News Hour").

32. *See, e.g.,* Sanford Levinson, *The Embarrassing Second Amendment*, 99 YALE L. J. 637 (1989); Akhil Reed Amar, *The Bill of Rights as a Constitution*, 100 YALE L. J. 1131 (1991); William Van Alstyne, *The Second Amendment and the Personal Right to Arms*, 43 DUKE L. J. 1236 (1994).

Columbia v. Heller,[33] the Supreme Court itself adopted this position in the course of striking down a strict gun control ordinance enacted by the District of Columbia. The *Heller* decision is so remarkable, and in some ways so problematic, that it is worth some attention, before we turn to the broader questions raised by the Second Amendment.

The basic question in the *Heller* case was the constitutionality, under the Second Amendment, of a District of Columbia (D.C.) ordinance that effectively forbade the possession of handguns within the city's boundaries, and that required any firearms stored within the city (including rifles) to be either disassembled, or equipped with a "trigger lock" mechanism. The Court struck down both provisions. At the broadest level, because the plaintiff in the case, Dick Heller (a D.C. special police officer, as it happens) wanted to keep a handgun in his home for his private use, the case required the Court to decide if the Second Amendment prohibited the federal government (since the District of Columbia is a federal entity) from preventing individuals from possessing firearms, independently of their service in a well-regulated militia. In a notably long majority opinion written by Justice Antonin Scalia, the Court delved deeply into the history of the Second Amendment. Crucially, the opinion begins by distinguishing between what Justice Scalia called the "prefatory clause" of the amendment (the reference to well-regulated militia), and the "operative clause," stating "the right of the people to keep and bear arms." Scalia concludes that the prefatory clause has little significance in interpreting the Second Amendment, because it is common for legal provisions to go beyond their stated purpose. The opinion then quickly concludes that the "Right of the People" granted by the operative clause is an *individual* right with no particular relationship to actual militia service, which individuals could exercise for any number of reasons, including hunting for game and self-defense of their homes. In reaching this conclusion, Justice Scalia emphasizes that (in his view) the rights "of the People" mentioned in other parts of the Bill of Rights (notably the First, Fourth, and Ninth Amendments) are all "individual rights, not 'collective' rights." He also concludes that the phrase "to keep and bear arms" had no particular military meaning in the founding era, and cites provisions of state constitutions similar to the Second Amendment, as well as the drafting history of the Second Amendment, to support his conclusion.

Heller was far from a unanimous decision. While five Justices (including Scalia) joined the Court's opinion, four Justices dissented, in another lengthy, historical opinion, authored by Justice John Paul Stevens. Stevens examined all of the same historical evidence canvassed by Justice Scalia, but reached almost diametrically opposite conclusions. Justice Stevens begins his opinion by conceding Justice Scalia's point that the Second Amendment right is an "individual"

---

33. 128 S. Ct. 2783 (2008).

one, in the sense that "[s]urely it protects a right that can be enforced by individuals." He concludes, however, that all of the historical context, and all of the evidence surrounding the drafting of the Second Amendment, supports the view that the Second Amendment protects only a right to keep and bear arms in the context of militia service. Because Dick Heller clearly was not claiming that he wished to use a handgun as a part of military service, for Justice Stevens this meant ipso facto that the D.C. regulation raised no serious constitutional concerns.

What are we to make of these sharp differences of opinion, arising from differing readings of *identical* (and largely undisputed) historical evidence? We should begin by identifying the points on which the majority and dissent (and all serious students of this issue) seem to agree. First, there is no doubt that the primary concern that drove the adoption of the Second Amendment was a military one. In particular, for historical reasons having to do with the use of professional armies to oppress civilian populations during both the English Civil War of the seventeenth century, and during the period leading up to the American Revolution, the framing generation had a deep and abiding mistrust of standing, professional armies. That generation also largely agreed that maintenance of a popular militia was the essential solution to this problem, both because the existence of a militia lessened the need for a standing army for national defense, and because if rulers decided to use the professional military against its own population, the militia could resist the army through force of arms. That this was the underlying motivation for the Second Amendment cannot be seriously doubted. As Justice Stevens points out (and Justice Scalia does not deny), essentially *all* of the proposals for a Bill of Rights advanced during the debates over ratification of the Constitution, which eventually inspired our Bill of Rights,[34] contained provisions that mentioned a right to bear arms in the context of listing the dangers posed by a standing army and the need for national defense. This included, crucially, the proposal drafted by George Mason at the Virginia Ratifying Convention, which provided the blueprint for the proposals of not just Virginia's, but also many other states' ratifying conventions.[35] Second, it is now widely understood that the "militia" referred to in the Second Amendment, and by the framing generation generally, was not a semiprofessional military body such as the modern National Guard; it was composed of all able-bodied male citizens of

---

34. The basic background here is that when the Constitution was originally drafted in 1787, it did not contain a Bill of Rights, a fact which became a source of controversy during the debates over whether the Constitution should be ratified. While the Constitution was ultimately ratified without a Bill of Rights, several of the state ratifying conventions proposed that a Bill of Rights be added, a demand to which supporters of the Constitution agreed, and acted upon soon after the Constitution came into effect. It is to these state proposals that the text refers. This history is discussed in more detail in Chapter 3.

35. *See* http://www.constitution.org/gmason/amd_gmas.txt.

fighting age. Of course, when the militia was called into action, not all members participated, and so what constituted the active, organized militia at any one time was a subset of the full militia. But the militia itself, the group referred to in the Constitution, was not so limited. Indeed, given the purposes of the Second Amendment, it could not be so limited, since granting the government (in 1789, the concern was the federal government) the power to pick and choose which citizens would be permitted to continue to be armed and serve in the militia, invited precisely the abuses that the Amendment was designed to prevent. Finally, there is no doubt that the Constitution envisioned a primary role for states in the process of training and organizing the militia, albeit Article I, section 8 of the Constitution grants the Congress the power to establish the rules ("the discipline") that state governments would enforce in training the militia.

It is now time to consider what all of this *means*—what reasonable conclusions can we reach about the meaning and reach of the Second Amendment. As it turns out, many questions are illuminated by recognizing the fundamental, structural nature of *all* constitutional provisions, including most especially the Second Amendment, as limits on power rather than grants of individual autonomy. Taking this perspective, it quickly becomes clear that many of Justice Scalia's basic conclusions are fundamentally wrong. Most importantly, his conclusion that the use of the phrase "the people" in the Second Amendment indicates an "individual right" is both a non sequitur and incoherent. First, Justice Scalia is simply incorrect that the use of the phrase "the people" elsewhere in the Bill of Rights indicates an "individual right" in the sense of a grant of individual autonomy. As we have already discussed, and will discuss in much greater detail in subsequent chapters, this is based on a basic, historical misunderstanding of what rights *meant* in the framing era (and indeed, even today). In fact, the very contrast Scalia draws between "individual" and "collective" rights makes no sense. All "rights" are individual, as Justice Stevens points out, in the sense that they can be invoked by individuals. How else could they be legally enforced? But that does not mean that their *function* is individual, in the sense of protecting individual autonomy. In our constitutional design, the *function* of rights is structural, to limit the power of the government, and in that sense it is collective, because limiting governmental power protects the liberties of *all* citizens, not just those individuals who happen to bring a lawsuit. Second, Justice Scalia's reading of the purposes of the Second Amendment makes no sense. Remember, during the founding era, the framers were creating the structure for a new government. The enactment of the Bill of Rights was an important part of that process, because it was triggered by concerns that the original Constitution granted the new, federal government too much power, without imposing necessary restrictions, thereby creating the danger of tyrannical misuse of that power. In that context, concerns about hunting and defense against criminals make no sense. The new, central government would have no reason to interfere with citizens' ability to hunt or act in personal self-defense. The concern was that the government would seek to disarm the militia—i.e., the citizenry, because remember, those terms were coterminus—in order to remove a barrier to oppression by a standing army. In short, the concern driving the Second Amendment was not protection of individual autonomy with respect to weapons, it was collective self-defense, against both foreign invaders *and* (even more significantly) an oppressive domestic government. All of which explains why Justice Scalia's reading of the history of the Second Amendment as protecting a right to keep and bear arms for the purposes of hunting and personal self-defense, which relies heavily on a few trivial references while ignoring the vast majority of evidence to the contrary, is utterly unconvincing.

But this does not mean that Justice Stevens and the dissenters are correct. The problem with Justice Stevens' reading of the Second Amendment is that, by granting the government essentially unlimited power to disarm citizens whenever they are not actually serving in an organized militia, it makes a mockery of the amendment's underlying purpose. Stevens' approach would permit the government to replace the organized militia with an elite, selective military organization of the government's choosing and under its control (i.e., the National Guard), and then to disarm everyone who has not been recruited to the National Guard. But at this point, the Amendment's purpose of ensuring a popular defense to standing armies has been eviscerated. Indeed, by condoning limiting the militia to "select" groups chosen by the government, Justice Stevens turns the history that drove the framers of the Constitution on its head, because as Justice Scalia points out correctly, the use of such select militias by the Stuart Kings of England, prior to the Glorious Revolution of 1688, was one of the abuses that the framers were responding to. For the Second Amendment to be able to achieve its goals, it must protect *all* households from being disarmed, and must permit those households to "keep" arms—i.e., to hold them in their homes. Finally, to meet those purposes, the protection must extend to all weapons with normal, military uses, which in the framing era meant muskets and pistols.

Thus it seems clear that both the majority and the dissent in *Heller* made serious errors of analysis—errors which, unfortunately, appear to have been driven more by the Justices' policy and political preferences than by analysis of the Constitution. But, one might ask, given the above analysis, what can we say with confidence about the meaning of the Second Amendment in the twenty-first century? One conclusion that does follow easily is that the Second Amendment clearly does *not* prevent the government from some regulation of the militia (the text does, after all, refer to a "well-regulated Militia"), including reasonable regulation of what firearms are stored in homes, and how they are stored. At the most obvious level, no one ever thought that the Second Amendment permitted citizens to store cannons in their homes—as Justice Scalia points out, "dangerous and unusual" weapons were historically banned. Moreover, as Justice Stevens points out, state regulation of how firearms were stored, including requirements that they be stored unloaded (because of fire concerns) were commonplace during the framing period. This strongly suggests that the majority in *Heller* was simply wrong to strike down the D.C. trigger lock requirement, since it is hard to see how an easily removed trigger lock interferes with the use of a weapon in the context of militia service (even if, as the majority concludes, it might interfere with its use for self-defense). Also, presumably some narrow, reasonable restrictions on who constitutes the militia and so is shielded by the Second Amendment, such as exclusion of felons or the mentally ill, is surely permissible.[36] Beyond these narrow conclusions, however, the going gets rough.

The fundamental difficulty one faces in translating the Second Amendment to the modern context is that during the framing era, the militia in principle could act as a counterbalance to an organized military because the weapons in common use by the military were also in common use personally, and so were commonly possessed by citizens. Moreover, during this period standing armies were sufficiently small that it was plausible to imagine a citizen militia providing serious resistance to the army—as one of the most influential framers (and later president) James Madison put it, no national army could exceed "twenty-five or thirty thousand men. To these would be opposed a militia amounting to near half a million of citizens with arms in their hands. . . . It may well be doubted whether a militia thus circumstanced could ever be conquered by such a proportion of regular troops."[37] These assumptions, however, clearly do not hold today. The *Heller* case, for example, was primarily about handguns, which are certainly the most common weapons in personal use in the modern United States. Handguns, however, are clearly *not* the primary weapons used by modern militaries. Those are automatic rifles, and it is difficult to imagine a citizenry armed only with handguns being able to fend off a modern military. For the Second Amendment to have meaning, therefore, it must be read to protect the right of essentially all citizens to own and possess automatic weapons in their home— but that seems a step too far even for most mainstream defenders of gun rights. More fundamentally, given the enormous size of the modern military establishment, and the complexity of modern warfare, with its dependence on highly destructive weapons, air power, and advanced technology, is it truly feasible to imagine *any* citizen militia fighting off a military and government determined to act tyrannically?

It is tempting to conclude from the above argument that the Second Amendment is essentially dead letter, with no real relevance or reach in the

---

36. It should be noted that given Justice Scalia's self-defense and hunting rationales, he is hard-pressed to explain why the disarming of felons is permitted by the Second Amendment, so he simply announces his conclusion by fiat. A structural reading of the Constitution clearly provides a better rationale for disarming felons than Justice Scalia's ipse dixit.

37. Alexander Hamilton, James Madison, and John Jay, THE FEDERALIST PAPERS (Garry Wills ed., Bantam 1982), FEDERALIST No. 46 at 242.

modern world. But that too is a troubling step, because it is an argument that might be made forcefully about any number of the Bill of Rights. It seems incumbent on us to work with the Constitution we have, not the one we want, and to strive to give meaning to all provisions of the Constitution. Furthermore, as a counterpoint to the pessimism expressed above about the value of a citizen militia under modern conditions, it should be recognized that an armed citizenry can in fact provide a great deal of effective resistance to an occupying army, even if it cannot defeat such an army in open battle; and when the army is drawn from the very population that seeks to resist it, that resistance can be a summons to disobedience within the army itself. Regardless of how convincing one finds these arguments, moreover, that a citizen militia was "necessary to the security of a Free state" was as much a founding assumption of our Constitution as the assumption, underlying the First Amendment, that free political debate was essential to a well-functioning democracy. We must therefore accept that assumption as a given, which in turn means that we must accept the corollary conclusion that the Second Amendment forbids the government from disarming the population at large. The only question that remains is *what* weapons, what "arms," are shielded by the Second Amendment. The difficulty here is that the weapons that provide the backbone of a modern military, such as automatic rifles, mortars, rocket launchers, and tanks, are surely also "dangerous and unusual" weapons that historically were not possessed by individuals because they posed too great a threat to general society. There is no easy solution to this conundrum, unfortunately, and so we must pick between two policies that in modern circumstances (though not during the framing period) are in direct conflict. Ultimately, given the complete chaos that would result if the general citizenry possessed military weapons, there seems little doubt and essentially all reasonable people seem to agree that the balance here must be drawn in favor of regulation, including if the legislature desires a complete ban on the private possession of such weapons. With respect to other weapons such as handguns and rifles that are in general use and are not, by any stretch of the imagination, "dangerous and unusual" under modern circumstances, however, the only reasonable conclusion is that the Second Amendment forbids government from flatly denying citizens the right to possess such weapons in their homes.

As a concluding point, however, it must be emphasized that even though the Second Amendment prevents a flat ban on common weapons, many reasonable regulations of such weapons are permissible, so long as such regulations do not undermine the concept of the citizen militia. So, as we noted earlier, rules on storage are surely permissible. Similarly, regulation of transactions in such weapons such as waiting periods before purchase, as well as broader regulations such as registration requirements, in no way interfere with that ultimate purpose. Indeed, given our rejection of the self-defense and hunting rationales for the Second Amendment, there seems no constitutional objection to a ban on carrying of firearms outside the home, whether concealed or otherwise. In short, a structural approach to the Second Amendment, focused on limits on power rather than individual autonomy, suggests that while the Second Amendment is not meaningless, as many modern advocates of gun control argue, it is also not the broad, libertarian grant of absolute individual autonomy with respect to firearms that gun-rights advocates defend. As is often the case, our Constitution adopts a much more modulated, structural approach to the fundamental problem of how to create a government that is effective, but not all-powerful.

2. THE NATURE OF RIGHTS
A Theoretical and Historical Overview

It is often said that the United States is the home of individual liberty and rights. But what is a "right"? What does it mean to say that someone has a "right," or that her "rights" have been violated? This chapter will show that there are many possible answers to these questions, and that the widely accepted answers have changed substantially over the course of American history. But at the same time, today among the American people it seems that there is a fairly wide consensus about what constitutes a "right," and what it means to have rights. The American people know what individual rights are, they know that the Constitution gives them rights, and they know that those rights cannot be taken away from them. The problem, as this book will argue, is that this consensus is fundamentally wrong.

THE POPULAR VIEW OF RIGHTS

Let us begin by considering what it is that most people in this country mean when they talk about rights. Most Americans would say, I think, that at its most basic level, a right is a specific kind of freedom. A right is an entitlement to behave in particular ways, to *act*, or to *refuse to act*, free from interference or punishment by others. In other words, a right is an *entitlement* to a specific kind of autonomy. So we say that individuals have the right to burn the American flag because they are entitled to do so, meaning that they cannot be stopped from doing so and cannot be criminally prosecuted after the fact for their actions. More generally, the "rights" of free speech and a free press mean that citizens cannot be stopped from saying and publishing what they want to, and cannot later be punished for what they have said or published. And the right recognized in the *Roe v. Wade* decision[1] is the right of a woman to obtain an abortion without interference or subsequent punishment.

Of course, everyone knows that rights are not absolute. Thus one can be punished for falsely shouting fire in a crowded theater[2] or stopped from publishing the sailing dates of troop transports,[3] and abortions may be forbidden once a

---

1. 410 U.S. 113 (1973).
2. *See* Schenck v. United States, 249 U.S. 47 (1919).
3. *See* Near v. Minnesota, 283 U.S. 697 (1931).

fetus has reached viability.[4] Americans are and have always been a practical people (at least outside the universities) who recognize that liberty can be abused, and that any sort of autonomy must have some limits within a complex, interdependent, and organized society. But within their scope, rights are at their essence a grant of autonomy to individuals, an entitlement to act as they see fit.

RIGHTS AS TRUMPS

Within the academic legal literature, the above concept of rights has probably been best expressed by Professor Ronald Dworkin, a professor at both Oxford and New York University, and one of the leading constitutional theorists of our time. In his path-breaking book, *Taking Rights Seriously*, Professor Dworkin describes rights as "political trumps held by individuals," and goes on to argue that the essence of a right is that it entitles an individual to act as he or she chooses even though society as a whole might have some valid reason (what Dworkin calls a "collective goal") for opposing the individual's choice.[5] Dworkin of course provides extensive explanations and justifications for his definition of rights and also makes some more controversial arguments about the nature of rights. For example, Dworkin argues that modern constitutional rights are rooted in prelegal *moral* rights, which exist independent of any particular legal system, and he also argues that at their essence rights are rooted in concepts of equality. Nonetheless, Dworkin's basic argument, his basic definition and understanding of rights, is a straightforward one.

Thus according to Ronald Dworkin, rights are trumps that an individual may "play," thereby overcoming any attempts to interfere with her behavior. Moreover, this view is one that fits very nicely with widely held views on rights—which is what makes Dworkin's analysis so attractive. The notion of a trump is very much consistent with the generally shared idea that rights are powerful *entitlements*, something that individuals possess that defeats attempts by others to interfere with their choices. Of course, Dworkin's definition refers only to *collective*, which is to say official, governmental efforts to interfere with individuals, but this is natural because Dworkin's focus (like the focus of this book) is on *constitutional* rights, and it is a widely accepted postulate among legal thinkers that the Constitution applies only to actions of the government. But with that limitation, Dworkin's notion of rights as trumps, and indeed his broader theory of moral rights, is very much in line with the common American view of what it means to have a right. Henceforth, I will refer to this view as the trump/entitlement theory of rights, or as the popular view of rights.

---

4. Planned Parenthood v. Casey, 505 U.S. 833, 846 (1992).
5. RONALD DWORKIN, TAKING RIGHTS SERIOUSLY xi (1977); *see also id.* at 133, 188.

CRIMINAL PROCEDURE AND RIGHTS AS TRUMPS

The broad view of rights as trumps provides a quite coherent explanation of most of what are widely considered the core constitutional rights, such as the rights to free speech, free exercise of religion, freedom from arbitrary search or arrest, privacy and intimate association (encompassing contraception, abortion, and sexual autonomy), and freedom from discrimination. Many of the other specific provisions of the Bill of Rights, however, do not fit comfortably within this model because these provisions do not create a sphere of autonomy within which individuals may act free from interference. Instead, provisions such as the Fifth Amendment's rights to due process of law and right against self-incrimination, the Sixth Amendment's rights to counsel and to confront witnesses, and the Eighth Amendment's prohibition on cruel and unusual punishment, impose rules that the government must follow in the course of criminal prosecutions against citizens. Furthermore, some of these provisions have been read to provide defendants with a positive right to *assistance* from the government, rather than merely freedom from interference—in particular, the right to counsel has been interpreted to require the government to provide indigent defendants with a lawyer,[6] and the right against self-incrimination has been interpreted to require the police to warn suspects of their rights prior to interrogation.[7] Such positive assistance is in deep tension with the idea of rights as entitlements to autonomy, or as trumps.

Can criminal procedure rights be reconciled with the model of rights as trumps? To a substantial degree, they cannot—indeed, it is the whole thesis of this book that the constitutional Bill of Rights does *not* create rights as defined by Ronald Dworkin and as popularly conceived. However, there is a way in which the popular understanding of rights is consistent with these provisions. Consider the fact that if the ultimate purpose of rights is to protect individual autonomy, and the purpose of constitutional rights in particular is to protect individual autonomy against governmental interference, then criminal prosecution by the state threatens the *ultimate* potential violation of that intent, since the end result of such prosecution is likely to be imprisonment or even death, the greatest possible intrusions on autonomy. But at the same time, of course, there can be no general "right" against criminal prosecution, since the government has a legitimate interest in punishing, indeed the government *must* punish, conduct that violates its laws (so long as that conduct itself does not enjoy constitutional protection, in which case a law criminalizing it would be unconstitutional). But nonetheless, the risk to individual liberty posed by the criminal justice system is clear enough.

---

6. Gideon v. Wainwright, 382 U.S. 335 (1963).
7. Miranda v. Arizona, 384 U.S. 436 (1966).

In that context, the granting of positive, procedural protections in the Bill of Rights, as part of a broader scheme of protecting individual autonomy, makes perfect sense. The criminal procedure provisions of the Bill of Rights exist as a sort of compromise, recognizing that some level of state power to punish criminalized activity, and thus some restrictions on individual autonomy, are inevitable in an organized society; but that at the same time some limits on criminal prosecutions, and even some positive obligations on government in the course of criminal proceedings, are essential if the criminal process is not to become a covert means to eliminate the liberties and autonomy that citizens retain. Nonetheless, it remains true that criminal procedure provisions of the Bill of Rights do not truly operate as "trumps," or as grants of autonomy, since they do not shield any individual conduct from state interference. As such, they represent the first fissure we have seen between the popular conception of rights and the constitutional Bill of Rights.

OTHER THEORIES OF RIGHTS

Ronald Dworkin's theory and definition of rights is not of course the only existing theory of rights. Indeed, there are probably as many theories of rights in this country as there are legal writers who think about rights. Some of the more prominent approaches will be briefly described here, to give a more complete idea of what "rights" might mean in our modern society.

The primary modern alternatives to the view of constitutional rights as trumps can be grouped together under the umbrella of "balancing." Balancing is less a *theory* of rights than it is a methodology for enforcing and adjudicating rights; but because it is (or at least purports to be) the dominant approach to constitutional decision-making within the courts,[8] it requires some consideration. The basic approach of balancing is to begin with a presumption that individuals possess certain rights derived from the Constitution (either directly from the text or by implication), but that these rights are not absolute and must sometimes yield to countervailing societal interests. Of course, there is a presumption that society must respect an individual's right to engage in particular behavior, but if society in the form of the government can come up with a powerful reason why it needs to limit specific rights, it is permitted to do so. Even the most committed balancers, however, recognize that not any reason will do in limiting important rights— otherwise it would not be a right. Furthermore, the more "fundamental" the right, the stronger the reason the government must give before the right is forced to yield, an idea that is captured by the metaphor of placing a thumb on the

---

8. The dominance of balancing methodologies in modern constitutional jurisprudence is documented and described in a very famous law review article: T. Alexander Aleinikoff, *Constitutional Law in the Age of Balancing*, 96 YALE L. J. 943 (1987).

rights side of the scale during balancing. But at the core of balancing lies the assumption that rights are not absolute, and that judges can and must decide when individual rights should yield to society. Thus in two of the most famous (or infamous) balancing cases in the history of the Supreme Court, individuals rights were found to be outweighed by societal needs: In the Japanese-American internment case the Court upheld against a claim of racial discrimination the forced resettlement and internment in concentration camps of Japanese-Americans during World War II, in the name of national security;[9] and in the McCarthy era prosecutions of Communist Party leaders, the Court upheld convictions against a free speech challenge, again on grounds of national security[10] (similar questions have of course arisen in the modern War on Terror, a topic examined in detail in Chapter 11).

In many ways, balancing approaches and the trump/entitlement view of rights have very similar basic understandings of what it means to have a right. Both share the fundamental understanding that rights constitute entitlements to engage in particular conduct, and both view rights as belonging to *individuals*. However, balancing tends to emphasize the *legal* rather than the *moral* roots of rights, and also (perhaps as a consequence) is more willing to sacrifice rights for the greater good. Thus for balancers, rights are not true trumps since they do not always win, they are rather weights to be placed on the scales of justice along with society's needs.

The trump and balancing approaches to rights are undoubtedly the leading modern theories of how rights should and do operate. These approaches together dominate both the language of courts when adjudicating rights, and legal discourse more generally. Legal scholars, however, have offered a number of alternative theories of rights. For example, Professor Linda Meyer of Quinnipiac University has suggested that rights should be understood as "practices of respect."[11] Meyer argues that the moral and philosophical roots of rights suggest that at the core of all rights are concepts of human dignity, and therefore rights are violated when the government fails to respect equally the human dignity of all citizens. The quintessential example she provides of a rights violation is the government searching one's home without cause, which is unconstitutional (under the Fourth Amendment) not simply because of one's property rights, but because the invasion of privacy entailed by such a search fails to treat the resident with proper respect.[12] Meyer, like most others, defines rights in *personal* terms, as belonging to individuals. But unlike those approaches, she does not see rights as primarily relating to individual conduct and spheres of autonomy, but instead as focused on the *relationship* between individuals and the government.

---

9. Korematsu v. United States, 323 U.S. 214 (1944).
10. Dennis v. United States, 341 U.S. 494 (1951).
11. Linda Ross Meyer, *Unruly Rights*, 22 CARD. L. REV. 1, 13–15 (2000).
12. *Id.* at 28–30.

In this respect, as we shall see, Professor Meyer is right on the mark, even if her focus on dignity and respect might not accurately describe the fundamental purpose of *constitutional* rights.

In contrast to Professor Meyer, Professor Matthew Adler of the University of Pennsylvania has propounded a theory of rights that *does* abandon the notion of rights as primarily individual entitlements. In an article entitled "Rights Against Rules"[13] Adler argues that rather than focusing on individual rights as such, modern constitutional doctrine is "rules dependent," meaning that courts understand the Constitution to forbid certain kinds of legal rules rather than protecting particular individual conduct. The primary example Adler offers is the famous flag-burning case, *Texas v. Johnson*. Adler points out that burning a flag is *not* protected conduct under the Bill of Rights. Flag burners can be prosecuted under any number of laws ranging from arson to public safety regulations. The reason that Johnson's prosecution for flag-burning violated the First Amendment was that the *law* under which he was prosecuted—a law that specifically criminalized defacing the American flag in a way that would offend others—was unconstitutional because it singled out for punishment speech of which the government disapproved. Adler's argument is powerful, and one with which I largely agree, especially the crucial point that constitutional adjudication must focus on the *government*, and not on individual conduct (why I believe this is so is the primary topic of the first part of this book, and will be discussed in detail in the next two chapters). However, Adler's focus on rules alone is inadequate to explain the full scope of constitutional doctrine, including especially prohibitions on individual acts of discrimination and even certain free speech issues, a point that Adler himself concedes. Furthermore, Adler's analysis, while a very important and useful contribution to the legal literature, does not seek to explore in detail *why* certain government actions, whether rules or otherwise, are unconstitutional. This book seeks to provide such an account, and in the process to go one step beyond Adler and demonstrate that not only are constitutional rights not "personal" in any meaningful sense, but that the very concept of rights (as generally defined) has little to contribute to constitutional discourse.

Some discussion is necessary here of the work of John Hart Ely. In his seminal book *Democracy and Distrust* Ely (who was at the time Dean of the Stanford Law School) presented a not a theory of rights as such, but rather what he called a "Theory of Judicial Review."[14] Nonetheless, Ely's work has profound implications for an understanding of constitutional rights, and has deeply influenced my

---

13. Matthew D. Adler, *Rights Against Rules: The Moral Structure of American Constitutional Law*, 97 MICH. L. REV. 1 (1998); *see also* Matthew D. Adler, *Rights, Rules, and the Structure of Constitutional Adjudication: A Response to Professor Fallon*, 113 HARV. L. REV. 1371 (2000).

14. JOHN HART ELY, DEMOCRACY AND DISTRUST: A THEORY OF JUDICIAL REVIEW (1980).

own approach to these questions. Ely's basic argument is that when judges assess the constitutionality of laws passed by democratically elected legislatures, they must carefully avoid reading their own values and opinions into the Constitution. Instead, Ely proposes that the judges' primary task is to police the process of representation—i.e., to ensure the fair and effective functioning of democratic politics.[15] This "representation-reinforcing orientation" requires courts, Ely argues, to take a number of steps including protecting political speech,[16] protecting the integrity of the electoral and representative process,[17] and ensuring that minority groups are not excluded from or victimized by democratic politics.[18] It should be obvious by now that Ely's approach to constitutional interpretation is, at heart, a structural approach, and that my arguments here have clear parallels to Ely's analysis. There are, however, also important ways in which my views differ from Ely's. Ely's theory is at heart a procedural one, focused on the processes by which our society governs itself. Mine is a much more substantive approach, based as it is on the premise that the Constitution implements a particular model of the relationship that should exist in a free society between citizens and the State. Reflecting this distinction, equality principles play a central role in Ely's view of the role of the judiciary and the function of the Constitution, while I, as well shall see in later chapters, tend to emphasize more specific, substantive values such as the importance of preserving civil institutions which are independent of the influence of the government. There is no question, of course, of the intellectual debt that I and all contemporary constitutional thinkers owe to Ely; but my work nonetheless departs in significant ways from his.

Finally, any discussion of theories of rights must take note of the Hohfeldian taxonomy of rights. During the first part of the twentieth century Wesley Hohfeld, a professor at the Yale Law School, developed the first, and to some extent still the leading, thorough jurisprudential analysis of rights. Hohfeld argued that the word "right" was (even then!) regularly misused in legal discourse, and that a more exact description was necessary to support careful discussion. To that effect, Hohfeld identified four distinct legal relationships that sometimes go under the name "right": rights, privileges, powers, and immunities.[19] It should be noted that Hohfeld is discussing *all* legal rights, not just constitutional rights, and thus his analysis contains much that is irrelevant to us. The most important aspects of Hohfeld's system for our purposes are that Hohfeld defines a *right* as a legal relationship arising out of a corresponding *duty* of another. Thus I have a right to something only if another person has a duty to me regarding that thing— for example, if someone owes me a debt, I have a right to a payment of that debt

---

15. *Id.* at 73–104.

16. *Id.* at 105–117.

17. *Id.* at 117–125.

18. *Id.* at 135–170.

19. Wesley Hohfeld, Fundamental Legal Conceptions 36 (1923).

because the debtor has a legal duty to pay me the money. *Privilege*, on the other hand, Hohfeld defines as an *absence* of a duty, a lack of obligation to do or refrain from doing something. Thus Hohfeld associates privileges with liberty and freedom, in other words with concepts that in modern constitutional discourse we tend to associate with rights.[20] Finally (skipping Hohfeld's understanding of powers, which are not relevant here), Hohfeld defines an *immunity* as freedom from liability, which is to say freedom from the legal power of another. One has an immunity, for example, if one is exempt from a particular law such as a taxation requirement.

Why does all of this matter? What does this dense and perhaps overcomplicated system contribute to our understanding of modern rights? The key point is that the modern conception of rights, especially constitutional rights, does not fit within the traditional, Hohfeldian conception of a right. When we talk about rights, or someone having a right, we do *not* have in mind some sort of corresponding duty. Instead, the modern notion of rights as trumps seems to fit better within the definition of a *privilege*, and sometimes an immunity. Most constitutional rights in the modern understanding are freedoms possessed by individuals; they are an absence of duty. Occasionally, a constitutional right might be an immunity, an exemption from general legal requirements (especially with respect to property-based rights, a point that Hohfeld made[21]), but again, there is no notion of a duty on another party as the essence of a right. All of this might be a mere difference in language, with no real consequences, but it suggests a potential gap between modern and traditional understandings of rights. I will argue next, and in the following chapter, that this gap is in fact a very real one. What we think of when we discuss constitutional rights today is something very different from what authors of the Bill of Rights thought of, and indeed what most legal and political thinkers in the nineteenth century thought of when they discussed rights. However, our legal system, and especially our system of constitutional adjudication, is necessarily rooted in an older conception of constitutional rights, since it is those kinds of rights, not modern individual privileges, liberties, and freedoms, that the Constitution protects. As a result, there is today a deep disconnect between the public rhetoric of rights, even in legal arenas, and the reality of constitutional rights.

RIGHTS DURING THE FOUNDING PERIOD: COLLECTIVE VERSUS INDIVIDUAL RIGHTS

Not only is there a serious disconnect between the modern concept of the nature of rights and traditional legal theory, the roots of that disconnect lie deep in

---

20. *Id*. at 42–43, 47–48.
21. *Id*. at 62.

American history. Our Bill of Rights was ratified in 1791, two years after the Constitution came into effect and fifteen years after the Declaration of Independence was enacted, signaling the break from Great Britain. As discussed earlier, the amendments constituting the Bill of Rights were proposed by the First Congress (under the leadership of James Madison) because objections had been raised in the state conventions elected to consider ratification of the new Constitution to the fact that the original Constitution failed to incorporate a Bill of Rights. The American attachment to rights thus goes back to the very beginnings of our history, and has remained at the center of our national consciousness since then. It turns out, however, that the meaning and concept of a right, and its function in our democracy, have shifted in fundamental ways over the past two centuries.

When the founders of our country discussed rights, and enacted a Bill of Rights, what did they mean, what did they have in mind? As we have seen, in our time the function of rights is seen to be protecting individual freedom of action. Rights are viewed as creating spheres of autonomy within which individuals may choose to engage in conduct without interference. To the founders, however, rights had a very different meaning and purpose. To understand what the relevant differences are, one must have some awareness of the very different historical context in which the founders lived. In the 1770s and 1780s, it must be remembered that Americans had just thrown off a powerful tyrant who had sought to subjugate the colonists by depriving them of self-rule as well as various civil liberties. Furthermore, during this time Americans were just creating the concept of popular sovereignty, which has since become the foundation of our system of government. Finally, the political science of this period viewed the structure of government as a whole, and the rights of the people in particular, as emerging from a political compact between rulers and ruled, who remained clearly distinct entities. It is not surprising, then, that when most people thought of freedom, liberty, or rights during this period, they saw these concepts as profoundly *political* in nature, and arising from a perhaps inevitable struggle between the People, as a collective entity, and tyrannical central authority in the shape of the king. As Gordon Wood, the leading modern historian of the founding period, puts it:

> In 1776 the solution to the problems of American politics seemed to rest not so much in emphasizing the private rights of individuals against the general will as it did in stressing the public rights of the collective people against the supposed privileged interests of their rulers.[22]

The historian Jack Rakove makes a similar point, arguing that "[i]n the eighteenth century . . . many authorities would still have held that the primary

---

22. GORDON S. WOOD, THE CREATION OF THE AMERICAN REPUBLIC, 1776–1787 at 61 (1969).

holders of rights were not individuals but rather the collective body of the people" because the point of rights was "to protect the people at large from tyranny."[23] Thus the entire orientation of the American people toward rights was fundamentally different during this time. Rights were not directed at or concerned with individuals or individual conduct at all. Rather, they were a bulwark enjoyed by the People as a group, against the hostile forces of the State, and in particular the king.

Of course, by 1791 there was no longer a king in America, but the fear of tyrannical central authority remained and in some ways had been increased by the chaotic politics at the state level during the 1780s. The focus had merely shifted from a nonexistent king to the new and often arbitrary legislatures of the several states.[24] Moreover, the new Constitution, by creating a new, powerful, and distant legislature and Chief Executive, generated heightened concerns about despotism. As a result, Americans during the period up to and including the ratification of the Bill of Rights continued fundamentally to view rights as concerned primarily with protecting the People collectively from tyrannical central authority.

There is much else in the history of this period that supports the conclusion that during the founding period, rights were primarily viewed in collective terms. The federal Bill of Rights of course did not emerge from a vacuum, and the precedents on which our Bill of Rights was built clearly incorporate a collective view of rights. The most important of those precedents was undoubtedly the English Declaration of Rights of 1689, which was enacted by Parliament in the course of inviting William and Mary to take the throne vacated by the ousted James II. The English Declaration, despite its title as a Declaration of *Rights*, is preeminently a document concerning governmental structure and the relationship between King and Parliament.[25] Of what today would be considered crucial rights such as speech and assembly one finds no mention except for a guaranty of free speech for *members of Parliament*. Indeed, the only *individual* protections found in the Declaration relate to petitioning the king, and to preserving jury trials; but during this period both of these "rights" were understood in fundamentally structural and collective terms, as means for the People as a whole to protect themselves from the king and, more importantly, from his servants (notably judges, who were profoundly mistrusted). Thus insofar as the English Declaration of Rights provided the model for future Bills of Rights, that model was entirely a collective and political one, with essentially no element of individual liberty or autonomy.

The other important precedents for the federal Bill of Rights came out of the various states that were to make up the federal union. During the period

---

23. JACK RAKOVE, DECLARING RIGHTS: A BRIEF HISTORY WITH DOCUMENTS at 22 (1998).

24. *See* WOOD, *supra*, at 267–273.

25. The full text of the Declaration of Rights is set forth in RAKOVE, *supra*, at 41–45.

immediately preceding the adoption of the Constitution and Bill of Rights, many states also adopted constitutions and many of these constitutions contained bills or declarations of rights, the most important of which were the Virginia and Pennsylvania declarations, both adopted in 1776. Two things are noteworthy about these declarations, however. First, almost all of them were written in broad, hortatory language rather than in terms of specific prohibitions. Thus the state declarations tended to *urge* the legislature or other branches of government to act in certain ways, but without establishing any firm rules, an approach quite inconsistent with the modern view of rights as individual, *legal* entitlements.[26] Second, the state declarations and bills were primarily concerned, like the English Declaration of Rights, with matters of structure and governance rather than individual conduct. For example, the Virginia declaration commits most of its length to discussing the concepts of popular sovereignty, separation of powers, and election of representatives, with only brief mention of freedom of press and of religion (though criminal procedure does get extensive attention, no doubt because of the crucial role of criminal prosecution and the jury in mediating between rulers and the ruled in this period).[27] Similarly, the Pennsylvania Declaration of Rights, while paying greater attention to freedom of religion and conscience, is also primarily a primer on proper political principles for running a government founded in the concept of popular sovereignty.[28] Thus while by 1776 Americans seem to have become aware that protection against governmental tyranny requires not only representative government but also guarantees regarding religion, speech, the press, and the criminal process, the *focus* of the state declarations of rights, like the original English Declaration, remained firmly on principles of governance and the ability of the People collectively to protect themselves against tyranny, rather than on individual autonomy.

If there remains any doubt that the founding generation that produced the Bill of Rights viewed rights in fundamentally different ways from us, an examination of the very sparse discussion of rights during the Constitutional Convention in Philadelphia in 1787 that produced the Constitution should remove them. Interestingly, the Convention barely considered a Bill of Rights during its deliberations. The sole mention was a brief motion by George Mason to draft a Bill of Rights, which was roundly rejected.[29] When the members of the Convention (many of whom were also members of the first Congress that enacted the Bill of Rights, including notably James Madison, who first brought the Bill of Rights to the floor of Congress) did discuss rights, however, their

---

26. Wood, *supra*, at 271–273.

27. The most influential version of the Virginia Declaration of Rights, the Committee draft, is reprinted in Rakove, *supra*, at 81–84. The enactment history of the Declaration is described by Rakove at *id.* at 75–78.

28. *Id.* at 85–87.

29. *See* Rakove, *supra*, at 113–114.

primary focus was on the rights of *states* as against the national government, which they viewed as part and parcel of the collective rights of the People to protect themselves against that central government by limiting its power.[30] Thus for the framers of the Constitution, as for most of their contemporaries, rights were a means for limiting central, governmental power and avoiding tyranny rather than an embodiment of individual autonomy.

Like the historical accounts discussed above, recent legal scholarship has also tended to support this understanding of the founding period. Notably, the legal scholar Akhil Reed Amar has argued extensively that during the founding period rights were viewed in collective terms, and he has supported his position with analysis of the text of the Bill of Rights as well as of contemporary judicial decisions and other evidence.[31] Amar demonstrates the profoundly *structural* rather than individualistic focus of the original Bill of Rights by pointing out that of the original twelve amendments submitted by the Congress to the states (of which only ten were then ratified, becoming the Bill of Rights), the first dealt with the completely structural issue of allocation of seats within Congress, and that even many of the seemingly individualistic provisions such as the Fourth Amendment prohibition on unreasonable searches and seizures was based fundamentally on structural understandings (in this case that the People, in their roles as jurors, would limit arbitrary governmental behavior by punishing government officials who conducted unreasonable searches).[32] Indeed, Amar argues that *all* of the amendments constituting the original Bill of Rights were at their heart structural and collective in nature, a conclusion fully supported by the evidence he provides. Ultimately, however, Amar argues that the nature of constitutional rights shifted from collective, structural measures to individual entitlements during the period following the Civil War. I will argue in the next chapter, however, that Amar greatly overstates the extent of this transformation in modern constitutional law.

The above discussion, suggesting as it does that at the time of the founding of this country *individual* rights were largely nonexistent, must seem extremely peculiar in light of the common wisdom regarding that period. After all, the founders were immersed in the language and philosophy of rights growing out of the Enlightenment, and much of that philosophy undoubtedly understood rights in individualistic terms. Furthermore, the founding document of this nation, the Declaration of Independence, speaks in ringing terms of the "inalienable Rights" of "Life, Liberty, and the Pursuit of Happiness," which certainly sound like individual entitlements. The key to resolving this seeming contradiction is to

---

30. *See* WOOD, *supra*, at 536; RAKOVE, *supra* at 114 (discussing the views of Edmund Randolph, a leading Virginia politician and member of the Constitutional Convention who ultimately refused to sign the Constitution).

31. AKHIL REED AMAR, THE BILL OF RIGHTS at 120, 152–55 (1998).

32. *Id.* at 72–73, 86–87.

understand a basic distinction drawn by the founding generation between *natural* rights and rights within an organized society. The types of rights discussed by Thomas Jefferson in the Declaration of Independence, like the broad rights of conscience and autonomy, were understood to be natural rights enjoyed by all individuals in the state of nature, independent of (and indeed, predating) their joining any organized society. This understanding of natural rights has obvious parallels with the modern view of rights, since natural rights necessarily belong to the individual (because they predate the State), and relate to freedom and autonomy—and indeed Ronald Dworkin has argued that modern rights must be based in natural rights principles.[33] Crucially, however, the founding generation did *not* generally consider natural rights to be legally enforceable; indeed, it was assumed that when individuals entered society they gave up those rights in exchange for the benefits of organized society. Within such an organized society, which the United States surely was by the late eighteenth century, natural rights were not central as a *legal* and constitutional matter, even though they provided important background principles that—as the Declaration of Independence indicates[34]— should guide governmental actions.[35] As we will discuss in more detail in Chapter 10, there existed disagreement within the founding generation, and there remains disagreement today, about whether natural rights were legally enforceable *at all;* but it is clear that such rights, even if enforceable, were not central to the constitutional system of government that was coming into existence. Within such an organized society, the rights that mattered were *collective* rights designed to keep governmental authority constrained and within the control of the People.

Of course, it would be highly deceptive to suggest that the founding generation was unconcerned with concepts of liberty, individual autonomy, and natural rights. Indeed, such concerns lay at the heart of what they were seeking to accomplish, which was to establish a free, limited, and accountable government precisely because such a government would protect those rights and liberties—an idea with roots in English political thinking.[36] During most of the relevant period, however, *rights* as we understand them today had little or no role as a means toward that end—rather, the sole means of protecting liberty was perceived to be popular participation in government through the vehicles of electing representatives

---

33. DWORKIN, *supra*, at 147, 176–77.

34. "We hold these truths to be self-evident, that all men were created equal, that they are endowed by their Creator with certain unalienable rights, that among these are life, liberty, and the pursuit of happiness. That to secure these rights, governments are instituted among men, deriving their just power from the consent of the governed. . . ."

35. *See* RAKOVE, *supra*, at 114, discussing the views of Edmund Randolph. *See also id.* at 96, quoting the Virginia Statute for Religious Freedom (the joint work of Thomas Jefferson and James Madison), also drawing a distinction between natural and legal rights.

36. *See* WOOD, *supra*, at 21–22.

(originally solely in the legislature) and the jury system. At least part of the reason why legally enforceable rights were given little attention was because in England and during the colonial period in America the judiciary was not seen as a defender of popular liberty, but rather as a tool of a tyrannical monarch. One of the great innovations of American political thought during the founding period was the recognition that in a popular government with separated departments, legal rights enforceable by an independent judiciary might play an important (albeit still somewhat peripheral) role in constraining abuse of governmental power. This extraordinary insight, which Thomas Jefferson shared with James Madison in the course of correspondence regarding the need for a Bill of Rights in the federal Constitution,[37] clearly constituted the first, critical step toward the modern system of judicial review and legal rights. It remains the case, however, that the founders, including Jefferson and Madison, continued to draw a distinction between natural and legal rights. For that generation, *legal* rights, including most especially *constitutional* rights, were viewed almost entirely as instruments for protecting the People collectively against an arbitrary or tyrannical government, and *not* as individual entitlements to autonomy. We turn now to a closer look at how these collective rights were intended to, and have, functioned in our constitutional system.

---

37. *See* RAKOVE, *supra*, at 165; WOOD, *supra*, at 543.

3. CONSTITUTIONAL RIGHTS AND THE STRUCTURE OF GOVERNMENT

In the last chapter, I argued that contrary to the modern understanding of rights, reflected both in popular perception and among leading theoreticians, constitutional rights (as opposed to unenforceable natural rights) were conceived by the framing generation not as a source of individual autonomy, but as a tool for the People collectively to protect themselves against an oppressive government. One might ask, however, why it matters what the founders believed rights meant. After all, today we seem to have a widely shared understanding of rights as individual entitlements to autonomy, and that understanding is reflected everywhere from the courts to political debate to legal theory. In this chapter I will argue that the gap between historical and modern understandings of rights matters a great deal, because when modern courts actually enforce the Bill of Rights and the rest of the Constitution (notably the Thirteenth, Fourteenth, and Fifteenth Amendments, generally called the Civil War Amendments), their decisions are heavily shaped by the traditional understanding of rights as collective measures designed to control governmental abuse of power. In fact, the influence of the original, collective view of rights on modern law remains profound, indeed overwhelming. To explain this point fully I am required to further develop two topics. First, I will discuss in more detail how and why legal, constitutional rights differ from natural, individual rights of autonomy, focusing in particular on the close relationship between rights and structural limits on governmental power. Second, I will argue that despite the other, radical changes that occurred in our constitutional system as a consequence of the Civil War and Reconstruction, the role of rights in our legal system did not change fundamentally. In particular, even though for a period of time in the early twentieth century the Supreme Court was enforcing a more individualistic version of constitutional rights, that approach has largely (but not entirely) been abandoned in the modern, post–World War II era.

CONSTITUTIONAL STRUCTURE AND CONSTITUTIONAL RIGHTS

It is commonly understood that, when the Constitutional Convention convened in Philadelphia in the summer of 1787, its objective was to create a national government that would possess the power, energy, and tools to govern the nation and achieve the collective goals of the United States, without tyrannizing the American people. The Preamble to the Constitution describes the reasons why

"We the People" were creating this new Constitution as follows: "to form a more perfect Union, establish Justice, insure domestic tranquility, provide for the common defense, promote the general Welfare, and secure the Blessings of Liberty to ourselves and our Posterity."[1] Thus from the beginning, the framers saw the Constitution as serving the twin goals of creating an effective government *and* securing individual liberty. Yet as noted in the previous chapter, the framers gave almost no attention to incorporating a Bill of Rights into the new document. Why? The answer can be found in the arguments made by the framers in defense of the proposed Constitution during the subsequent ratifying debates, when opponents of the Constitution, called anti-federalists, criticized the document for its omission of a Bill of Rights. The stock answer provided by the federalist defenders of the Constitution was that a Bill of Rights was necessary only as a guard against unlimited power of the sort wielded by kings. The government created by the Constitution, however, was a government of limited powers delegated by the sovereign People. As such, no further limitations on power were necessary.[2] Indeed, the federalists argued, enacting a Bill of Rights was not only unnecessary, it was positively dangerous in that it might be read to *increase* the powers delegated to the national government, by suggesting through negative implication that those powers not limited by a Bill of Rights were in fact granted.[3] In short, the framers viewed rights as the mirror of power, necessary to limit unrestricted powers. In a government of inherently restricted powers, rights simply had no role to play.

But the federalists' arguments did not end with the fact that the new government would possess only limited, enumerated powers. Insofar as limiting the national government to specific, listed powers would not alone be sufficient to prevent tyranny, the new Constitution was chock full of *other* mechanisms for limiting power, which together would accomplish the same purpose. As Alexander Hamilton put it in *Federalist* No. 84, "the constitution is itself in every rational sense, and to every useful purpose, A BILL OF RIGHTS."[4] How so? Because, according to Hamilton, the purposes of a Bill of Rights are to "declare and specify the political privileges of the citizens in the structure and administration of the government," and to "define certain immunities and modes of proceeding, which are relative to personal and private concerns"; but these purposes

---

1. U.S. Constitution, Art. I, Preamble.

2. *See* WOOD, THE CREATION OF THE AMERICAN REPUBLIC at 539–540 (discussing in particular the views of James Wilson).

3. This argument was most famously made by Alexander Hamilton in FEDERALIST No. 84. *See* Alexander Hamilton, James Madison, and John Jay, THE FEDERALIST PAPERS (Garry Wills ed., Bantam 1982), FEDERALIST No. 84 at 437; *see also* LEONARD W. LEVY, ORIGINS OF THE BILL OF RIGHTS 21 (2001) (similar argument made by James Wilson); RAKOVE, DECLARING RIGHTS at 149 (James Iredell).

4. FEDERALIST No. 84 at 438–439.

were fully accomplished by the Constitution itself.[5] Presumably, what Hamilton meant by this statement was that the structure of the national government, and the inherent limits on its power, were a far more effective protection for the People than any Bill of Rights. Such limits include the division of the legislative branch into two, independent chambers, the House and the Senate; the electoral accountability of members of the House; the creation of independent executive and judicial branches (the former with a veto on all legislation) to further check Congress; and various specific restrictions on congressional power such as the bars on bills of attainder and ex post facto laws,[6] the elimination of titles of nobility,[7] and the severe limits on suspension of the writ of habeas corpus.[8] In toto, Hamilton concludes, such provisions along with the core concept of popular sovereignty enshrined in the Constitution, including notably the Preamble, would be far more effective in protecting "popular rights, than volumes of those aphorisms which make the principal figure in several of our State bills of rights, and which would sound much better in a treatise of ethics than in a constitution of government."[9]

The key point here is that for Hamilton and his fellow framers, there was no clear distinction between a Bill of Rights and structural provisions of the Constitution aimed at restricting the arbitrary use of power. Even the limitations on congressional power cited by Hamilton, such as the bar on ex post facto laws (laws that criminalize conduct *after* it has occurred) or the protection of the writ of habeas corpus, do not identify spheres of individual autonomy to protect. Rather, they are restrictions on the misuse of official power. Rights, like structural constitutional provisions, were designed to protect the People against the tyrannical use of power by rulers, and as such were interchangeable with structural limitations on power of the sort that did not exist in absolute monarchies (or even, to the same degree, in the English system of mixed, parliamentary government).

Of course, the federalists eventually lost their argument against the need for a Bill of Rights. When it became clear during the ratification debates that the absence of a Bill of Rights was placing ratification of the Constitution at risk, the federalists agreed that that upon ratification, a Bill of Rights should be added to the Constitution. Carrying through on these commitments, one of the first steps taken by the newly elected Congress following ratification was to propose a series of amendments that became our Bill of Rights. Do those developments represent a victory for an individualistic view of rights, as opposed to the collective, structural vision of Hamilton and his ilk? An examination of the background

---

5. *Ibid.*
6. U.S. Constitution, Art. I, Sec. 9, cl. 3.
7. U.S. Constitution, Art. I, Sec. 9, cl. 8.
8. U.S. Constitution, Art. I, Sec. 9, cl. 2.
9. FEDERALIST No. 84 at 437.

and text of those amendments makes it clear that even though some ambiguity regarding the role of rights is evident in the thinking of a very few members of the framing generation (including notably James Madison, the original proponent of the amendments), on the whole there can be no doubt that the collective vision of rights permeates and motivates those amendments.

The constitutional amendments that eventually became the Bill of Rights have their genesis in objections raised to the proposed Constitution in the ratifying conventions of various states. Many of these conventions were in turn critically influenced by a "Master Draft" of a Bill of Rights created and circulated by George Mason of Virginia.[10] Based on the proposals of these state conventions, on June 8, 1789, James Madison introduced in the House of Representatives a series of nine constitutional amendments, which, after many revisions, would eventually become our Bill of Rights.[11] The form of those amendments was very different from the eventual Bill of Rights (for example, they were styled as making changes to the enacted constitutional text itself, rather than as amendments to be listed after the text, which was the practice eventually adopted), and many of Madison's specific proposals were never adopted. Nonetheless, the essence of almost all of the eventual Bill of Rights can be found in Madison's proposals. What stands out clearly from Madison's proposals, as from Mason's original draft, is that the focus of the proposed amendments was clearly on restraining governmental power and ensuring its democratic qualities, rather than on individual autonomy as such. Most notably, Madison's *first* proposed amendment, which Madison himself described as "what may be called a bill of rights," was a simple statement of popular sovereignty (to be affixed to the Preamble), which clarified that all power was derived from the people, that power must be exercised for the benefit of the people, and that the people retained the authority to alter the form of their government if they so chose. The second proposed amendment dealt with apportionment of seats in the House of Representatives. And the third imposed limits on members of Congress raising their own salaries between elections (after languishing for two centuries, this provision eventually became our Twenty-Seventh Amendment in 1992). None of these provisions concern "rights" as understood in modern parlance, yet they formed an important part of Madison's proposals (though admittedly, their placement at the head of the list has no special meaning—that was simply because they proposed amending earlier parts of the Constitution). Further on in Madison's proposals we find an amendment explicitly inserting into the constitutional text the principle of separation of powers (i.e., that each of the three

---

10. Mason's Master Draft can be found at http://www.constitution.org/gmason/amd_gmas.htm (last visited July 12, 2006).

11. The text of Madison's speech can be found at http://www.constitution.org/ac/001/r01-1/bill_of_rights_hr1789.htm (last visited July 12, 2006). The speech is also discussed in RAKOVE, DECLARING RIGHTS at 170 and following.

branches of government may exercise its own powers only, not those of the other branches). Again, we see a clearly structural provision interspersed among more obvious "rights-granting" ones. Finally, Madison's explanation for why these amendments were necessary focused not on individual autonomy, but on the need to restrain governmental power for the collective good. As Madison put it, whatever the precise form or precise roots of a Bill of Rights, its principle purpose is always "to limit and qualify the powers of government, by excepting out of the grant of power those cases in which the government ought not to act, or to act only in a particular mode."[12]

In September 1789, after debate, compromise, and many changes to Madison's proposals, Congress eventually sent twelve proposed amendments to the states for ratification. The first two proposed amendments, dealing with House apportionment and congressional compensation, were not ratified at this time (though as noted above, the second was ratified in 1992). The third through twelfth amendments were ratified by the requisite three-quarters of the states on December 15, 1791, becoming the Bill of Rights. At first glance, it might appear that the ten amendments that eventually *were* ratified (or at least the first eight of them) are more clearly directed at individual autonomy than on a need to protect the collective people against tyrannical government. On closer examination, however, that turns out not to be the case. As a whole, the focus of the ten ratified amendments is clearly structural and collective. While I will defer a close examination of the structure and purposes of the most important of these amendments until the second part of this book, it is valuable at the outset to look at the ten amendments as a whole, to understand how they fit together, and how they reflect the structural and collective vision of the framing generation.[13]

THE STRUCTURAL BILL OF RIGHTS: A FIRST LOOK

The First Amendment reads as follows: "Congress shall make no law respecting an establishment of religion, or prohibiting the free exercise thereof; or abridging the freedom of speech, or of the press; or the right of the people peaceably to assemble, and to petition the Government for a redress of grievances." The amendment thus addresses three topics: speech and the press, religion, and assembly and petition. Taking the last first, it is immediately obvious that the "right of the *people*" to assemble and petition is a collective right, deeply intertwined with the democratic structure of the constitution. Assembly and petition are not exercises of individual autonomy, they are a collective means for the People to involve themselves in government, as a supplement to voting in

---

12. *Ibid.*

13. As will become obvious, my discussion here draws heavily upon Akhil Reed Amar's path-breaking book THE BILL OF RIGHTS (Yale University Press 1998).

biannual elections. But what of freedom of speech and of the press? Surely free speech is the quintessential right of autonomy, a bulwark for individuals against majority rule? Not necessarily. For one thing, there is a substantial argument to be made that when adopted, the First Amendment was understood only to prohibit so-called "prior restraints" on speech and the press, which is to say, laws forbidding speech before it occurred (typically through a licensing scheme); punishing speakers after the fact because of what they said, under this view, was entirely unproblematic.[14] Such a reading provides little meaningful protection to individual autonomy, but it does substantially restrain the power of an incumbent government to protect itself from criticism—most significantly by interposing a criminal jury, composed of ordinary citizens, between the government and its critics. Even if First Amendment protections are not limited to prior restraints—as we now believe—that does not mean that the purpose of the speech and press clauses is to defend individual autonomy. Rather, as Supreme Court Justice Louis Brandeis and the philosopher Alexander Meiklejohn argued in the early to mid-twentieth century, the better understanding is that purpose of those clauses is to protect *democracy*—i.e., to enable the People in their collective capacity to maintain oversight and control over their elected representatives.[15] It is for this reason that political speech has always been considered the most valuable and highly protected speech for First Amendment purposes, and it is for this reason that under modern free speech law, the critical determinant of whether a free speech claim will be upheld is not the impact of a law on free speech or individual autonomy, but rather is the government's censorial intent.[16] No individual-autonomy based theory can explain this structure. None of which is to say that *only* political speech should be protected by the First Amendment; there are good arguments to be made that a proper understanding of the functioning of democracy and popular sovereignty requires a broad definition of free speech.[17] But it does argue strongly in favor of a collective, structural understanding of the *purposes* of the speech and press clauses of the First Amendment.

---

14. The position that free speech consists of nothing more than freedom from prior restraints has its roots in the writings of William Blackstone, and was accepted by, among others, Supreme Court Justice Joseph Story, the author of the premier commentaries on the Constitution in the early Republic. J. STORY, COMMENTARIES ON THE CONSTITUTION OF THE UNITED STATES §1879 (1833). This interpretation was also put forward by no less than Justice Oliver Wendell Holmes in *Patterson v. Colorado*, 205 U.S. 454, 462 (1907), though Holmes later abandoned this position.

15. *See* Whitney v. California, 274 U.S. 357, 374–377 (1927) (Brandeis, J., concurring); ALEXANDER MEIKLEJOHN, FREE SPEECH AND ITS RELATION TO SELF-GOVERNMENT (1948).

16. I explain and develop this proposition, and its implications, further in Chapter 4.

17. Alexander Meiklejohn expounded this position in *The First Amendment is an Absolute*, 1961 S. CT. REV. 245. I have also defended a similar position in an earlier article. Ashutosh Bhagwat, *Of Markets and Media: The First Amendment, the New Mass Media, and the Political Components of Culture*, 74 N.C. L. REV. 141, 176–187 (1995).

Finally, we come to the two religion clauses: the Establishment Clause and the Free Exercise Clause. That the Establishment Clause is structural and collective in nature is clear from its text and history. As originally enacted and understood, the Establishment Clause provided absolutely no protection for individual religious worship or worshippers. Instead, the Clause ensured that the national government would not align itself with a particular church and also would not interfere with state governments that had established their own churches. As such, the Establishment Clause not only did not protect members of minority religions, it acted to their detriment, by protecting state establishments. As a result of a complex set of developments that we will examine shortly, in modern times the Establishment Clause has been applied to prevent state as well as federal religious establishments (to use the jargon, has been "incorporated" against the states), but as we shall see when we examine modern law in more detail (in Chapter 6), its primary role remains to maintain a structural separation between church and state, rather than to protect individuals as such. In this respect, the Establishment Clause might seem a clear contrast to the free exercise clause, which on its face does seem to protect individual religious worship. As Yale Professor Akhil Amar points out, however, that is not necessarily so. Professor Amar argues convincingly that both at the time of the framing and under modern law, the free exercise clause only prohibits Congress (and now state legislatures) from passing statutes specifically targeted at religious worship. It does not grant individuals any right to worship in violation of general laws with secular purposes.[18] Furthermore, from a historical perspective this reading makes some sense. Looking at the European experience over the two centuries prior to the ratification of the Constitution and Bill of Rights, the framers would have been able to point to countless examples of governments suppressing disfavored religious groups, resulting in endless conflict and civil war. It was that concern—the misuse of governmental power to create social division—that explains the free exercise clause, and the religion clauses generally. Again, this is not to say that the framing generation did not believe in a *natural* right, held by individuals, to freedom of conscience and religious exercise; but the focus of the First Amendment's religion clauses was not that, it was the relationship between religion and the government.

Let us now move on from the First Amendment to the rest of the Bill of Rights, and to the Fourteenth Amendment. We have already discussed in detail, in Chapter One, the fundamental structural purposes, and structural design, of the Second Amendment's "right . . . to keep and bear Arms." As we there noted, there can be no doubt that the Second Amendment's primary purpose, and during the framing period entire significance, lay in providing a collective

---

18. AMAR, THE BILL OF RIGHTS at 42–44 (citing *Employment Division v. Smith*, 494 U.S. 872 (1990).

defense for the People (acting in their capacities as citizen soldiers, under the aegis of their state governments) against a potentially tyrannical national government possessing a dreaded standing, professional army. Fear of a standing army, and what it might mean for a democratic society, also explains the structural context of the ever-obscure Third Amendment. The Third Amendment provides that "[n]o Soldier shall, in time of peace, be quartered in any house, without the consent of the owner, nor in time of war, but in a manner prescribed by law." While on its face the amendment might be read to protect an individual's privacy in his or her home, upon closer look that is a distinctly odd explanation. Notice, for one thing, that during times of war (when presumably quartering would be most likely), the amendment provides *no* privacy protection, it merely ensures that soldiers be quartered in accordance with "law"—i.e., the amendment restrains the president, or the military, acting alone, but it does not restrain Congress. During times of peace the amendment does absolutely bar the involuntary quartering of soldiers, but again, this is a most narrow and peculiar defense of privacy. Why soldiers in particular? Note that the Third Amendment does not protect the home from search or seizure (that is done in the Fourth Amendment) or from simple dispossession (to the extent that that is addressed, it is in the Takings Clause of the Fifth Amendment). The answer, unsurprisingly, lies in history. During the years leading up to the Revolutionary War, British troops were involuntarily quartered with colonial families pursuant to the Quartering Act of 1774, as a means of exercising control and (to some extent) punishing colonials for acts of disobedience such as the Boston Tea Party.[19] These actions were specifically cited in the Declaration of Independence as one of the grievances that had led the colonies to "dissolve the Political Bands" binding them to Great Britain; and ultimately, of course, the Third Amendment was enacted to prevent the recurrence of such behavior. Seen in this light it becomes clear that the Third Amendment was not about privacy as such, it was about erecting a barrier to military occupation by a professional, standing army— originally one controlled by the king of Great Britain, but now one controlled by a distant, national government.[20]

The Fourth Amendment prohibits "unreasonable searches and seizures" in order to protect "[t]he right of the people to be secure in their persons, houses, papers, and effects," and also imposes limitations on the issuance of warrants. Like the Third Amendment, this provision at first glance would appear to be a straightforward effort to protect individual privacy and autonomy. Notice, however, that the amendment does not prohibit searches and seizures as such, nor

---

19. AMAR, THE BILL OF RIGHTS at 59; DAVID HUTCHISON, THE FOUNDATIONS OF THE CONSTITUTION 292–293 (University Books 1975).

20. For an interesting argument interpreting the Third Amendment as forbidding the conscription of the People's property for military purposes, just as the Second Amendment forbids the conscription of the militia itself, *See* AMAR, THE BILL OF RIGHTS at 59–63.

even searches and seizures without warrants (though it has sometimes been so interpreted in modern times), it prohibits only *unreasonable* searches and seizures. What makes a search unreasonable? Is it the degree of the intrusion on personal privacy? To some extent it is, but the primary focus of a reasonableness inquiry must be the government's justifications and motivations for the search if society is to function. Once again, therefore, the focus is on the misuse of governmental power to oppress "the people," not on individuals as such. Moreover, Professor Akhil Amar has made a highly persuasive argument that one of the primary purposes of the Fourth Amendment was to interpose a *jury* between the government and private citizens, by permitting citizens subject to search or seizure to litigate the reasonableness of the government's actions before a jury of their peers.[21] Juries, of course, are a cross-section of, and represent the People; they are indeed the embodiment of collective, popular participation in our system of government.[22] Finally, one might ask *why* the framers chose to address searches and seizures in the Bill of Rights. One might think that the purpose was to protect citizens' privacy from marauding government officials, but remember that in the late eighteenth century, large, professional police forces of the modern sort did not yet exist. Moreover, in a functioning democracy one would think that elected officials who permitted random, oppressive searches of innocent people might face some consequences! If, however, government officials were to misuse their search and seizure authority to selectively harass their political opponents, such behavior might escape political consequences; yet in the long run, such behavior could substantially undermine democracy and the ability of the collective People to control their government.[23] Seen in this light, the Fourth Amendment, like the First Amendment, is a critical tool in protecting the structure of democratic government from being undermined by the misuse of power.

The rest of the substantive amendments of the Bill of Rights—the Fifth, Sixth, Seventh, and Eighth—can be discussed quickly. Most of the provisions of those amendments address the criminal justice process by ensuring that the government follows fair procedures when prosecuting citizens for crimes. The Due Process Clause is the most obvious statement of this principle. Other such provisions are the Double Jeopardy and Self-Incrimination Clauses of the Fifth Amendment (which respectively provide that a defendant may not be retried

---

21. AMAR, THE BILL OF RIGHTS at 68–77.

22. For an excellent discussion of the political role of juries in the founding era, *see* Vikram David Amar, *Jury Service As Political Participation Akin to Voting*, 80 CORNELL L. REV. 203, 218–221 (1995).

23. There is indeed historical evidence that the Fourth Amendment was inspired in part by just such uses of searches and seizures in Great Britain. *See* Akhil Reed Amar, *The Fourth Amendment, Boston, and the Writs of Assistance*, 30 SUFFOLK U. L. REV. 53, 65 (1996) (discussing the cases of *Wilkes v. Wood* and *Entick v. Carrington*).

after being acquitted by a jury, and may not be required to testify against him-self), as well as Confrontation and the Compulsory Process Clauses of the Sixth Amendment (which require, respectively, that defendants be informed of the charges against them and face their accusers, and themselves have the ability to require witnesses to appear on their behalf). None of these provisions contribute to autonomy in any meaningful way—they do not let citizens *do* anything, nor do they protect against ultimate conviction. Rather, they ensure that the govern-ment, when employing its ultimate coercive mechanisms, does not abuse its power or illegitimately target its enemies, just as the Eighth Amendment's pro-hibition on excessive bails and cruel and unusual punishments ensures that the state does not use the excuse of a trivial infraction to impose disproportionate harms on its enemies. Indeed, the most significant of the criminal procedure protections, the right to a Grand Jury indictment, and to a public trial before a local jury, are paradigmatic examples of interposing the collective People, acting through their representative jurors, into the criminal process to provide a check against the power of the State. Finally, the Seventh Amendment's guaranty of a civil jury interposes the People into dispute resolution, again forestalling the possibility that the government (acting through partisan or biased judges) will favor its friends and punish its enemies.

There is one provision in this series of amendments, however, that does not fit well into this clear pattern—the Takings Clause at the end of the Fifth Amendment. The Takings Clause reads as follows: "nor shall private property be taken for public use without just compensation." The clause requires than when the government employs the power of eminent domain—i.e., the power to take ownership of citizens' property against their will—it must meet two require-ments: that the property must be taken "for public use," and that the owner be paid "just compensation." In truth, it is quite difficult to reconcile this provision, focusing as it does on the property rights of individuals, with the broader, collec-tive themes of the rest of the Bill of Rights (though Professor Amar does try val-iantly[24]). Rather, the Takings Clause may represent an important, though minor, countercurrent in the otherwise intensely structural and collective zeitgeist of the Bill of Rights—and a distinctly Madisonian one at that. It should be noted that there was no precursor to the Takings Clause in George Mason's Master Draft of the Bill of Rights. Rather, this clause appears to have been the work of James Madison alone, slipped into the Fifth Amendment (which otherwise deals with the quite distinct subject of criminal procedure) and adopted by stealth (or as Amar calls it, by "clever bundling"[25]). It is clear from his writings that by the late 1780s, James Madison had become seriously disenchanted by popular gov-ernment. He, unlike most of his contemporaries, no longer saw popular control

---

24. Amar, The Bill of Rights at 77–80.
25. *Id.* at 78.

over government as the solution to despotism; he saw it as a potential source of despotic policies. In particular, in *Federalist* No. 10 Madison expounded a detailed theory of democratic "factions," which he defined as "a number of citizens, whether amounting to a majority or a minority of the whole, who are united and actuated by some common impulse of passion, or of interest, adverse to the rights of other citizens, or to the permanent and aggregate interests of the community." Factions, in Madison's view, were the bane of popular, democratic governments, leading to majoritarian tyranny and unstable government. Later in *Federalist* No. 10, and then again in *Federalist* No. 51, Madison sought to explain how the federal Republic created by the Constitution, because of its great size, because of its reliance on representative rather than direct democracy, and because of its division of power between federal and state governments, as well as between the branches of the national government, was likely to be less prone to the problem of factions than existing state governments. It should be noted in passing that even Madison, the most "libertarian" of the framers, relied primarily on *structural* provisions to ameliorate the flaws of popular government. For our purposes, however, the crucial point is what Madison saw as the source of faction, which he identifies as "[t]he diversity in the faculties of men, from which the rights of property originate," and which results in "the possession of different degrees and kinds of property."[26] Elsewhere Madison identifies as potential results of faction "[a] rage for paper money, for an abolition of debts, for an equal division of property, or for any other improper or wicked project."[27] In short, by the late 1780s Madison had become convinced that property owners were highly vulnerable to abuse (or what Madison thought was abuse) at the hands of democratic government. Seen in this regard, the Takings Clause makes sense. In an otherwise overwhelmingly collective, structural set of measures, it is the one provision designed to protect a form of minority autonomy against majoritarian oppression, and it protects the only form of autonomy that Madison seemed truly concerned about—the autonomy to hold and control property in the face of redistributive legislation.

Finally, we come to the Ninth and Tenth Amendments, the structural coda to the Bill of Rights. The Ninth Amendment reads, "the enumeration in the Constitution of certain rights shall not be construed to deny or disparage others retained by the People," while the Tenth states that "the powers not delegated to the United States by the Constitution, nor prohibited by it to the States, are reserved to the States respectively, or to the people." The Tenth Amendment is obviously a structural provision, addressing the distribution of governmental powers in a federal system, and in particular, reaffirming the critical principle that the national government was one of limited, enumerated powers only.

---

26. THE FEDERALIST PAPERS, *supra*, FEDERALIST No. 10 at 43–44.
27. *Id.* at 49.

As our discussion to this point should make obvious, for the framers this provision was a natural complement to the rest of the Bill of Rights, confirming that not only were the national government's powers limited in the ways identified in the earlier amendments, they were also limited by the principle of enumeration. It should be noted in this regard that the reference to "the people" in the Tenth Amendment is necessarily a collective one, since obviously *individuals* cannot exercise "powers" not given to the national government; such powers could only be exercised by the people collectively. But what of the Ninth Amendment, with its explicit reference to "rights"? The Ninth Amendment is frankly one of the most obscure, ill-understood provisions of the Constitution. It has never been the explicit basis for *any* decision of the Supreme Court, and has largely been treated as hortatory only. Indeed, the only significant cases in which the Court has relied even partially on the Ninth Amendment are the modern "privacy" cases dealing with reproductive and sexual freedom, including abortion.[28] Whatever the Ninth Amendment means, however, it *cannot* be read to create a broad, undefined sphere of individual autonomy, enforceable by the courts against the legislative power. How could such a sphere of autonomy be defined, and more to the point, how could government function in the face of such an undefined sphere? After all, it is the very function of law to limit autonomy, to impose constraints on individuals, in the name of the common good. The Ninth Amendment conundrum clears up, however, when one recognizes that the phrase "the people," in the Ninth Amendment *must*, like the phrase "the people" in the Tenth Amendment and in the preamble, refer to the People of the United States in their collective, sovereign capacity. Seen in this way, the Ninth Amendment makes perfect sense. Just as the framers saw "rights" as the converse of power, the Ninth Amendment is the logical converse to the Tenth. If the Tenth Amendment recognizes that the States and the People collectively retain legislative powers not granted to the national government, the Ninth recognizes that the first eight amendments do not necessarily identity *all* of the structural limitations on the powers of the government that may be necessary to protect the ultimate authority of the sovereign People. Akhil Amar argues that the most important of the limitations is the fact that the People retain the right "to alter and abolish it, and to institute new Government," in the words of the Declaration of Independence.[29] Regardless of whether this is true, it is clear that the Ninth and Tenth Amendments announce principles of structure and control, about the distribution of power in a republican system of government, and not individual autonomy.

If there is any doubt remaining about the fundamentally collective and structural goals of the Bill of Rights, it disappears when one takes account of a gaping

---

28. *See* Griswold v. Connecticut, 381 U.S. 479, 484 (1965).
29. AMAR, THE BILL OF RIGHTS at 120–122.

hole in the Bill of Rights—the fact that the Bill of Rights as originally enacted imposed *no* limits on the authority of *state* governments. That this was the case is not seriously disputed. Despite the fact that most of the provisions of the Bill of Rights (except for the First Amendment) impose prohibitions on general terms (e.g., the Second Amendment states "the right of the people to keep and bear Arms, shall not be infringed"), it was well understood by the framers that the Bill of Rights limited only the power of the *federal* government, not state governments—a point that the Supreme Court confirmed in its 1833 decision in *Barron v. Mayor & City Council of Baltimore*,[30] written by Chief Justice John Marshall. But how could limits on national power alone protect individual autonomy? After all, in the early Republic (and even today, to a great extent) most laws, and most powers, were the province of state governments, not the national one. As such, by far the greatest threat to individual autonomy lay in those governments, not a national government of highly limited powers (most of which operated in the realm of foreign affairs, and so had little impact on individuals). James Madison certainly understood this point, and indeed, given Madison's now-jaundiced views on popular government, he saw state governments as greater threats to liberty than the national government, precisely because of their greater democratic accountability. As such, at the Constitutional Convention he argued in favor of a national negative on state laws, and in his original, proposed Bill of Rights he included a provision that stated: "No state shall violate the equal rights of conscience, or the freedom of the press, or the trial by jury in criminal cases."[31] Neither of Madison's proposals, however, were adopted (or even garnered serious support). Moreover, while the original Constitution (in Article I, Section 10) did contain some restrictions on state authority, almost all of them were structural in nature, designed to ensure and defend Congress's preeminence in areas of policy (such as trade and foreign affairs) where the new Constitution vested the national government with broad powers. Again, with the possible exception of the provision forbidding states from "impairing the Obligation of Contracts," individual autonomy was simply not the focus. For most of Madison's generation, then, the primary focus in framing a Constitution was not individual autonomy as such (though certainly that was an *ultimate* goal), but rather how to maintain a balance between the need for an effective government, and the need to maintain the collective People's control over that government. The structural provisions of the original Constitution constituted one solution to that conundrum, while the Bill or Rights constituted another, complementary one.

---

30. 32 U.S. (7 Pet.) 243 (1833).
31. Http://www.constitution.org/bor/amd_jmad.htm (last visited Aug. 10, 2006).

THE CIVIL WAR AND THE REVOLUTIONARY FOURTEENTH AMENDMENT

The above discussion demonstrates that from the perspective of the framing generation, the purpose and operation of the Bill of Rights was fundamentally structural; the Bill of Rights was a tool designed to protect the collective People against a potentially tyrannical national government, and concomitantly, to maintain their control and supremacy over that government. Protecting individual autonomy and the "natural rights" of individuals may have been an ultimate goal of this enterprise, but it was not the central, or even a significant, consideration in framing the textual Constitution, including the first ten amendments. But of course, constitutional history did not end in 1789 or in 1791. In particular, since that time we have lived through at least one, and perhaps two constitutional revolutions. The first was the Civil War and its constitutional aftermath, the enactment of the Thirteenth, Fourteenth, and Fifteenth Amendments. The second, arguable revolution was the New Deal of President Franklin Delano Roosevelt, which resulted in no significant constitutional amendments, but which fundamentally changed the structure of American government as well as of constitutional jurisprudence.[32] Might it be that even if the original Constitution and Bill of Rights were not focused on individual autonomy, the Constitution that emerged from one or both of those revolutions was? This is the argument that has been advanced by Professor Akhil Amar, referring in particular to the changes made to the Constitution by Reconstruction and the Fourteenth Amendment,[33] and it is a plausible one. Indeed, Professor Amar makes a compelling case for the position that the drafters and ratifiers of the Fourteenth Amendment understood the Fourteenth Amendment to reconceptualize the concept of rights into one focused much more on individual liberties and protection of minorities against majoritarian oppression and, as part and parcel of this, to "incorporate" against the states the provisions of the Bill of Rights that created individual liberties. While I have no quarrel with the historical story that Amar tells, and indeed have no doubt that the Fourteenth Amendment was intended to incorporate the Bill of Rights against state governments, I do believe that with one important qualification, Professor Amar's argument vastly overstates the extent to which *in practice* the Fourteenth Amendment transformed the content and character of constitutional law, including the function and operation of the Bill of Rights.

In the wake of the Civil War, the Reconstruction Congress proposed, and the states ratified, three constitutional amendments: the Thirteenth Amendment in 1865, the Fourteenth Amendment in 1868, and the Fifteenth Amendment

---

32. The primary academic proponent of the position that the New Deal constituted a true constitutional revolution is Professor Bruce Ackerman of Yale University. *See* BRUCE ACKERMAN, WE THE PEOPLE: FOUNDATIONS ch. 5 (Belknap 1991).

33. *See generally* AMAR, THE BILL OF RIGHTS (Yale University Press 1998).

in 1870. The Thirteenth Amendment codified and expanded President Lincoln's Emancipation Proclamation, ending slavery in the United States—an obviously epochal event, but not central to our story. The Fifteenth Amendment prohibited racial discrimination in voting—again, an important event, but a relatively narrow one. By far the most significant of the Reconstruction amendments for modern purposes was the Fourteenth Amendment, and in particular, Section One of the Fourteenth Amendment, which fundamentally changed the relationship between the national and state governments in our constitutional system. The first sentence of Section One grants state and national citizenship to all persons born or naturalized in the United States, thereby reversing the Supreme Court's infamous *Dred Scott* decision[34] and (theoretically) granting African Americans full rights of citizenship. The second, critical sentence reads as follows: "No State shall make or enforce any law which shall abridge the privileges or immunities of citizens of the United States; nor shall any State deprive any person of life, liberty, or property, without due process of law; nor deny any person within its jurisdiction the equal protection of the laws." This sentence thus imposes three distinct restrictions on state governments: they may not (1) abridge the privileges or immunities of U.S. citizens; (2) deprive any person of life, liberty, or property without due process; or (3) deny any person equal protection of the laws.

Note immediately that of these three restrictions, the latter two *on their face* (the subsequent history is more complicated) do not create any substantive rights. Rather, the due process clause merely imposes *procedural* restrictions on states, and the equal protection clause states that citizens cannot be treated unequally—i.e., discriminated against (for obvious historical reasons, the primary, some have argued exclusive, focus of the Equal Protection Clause has always been understood to be racial discrimination). If the Fourteenth Amendment augured in a new system of individual liberties, then, it had to be through the Privileges or Immunities Clause. And indeed, Professor Amar makes a powerful case that at least some of the framers of the Fourteenth Amendment (including its primary sponsors in the House and Senate) intended that this clause would transform many of the provisions of the Bill of Rights into enforceable, individual rights, applicable against state governments and designed to protect individuals against abuse by hostile majorities.[35] While this understanding of the purpose and effect of the Fourteenth Amendment was contested at the time the amendment was enacted, as it is today, Amar's defense of it is quite persuasive. No matter how persuasive, however, this interpretation is *not*

---

34. Dred Scott v. Sandford, 60 U.S. (19 How.) 393 (1857).

35. To be precise, Amar reads the Privileges and Immunities Clause as designed to a form of "refined incorporation," through which some, but not all, of the provisions of the first eight amendments were made applicable against the states. *See generally,* AMAR, THE BILL OF RIGHTS, chs. 9 and 10.

the one that has *ever* prevailed in the courts. Instead, in its important 1873 decision in *The Slaughter-House Cases*,[36] the Supreme Court largely emasculated the Privileges or Immunities Clause, interpreting it to protect only those rights, privileges, and immunities that are distinctly national in character, such as the right to travel to the national capital, or the 'right of free access to . . . seaports." In so holding, the Court specifically rejected that idea that the clause protected natural rights of autonomy. This conclusion has since been heavily criticized, and indeed is almost certainly incorrect; but it remains binding precedent today. As a consequence, the Privileges or Immunities Clause has been a dead letter almost since its adoption, and certainly has not been invoked as the basis for a broad, new jurisprudence of individual rights and autonomy.

The death of the Privileges or Immunities Clause, however, does not end our story. Instead, we come to the next chapter, an odd plot twist indeed: the resurrection of incorporation through the unlikely auspices of the Due Process Clause of the Fourteenth Amendment. It is obvious from the text of the Due Process Clause that its primary function is to impose a *procedural* constraint on state governments (just as its cousin, the Due Process Clause of the Fifth Amendment, imposes a procedural constraint on the federal government). The Clause does not by its language seem to deprive states of any substantive power, or to grant individuals any substantive right; it merely requires that if a state wishes to punish an individual, it must accord that individual procedural protection—in essence, a fair trial. Nonetheless, at least since the Supreme Court's *Dred Scott* decision in 1857, there have been hints in judicial decisions that the Due Process Clauses also have a substantive component to them, imposing actual, substantive constraints on legislative power. In the late nineteenth century the Supreme Court began to suggest with increasing frequency that due process was indeed substantive in part. All of this culminated in the Court's path-breaking decision in *Lochner v. New York* in 1905,[37] in which the Court relied on the Due Process Clause to strike down a state law regulating the working hours of bakers on the grounds that the law unconstitutionally burdened the freedom of contract of bakers and their employers, one of the liberties accorded substantive protection by the Due Process Clause. At least since *Lochner*, and to this day, the Court has consistently and unambiguously held that the Due Process Clause does indeed have a substantive component. This interpretation has had two important consequences: First, it has resulted in the "incorporation" against the states of most of the substantive prohibitions of the Bill of Rights, through the Due Process

---

36. 83 U.S. (16 Wall.) 36 (1873). These cases involved a constitutional challenge pursuant to the Fourteenth Amendment to a Louisiana statute that granted a particular company (the Crescent City Live-Stock Landing and Slaughter-House Company) a legal monopoly within the City of New Orleans over the businesses of landing livestock and operating a slaughterhouse. The Court upheld the statute.

37. 198 U.S. 45 (1905).

Clause; and second, it has resulted in the enforcement, against both the state and the federal government, of certain nontextual rights such as the freedom of contract at issue in *Lochner*, and the right of "privacy" that forms the basis of the modern abortion cases. Each of these developments must be considered in turn, to understand the full impact of so-called "substantive due process" on the jurisprudence of rights.

The basic idea behind incorporation is a simple one. Even though prior to the Civil War, and pursuant to the *Barron* case, the Bill of Rights restricted only the national government's power, after the Fourteenth Amendment it restricts the states as well. As a matter of text and history, the natural textual vehicle for incorporation was the Privileges or Immunities Clause, but that path was closed by the *Slaughter-House Cases*. Once the Court accepted that the Due Process Clause had substantive content, however, it was natural that at least some of the substantive rights protected via due process would be those listed in the first eight amendments. And that is indeed what happened—the First Amendment's free speech clause, for example, was incorporated via due process in the *Gitlow v. New York* case in 1925.[38] The path to incorporation, however, was an uneven one. Instead of holding simply that the Bill of Rights applied against the states, during most of the twentieth century the Court adopted the position that only basic or fundamental rights were incorporated—the classic formulation was Justice Benjamin Cardozo's that the right must be "of the very essence of a scheme of ordered liberty."[39] Moreover, the fact that a right was listed in the first eight amendments was neither necessary nor sufficient to make it fundamental. In short, the Court during this period interpreted the Due Process Clause—or more precisely, the Due Process Clauses, since they did not distinguish between the Fifth and Fourteenth Amendments—to protect natural rights, precisely what the framers of the Bill of Rights did *not* understand their Constitution to do.

If the above approach to incorporation had prevailed, it might have resulted in a broad jurisprudence of natural rights, untethered to either text or history. But it did not. Instead, during the 1960s the Warren Court abandoned natural law incorporation, and replaced it with a system of mechanical, and almost automatic incorporation, under which almost all of the provisions of the first eight amendments have been incorporated against the states, and are applied against the states on precisely the same terms as they are applied against the federal government. The only exceptions to mechanical incorporation are the Third Amendment, the grand jury provision of the Fifth Amendment, and the Seventh Amendment, all of which are, in the modern world, peripheral provisions at best. The consequence of this transformation is profound. Today, there is no separation

---

38. 268 U.S. 652 (1925).
39. Palko v. Connecticut, 302 U.S. 319 (1937).

between the jurisprudence interpreting the Bill of Rights as applied to the national government, and the jurisprudence applying those provisions, through incorporation, against the states. The consequence is that at least the incorporation prong of the law of substantive due process is no longer a jurisprudence of natural rights. Instead, it is a body of law focused on the text, and history, of the Bill of Rights itself. But as we have already noted, the original Bill of Rights is not, as a textual or historical matter, primarily a body of individual rights or a source of protection for individual autonomy. In the second part of this book I will demonstrate that for this reason, modern judicial decisions interpreting and applying the Bill of Rights, both against the states and against the national government, ultimately are not focused on autonomy.

What then of the second prong of substantive due process, the law of nontextual (or "unenumerated") rights? There can be no doubt that during the heyday of the so-called "*Lochner* era," from 1905 to 1937, this part of the jurisprudence of substantive due process *did* protect natural rights and individual autonomy. In particular, the Supreme Court of this era gave primary protection to economic autonomy, through enforcement of the right of freedom of contract, invoking this right to strike down much workers' rights legislation. But the Court did not limit itself exclusively to economic autonomy; during this period it also provided protection for the natural rights of parents to control the raising and education of their children.[40] Again, if this approach had prevailed, a full-blown jurisprudence of natural rights might have blossomed. But it did not. In 1937 in a case named *West Coast Hotel Co. v. Parrish*,[41] the Supreme Court fully and finally abandoned the approach of *Lochner*. In particular, while the *West Coast Hotel* Court did not formally abandon the concept of substantive due process, Chief Justice Charles Evans Hughes's opinion had this to say about freedom of contract: "The Constitution does not speak of freedom of contract. It speaks of liberty and prohibits the deprivation of liberty without due process of law. In prohibiting that deprivation the Constitution does not recognize an absolute and uncontrollable liberty."[42] The death knell of substantive due process was clearly at hand; and in fact, the Supreme Court has not struck down a single economic regulation on substantive due process grounds since 1937. After *West Coast Hotel*, the libertarian Constitution was dead.

Or was it? While the 1937 revolution (or "switch in time," as it is commonly called) largely marked the end of the Court's experiment with a natural rights jurisprudence, there is one strand of modern cases where that form of reasoning

---

40. *See* Meyer v. Nebraska, 262 U.S. 390 (1923); Pierce v. Society of Sisters, 268 U.S. 510 (1925).

41. 300 U.S. 379 (1937).

42. *Id.* at 391.

lives on: the so-called "privacy" cases. The first[43] of those cases was the 1965 decision in *Griswold v. Connecticut*,[44] in which the Supreme Court struck down a Connecticut statute banning the use of contraceptives. While Justice Douglas's opinion for the Court in *Griswold* is notoriously vague, indeed baffling, regarding the precise textual basis for the decision (he refers to "penumbras, formed by emanations" from the specific provisions of the Bill of Rights), several concurring Justices relied squarely on substantive due process; and the case has been so understood since then. *Griswold* was in some ways a sport, a narrow decision with little apparent significance. The same cannot be said of *Griswold*'s most important progeny, *Roe v. Wade*,[45] in which the Court held that the *Griswold* privacy right (which the Court now squarely identified as rooted in substantive due process) "is broad enough to encompass a woman's decision whether or not to terminate her pregnancy." The holding in *Roe v. Wade*, constitutionalizing a woman's right to choose an abortion, is undoubtedly the most controversial judicial decision of the past half century. *Roe* has since spawned an entire body of privacy jurisprudence, most of which has involved abortion regulations (including the famous 1992 decision in *Planned Parenthood v. Casey*[46] reaffirming *Roe*), but has also encapsulated other fundamental rights including rights of family cohabitation,[47] parental rights to control their children's upbringing,[48] and most famously, a right to sexual intimacy for homosexuals as a result of the 2003 *Lawrence v. Texas* decision.[49] All of these decisions are rooted in a natural rights tradition, and so sit uncomfortably with both the text of the Constitution, which as we have seen has little to do with natural rights, and with the bulk of our constitutional jurisprudence outside of the *Lochner* era. The truth is that whatever the moral and social value of privacy rights (and I am personally highly sympathetic to the holdings in all of these cases), the privacy cases as the Supreme Court has tended to justify them have little or nothing to do with the primary concern of our constitutional rights tradition, which is to guard against the undermining of democratic self-government. The question of whether these decisions might otherwise be justified on structural grounds is the topic of Chapter 10.

---

43. Arguably, the actual first privacy case was *Skinner v. Oklahoma*, 316 U.S. 535 (1942), striking down an Oklahoma law prescribing forced sterilization as the penalty for certain repeat offenders. *Skinner*, however, did not rely on the Due Process Clause, and in any event was so poorly reasoned that it is hard to reconcile it with *any* consistent constitutional theory.

44. 381 U.S. 479 (1965).

45. 410 U.S. 113 (1973).

46. 505 U.S. 833 (1992).

47. *See* Moore v. City of East Cleveland, 431 U.S. 494 (1977).

48. *See* Troxel v. Granville, 530 U.S. 57 (2000).

49. 539 U.S. 558 (2003).

Finally, it is important to note that even if the concept of "substantive due process" is not salvageable, this is not to say that the *results* in the privacy cases are all necessarily incorrect. This is because there is in the Fourteenth Amendment, in addition to the Privileges or Immunities and Due Process Clauses, another critically important provision: the Equal Protection Clause. Regarding abortion, for example, even if natural rights provide a weak basis for a *constitutional* abortion right, it may be that abortion regulation constitutes a form of sex discrimination, violating the equality principle of the Equal Protection Clause. Indeed, such an argument has been made by many thinkers, including none other than Justice Ruth Bader Ginsburg.[50] Similarly, the sorts of sodomy statutes struck down in *Lawrence v. Texas* are very arguably rooted in sexual orientation discrimination, and so again may violate the equality principle; indeed, equal protection was the basis of Justice Sandra Day O'Connor's separate concurring opinion in that case.

The reach and meaning of the Equal Protection Clause is the topic of chapters 8 and 9, but some basic observations must be made here regarding the equality principle. I have argued that whatever the original intent of its framers (on which reasonable people differ), it seems relatively clear that the Fourteenth Amendment has not created a broad, constitutional jurisprudence of natural rights, with the occasional historical or doctrinal aberration. This is not to say, however, that the Fourteenth Amendment did not fundamentally change our constitutional juris-prudence; it surely did, in two independent ways. First, as discussed above, the Fourteenth Amendment resulted in the incorporation of the Bill of Rights against state governments, thereby extending the People's constitutional protec-tions against *all* of our governments, not just the national one. Second, the Fourteenth Amendment introduced a whole new concept of, and approach to, constitutional jurisprudence: the concept of equal treatment. Underlying this concept was a realization, reached by the authors of the Fourteenth Amendment, that the original Constitution's protections accorded to "the People" collectively were inadequate to protect against oppressions *within* the People. It is important to remember that these framers were Republican members of Congress, acting in the wake of the Civil War, and in response to the efforts by the governments of Southern states after the war to retain the essential structure of slavery, undo-ing the work of the Thirteenth Amendment, through highly oppressive pieces of legislation known as the "Black Codes," which sought to strip African Americans of essentially all economic and social independence. In the face of such misuse of power by electoral majorities (for there was no doubt that White, Southern voters fully supported their governments' actions), it became clear that the

---

50. Ruth Bader Ginsburg, *Some Thoughts on Autonomy and Equality in Relation to* Roe v. Wade, 63 N. C. L. Rev. 375 (1985); *see also* Cass Sunstein, *Neutrality in Constitutional Law (with Special Reference to Pornography, Abortion, and Surrogacy)*, 92 Colum. L. Rev. 1 (1992).

Constitution and Bill of Rights' original focus on the balance of power between rulers and the collective People no longer sufficed to protect the nation's constitutional aspirations, because it failed to protect minorities from majorities. This insight was the great constitutional innovation of the Reconstruction era. Of course, concerns about majoritarian abuse of power were not entirely unknown in the early Republic. We have already noted James Madison's concerns in this regard—though as a slave-owning aristocrat, the minority for whom Madison reserved his concerns was property owners. But as we have also noted, Madison's views were outliers during the founding era. During Reconstruction, such concerns finally took constitutional center stage, with the important refinement that the minorities that were now seen to need constitutional protection were racial (and perhaps other disempowered) minorities, rather than the wealthy.

The Equal Protection Clause of the Fourteenth Amendment was clearly the Reconstruction Congress's primary response to this newly discovered problem of majoritarian tyranny. This is not to say that the rest of the Fourteenth Amendment, along with the later-adopted Fifteenth Amendment prohibiting the denial of the right to vote on the basis of race, did not also respond to this problem. But the equality principle was the heart of the matter. Justice Robert Jackson, writing some eighty years later, described the genius of the equality principle, and its superiority to more substantive protections such as substantive due process, as follows:

> Invocation of the equal protection clause . . . does not disable any governmental body from dealing with the subject at hand. It merely means that the prohibition or regulation must have a broader impact. I regard it as a salutary doctrine that cities, states and the Federal Government[51] must exercise their powers so as not to discriminate between their inhabitants except upon some reasonable differentiation fairly related to the object of regulation. This equality is not merely abstract justice. The framers of the Constitution knew, and we should not forget today, that there is no more effective practical guaranty against arbitrary and unreasonable government than to require that the principles of law which officials would impose upon a minority must be imposed generally. Conversely, nothing opens the door to arbitrary action so effectively as to allow those officials to pick and choose only a few to whom they will apply legislation and thus to escape the political retribution that might be visited upon them if larger numbers were affected. Courts can take no better measure to assure that laws will be just than to require that laws be equal in operation.[52]

---

51. It should be noted that even though the Equal Protection Clause, by its terms, applies only to the states, in modern times the Supreme Court has consistently applied an equivalent, nontextual equality limitation on the federal government. *See, e.g.*, Korematsu v. United States, 323 U.S. 214 (1944); Bolling v. Sharpe, 347 U.S. 497 (1954); Adarand Constructors, Inc. v. Pena, 515 U.S. 200 (1995).

52. Railway Express Agency, Inc. v. New York, 336 U.S. 106, 112–113 (1949) (Jackson, J., concurring).

Furthermore, as Jackson's quote suggests, despite the Reconstruction Congress's original focus on racial discrimination, the principle they adopted was *not* one prohibiting race discrimination alone (as some modern scholars, and even Justices, have suggested), it was a general equality principle. After all, no where does the Equal Protection Clause mention the word "race," and if the authors of that amendment had meant to draft a prohibition on race discrimination alone, they surely knew how to do so—as demonstrated by the Fifteenth Amendment, adopted just two years later, which does focus on race. As a consequence, the Equal Protection Clause provides protection to *all* minorities whom those in power might seek to single out for unfavorable treatment, including some, such as women and homosexuals, who might not have been considered full citizens, with fully equal rights, during the Reconstruction era. Of course, recognizing the potential breadth of the equality principle does not end all interpretational problems because it does not resolve which groups, defined by which characteristics, are entitled to equal treatment (surely we do not think murderers are such a group!). But, subject to that qualification, the equality principle does provide a broad, substantively neutral yet institutionally powerful, mechanism to prevent abuse of power. As an illustration, consider what the willingness would be of electoral majorities to support sodomy statutes, if the consequence was that there own private, sexual practices were subject to close regulation, and prosecution by the state. As Justice Jackson states, however, the Equal Protection Clause does not deny the government any substantive powers, or concomitantly, protect any substantive, individual rights. As such, it does nothing to create or advance a natural rights jurisprudence.

4. HOW CONSTITUTIONAL RIGHTS LIMIT GOVERNMENTAL POWER

In the last chapter, I demonstrated that as a matter of text and history, the Bill of Rights and the Fourteenth Amendment do not create the system of individual autonomy and entitlements that much modern, constitutional discourse suggests that they do. In other words, we do not have a libertarian Constitution. Instead, our Constitution, both as originally drafted and as subsequently amended, is fundamentally a structural document, concerned with the exercise of, and limitations on, governmental power. In this chapter I will further develop this insight, explaining why a structural vision of the Bill of Rights and the Fourteenth Amendment, one focused on limits on power, fits well with both the rest of the Constitution, and with practical realities. I will also set forth a framework regarding precisely what *sorts* of limits on governmental power are implied by a structural vision of the Constitution.

LIMITS ON POWER

We begin with a truism: if one examines the original Constitution of the United States, the document that was drafted in Philadelphia in 1787 and implemented in 1789, there is no doubt that it is almost entirely a structural document, focused on the design and powers of the new national government that the Constitution created, and on the methods of selecting members of that government. Further attention is given to the relationship between the national government and the states compromising the new Union, as well as to the relationships between those states. Thus the first three articles of the Constitution, which are by far the most lengthy, establish and describe the three branches of government (the legislative, executive, and judicial branches, in that order), set forth detailed procedures for how its members will be selected, and list the powers of each branch. Article IV sets forth rules for how states must deal with each other, establishing in particular requirements of cooperation and nondiscrimination against citizens of other states, as well as empowering Congress to administer federal territory and create new states. Article V describes how the Constitution may be amended in the future. Article VI establishes the superiority of the new national government over state governments, whenever a conflict should arise. And Article VII sets forth rules for how the new Constitution shall come into force. There are essentially no references in this document to individual citizens, much less to their "rights." It is true that Section 9 of Article I (the article establishing

Congress and setting forth its powers) does impose some limits on congressional authority; but the focus of those limits is on structural concerns such as how Congress may spend, or exercise its taxing powers, and forbidding Congress to play favorites among states. The closest we can find to provisions that today might be considered to protect "rights" are the clauses permitting the writ of habeas corpus to be suspended only in times of emergency, and prohibiting bills of attainder and ex post facto laws (bills of attainder are laws that impose penalties on named individuals, while an ex post facto law is one that criminalizes behavior after it has occurred). None of these provisions, however, creates zones of autonomy for individuals. Rather, the suspension clause merely preserves an important remedy against abuse of power (notably, executive detention), while the other two clauses stop Congress from using its granted powers in a way calculated to target identified, political enemies. Just as Section 9 imposes limits on congressional power, Section 10 of Article I imposes limits on the legislative powers of the states. Once again, however, the focus is all on structure, identifying areas of legislation such as foreign affairs, international trade, war, and coinage, which are of exclusively national concern, and so where states are forbidden from acting. Protection of individuals is simply not the central purpose of either Section 9 or 10. (The only arguable counterexample is the provision of Section 10 forbidding the states to make any laws "impairing the obligation of contracts," which I will discuss in Chapter 7).

Should one infer from the nature of the original Constitution that the framers, gathered in Philadelphia, did not care about individual liberty? Obviously not. Rather, as the quotations from Alexander Hamilton discussed at the beginning of the previous chapter indicate,[1] in the framers' view the structure of the government that they were creating provided the best defense of liberty possible, far more effective than the unenforceable assurances that were typical of existing bills and declarations of rights. The most important of these defenses was, of course, the principle of popular sovereignty, implemented by the People's participation in government through elections and through jury service. It should be noted in this regard that the institution of criminal juries is preserved in Article III itself, the article creating the judicial branch. The Bill of Rights, through the Sixth Amendment, merely reiterates and clarifies this decision, renaming it a "right."

Needless to say, however, the framers recognized that democracy and juries are not enough to prevent a tyrannical government. The other, primary mechanisms they adopted to this end were enumeration and separation. Enumeration is the concept the powers of the new national government, and of Congress in particular (the most important and dangerous branch, because the only branch empowered to make law), were limited to those listed in the Constitution.

---

1. *See* Chapter 3, *supra*, notes 4 to 9 and accompanying text.

Article I begins by emphasizing that Congress's legislative powers are limited to those "herein granted," a point later reiterated in the Tenth Amendment; and Section 8 then lists the specific powers granted to Congress. Notably, while the powers granted to Congress encompass such important topics as bankruptcy, coinage, intellectual property, and (most importantly) interstate and foreign trade, they do *not* include general police and criminal powers. As such, after the framing and to this day, most important criminal and civil laws remain the product of state, rather than the federal, governments, making the very possibility of abuse of power by the national government (the main concern of the framers) far smaller.

The other tool chosen by the framers was the separation of powers, or as James Madison put it in *Federalist* No. 51, "that separate and distinct exercise of the different powers of government, which to a certain extent, is admitted on all hands to be essential to the preservation of liberty."[2] As Madison further noted, in the American system, power was separated not only horizontally, among the different branches of government, but also vertically, between the national and state governments, providing "a double security . . . to the rights of the people."[3] While a full discussion of the ways in which horizontal and vertical division of authority—i.e., the separation of powers and federalism—work to protect individual liberty is beyond the scope if this book, it is essential to recognize that for the framers, the structure of the governmental system created by the new Constitution was *the* critical defense of individual liberty in the Constitution; and indeed, that the entire point of that structure was to enable effective government while minimizing the risk of arbitrary government. Justice Anthony M. Kennedy made this point eloquently, in a 1998 decision in which the Supreme Court held unconstitutional the so-called "Line Item Veto," which permitted the president to strike individual spending items out of appropriations bills passed by Congress:

> In recent years, perhaps, we have come to think of liberty as defined by that word in the Fifth and Fourteenth Amendments and as illuminated by the other provisions of the Bill of Rights. The conception of liberty embraced by the Framers was not so confined. They used the principles of separation of powers and federalism to secure liberty in the fundamental political sense of the term, quite in addition to the idea of freedom from intrusive governmental acts. The idea and the promise were that when the people delegate some degree of control to a remote central authority, one branch of government ought not possess the power to shape their destiny without a sufficient check from the other two.[4]

---

2. Alexander Hamilton, James Madison, and John Jay, The Federalist Papers (Garry Wills ed., Bantam 1982), Federalist No. 51.

3. *Ibid.*

4. Clinton v. City of New York, 524 U.S. 417, 450 (1998).

In other words, structure *is* liberty insofar as it ensures that government operates with the consent of the governed.

That at least was the theory of the original Constitution—so much so that as noted above, the framers consciously chose to not include a Bill of Rights in their Constitution, deeming it unnecessary. Of course, they lost that argument, and the First Congress took up the task of amendments. Many of the members of the First Congress, however, had also sat in the Constitutional Convention, and it is surely to be expected that their fundamental approach to constitutionalism had not shifted dramatically in the two years between the Convention and the convening of the new Congress. It should therefore come as no surprise that the First Congress's approach to amendment reflected the same basic approach as the original Constitution. Indeed, as we have seen, in at least two instances the Bill of Rights merely reiterates protections established in the original Constitution: thus the Sixth Amendment reiterates Article III's retention of jury trials in criminal cases, albeit restating the principle as a "right"; and the Tenth Amendment reiterates the principle established in the first sentence of Article I, that Congress (or now more generally, the United States) is limited to powers delegated to it in the Constitution. With respect to jury trial, in particular, it is noteworthy that renaming it as a "right" in the Sixth Amendment does not in any way alter the fact that juries are in fact an aspect of the institutional design of the judiciary created in Article III.

Having emphasized the similarity in basic approach between the original Constitution and the Bill of Rights, it is important to acknowledge that there are, of course, important differences as well. In particular, while the general structural protections of the original Constitution were designed to create a *generic* assurance that the new government would not use its powers to treat citizens unfairly, or more generally to undermine the system of popular, representative government created by the Constitution, the Bill of Rights identifies and forbids *specific*, particularly threatening ways in which the government might abuse its powers. Thus the First Amendment is built on the recognition that when the government chooses to regulate speech, the press, or religion, particularly great dangers of abuse and particularly severe threats to representative democracy are posed. The Second Amendment implements a similar insight with respect to possession of firearms. The Third and Fourth Amendments, respectively, restrict the government's power to use a standing military, or a police apparatus, to cow the people to whom the government is in principle responsible. Indeed, as discussed in detail in the previous chapter, each of the ten provisions of the Bill of Rights can be understood to implement a particular barrier to the abuse of governmental power, each targeted at a particular area of special risk. The specific concerns underlying each of the amendments are, of course, varied; but they share in common this basic understanding, that they act in areas where it is especially important to restrict governmental power, in order to preserve popular government.

Here, a word is necessary about the Fourteenth Amendment. As noted previously, the Fourteenth Amendment was ratified in 1868, in the wake of the Civil War, over three quarters of a century after the ratification of the Bill of Rights. As such, it is quite conceivable that the drafters of the Fourteenth Amendment intended to take a somewhat different approach to constitutional design, incorporating a more explicitly libertarian element into the Constitution. If so, however, because of the judicial interpretations imposed on that amendment in subsequent years, those efforts largely failed. Instead, the primary impact of the Fourteenth Amendment has been twofold. First, through the process of incorporation, it has resulted in the Bill of Rights' limitations on *federal* power being imposed on state governments as well, on the belief that the same abuses of power that might occur at the national level pose risks to republican government at the state level, too. Second, the Fourteenth Amendment, through the Equal Protection Clause, introduced a new, structural feature into the constitutional system—the concept of equality and protection of minorities. That this is a structural feature cannot be in doubt; equality, after all, protects no particular zone of autonomy, it rather restricts the *ways* in which government can regulate, by requiring even-handedness. Underlying this new, structural restriction was a realization that democratic failure could occur not only when rulers acted against the People, but also when a majority of the People systematically disempowered a minority of the same. Interestingly, this new structural principle was originally imposed on state governments only; but in the modern era the Supreme Court has required the federal government to abide by it as well.[5] The key point is that while the Equal Protection Clause was motivated by concerns that were in important ways different from those that drove the original Bill of Rights, those concerns were no less structural, and the Equal Protection Clause is no less at bottom a limitation on governmental power.

Till now, our consideration of the methodology and purposes of the Bill of Rights and the Fourteenth Amendment have been necessarily abstract. Does such abstraction have anything useful to contribute to our practical understanding of constitutional rights? I will argue that it does. The difficulty is as follows. If the important limitations on governmental power imposed by the Bill of Rights and Fourteenth Amendment were self-defining, understanding their underlying purposes would be of theoretical interest, but of little other value. In fact, however, if there is one thing that is clear, it is that the scopes of constitutional limitations are notoriously unclear. Debates over the meaning of those limitations in fact pervade our history, from the time of the framers to today, and there is no sign that the intensity of those debates is in any danger of lessening. It is fine to say that government shall not "abridg[e] the freedom of speech" or that "the right of the people to keep and bear Arms, shall not be infringed," but

---

5. *See* Bolling v. Sharpe, 347 U.S. 497 (1954).

what does that *mean?* These questions, and others like them, are of course the lifeblood of modern constitutional law. We now turn to the question of how understanding the nature of constitutional rights helps provide some answers to such questions.

The key insight into modern constitutional disputes that flows from a structural understanding of rights as limits on government power is simply this: in any situation where it is alleged that the government has infringed upon a person's constitutional "rights," the key question should always be whether the government has exceeded a definable limit on its power, *not* whether it has deprived the individual of some sort of entitlement. The impact of the government's action on the autonomy of affected individuals might sometimes be a relevant factor in considering whether the government has abused its power, but it is *not* the central concern, and indeed it will not always be a particularly important factor in the analysis. In short, constitutional rights guard against abuse of power, not infringement on autonomy.

ACTIONS AND PURPOSES

Once it becomes clear that constitutional disputes center around misuse of power, it becomes clear that constitutional disputes must be resolved by focusing on *what* the government is doing, and *why* it is doing it—in other words, it must focus on governmental actions and purposes. To understand why this is so, it is useful to think back to the framework established by the framers to ensure that the new, national government did not develop tyrannical tendencies. In addition to dividing power, another key mechanism was enumeration. While division of power limits how the government operates, enumeration limits why it operates—it limits the objectives that the national government may pursue. As it turns out, however, enumeration is not a terribly strict limit on federal authority because the Constitution, through the key "necessary and proper" clause of Article I, Section 8, grants Congress great discretion in choosing means, which is to say in choosing what specific legislation to enact, so long as its ultimate objective remains one of the powers committed to Congress by the Constitution. As Chief Justice John Marshall famously put it in the landmark *McCulloch v. Maryland* decision interpreting the necessary and proper clause, "[l]et the end be legitimate, let it be within the scope of the constitution, and all means which are appropriate, which are plainly adapted to that end, which are not prohibited, but consist with the letter and spirit of the constitution, are constitutional."[6] Given the broad scope of federal authority, therefore, further restrictions on federal power were deemed necessary, and so the Bill of Rights was enacted.

---

6. McCulloch v. Maryland, 17 U.S. (4 Wheat.) 316, 421 (1819).

While enumeration lists certain permissible objectives for the federal government, the Bill of Rights acts by identifying other powers, other objectives, and other means of pursuing those objectives that are specifically *forbidden* to the federal government. Understood this way, rights are really the mirror-image of powers, an exception to rather than a grant of authority. James Madison himself, in introducing to the First Congress his proposed amendments that would eventually become the Bill of Rights, stated that "the great object in view" of all Bill of Rights "is to limit and qualify the powers of government, by excepting out of the grant of power those cases in which the government ought not to act, or to act only in a particular mode."[7] This description of the function of rights is also consistent with the arguments made by many of the framers, including notably Alexander Hamilton in *The Federalist*, that it would be a mistake to incorporate a Bill of Rights into the new Constitution because to include in it "various exceptions to powers which are not granted . . . would afford a colourable pretext to claim more than were granted."[8]

A focus on governmental actions and purposes in constitutional analysis also makes sense from a functional perspective. Actions are the easiest to understand—certain kinds of government actions are explicitly forbidden by the Bill of Rights, and simply may not be done. Thus the Third Amendment forbids the quartering of soldiers in homes, without the owner's consent, during peacetime, and the Fifth Amendment states that the government may not compel a person "in any criminal case to be a witness against himself." These are things that the government simply may not do, period. Note in this regard that these things are forbidden regardless of the impact on the individual whose "right" is being infringed. For example, an owner of a mansion cannot be compelled to quarter soldiers during peacetime, even if they were going to occupy a vacant wing of the mansion, with little or no burden on the owner.

Unfortunately, however, a focus on forbidden actions does not take us very far in constitutional analysis, because rarely is it clear exactly *what* a particular amendment forbids the government to do. The prohibition on quartering soldiers may have a clear meaning (which is perhaps why the Third Amendment has never been litigated), but what does it mean to say that Congress may not "abridge[e] the freedom of speech," or infringe "the right of the people to keep and bear Arms," as the First and Second Amendments provide? Similarly, what does it mean to say that no state shall "deny any person . . . the equal protection of the laws," as the Fourteenth Amendment commands? These are not self-defining limits, and moreover, the literal language of these amendments leads to absurd results. For example, does the free speech clause of the First Amendment

---

7. RAKOVE, *supra*, at 176.

8. FEDERALIST No. 84; *see also* LEVY, ORIGINS OF THE BILL OF RIGHTS at 21 (quoting a similar argument made by James Wilson); RAKOVE, *supra*, at 146 (quoting a similar argument made by James Iredell).

mean that Congress may not pass a law criminalizing threats against the president, or that states may not (postincorporation) make it a crime to solicit murder? Of course not. At the same time, criminalizing *criticism* of the president surely is forbidden. Another problem is that government actions that are not targeted at specific kinds of speech can often have an impact on speech, sometimes a dramatic one. Thus when the government forbids camping in a park, a protest against homelessness may be disrupted;[9] or when the government forbids the placing of signs in front of homes, a homeowner may be prevented from expressing her political views.[10] Again, some principle is needed to distinguish between permissible and impermissible burdens on speech (the answers given by the Court, by the way, were that the sleeping ban was permissible, but the sign ban was not). Equal protection is even more problematic, because at some level, the government treats people unequally whenever it acts with specificity. Thus when the government permits a tax deduction for mortgage interest, it treats homeowners and renters unequally; and when my town repaves my neighbor's street but not mine, it is treating us unequally. Why such inequalities are permissible, but requiring African American children to attend segregated schools is not, or why threats against the president may be forbidden, but criticism may not, are the kinds of questions that sit at the core of modern constitutional analysis.

To answer these questions, to determine why some restrictions on speech are permissible but others are not, and why some inequalities are permitted but not others, we must return to first principles. We must, in short, remember why the Bill of Rights and the Fourteenth Amendment exist, and what role they are designed to play in our constitutional system. That role, as we have established, is a structural one—these provisions seek to ensure that the government does not misuse the power granted to it by the People, by acting against them. In other words, making the distinctions that we must requires us to ask, which government actions constitutes an *abuse* of power, as opposed to an exercise of it. Alternatively, one must ask which uses of power threaten to undermine the supremacy of the People, or (in the case of equal protection) the political and social status of minority groups, and which do not. It is here that the focus must shift from actions to purposes. If in fact one's concern, in imposing limits on governmental power, is to check abuse, surely a critical question is *why* the government is acting as it is. If the government is acting for legitimate, permissible reasons—i.e., for the public good—then it is much less likely that its power is being abused, or poses a threat to the People (or to minority groups). When rulers, or electoral majorities, seek to use the tools of government in illegitimate ways, to undermine our institutions or to harm vulnerable groups, however, the

---

9. *See* Clark v. CCNV, 468 U.S. 288 (1983).
10. *See* City of LaDue v. Gilleo, 512 U.S. 43 (1994).

threat to our system of government is clearly very serious. It is then that courts must step in, and the government must be prevented from acting.

Of course, to implement the framework described above, one needs some way to distinguish between permissible and impermissible governmental objectives. It must be remembered, however, that our analysis in this respect is not an abstract one. The Bill of Rights and the Fourteenth Amendment, after all, were *designed* to place specific, identifiable limits on governmental actions and objectives. As such, coming up with a framework through which to judge the constitutionality of governmental objectives is ultimately a task of interpretation, of determining what tasks specific constitutional provisions are designed to accomplish, and what governmental purposes are consistent, and inconsistent, with those tasks. In the following pages, I will lay out a general framework, a typology within which that analysis can proceed, providing some examples for clarification.[11] In future chapters I will apply that typology to specific provisions of the Bill of Rights and the Fourteenth Amendment.

ILLEGITIMATE PURPOSES

We start with a simple premise—certain governmental objectives, certain purposes, are simply forbidden by the Constitution. Just as the Bill of Rights and the Fourteenth Amendment prohibit certain governmental actions (e.g., quartering soldiers during peacetime), it also prohibits certain governmental purposes. Governmental action taken for such purposes violates the constitutional provision that prohibits the purpose, regardless of the impact of the action on individual autonomy, and regardless of the social "good" that the government claims is advanced by that action. This idea, that certain governmental purposes are illegitimate, should not be controversial; it seems to follow naturally from the nature of particular provisions, and has been recognized in the Supreme Court on a number of occasions.

Consider in this respect *Romer v. Evans*,[12] a 1996 decision in which the Supreme Court held unconstitutional Colorado's "Amendment 2," a voter-enacted provision of the Colorado state constitution that forbade the state, or any local government within the state, from protecting gays and lesbians from discrimination. The Court concluded that the only purpose of Amendment 2 was "to make [gays and lesbians] unequal to everyone else," a purpose that the Court held was illegitimate under the Equal Protection Clause of the Fourteenth Amendment. In reaching this conclusion, the Court drew upon two of its earlier decisions

---

11. My analysis here draws heavily upon an article I published some years ago, Ashutosh Bhagwat, *Purpose Scrutiny in Constitutional Analysis*, 85 CAL. L. REV. 297 (1997).

12. 517 U.S. 620 (1996).

raising similar issues. One was *City of Cleburne v. Cleburne Living Center*,[13] in which the Court was faced with a municipal zoning ordinance, in the City of Cleburne, Texas, which permitted a particular parcel of land to be used to house a hospital, a nursing home, or another type of group living facility, but forbade its use for a home for the mentally retarded. Based on these facts, the Court concluded that the city's actions were motivated by simple, irrational fear and hostility toward the mentally retarded, and so struck it down. Similarly, in *U.S. Department of Agriculture v. Moreno*[14] the Court struck down a congressional statute denying food stamps to households containing unrelated individuals, because the legislation had been motivated by hostility toward "hippies." Together, the *Romer, Cleburne*, and *Moreno* cases stand for the proposition that "a bare . . . desire to harm a politically unpopular group cannot constitute a legitimate governmental interest,"[15] and so violates the Equal Protection Clause. In other words, the Fourteenth Amendment forbids government to act out of fear of, or hostility toward, definable groups of people, a rule that has been called an "anti-animus" principle.

Illegitimate purpose analysis is not limited to the equal protection context. In the area of free speech, the Court has long recognized that it is inherently illegitimate for the government to regulate because of hostility to the message that a speaker is seeking to deliver, even when there might be good reasons for that hostility. Thus in *Simon & Schuster, Inc. v. Members of New York State Crime Victims Bd.*,[16] the Supreme Court held unconstitutional a New York statute (known as the "Son of Sam" law after the serial killer whose conduct lead to its adoption) that required any income from books or other works written by an accused or convicted criminal, describing his or her crime, to be placed in escrow for the benefit of the crime's victims. The reason the Court struck down this law was, simply, that by targeting only speech describing the author's crimes the law expressed hostility to that speech, even though the overarching goal of the statute, to compensate crime victims, is of course entirely permissible. The Court has also held that in regulating so-called "commercial speech"—i.e., advertising—the government may not act with the purpose of keeping consumers ignorant of truthful information, for fear that they will misuse it by making bad decisions.[17] Indeed, as we shall see in subsequent chapters, illegitimate purpose analysis pervades constitutional analysis in the area of free speech, as well as other areas including the religion clauses of the First Amendment and antidiscrimination law.

---

13. 473 U.S. 432 (1985).

14. 413 U.S. 528 (1973).

15. *Moreno*, 413 U.S. at 534; *Cleburne*, 473 U.S. at 447; *Romer*, 517 U.S. at 634.

16. 502 U.S. 105 (1991).

17. *See, e.g.*, Thompson v. Western States Medical Center, 535 U.S. 357 (2002); 44 Liquormart, Inc. v. Rhode Island, 517 U.S. 484 (1996).

The concept of illegitimate governmental purposes is thus well established in constitutional law and seems to follow easily from the structure and functions of particular constitutional provisions. It should be noted, however, that the acceptance of such an analysis belies the possibility that constitutional rights are designed to protect individual autonomy. After all, if the function of a constitutional "right" such as free speech is to protect the autonomy of individuals to speak, what difference does it make *why* the government is banning speech? What should matter, rather, is the impact of the law on an individual's ability to communicate his or her message. In fact, however, it is clear that the Supreme Court's analysis in illegitimate purpose cases does not turn on individual impact, it turns on governmental intent. Thus in *Simon & Schuster*, the Court did not inquire seriously into whether the effect of the Son of Sam law was to silence much, if any, speech; and in *Cleburne* and *Moreno* the Court's finding of unconstitutionality was not based on any conclusions regarding the actual harm imposed on the harmed groups. Indeed, in *Moreno* the plaintiffs injured by the food stamp law were not even "hippies" and so had not suffered the relevant "harm" of being the target of official animus.

Another important point about the illegitimate purposes identified by the Court is the generality at which they are identified, resulting in decisions far removed from the narrowly defined "Original Intent" of the framers of the relevant constitutional provisions. Thus in the *Romer/Cleburne/Moreno* line of cases, the idea that equal protection requires an anti-animus principle seems entirely consistent with the general purposes of the Fourteenth Amendment (as we shall discuss in more detail later); but the application of that principle to protect homosexuals, the mentally retarded, and "hippies" would surely not have been imagined, or probably condoned, by the authors of that amendment. Similarly, in the free speech area the "anti-ignorance" principle that the Court has applied in commercial speech cases also seems to follow naturally from the broader philosophy of the First Amendment, but it seems most unlikely that James Madison and his fellow members of the First Congress imagined that their creation protected the right of liquor stores to advertise prices! It should be noted that even Justices Antonin Scalia and Clarence Thomas, the foremost advocates on the current Court of interpreting the Constitution based on "Original Meaning," have joined the Court's anti-ignorance decisions, suggesting that at least in some areas such as free speech (and, as we shall see, affirmative action), they are willing to define principles extracted from constitutional provisions at a high level of generality.

DIRECT INTRUSIONS AND LIMITED PURPOSES

While the identification and invalidation of governmental actions with illegitimate purpose plays an important, even pivotal role in constitutional analysis, the analysis cannot end there. The reason is this: the key provisions of our Bill of Rights and of the Fourteenth Amendment do not simply identify certain governmental purposes as out of bounds, they also identify certain types of governmental action, touching on certain areas of human behavior, which are inherently suspect because of the threat they pose to a functioning, democratic society. In such areas, good motives are not enough to justify governmental action, something more is needed. To use a familiar (and unlikely) example, suppose the government chose to quarter troops in homes during peacetime, not in order to occupy and intimidate a civilian population, but rather to save money during a fiscal crisis. The government's motives in this regard would be unobjectionable, but surely the Third Amendment would still forbid the quartering. The reason is that the framers of the Third Amendment identified quartering troops as a form of governmental action that is so fraught with danger, because of the power imbalance it creates between the sovereign People and their government, that it is normally forbidden. Quartering troops is hardly unique in this regard.

This point might be illustrated by examples from the free speech area. Consider the facts of *Schneider v. State*,[18] one of the Supreme Court's critical, early cases implementing the First Amendment's free speech clause. In *Schneider*, the Court invalidated an ordinance prohibiting the distributing of leaflets "on any street or way." The stated purpose of the law, which no one seemed to question, was to limit littering on public streets (because recipients sometimes throw leaflets onto the ground)—a purpose that is surely legitimate and poses no free speech concerns as such. Consider also *Turner Broadcasting System, Inc. v. FCC*,[19] in which the Court upheld a congressional statute, the so-called "must-carry" law, which required cable television operators to carry the signals of local over-the-air broadcast television stations. Congress defended the law, again without much dispute, as a means to ensure that free, over-the-air television stations remained economically viable and available to those who could not afford, or for some other reason did not subscribe to, cable television. Again, the apparent purpose of this law was unproblematic, so that if constitutional analysis ended with a search for illegitimate purposes, it would be upheld. Regulations directed at speech (and at the press), however, are obviously a form of government action that raises profound constitutional concerns, because of the deep, intrinsic relationship between free speech and self-governance (a point we will elaborate on in the next chapter). As such, *some* constitutional scrutiny of such laws seems essential, if free speech is to play its structural role in our society.

Equal protection law also provides a useful illustration of the limitations of motive analysis. *Korematsu v. United States*[20] is one of the most notorious cases in

---

18. 308 U.S. 147 (1939).
19. 520 U.S. 180 (1997).
20. 323 U.S. 214 (1944).

the history of the Supreme Court. In that case, the Court upheld the constitutionality of the U.S. government's decision to exclude from the West Coast of the United States all persons of Japanese ancestry, including U.S. citizens of such ancestry, in the wake of the Japanese attack on Pearl Harbor that brought the United States into the Second World War (most of the excluded Japanese Americans were then forced to move to concentration camps, called "relocation centers," but the constitutionality of the camps was not technically before the Court in *Korematsu*). The reason that *Korematsu* is a difficult case under illegitimate purpose analysis is that the government's stated purpose for the exclusion was not hostility to Japanese Americans, but rather national security—the military claimed that there were potential saboteurs among the group, who could not easily be identified. In fact, today many people (including myself) believe that the real purpose behind the relocation was simple racial animus and prejudice, making *Korematsu* an easy case. In the wartime context in which it was decided however (the case was handed down in 1944, when World War II was still ongoing), it was extremely difficult, and unlikely, for the Court to second guess the government's stated, military concerns. Nonetheless, the government's actions in *Korematsu* should have triggered careful review, because as the *Korematsu* Court itself recognized (but then failed to heed), "all legal restrictions which curtail the civil rights of a single racial group are immediately suspect." Why? Because the Equal Protection Clause, drafted and enacted in the wake of the Civil War and Emancipation, and in the midst of Reconstruction, incorporates the judgment that race-based government actions should be highly disfavored, because of their tendency to systematically divide society and undermine democratic politics. As in the free speech cases, then, cases like *Korematsu* demand careful judicial scrutiny, even absent proof of illegitimate governmental motives.

What then is the proper analysis in cases such as Schneider, Turner, *Korematsu*, and countless others? These are cases in which the government is not (or cannot be proven to be) acting with illegitimate motives, but is nonetheless taking actions that intrude directly on core, constitutional principles—in *Schneider* and *Turner*, the government is directly regulating private, fully protected speech; and in *Korematsu* the government is explicitly imposing burdens (and denying benefits) based on people's race. These are actions that the Constitution should be read to presumptively invalidate, in the case of speech regulations because of the plain language of the First Amendment, and in the case of racial classifications because of the undisputed history of the Fourteenth Amendment. One might argue that such actions should not just be presumptively unconstitutional, they should be flatly so. That, however, goes too far. There are clearly times when the government will need to regulate speech, and there are times when it will have good reasons to take race into account. I would argue that in these circumstances, when core constitutional principles are at stake, the government should be permitted to act *only* if the ultimate objective, the purpose of the action is consistent with the principles underlying the constitutional provision it appears to be violating.

Thus in the speech area, regulation of speech should be permitted only if the ultimate purpose of the regulation is to enhance speech; and in the race area, if the purpose is to enhance equality (the ultimate objective, after all, of the Equal Protection Clause). The key point here is that not any valid governmental purpose would do; if it did, we would largely emasculate the limitations set by the Constitution by balancing them away (as in *Korematsu*), and thereby abandon the principle established by these constitutional provisions, that the type of governmental action at issue poses a serious risk to our system of government. Instead, the government should be permitted to act in these areas only if it is seeking to advance the goals of the relevant constitutional provision. In the area of direct intrusions, the universe of permissible governmental objectives must be sharply limited by the Constitution itself.

Under the limited-purpose analysis described above, *Korematsu* would appear to be an easy case. After all, as even the Court conceded, the government's decision to impose severe burdens on an identified racial group implicates core equal protection concerns, and under no conceivable definition did the Japanese-American Internment advance equality. The one caveat here is the wartime context. As many scholars have noted, constitutional restrictions on government power tend to be weakened or ignored during wartime,[21] and it may be that a strong limited-purposes analysis cannot realistically be followed strictly in circumstances where national security is (or is claimed to be) at risk. We will come back to the topic of the Constitution during wartime in the final chapter of this book, when I address the War on Terror. For now, however, it is sufficient to note that under any reasonable view of what kinds of powers the Equal Protection Clause is designed to strip government of, the treatment of Japanese Americans during World War II *must* be understood as unconstitutional. The wartime context is relevant not because it changes the meaning of the Constitution, but because it may be that when national security is at issue, the courts cannot realistically be expected to enforce those limitations—a point that, indeed, Justice Robert Jackson specifically made in his dissenting opinion in *Korematsu*.[22]

If *Korematsu* is an easy case under a limited-purpose approach to constitutional analysis, *Turner* and *Schneider*, the two free speech cases mentioned above are not. In *Turner*, the difficulty arises because Congress's precise purpose in enacting the must-carry laws was disputed. The effect of the must-carry law was to force cable television companies to let broadcasters use some of their channel capacity free of charge, a burden that was not trivial given that the law was enacted in 1992, when cable television had far less channel capacity than the hundreds of channels possible in today's digital world. Proponents of must-carry

---

21. *See* WILLIAM H. REHNQUIST, ALL THE LAWS BUT ONE: CIVIL LIBERTIES IN WARTIME (Vintage 2000); RICHARD A. POSNER, NOT A SUICIDE PACT: THE CONSTITUTION IN A TIME OF NATIONAL EMERGENCY (Oxford 2006).

22. *Korematsu*, 323 U.S. at 244–246 (Jackson, J., dissenting).

argued that the purpose of the law was to maintain a diverse range of television outlets, accessible to the entire public. This would appear to be a speech-enhancing rationale, which would pass even a limited-purpose analysis. Opponents of must-carry (notably the cable companies), however, argued that Congress was merely favoring one part of the media—broadcasters—over another, perhaps because Congress had greater regulatory control over broadcasters than over cable companies. The latter purpose is, of course, probably illegitimate, and in any event certainly cannot be claimed to enhance free speech. Ultimately, a bare majority of the Supreme Court accepted Congress's claim that it was merely seeking to enhance diverse speech, and so upheld the law.

Schneider would appear to be an easier case than *Turner*. After all, the justification for the antileafleting rule, preventing litter, can hardly be described as speech-enhancing. The difficulty arises because in *Schneider* the government did not prohibit leafleting everywhere, it only prohibited it on its own property ("streets and ways'), where the government necessarily enjoys enhanced regulatory powers. Thus, the defenders of government power in this situation would argue that this is not a "core" intrusion on free speech principles, because it is not simple regulation of private speech. Ultimately, however, this argument is unconvincing, because it does not explain why the government chose to single out *speech* on its property, for unfavorable treatment. After all, leaflets are hardly the only source of public litter. What about cigarettes, or food containers? Given the specific targeting of speech, with no particular justification, I would argue that it remains appropriate to think of the ordinance in *Schneider* as directly intruding on a sphere of authority denied to the government by the First Amendment, thereby justifying heightened, limited-purposes analysis, which the ordinance surely cannot satisfy.

INCIDENTAL BURDENS AND BALANCING

The above two types of constitutional cases, when the government is either acting for illegitimate reasons, or is directly intruding on an area of authority explicitly denied it by the Constitution, capture the vast majority of situations where the government can reasonably said to be abusing its power in ways forbidden by the Bill of Rights and the Fourteenth Amendment. There is, however, another category of cases that we must consider: cases where the government acts in a way that impinges on the autonomy of individuals in ways which seem, on their face, to be constitutionally problematic, but where such a result is neither the purpose nor the direct thrust of the government's actions. Instead, the impact is merely incidental. As an example of such a situation, consider the facts of the *Clark v. CCNV* case discussed above,[23] in which homeless advocates argued

---

23. 468 U.S. 288 (1984).

that a federal regulation banning camping in certain parks violated their free speech rights because they wanted to sleep overnight in Lafayette Park in Washington, D.C. (which is located across the street from the White House) in order to dramatize the plight of the homeless. It seems fair to assume that the camping regulation had no illegitimate purpose; nor does it directly regulate speech, thereby invading a forbidden sphere of power (a camping ban, after all, is on its face a regulation of conduct, not speech). In situations like this, when the government is enforcing general rules with no ill intent, but the rules have the effect of substantially interfering with an individual's ability to speak (or with some other protected constitutional "right"), the Supreme Court's traditional solution has been to purport to "balance" the burden on free speech against the strength of the government's interest. In fact, however, this balancing is something of a farce. As Justice Antonin Scalia pointed out in two cases involving the application of public nudity statutes to nude dancing in adult clubs, while the Supreme Court purports to balance in such cases, it has in fact *never* invalidated a general regulation of conduct because of its impact on an individual's ability to express himself or herself. He therefore argues that in these situations, no constitutional issues are implicated.[24]

A view of rights as limitations on power suggests that Justice Scalia *must* be correct on this point (though there was evidence in at least one of the nude dancing cases that the government's purpose in adopting its nudity ordinance was to eliminate nude dancing, a form of express, suggesting that this case may have been incorrectly decided even under Justice Scalia's rule). The reason, quite simply, is that when the government adopts a general regulation of conduct, in an area not otherwise forbidden to it by the Constitution, it is difficult to see how the government's actions can be characterized as an abuse of power, or otherwise an invasion of territory forbidden to it. And absent an abuse of power, a structural understanding of rights suggests that it is entirely irrelevant that the government's actions are burdening some individual's autonomy. The fact that the Supreme Court in fact does *not* protect individual autonomy in this situation strongly suggests that whatever the Court's rhetoric regarding the nature of the free speech "right," its practice in this area reflects a structural understanding of the First Amendment (and as we shall see, of constitutional rights generally).

An important caveat is necessary here—if incidental burdens on autonomy are to be considered irrelevant to constitutional analysis, it is very important to distinguish carefully between situations where burdens are truly incidental, and situations where the government is exceeding its authority. To that effect, courts must always take a close look in such cases, to ensure that the government's purposes, either in enacting a law or in choosing to enforce it as it does, are not

---

24. Barnes v. Glen Theatre, Inc., 501 U.S. 560, 576–577 (1991) (Scalia, J., concurring in the judgment); City of Erie v. Pap's A.M., 529 U.S. 277, 307–308 (2000) (Scalia, J., concurring in the judgment).

illegitimate—an inquiry that the Court arguably failed to undertake honestly in the nude dancing cases. In addition, it must be made clear that when a law directly *targets* either speech or conduct that is traditionally associated with expression (such as marching, holding signs, waving a flag, or burning a flag in public), such cases cannot be treated as involving merely incidental burdens, but rather should be seen as directly intruding on a prohibited sphere of power. Thus in *City of LaDue v. Gilleo*,[25] the case mentioned above in which a city banned essentially all signs outside residences, the Supreme Court did *not* uphold the law. Instead, after only cursory review, it struck down the statute because it directly regulated speech. The Court's opinion in *LaDue* is rather unclear about the extent to which the government may regulate signs to advance social interests such as aesthetics, but its ultimate (and unanimous!) conclusion that the city's rule was invalid suggests that the Court recognizes this important distinction.

DEMOCRACY, CONSTITUTIONALISM, AND JUDICIAL LEGITIMACY

The above discussion of balancing points to a broader truth regarding why a structural approach to constitutional rights, which seeks to restrain government rather to protect individual autonomy, is the best approach to implementing the Constitution. The reason is in part a practical one. Under an individual autonomy–based approach to constitutional rights, constitutional concerns are raised whenever the government acts in a way that substantially limits individual autonomy, at least in any area of special protection such as free speech, religion, or reproductive liberty. In fact, however, government action *constantly* intrudes on autonomy, often in very significant ways. Thus when the government closes a park for maintenance, many speakers are potentially silenced; when the government bans particular drugs or alcohol, some individuals' religious autonomy may be burdened; and when the government refuses to fund nontherapeutic abortions, poor women are effectively denied their reproductive autonomy. In principle, in each of these situations an autonomy-based approach to rights requires courts to "balance" the strength of the government's interest in acting, against the burden on individual autonomy, with unpredictable results. Yet it is well-accepted today that none of the above situations pose serious constitutional questions.[26] Why? The answer, quite simply, is that it is unrealistic to expect courts to constantly engage in this sort of second-guessing of the decisions of democratically elected government officials. It is a role that the courts are not institutionally capable of

---

25. 512 U.S. 43 (1994).

26. *See* Employment Division, Department of Human Resources v. Smith, 494 U.S. 872 (1990); Maher v. Roe, 432 U.S. 464 (1977); Harris v. McRae, 448 U.S. 297 (1980).

performing, and it is hard to believe that the Constitution really contemplates such a role of the courts.

Not only is constant judicial balancing impractical, it is also institutionally illegitimate. To understand why, it is worth considering what role balancing expects judges to play. In every case where government action intrudes on constitutionally protected autonomy, judges would be expected to assess the impact of the law on an individual, assess the strength of the public policy behind the law, and then decide whether the public policy is strong enough to justify the burden on individual autonomy. Indeed, at least in theory that is what the Supreme Court's current set of constitutional doctrines expects courts to do. This balancing may not be neutral—it might be that certain kinds of autonomy are so strongly protected that only a very powerful public policy (what the Court calls a "compelling interest" in the current jargon) outweighs the individual's autonomy. But in every case, some comparison is necessary. The difficulty is, it has never been clear, and the Supreme Court has never explained, on what basis courts are to assess the strength, or lack thereof, of particular public policies. In our system of government, it is the task of democratically elected legislatures, at both the state and federal levels, to establish public policy and determine which policies are most important to society. Given the lack of any objective basis for determining what are "good" or "bad," or "strong" or "weak" public policies, the reason that we respect legislatures' judgments in this regard is their democratic pedigree, making their judgments expressions of the will of the sovereign People. Federal judges, of course, have no such democratic pedigree, because they are not elected.

Another problem with the "balancing" approach is that presumably, every statute enacted by a legislature, including most especially a statute intruding on a constitutionally excluded area of authority such as free speech, reflects a judgment that the policy advanced by the statute is a powerful one. On what basis are unelected federal judges to second-guess that judgment? What is the constitutional calculus, the "rule of law," that permits them to say to a legislature that while you think this goal is important to the public good, we're telling you that you are wrong? In short, judgments about the strength of public policies are not legal judgments, they are political ones—and as such, are judgments which in our system of government unelected judges have no business making.

All of the above suggests that a true, autonomy-based system of constitutional rights is not only impractical, it is illegitimate. A structural approach to rights, however, which does not seek to balance individual autonomy against public policy but rather expects judges to enforce specific, definable limits on governmental authority, is one that is entirely consistent with our system of government, and with the role of an unelected judiciary in that system. Our Constitution defined and created a new national government and empowered it in specified ways. A Bill of Rights was added to that Constitution to disempower that government, again in specified ways. And finally, in the wake of the Civil War the

Fourteenth Amendment was added to the Constitution, extending those areas of disempowerment, as well as others, to the governments of the several states. The job of the courts, in this system, is to identify what powers are granted to governments, what powers are denied to them, and to enforce those limits. When courts, following such an approach, hold the acts of elected officials unconstitutional, they are not expressing a judgment about the strength of the policies the government is seeking to advance, they are simply enforcing preexisting limits on the government's authority, limits that the People themselves imposed on government through the process of constitutional formation and amendment. This, unlike balancing, is a role that judges should feel comfortable playing.

Once one accepts this vision of the important but limited role that judicially enforceable constitutional rights play in our society, some important implications follow. In the balance of this book, I will endeavor to explain some of those implications in specific constitutional contexts. Before turning to these matters, however, one broad point must be kept in mind. When we say that the role of constitutional rights in our system is a limited one, it is important to remember that the Constitution is not only a disempowering document, it is also an empowering one. Even if constitutional rights do not protect individual autonomy, and (as discussed in Chapter 1) do not create rights to positive assistance from the government, that does not mean that autonomy, or an active government, are not important values. Indeed, the framers themselves clearly considered natural rights and liberty to be critical, perhaps the most significant, values that a democratic society might choose to support. The point is, however, that the Constitution, as enforced by judges, will not do that work for us. Instead, the Constitution creates a system of government that permits us to express our preferences, and envisions an active citizenry that engages with that system. If we as citizens value individual autonomy, and if we believe that the government should assist individuals in achieving liberty and human dignity, we must pursue those goals through the democratic process.

5. FREE SPEECH AND SELF-GOVERNANCE

The Free Speech Clause of the First Amendment states that "Congress shall make no law . . . abridging the freedom of speech, or of the press, or of the right of the people peaceably to assemble, and to petition the Government for a redress of grievances." As we have already seen, the Bill of Rights and the Fourteenth Amendment, like the rest of the Constitution, are not generally intended to protect individual liberty, but rather to organize and place limits upon government. Yet the First Amendment on its face, by singling out freedom of speech, press, and assembly (and, as we shall see in the next chapter, of religion) for special protection, does appear to be concerned with rights of the individual. Is this so? Why did the framers choose to single out speech, the publication of writings, and assembly, among the myriad of activities that human beings engage in, for special constitutional protection? And why did they combine and juxtapose these three particular activities in the First Amendment? In short, what is the *role* of the Free Speech Clause in the constitutional structure? These are questions that have been debated by judges and academics for decades, and the answers to these questions have important implications for the great free speech issues that our society has confronted over the years. A structural understanding of the Bill of Rights, unsurprisingly, yields important and valuable insights in this debate.

THEORIES OF FREE SPEECH

Over the years, three distinct schools of thought have emerged regarding the "purposes" of the constitutional protection of free speech. Probably most famously, early in the twentieth century, Justice Oliver Wendell Holmes, Jr., created the metaphor of "the marketplace of ideas" to describe the First Amendment's social function. Dissenting from a 1919 decision in which the Supreme Court affirmed the convictions for espionage of a group of Russian émigrés who supported the Communist Revolution in Russia, Justice Holmes posited that the Constitution protects free speech because "the best test of truth is the power of the thought to get itself accepted in the competition of the market," and that therefore ideas such as those espoused by the defendants in the case should not be suppressed simply because a judge and jury found them false, or even reprehensible.[1] Thus for Holmes, we protect free speech as a means to pursue truth because the discovery of truth creates a better society.

---

1. Abrams v. United States, 250 U.S. 616, 630 (1919) (Holmes, J., dissenting).

In recent decades, another quite distinct view of the First Amendment has emerged. A group of scholars including notably Thomas Emerson and C. Edwin Baker have argued that the importance of free speech, and the reason for the special constitutional protection it receives, is the fundamental significance of free speech for individuals, in their quest for autonomy and self-fulfillment.[2] In other words, speech is protected because it is an important part of individual identity. This approach, which we might call the "self-fulfillment" theory of free speech, thus sees the value of speech in its ability to permit individuals to express themselves, and to shape their own lives and values.

Both the marketplace of ideas and the self-fulfillment theories of free speech have obvious attractions and have been ably defended. What is notable about these theories, however, is that neither if them fits well with a structural understanding of the Constitution, one focused on the powers and limits of organized government. The search for truth, after all, is not in any way an inherent function of the *government*, as opposed to civil society. The self-fulfillment rationale is even more distant from any structural model, focused as it is on individual liberty and happiness. Neither of these theories fits well with the general purposes and organizational principles of the Constitution. There is, however, a third approach to free speech, one that better reflects the structural values of the Constitution. This approach emphasizes the close, symbiotic relationship between free speech and democratic self-governance. The origins of this understanding of free speech can be found in an opinion of another great Supreme Court Justice, Louis Brandeis (who was a contemporary and ideological ally of Justice Holmes). Writing in 1927, Justice Brandeis had this to say about free speech: "Those who won our independence believed . . . that the greatest menace to freedom is an inert people; that public discussion is a political duty; and that this should be a fundamental principle of the American government."[3] Some years later, the philosopher Alexander Meiklejohn expressed a similar sentiment. He argued that "[t]he First Amendment does not protect a 'freedom to speak.' It protects the freedom of those activities of thought and communication by which we 'govern.' It is concerned, not with a private right, but with a public power, a governmental responsibility."[4] Meiklejohn also said that "the First Amendment, as seen in its constitutional setting, forbids Congress to abridge the freedom of a citizen's speech, press, peaceable assembly, or petition, whenever those activities are utilized for the governing of the nation."[5] In short,

---

2. *See* C. Edwin Baker, Human Liberty and Freedom of Speech 47–69 (1989); Thomas I. Emerson, Toward a General Theory of the First Amendment 4–7 (1966).

3. Whitney v. California, 274 U.S. 357, 375 (1927) (Brandeis, J., concurring).

4. Alexander Meiklejohn, *The First Amendment Is an Absolute*, 1961 S. Ct. Rev. 245, 255 (1961).

5. *Id.* at 256.

Meiklejohn and (albeit a bit more ambiguously) Brandeis argued that free speech is accorded special constitutional status not because of its significance to individuals, but rather because of its critical importance to the democratic process. Free speech is important, in other words, because it permits citizens to vote intelligently and otherwise to participate in the political process. Without free speech, democracy would be impossible, because without free and open discussion citizens could never achieve "the knowledge, intelligence, sensitivity to human values: the capacity for sane and objective judgment which, so far as possible, a ballot should express."[6] In modern times, a similar approach has been espoused by figures as diverse as former judge and (Republican) Supreme Court nominee Robert Bork,[7] and the highly respected (liberal) law professor Cass Sunstein.[8] It is, I think, safe to say that in recent years the democracy-centered approach to free speech has become the dominant, though not uncontested, view of why the Constitution protects free speech.

SELF-GOVERNANCE AND RESISTANCE

The self-governance theory of free speech is, of course, at its heart a structural approach, focused on the nature of government rather than on individual autonomy. Free speech is protected not for its own sake, nor for its importance to individuals. It is protected because of its role in the workings of government. Voting, after all, is at its core a governmental function, in the sense that when citizens vote, they are acting in their sovereign capacity, to create or constitute their government. The self-governance rationale also explains, as the other approaches cannot, the juxtaposition in the First Amendment of protection for free speech, a free press, and the rights of peaceable assembly and petition. (And it explains the protection for religion in the First Amendment, a subject we will explore in the next chapter). Admittedly, free speech and a free press do seem logically linked, since one protects the spoken word and the other the written word, though even here, protection of the institutional press seems in some tension with at least the self-fulfillment rationale for free speech, since surely Fox and CNN do not seek "self-fulfillment." When one considers the rest of the First Amendment, moreover, the conundrum seems clear. It is hard to conceive of what relationship peaceable assembly, or petitioning the government for a redress of grievances, have to either individual self-fulfillment, or to the search for truth. Both of these activities, however, are obviously and intimately tied with self-governance. To be able to form views, and to express them effectively and

---

6. *Ibid.*

7. Robert H. Bork, *Neutral Principles and Some First Amendment Problems*, 47 IND. L. J. 1, 20 (1971).

8. CASS SUNSTEIN, DEMOCRACY AND THE PROBLEM OF FREE SPEECH 121–166 (1993).

meaningfully, citizens must be able to assemble publicly, to form groups and associations. Furthermore, to participate in government citizens must be able not only to organize independently of the government, but also to communicate with their elected leaders about the actions of their government (remember, the First Amendment was written in an era before electronic communications of any sort). How else could the People ensure that their leaders were aware of, and held accountable for, the actions of the government that they led? How else could democracy and voting be utilized to ensure that the balance of power between organized government and the People remains favorable to the latter? In short, the protection for free speech, a free press, assembly, and petition, are best understood not as distinct, individual rights, but as a unitary principle, protecting the process through which the People participate in, and control, their government.

All of this points to a broader truth about the role of First Amendment freedoms in our system of democratic self-government. If our government is to be one that is controlled and kept within its proper bounds by the People, rather than one that controls and shapes the People, the public must have a means to speak, think, and organize free of public influence or control. While Alexander Meiklejohn emphasized the relationship of free speech to *voting*, that is undoubtedly too narrow a view of the role of First Amendment in protecting popular government. Certainly in our representative democracy voting is the most obvious way in which citizens shape, check, and participate in government. And certainly freedom of speech is essential to effective voting. But voting to choose representatives is far from the only way in which citizens can influence government, and (more importantly) restrain misuses of governmental power. Justice Louis Brandeis captured this point when he pointed out the dangers of an "inert people," because surely citizens who do nothing more than vote every two years qualify as inert citizens. An active citizenry must do more than that. It must discuss, form organizations and associations, communicate their views to governmental officials (both elected and appointed), and generally create public institutions independent of the government within which views about government can be formed and expressed free from the influence and coercion of public officials. Ultimately, moreover, such organizations can also act as centers of resistance to governmental power—though that eventuality, like the military resistance envisioned by the Second Amendment (as discussed in Chapter 1), is of course a last, hopefully rare, resort. In the revolutionary era, organizations such as the Sons of Liberty played that role. Today, there exists a vast array of public groups, ranging from Code Pink to the National Rifle Association, which do the same. And these groups are as essential a part of our system of government as the Democratic and Republican parties.

Once the importance of public groups, which is to say citizens' organizations, to the democratic process is accepted, the role of the First Amendment becomes clear. In order for such groups to organize themselves and to participate in the process of governance, citizens belonging to such groups *must* be able to speak to each other, to spread their views through pamphlets and books, and to gather together in private and in public—note that in the era of the framers public assembly was the only feasible way to organize groups of any substantial size, given the limits of communications technology. Finally, to be able to participate in government, such groups must have the right to present their views to public officials—i.e., to "petition the Government for a redress of grievances." That is the liberty that the First Amendment, in all of its aspects, protects. The First Amendment states that the State may not interfere with any of these activities—speech, press, assembly, and petition—and indeed lumps them together as part of a single principle. This combination is consistent with the structural vision set forth here, but not consistent with either the marketplace of ideas or the self-fulfillment explanations for the protection of free speech. The last point to recognize is that while the First Amendment does not explicitly protect the right to resist unjust governmental actions (any more than the Second Amendment explicitly authorizes militias to resist the federal armed forces), such a possibility, in extremis, is implicit in the protections that are accorded by the First Amendment. It should be remembered in this regard that the Sons of Liberty, the quintessential example for the framers of a public resistance organization (indeed, many of the framers were members) graduated, over time, from written propaganda, to protests, to substantial acts of violence directed at the British government. Of course, the framers hoped and expected that the new, republican government that had come into being in 1789 would not act in a way to require such active resistance; but their recent history strongly suggested that the possibility had to be kept alive.

In summary, properly understood, the speech, press, and assembly provisions of the First Amendment are as much a part of the structural constitution of the framers as the parts of Article I organizing the Congress. The First Amendment, however, deals not with the formal structures of government, but with the means by which citizens—the People in whose name the new government was being organized—could participate in, and if necessary control and resist, that government. The question to which we now turn is how this understanding contributes to the resolution of practical, modern free speech disputes.

ANTI-ORTHODOXY: OF FLAGS, COMMUNISTS, AND RACISTS

Combining the insights about the purposes of the First Amendment discussed above with the theoretical framework set forth in Chapter 4, what principles can we derive regarding the prohibitions imposed on government by the Free Speech Clause? One conclusion follows immediately: that neither the federal government, nor (after the First Amendment was extended to the states) any state government, may suppress speech, writings, or organizations simply because the government disapproves of the message communicated or espoused by the communication or organization; and concomitantly, the government may not, ever, require citizens to express or adhere to any ideas or values simply because the government supports them. Any attempt to suppress a particular message, or to impose a particular message on citizens, is an illegitimate action that automatically violates the First Amendment, and any action motivated by such a purpose is similarly invalid, because its purpose is illegitimate. We might call this the "anti-orthodoxy" principle. The derivation of this principle is straightforward. As noted above, the core purpose of the Free Speech Clause (along with the press, assembly and petition provisions) of the First Amendment is to permit citizens to shape their beliefs and values and to organize themselves, free of governmental interference. When a government suppresses speech, writings, or organizations because of hostility to a message or belief, it is acting contrary to that core purpose because it is trying to usurp and control the process by which the sovereign People form their beliefs and values, biasing that process toward beliefs and values favored by the government. Similarly, when a government requires citizens to adhere to values chosen by the government rather than the citizens themselves, it is once again usurping a power that belongs to the People, not to the government. In both cases, by acting as it does the government is undoing the balance of power between citizens and the State established by the First Amendment.

The judicial roots of the anti-orthodoxy principle can be found in the Supreme Court's 1943 decision in *West Virginia Board of Education v. Barnette*.[9] In *Barnette*, the Court invalidated a West Virginia School Board regulation requiring all school children in the state to salute the American flag and to recite the Pledge of Allegiance, and further held that the plaintiff students, Jehovah's Witnesses who refused to salute the flag for religions reasons, could not be expelled for their refusal. In explaining why the law was unconstitutional, Justice Robert Jackson, one of the great Justices of the twentieth century, had this to say about the nature of American government:

> There is no mysticism in the American concept of the State or of the nature and origin of its authority. We set up government by the consent of the governed, and the Bill of Rights denies those in power any legal opportunity to coerce that consent. Authority here is to be controlled by public opinion, not public opinion by authority. . . .
>
> If there is any fixed star in our constitutional constellation, it is that no official, high or petty, can prescribe what shall be orthodox in politics, nationalism, religion, or other matters of opinion or force citizens to confess by

---

9. 319 U.S. 624 (1943).

word or act their faith therein. If there are any circumstances which permit an exception, they do not now occur to us.[10]

Note how, in this passage, Justice Jackson explicitly links the anti-orthodoxy principle with American concepts of popular sovereignty. If popular sovereignty is to have any meaning, Jackson is saying, the government may not tell the People what they may say or think. Rather, the reverse must be true.

It should come as no surprise, given the emotional significance of the American flag, that disputes over the flag have played a major role in the development and exposition of the anti-orthodoxy principle. During the Vietnam War and the Civil Rights era the Supreme Court was faced with a number of cases in which protestors were prosecuted for defiling or desecrating the flag. In each case, the Court managed to reverse the conviction, while avoiding the ultimate question of whether flag desecration may be outlawed at all.[11] Ultimately, however, in 1989 in the famous flag-burning case, *Texas v. Johnson*,[12] the Court was faced squarely with the question. During the 1984 Republican National Convention, Gregory Lee Johnson burned an American flag as a protest against the Reagan Administration's policies in Central America. He was convicted under a Texas statute forbidding the desecration of "venerated objects," including the national and state flags. The Supreme Court, albeit by a narrow 5–4 vote, reversed his conviction, holding that his prosecution, and the Texas statute, violated the First Amendment. In so holding the Court, in an opinion by Justice William Brennan, emphasized that the very reason for the State of Texas's decision to ban flag desecration was that the state disapproved of Johnson's message of contempt for the flag, and held that this motivation made the prosecution invalid, because "[i]f there is a bedrock principle underlying the First Amendment, it is that the government may not prohibit the expression of an idea simply because society finds the idea itself offensive or disagreeable."[13] Brennan then goes on to quote the language from the *Barnette* case reproduced above, as well as the passage from Justice Brandeis's opinion in *Whitney v. California* discussed earlier in this chapter, as support for his conclusion. In short, *Texas v. Johnson* is the mirror image of *Barnette*. Just as the government may not impose agreement with ideas it favors (*Barnette*), it also may not punish expression of ideas it disfavors (*Johnson*). A year later the Court reaffirmed this conclusion in striking down a federal law that also forbade mistreatment of the flag.[14]

---

10. *Id*. at 641–642.
11. *See* Street v. New York, 394 U.S. 576 (1969); Smith v. Goguen, 415 U.S. 566 (1974); Spence v. Washington, 418 U.S. 405 (1974).
12. 491 U.S. 397 (1989).
13. *Id*. at 414.
14. United States v. Eichman, 496 U.S. 310 (1990).

The anti-orthodoxy principle, and more generally an approach focused on limits of power rather than on individual autonomy, is particularly valuable in understanding the result in the flag burning cases, which was of course highly controversial at the time (and which elicited numerous, ultimately unsuccessful attempts to amend the Constitution to reverse the decisions). The truth is that seen through the lens of individual autonomy, the result in these cases is quite dissatisfying. After all, why should Gregory Johnson have been permitted to engage in public behavior that was *highly* offensive and hurtful to others, in order to express his views in this particular way when there were a myriad other, perfectly legal ways for him to state his disapproval of the Reagan Administration—a point that Chief Justice William Rehnquist made dissenting in *Johnson*?[15] Surely requiring a slightly different mode of expression would not be a serious burden on Johnson's "liberty," given the weighty interests on the other side? The answer to these questions is that Johnson's liberty, or autonomy, are frankly beside the point. The anti-orthodoxy principle, that the government may not coercively impose its values on citizens, is an absolute one, as Jackson pointed out, with no exceptions, because it follows from the very structure of our government. Just as Congress cannot enact laws unless both the House and Senate vote for it and it is presented to the president for his signature,[16] and just as a president cannot continue in office past his or her four-year term unless reelected, no matter how good the reason in either case, the government also may not claim for itself a power that rightfully belongs to the People. That, however, is what flag desecration statutes attempt to do.

Strong and clear as the anti-orthodoxy principle is, it must be acknowledged that the Supreme Court has not always honestly held to it. There were two significant eras in our constitutional history, in particular, in which those principles were discarded. Both, however, have been largely repudiated in modern times and provide an object lesson in why the anti-orthodoxy principle should not be abandoned lightly.

The first such era ran from 1918 to the late 1920s, encompassing World War I and the "Red Scare" that followed it, triggered by the 1917 Bolshevik Revolution in Russia. This was a politically turbulent era in the United States. Industrialization and the social dislocations it produced, combined with the lack of significant legal protection for workers, had led to the growth of a significant left-wing political movement, ranging from radicals to moderate socialists. Most of the upper classes, on the other hand, including most of the legal profession, were firmly wedded to a *laissez-faire* economic philosophy that emphasized protection of property rights and freedom of contract, and who were therefore highly hostile both to attacks on private property and to efforts on the part of workers to

---

15. *Id.* at 430–431 (Rehnquist, C. J., dissenting).
16. *See* INS v. Chadha, 462 U.S. 919 (1983); Clinton v. New York, 547 U.S. 417 (1998).

organize into unions. Into this volatile situation was thrown first the entry of the United States into World War I in April 1917, which socialists and communists strongly opposed, and then in late 1917 the Bolshevik Revolution. A wave of repression followed. During the war itself (which ended in November 1918), thousands of opponents of the war were prosecuted and imprisoned for sedition, on the theory that their opposition impeded the U.S. war effort, in particular by interfering with conscription. Among those imprisoned was Eugene Debs, the leader of the American Socialist movement, who ran for president from jail in 1920. Many of the defendants raised First Amendment defenses to their prosecutions, but they were uniformly rejected by the federal courts. One trial court judge, Learned Hand (who was later to become one of the most respected appellate judges in American history), did attempt to limit these prosecutions, but his efforts were rejected on appeal.[17] All of this culminated with three unanimous Supreme Court decisions in the spring of 1919, all written by Justice Oliver Wendell Holmes, which affirmed the convictions of opponents of the war, including that of Debs himself.[18] Holmes justified the convictions by arguing that while political speech is constitutionally protected unless it creates a "clear and present danger" of some illegal result, in the wartime context that danger existed.[19]

The end of World War I did not spell the end of political repression. After the war, socialists, communists, and anarchists were prosecuted in large numbers under both federal espionage statutes and under state "criminal syndicalism" statutes, which made it a crime to advocate or teach the need for, or legitimacy of, using violence or force to overthrow the government or change the ownership of property. Again, the justification for these "Red Scare" prosecutions was a stated fear that advocacy of such ideas would lead to political violence or revolution. And again, the Supreme Court consistently permitted the government to punish individuals' speech and publications on the grounds that speech that constitutes "incitement" is unprotected.[20] This time, however, the Supreme Court was not unanimous. Holmes and Justice Louis Brandeis wrote separate opinions in the important free speech cases of this era, disagreeing with the majority's conclusions because, according to Holmes and Brandeis, there was insufficient evidence that the speech being prosecuted was *likely* to produce any illegal action in the near future. As a result, they concluded that the defendants were merely being punished for their political beliefs, which was impermissible

---

17. *See* Masses Publishing Co. v. Patten, 244 F. 535 (S.D.N.Y. 1917), *rev'd* 246 F. 24 (2nd Cir. 1917).

18. Schenck v. United States, 249 U.S. 47 (1919); Frohwerk v. United States, 249 U.S. 204 (1919); Debs v. United States, 249 U.S. 211 (1919).

19. *Schenck, supra*, 249 U.S. at 52.

20. *See, e.g.*, Abrams v. United States, 250 U.S. 616 (1919); Gitlow v. New York, 268 U.S. 652 (1925); Whitney v. California, 274 U.S. 357 (1927).

under the First Amendment.[21] As we shall see, these great opinions are the source of modern free speech law.

To understand the errors made by the Supreme Court during this period, and the consequences of those errors, some context is necessary. At one level, the Court made no mistake at all—the Court was surely correct in arguing that the First Amendment's free speech guarantee does not protect violence, nor does it protect conspiracy or planning to engage in violence. No government could proceed on such a basis, and for all of their mistrust of authority even the framers would surely not have supported such a result (though Thomas Jefferson may have come close). Indeed, Robert Bork has on this very basis argued that the Supreme Court did *not* make any mistakes during this era, and concomitantly that Holmes and Brandeis were wrong.[22] But it is Bork who is wrong. The difficulty, as Holmes and Brandies (eventually) came to realize, was that in these cases the courts completely did away with any need for the government to *prove* that the speech they were suppressing risked causing real, social harm, and relatedly, made no serious attempts to probe the government's *true* motives for suppressing speech. The truth is that opponents of World War I appear to have had no effect on the ability of the United States to wage war, and it is even more clear that there was no risk at all of a Communist Revolution, or even of any serious uprising, in the United States in the 1920s (or at any time, for that matter). Furthermore, government officials during this period surely knew this—as demonstrated by their persecution of such "dangerous" figures as Anita Whitney, a fifty-two year old socialite turned communist who never in her life advocated violence.[23] As a result, it is impossible not to conclude that the defendants in these cases were being punished not because of the risk they posed to society, but because they were expressing, and organizing themselves to support ideas that the majority found abhorrent. But such governmental actions are the very essence of a violation of the anti-orthodoxy principle. Furthermore, the repressions of this era had consequences. During the war, opposition was silenced, leading to a false and fragile sense of unity. The results were first a failure to hold the government to account for its wartime decisions, which can be contrasted to the powerful effects of publicly stated opposition to modern wars such as Vietnam and Iraq, when free speech was protected. Second, when the war finally ended, there was a sharp counterreaction within the United States, resulting in the Senate's refusal to join the League of Nations and a rise of isolationism,

---

21. *See Abrams, supra,* 250 U.S. at 627 (Holmes, J., dissenting); *Gitlow, supra,* 268 U.S. at 672–673 (Holmes, J., dissenting); *Whitney, supra,* 274 U.S. at 374 (Brandeis, J., concurring).

22. Bork, *supra,* 47 IND. L. J. at 29–35.

23. For a more detailed discussion of Whitney's fascinating story, *see* Ashutosh Bhagwat, *The Story of* Whitney v. California: *The Power of Ideas* in CONSTITUTIONAL LAW STORIES (Michael Dorf ed., 2004).

which in turn may have contributed to the rise of Hitler and the outbreak of World War II. During the Red Scare, the suppression of leftists led to an uneven political landscape in which the conservative economic policies supported by the country's economic elite (and by a majority of the Supreme Court) could be entrenched. Such a result was (perhaps) acceptable during the economic boom of the 1920s, but it was an utter disaster during the Great Depression that began in November 1929. Ultimately, of course, many (though by no means all) of the reforms advocated by the left during this period, including notably the right to unionize, were adopted during President Franklin Delano Roosevelt's New Deal.

The Supreme Court eventually reconsidered its position on free speech. In the landmark 1931 decision in *Stromberg v. California*,[24] the Court invalidated a California statute making it a crime to display a red flag as a symbol of opposition to the government. Over the next two decades, the Supreme Court (reshaped by new, liberal appointees) provided substantial protection even to unpopular opinions (many of the defendants in this era were, as in the *Barnette* flag salute case, Jehovah's Witnesses), and adopted the Holmes/Brandeis approach to free speech. In the 1950s, however, repression and judicial failure reappeared, in the form of the McCarthy era. Once again, the United States was faced with an external threat (from the Soviet Union during the Cold War) and a perceived internal threat (from domestic communists), and once again the nation responded with a heavy-handed repression of communist organizations, as well as organizations and individuals perceived to be supportive of communists. These efforts included criminal prosecution of communist leaders, legislative investigations, black lists, and loyalty oath programs. During the crucial, early period from the later 1940s through the mid-1950s, the federal courts largely permitted the McCarthy-era persecution to proceed, including affirming the criminal convictions of the leaders of the Communist Party.[25] Again, the justification was that communist organizations posed a serious threat to the nation's security. As Justice William O. Douglas pointed out, however, the difficulty (as in the Red Scare era) was that there was simply no proof that domestic communists posed a serious threat to the United States, and indeed, all evidence and common sense pointed to the contrary conclusion.[26] As a consequence, in hindsight it becomes clear that during this era, the United States was punishing individuals purely because of the beliefs they held and espoused, in clear violation of First Amendment principles. The result was not only substantial individual suffering, but also a withering of political debate leading to unchecked governmental actions both domestically and abroad such as refusal among political leaders to confront the evils of racial segregation in this country, and support for military coups

---

24. 283 U.S. 359 (1931).

25. Dennis v. United States, 341 U.S. 494 (1951).

26. *Id.* at 588–591 (Douglas, J., dissenting).

overthrowing democratically elected governments in countries such as Iran and Guatemala.

Beginning in the late 1950s, and accelerating in the 1960s, the Supreme Court finally turned its back on tolerance for repression. The Court began, in a series of narrow decisions, by imposing limits on the persecution and prosecution of communists.[27] As the 1960s progressed, free speech conflicts began to center not on Communism, but on the Civil Rights movement and opponents of the Vietnam War. The Court during this period provided more and more protection to free speech, rejecting numerous claims that speech may be suppressed merely because of its potential to cause violence. This trend culminated with the Court's landmark 1969 decision in *Brandenburg v. Ohio*,[28] in which the Court reversed the conviction for criminal syndicalism of a Ku Klux Klan (KKK) leader, holding that such prosecution was impermissible absent strong proof of eminent, actual social harm—an approach that would surely have led to the reversal of convictions in all of the World War I, Red Scare, and McCarthy era cases. In a related series of cases during this period, the Supreme Court held that not only may the government not suppress "incitement" without proof of social harm, it also may not silence speakers because of fears that listeners might react with violence toward the speaker because of their hostility to the message conveyed—a conclusion that had obvious and important implications for civil rights demonstrators who could otherwise be silenced by segregationist mobs.[29] Eight years after *Brandenburg*, in 1977, state and federal courts applied the rules developed by the Supreme Court in this period to uphold the right of the National Socialist (Nazi) Party of America to hold a march through Skokie, Illinois, a suburb of Chicago with a large Jewish population, including thousands of survivors of Nazi concentration camps during World War II.[30] Clearly if Nazis are provided protection in modern America, the anti-orthodoxy principle without exceptions has come of age, protecting even the most vile ideas and organizations.

The history set forth above of this nation's treatment of unpopular speech not only demonstrates the power of the anti-orthodoxy principle, it also provides further grounds to understand why free speech law is best understood in structural terms, rather than in terms of individual autonomy. Consider the cases discussed above. It is no doubt clear (certainly today, but also at the time) that it

---

27. *See, e.g.*, Yates v. United States, 354 U.S. 298 (1957); Scales v. United States, 367 U.S. 203 (1961).

28. 395 U.S. 444 (1969).

29. *See* Edwards v. South Carolina, 372 U.S. 229 (1963); Cox v. Louisiana, 379 U.S. 536 (1965); Gregory v. City of Chicago, 394 U.S. 111 (1969).

30. The Skokie controversy produced many judicial opinions. *See, e.g.*, Skokie v. National Socialist Party of America, 373 N.E.2d 21 (Ill. 1978); Collin v. Smith, 578 F.2d 1197 (7th Cir. 1978).

was correct to protect civil rights protestors from persecution. But with respect to other speakers, communists and racists in particular, the answer is less obvious. I have no doubt that government officials during World War I honestly believed that opposition to American participation in the war was treasonous, and that officials in the 1920s and 1950s honestly believed that communist speech was worthless and potentially disruptive of society. More obviously, surely there is widespread consensus in modern American society that organizations like the KKK and the Nazi Party are valueless and provide no useful contribution to our political debate. Given the substantial social harm that racist speech produces (consider what it would have felt like, as an elderly Holocaust survivor living in Skokie, to have to witness a Nazi march in your home town), why should we protect such speech, at least when addressed to victims of racism? Surely in those circumstances the speaker's interest in autonomy is outweighed by the victim's interest in avoiding fear and psychic harm, and by society's interest in protecting those victims and maintaining social harmony? Under an individual autonomy approach that balances interests, a speaker's "rights" may well be outweighed. But from a structural perspective that is asking the wrong question. The correct question is whether the government can be trusted with the power to decide which speech, and which ideas, are valueless, and which ideas are worthy of protection. To that question, the answer is clear. The First Amendment allocates the power to decide which values and which ideas should be developed not to the State but to the People, acting individually and through their personal, private associations. Furthermore, the First Amendment does not permit certain subsections of the People to co-opt the State to suppress ideas of which they disapprove, because in that situation also the power to choose values has been centralized in the State, eliminating the possibility of multiple, competing sources of power and values among citizens. Thus the government may not suppress speech because of the hostility of audiences, just as it cannot suppress speech because of its own hostility. This principle is a bedrock element of our system of government, and as noted above permits no exceptions, even for racists and Nazis.

More generally, this structural perspective also explains why, in our system of government we provide full constitutional protection to such harmful and hurtful speech as hate speech and pornography that depicts women in a demeaning fashion. Consider hate speech first. The constitutional status of hate speech, which we might define as attacks directed at vulnerable groups such as racial minorities, religious minorities, women, and sexual minorities, has been a highly controversial issue in modern times. Beginning in the 1980s, a number of academics and commentators began presenting forceful arguments that government should be permitted to regulate hate speech because of its extremely low social value and the severe harm it imposes on victims. In particular, these writers argued persuasively that the effect of hate speech was often to silence and disempower already vulnerable minorities—a result that contradicts the purposes of provisions of the Constitution other than the First Amendment, including notably the Equal Protection Clause of the Fourteenth Amendment.[31] Furthermore, there are surely many ways to express disapproval of groups without directing epithets at individuals, the only kind of speech that these commentators sought to regulate. The burden on speakers' autonomy imposed by narrowly drawn hate speech regulations thus seems trivial.

These arguments, on their own terms, seem hard to refute. Nonetheless, when the issue of hate speech reached the Supreme Court in 1992, in a case called *R.A.V. v. City of St. Paul*,[32] the Supreme Court flatly rejected it. *R.A.V.* involved the prosecution of a White teenager, for burning a cross on the lawn of a Black family in St. Paul, Minnesota. R.A.V. (his name is not public, because he was a juvenile at the time) was charged under a St. Paul ordinance making it a crime to display various symbols, including a burning cross or a swastika, knowing that the symbol "arouses anger, alarm, or resentment in others on the basis of race, color, creed, religion or gender." The Court, in an opinion by Justice Scalia, held that this ordinance violated the First Amendment because of the fact that the government of St. Paul had chosen to single out particular viewpoints— bigotry on the basis of race, color, creed, religion, or gender—for suppression because of the city's hostility to those viewpoints. That was unacceptable under the First Amendment. What is notable about the Court's holding in *R.A.V.* was that the Court clearly was *not* holding that R.A.V. had a "constitutional right," in the sense of an autonomy right, to burn a cross on a family's lawn. Justice Scalia explicitly recognized that R.A.V.'s behavior was not only "reprehensible," but also potentially subject to prosecution under any number of other laws, such as laws prohibiting terroristic threats, arson, and damage to property (to say nothing of trespass).[33] Indeed, eleven years later the Court confirmed that even cross-burning may be specifically barred, so long as the law prohibited only cross-burning intended as a threat to an individual.[34] Justice Scalia also recognized that St. Paul had powerful, legitimate interests in protecting the victims of hate speech.[35] Nonetheless, a majority of the Court concluded that R.A.V.'s prosecution was unconstitutional. Why? The answer, simply, is because St. Paul was taking sides in a political debate, by suppressing some (though by no means all) expressions of one viewpoint, while leaving the opposite perspective (tolerance) unregulated. St. Paul was perfectly welcome to adopt laws designed to protect

---

31. *See, e.g.*, Richard Delgado and David H. Yun, *Pressure Valves and Bloodied Chickens: An Analysis of Paternalistic Objections to Hate Speech Regulation*, 82 CAL. L. REV. 871 (1994); Mari Matsuda, *Legal Storytelling: Public Response to Racist Speech: Considering the Victim's Story*, 87 MICH. L. REV. 2320 (1989); Richard Delgado, *Words that Wound: A Tort Action For Racial Insults, Epithets and Name-calling*, 17 HARV. C.R.–C.L. L. REV. 133 (1982).

32. 505 U.S. 377 (1992).

33. *Id.* at 380 n.1, 396.

34. Virginia v. Black, 538 U.S. 343 (2003).

35. *R.A.V*, 505 U.S. at 395–396.

individuals from harm, but it had to do so in a way that did not favor one particular viewpoint, and the individuals and groups who advocated that perspective, over others—i.e., which did not establish an orthodoxy. That conclusion is correct, in my view, but it only makes sense if one views the purposes of the First Amendment in structural terms. When viewed from the perspective of individual autonomy, it is nonsensical because R.A.V. had no "right" to terrorize his neighbors.

Finally, in considering the treatment of hate speech in this country, it is worthwhile to contrast it with the approach of other countries, which is often very different. For example, the Canadian Supreme Court has explicitly held that certain kinds of hate speech are not constitutionally protected because they conflict with democratic values.[36] Many other democratic nations, including Great Britain, France, and Germany, prohibit certain kinds of hate speech. So why not the United States? The short answer, I think, is that our Constitution, our system of government, and our free speech protections are based on different structural assumptions than elsewhere. In particular, the strong principle, encapsulated, in the First Amendment that the People must stand independent of, and above, the government in forming their values, and the strong belief in a need for power centers independent of the State to make this possible, is a value distinctly associated with the United States. It is rooted both in distrust and hostility toward government, *and* in a strong faith in private, civic groupings of citizens (the combination is crucial). In many other countries, the State is less feared, and the role of the State in cultural and political value formation is more accepted (this is especially true in France, but not uniquely so). Thus in much of the world free speech is valued as one important aspect of autonomy, to be balanced against others. Our Bill of Rights is a structural document reflecting *our*, and no other, structure of government.

The constitutional treatment of hate speech in this country is paralleled by its treatment of pornography and other sexually explicit speech. The Supreme Court has long held that other than a very narrowly defined category of sexually explicit speech called obscenity (on which more later), sexual and other "indecent" speech (e.g., foul language) generally enjoys constitutional protection. Famous examples of cases confirming this principle include *Cohen v. California*,[37] in which the Supreme Court reversed the conviction of a man who (during the Vietnam War) wore a jacket into a courthouse with the words "Fuck the Draft" written on the back, and *Reno v. American Civil Liberties Union*,[38] in which the Court struck down a federal statute, the "Communications Decency Act," which forbade the transmission or posting of "indecent" message over the Internet if they would be accessible to anyone less than eighteen years old. In the 1980s a

---

36. Regina v. Keegstra, 2 W.W.R. 1 (1991).
37. 403 U.S. 15 (1971).
38. 521 U.S. 844 (1997).

strong movement emerged, lead by feminists such as Catherine MacKinnon and Andrea Dworkin, seeking to ban pornography that demeaned women by treating them as sexual objects deserving of violence or mistreatment. The laws proposed by this movement would *not* have banned all pornography, only demeaning pornography. Many prominent commentators supported this approach, on grounds that strongly paralleled the arguments against protection of hate speech more generally.[39] When the City of Indianapolis attempted to implement this approach in a statute, however, the U.S. Court of Appeals for the Seventh Circuit struck down the law. In an opinion by the highly respected judge, and former University of Chicago law professor, Frank Easterbrook, the court conceded the harm to women documented by Catherine MacKinnon that such pornography causes, and also conceded that it may be difficult to "respond" to such a message with more speech. Nonetheless, the court held the Indianapolis law unconstitutional, describing it as "thought control" and concluding that "[a]ny other answer leaves the government in control of all of the institutions of culture, the great censor and director of which thoughts are good for us."[40] In short, the Court (citing *Barnette*, the famous West Virginia flag salute case) recognized that commendable as Indianapolis's goals were, its approach to the problem violated the anti-orthodoxy principle.

As noted above, while the First Amendment has been held generally to protect sexually explicit speech, there are two significant exceptions to that rule. The Supreme Court has long held that the First Amendment provides no protection to either child pornography (defined as a visual depiction of an actual minor engaging in sexual conduct) or "obscenity." The exception for child pornography does not pose any difficulties under the anti-orthodoxy principle, because as the Court has recognized, the reason why the government prohibits (or at least why the Court permits the government to prohibit) child pornography is not because of hostility to its "message," but because of the desire to protect the actual children used in making child pornography.[41] That purpose has nothing to do with suppressing ideas, or interfering with people's desire to speak and organize in order to express a different view regarding sexuality and minors. Thus speech merely advocating for the repeal of statutory rape laws would be protected, and the Court has also held that *virtual* child pornography—i.e., sexually explicit depictions that *appear* to show minors engaged in sexual acts, but which in fact are produced using either computer morphing or adult actors—is fully protected speech.[42] Since such speech sends precisely the same "message" as actual child

---

39. *See, e.g.*, Cass Sunstein, *Pornography and the First Amendment*, 1986 DUKE L. J. 589.

40. American Booksellers Association v. Hudnut, 771 F.2d 323, 328, 330 (7th Cir. 1985).

41. *See* New York v. Ferber, 458 U.S. 747 (1982).

42. Ashcroft v. The Free Speech Coalition, 535 U.S. 234 (2002).

pornography, it is clear that the Court is not permitting governments to suppress that message.

Obscenity, however, poses a different problem. The Supreme Court has long recognized a category of sexually explicit speech, called obscenity, that enjoys no constitutional protection. In its landmark 1973 decision in *Miller v. California*,[43] the Court defined obscenity as material which, under community standards, appeals to the prurient interest (i.e., invokes sexual feelings), depicts or describes sexual conduct in a patently offensive way, and lacks serious social value. In a companion case to *Miller*, the Court clarified that distribution of obscene material could be prosecuted even if the transaction was between consenting adults, with no minors or unwilling viewers being exposed to it.[44] Why is obscenity unprotected? Chief Justice Warren Burger, writing in 1973, explained that it was because of "the interest of the public in the quality of life and the total community environment, the tone of commerce in the great city centers, and, possibly, the public safety itself."[45] He also argued that obscenity may be banned because "a sensitive, key relationship of human existence, central to family life, community welfare, and the development of human personality, can be debased and distorted by crass commercial exploitation of sex."[46] Insofar as the justification for banning obscenity is protection of the "public safety" (i.e., the prevention of crime caused by obscene material), that appears permissible, since it does not turn on hostility to ideas. The problem is that, as Burger himself conceded, there was in 1973 no substantial evidence that obscene materials in fact cause crime or other social harm in any direct way[47]—something that remains true today. Thus this justification founders on the same lack of proof that undermined the Red Scare and McCarthy era prosecutions, demonstrating that it is a make-weight, a pretext for the government's *true* motives. A further difficulty with Burger's explanation should also be clear. In essence, in adopting Burger's rationale the Supreme Court was itself adopting—and permitting governments to adopt—a particular view of the proper nature and social role of sexuality, as centered on family life. By making obscene speech unprotected, the Court was permitting the government to impose this view by force on private individuals and groups. That is a clear violation of the anti-orthodoxy principle. Furthermore, the fact that the topic of the speech was sexuality rather than an overtly political topic cannot matter; after all, the role of sex and sexuality in our society is hardly a topic free of political implications, as illustrated by modern debates over homosexuality, sex education in schools, and any number of other subjects. Finally, the fact that obscenity laws do not prohibit *all* speech adopting a particular

---

43. 413 U.S. 15 (1973).

44. *See* Paris Adult Theatre I v. Slaton, 413 U.S. 49 (1973).

45. *Id.* at 58.

46. *Id.* at 63.

47. *Id.* at 60–61.

attitude or approach to sexuality, only certain sexually explicit types of speech that "lack value," also does not matter. The availability of alternative ways to communicate is irrelevant for the same reason that the argument was rejected in the hate speech and flag burning contexts—the anti-orthodoxy principle is a bedrock structural principle, without exceptions. To say that obscene materials lack value is even more problematic, because it empowers the government, in the form of prosecutors and judges, to judge the worth of speech based on what is being expressed; but such a judgment is in itself a violation of anti-orthodoxy principles, because it permits the State to impose its values on individuals by regulating not their actions, but their communications.

It is thus extremely difficult to justify the modern law of obscenity in rational terms, and indeed, few modern scholars even try to do so. Instead, the obscenity exception is usually justified on historical grounds, because of the supposed traditional intolerance in England and the United States of pornographic materials. In fact, this history is questionable—widespread suppression of pornography did not start in this country until the nineteenth century, well after the adoption of the First Amendment.[48] And regardless of history, the truth is that adherence to the anti-orthodoxy principle as a bedrock element of our structural Constitution requires abandonment of the "obscenity" exception to the First Amendment.

To conclude, the most important free speech principle that emerges from a structural view of the First Amendment is the anti-orthodoxy principle—that the government may not suppress communication because it does not want citizens to adopt ideas in those communications, and it may not require citizens to espouse or adopt particular viewpoints. In modern times, the Supreme Court has held onto this principle fairly consistently, though historically it sometimes bobbled. The primary modern deviation from this principle is the Court's tolerance of "obscenity" prosecutions against sexually explicit speech and publications. The reason why this exception exists is unclear, however. It would appear that sex is different; why, we do not know.

THE MASS MEDIA: ENHANCING SPEECH THROUGH REGULATION

The anti-orthodoxy principle provides the core of the prohibitions upon government imposed by the First Amendment, identifying those actions that are inherently illegitimate. It is, however, only a beginning, not an end. As discussed in Chapter 4, the various provisions of the Bill of Rights do not only disallow certain governmental purposes, they also identify certain kinds of governmental action, certain areas of regulation, that are inherently suspect. Generally, the speech and

---

48. *See generally* Geoffrey R. Stone, *Sex, Violence, and the First Amendment*, 74 U. CHI. L. REV. 1857, 1861–1863 (2007).

press clauses indicate that when the government directly singles out communication, either oral or written, for unfavorable treatment, the government is treading on dangerous ground. This bald statement, however, requires many caveats. First, it does not cover laws that do not target speech, but merely incidentally burden it—including, as we shall see, some laws that appear to regulate speech but are better understood as conduct regulations. Second, the presumption against regulation cannot hold when the government is acting in a proprietary capacity—i.e., as an owner or as an employer. Under those circumstances, more complex issues are raised, as we shall also see. Finally, not even all direct regulations of speech or the press are prohibited even if they are inherently suspect. In this section, I will consider one category of such regulations, those directed at the mass media. Later, we will consider regulations of private speech that impose noncommunicative harms on others.

Regulation of the mass media, of the "press" in constitutional terms, poses some of the most important, and difficult, dilemmas of modern free speech. First a clarification. During the framing period, the term "press" referred of course to the use of printing presses, creating books, newspapers, and pamphlets. Today, however, the term must be understood more broadly, to include all forms of nonoral communication, including radio, broadcast and cable television, the Internet, and any other technologies that exist or develop over time. Any other reading would be an absurdity (ponder in this regard if we read the constitutional phrase authorizing Congress to raise an army and a navy to exclude an air force). Moreover, the term press (or media) should not be limited to the institutional, organized media such as major newspapers and broadcast networks. In the framing period, a lone pamphleteer would surely have been protected by the First Amendment, and today a lone blogger deserves no less.

With that understanding, and in light of the purposes of the First Amendment discussed earlier, it should be clear that *any* governmental regulation of the media poses profound constitutional concerns. The reason is obvious—insofar as the core purpose of the First Amendment is to permit the People to shape their beliefs and views, and to organize themselves free of governmental intrusion, freedom of the press from governmental interference is absolutely essential if that purpose is to be carried out. The vital role that the press plays in that process is twofold. First, it provides the means by which citizens can communicate with each other in numbers, to share their views, persuade others to join them, and generally to organize themselves. To put it in obvious terms, how can citizens "assemble" unless they can publicize the time and place of assembly? And even more basically, can assembly and petition have any real value unless citizens have had a prior opportunity to identify those who share views and persuade others to join them? Liberty to communicate broadly, not merely face-to-face, is thus an inherent aspect of the overarching sphere of private power placed off-limits to the government by the First Amendment. Second, organized media entities—i.e., the institutional media—play an important role in our system of government, since they are themselves one of those independent associations of citizens, discussed earlier, through which the People may organize, form views, communicate them to the government, and ultimately resist unjust actions. It is noteworthy in this regard that in this country, there is a strong tradition of a media that is *not* State-owned and not subject to substantial political control (in many other countries the electronic media in particular is either State-owned, or subject to substantial political control). Other than a minor government involvement in public broadcasting, the independence of the media from the government still holds today. Given the institutional role of the media described above, that independence is essential. This is why describing the media as the "Fourth Branch of Government" is a bit of a misnomer; the media's significance lies precisely in the fact that it is *not* a part of government.

For all of these reasons, there must be a constitutional presumption against regulations that single out the media. Of course, this does not mean that the media must not obey generally applicable laws that regulate everyone evenhandedly. Reporters have no right to break the speed limit when racing to cover a story, and (as the Court has recognized) media entities must follow general labor and employment laws.[49] With respect to targeted laws, however, the Supreme Court has traditionally recognized such a presumption of unconstitutionality, at least with respect to the written media. It has thus invalidated rules requiring licensing of the press,[50] a law permitting the press to be enjoined (i.e., ordered by a judge) to refrain from publishing "scandalous and defamatory" stories about public officials,[51] and a law imposing higher taxes on the press.[52]

With respect to the electronic media, however, the Court's path has been less certain, at least in part because of technological differences. With respect to the oldest of the electronic media, broadcasting (radio and television), licensing is necessary because broadcasters use a common public resource, the airwaves, which the government must regulate to ensure rational use (for example, to ensure that broadcasters do not interfere with each other's transmissions). Therefore, throughout the modern era all broadcasters have been required to obtain a license from the Federal Communications Commission (FCC), an agency of the federal government, and no one believes this requirement raises any serious constitutional issues. In addition to licensing, however, the federal government also regulates the *content* of broadcast programming in many ways, to ensure that broadcasters serve the public interest. Thus broadcasters have traditionally been required to provide coverage of public issues, to provide suitable programming for children, and to refrain from broadcastings indecent

---

49. Associated Press v. NLRB, 301 U.S. 103 (1937).
50. Lovell v. Griffin, 303 U.S. 444 (1938).
51. Near v. Minnesota, 283 U.S. 697 (1931).
52. Minneapolis Star & Tribune Co. v. Minnesota Commissioner of Revenue, 460 U.S. 575 (1983).

materials (at least during daytime). Furthermore, for many years (though no longer) the FCC imposed a rule called the "fairness doctrine" on broadcasters, which required broadcasters to offer "fair" or balanced coverage of public issues and to permit anyone who has been subject to a "personal attack" a chance to respond on the air. The effect of these rules, in combination, is to impose substantial, government-imposed restraints on the editorial freedom of broadcasters. It should be clear that the above rules go far beyond what would be permitted for other media, since they interfere so clearly with the autonomy of the press. Indeed, the Supreme Court has specifically held that a "right of reply" comparable to the fairness doctrine may not be imposed on *newspapers*,[53] and as noted above has also generally provided strong constitutional protection to indecent speech outside the broadcast context. Nonetheless, the Supreme Court has upheld the constitutionality of both the fairness doctrine[54] and of indecency regulation[55] in the broadcast context, on the grounds that because of the "scarcity" of available airwaves, broadcasters receive less constitutional protection. The Court has made clear that this less-protected status does *not* apply to other electronic media, such as cable television or the Internet, limiting the modern significance of this rule. However, even with cable television the Court has upheld some regulation—for example, a rule requiring cable television providers to dedicate some of their channel capacity to carry, free of charge, the signals of over-the-air broadcast television stations[56]—which would probably not be permissible in the print context. In short, it is clear that because of their particular technological characteristics, the electronic media are subject to greater regulatory restrictions than print. The exact status of the Internet in this regard remains unclear, but the possibility remains that it too will be subject to greater governmental controls.

What are we to make of all of this? The answer is complex. On the one hand, given the dominance and peculiar effectiveness of the electronic media in today's society in distributing information, shaping the values and culture of the public, and influencing the electoral process, governmental intervention here raises a profound risk of undermining the basic separation of power and authority between the State and the People that underlies our democratic system of government. On the other hand, there seems little doubt that technological differences do sometimes require *some* weakening of the strong presumption against regulation. Licensing of broadcasters is probably one example—though even here, Nobel Laureate Ronald Coase proposed many years ago that licensing could be avoided by granting broadcasters property rights over portions of the

---

53. Miami Herald Publishing Co. v. Tornillo, 418 U.S. 241 (1974).
54. Red Lion Broadcasting Co. v. FCC, 395 U.S. 367 (1969).
55. FCC v. Pacifica Foundation, 438 U.S. 726 (1978).
56. Turner Broadcasting System Inc. v. FCC, 520 U.S. 180 (1997).

airwaves, that could be sold.[57] Coase's solution, however, does not solve the problem of scarcity. Because inevitably there will be only a handful of broadcast television stations in a particular locality (scarcity is less of an issue with radio), some governmental intervention is arguably necessary. Similarly, cable television poses special problems because local cable television operators (atleast for now) appear to be what is called a "natural monopoly," meaning that only one cable operator can survive economically in any single service area.[58] This too would seem to suggest a greater role for government, to avoid abuse of monopoly power, and to ensure that *multiple* sources of information remain available to the public.

The path the Court has trodden with respect to the electronic media is, however, a dangerous one. The problem is that once the door is opened to extensive governmental regulation, the risk that the institutional media will come under the dominance of the government, and lose their crucial independence, becomes severe. In the context of the broadcast industry, for example, there are good reasons to believe that extensive governmental regulation severely restricted the scope of controversial political coverage for many years. To solve this conundrum, we must return to first principles, and recall why the free speech and press clauses are in the Constitution. Instead of engaging in a sterile debate about the "rights" of broadcasters (who might be argued to have waived them, by accepting an FCC license), or the editorial "rights" of cable operators, we should remember that the objective here is to maximize speech by the public and to the public, so as to ensure the dialogue and diversity of opinion that makes for a vibrant democracy, while at the same time absolutely minimizing the risk that the *government* will be able to influence this conversation. To accomplish this, courts must take a very careful look at all media regulation, to ensure that it advances those goals. In particular, courts must ensure that any regulatory scheme imposed on the media has the specific purpose and effect of increasing competition and diversity within the media, without allowing the government to control the content of media speech or the day-to-day operations of the media. Put in terms of the "limited purpose" analysis set forth in Chapter 4, the only governmental purpose that can justify regulation of the media is to create an increasing competition and diversity within an *independent* media.

By this measure, the Court's treatment of regulation of broadcasters has been a disaster. By upholding stringent, recurring licensing requirements imposed on the industry by Congress (FCC licenses must be renewed every five years), the courts have permitted a regulatory scheme that brings an important element of the media under constant governmental scrutiny and control. By permitting the government to oversee the content of broadcast programming, the Supreme Court has opened the door to manipulation and intimidation of the media.

57. Ronald Coase, *The Federal Communications Commission*, 2 J. L. & ECON. 1 (1959).
58. *See* Omega Satellite Products v. City of Indianapolis, 694 F.2d 119 (1982).

In the radio context, where dozens of stations can coexist, there is simply no justification for this. Regarding television, the spectrum scarcity problem is (or at least was, as I will discuss) real enough, but the solutions adopted by Congress and the FCC, and endorsed by the Court, are absolutely the opposite of the non-substantive, competition-inducing, structural regulations that the First Amendment would permit. Instead, they have created a dependent, cautious media that by its nature cannot fulfill the functions intended by the First Amendment.

But the truth is that the debates over broadcast regulation are increasingly irrelevant, because of the decline of traditional, over-the-air broadcasting. According to the FCC, as of June 2005 almost 86 percent of U.S. households owning televisions subscribed to some sort of multichannel video service (primarily either cable television or direct broadcast satellite services such as Dish or DirectTV). This means that by that date, only 14 percent of T.V. households received their television through over-the-air broadcast.[59] This does not make the government's influence over broadcast television stations irrelevant, because cable and satellite services inevitably carry broadcast stations (indeed, they are required to do so by law, as noted previously), and the major network stations subject to FCC regulation remain the most popular channels even on cable. However, given the availability today to most American households of hundreds of purely cable television channels (such as CNN, Fox News, A&E, etc.) that are *not* subject to close FCC supervision, to say nothing of the rise of the Internet as an independent, unregulated source of information and communication, the risk of government control over a substantial portion of the media has largely disappeared. This is not to say that governmental influence over the broadcast industry is not still excessive—it clearly is—but the significance of that problem has faded.

That leaves cable and the Internet. Though distinct, both raise similar problems. As mentioned previously, the physical structure of the cable television network likely makes it a natural monopoly with real power. Since the turn of the twenty-first century the rise of direct broadcast satellite services such as Dish and DirectTV has substantially restricted cable's power (according to the cable industry's association, as of 2007 only 58 percent of U.S. television households subscribed to cable[60]), but there is no doubt that cable providers still have substantial power over the information available to the public. With respect to the Internet, the idea of control may seem absurd, given the multiplicity of Web sites, but again, a potential problem exists, which is the problem of access. Increasingly, effective access to the Internet requires a broadband connection. In practice,

---

59. *See Twelfth Annual Report on the Status of Competition in the Market for Delivery of Video Programming* at ¶8 (FCC 2006), available at http://hraunfoss.fcc.gov/edocs_public/attachmatch/FCC-06-11A1.doc.

60. *See* http://www.ncta.com/Statistic/Statistic/Statistics.aspx.

broadband Internet access is a duopoly, dominated by two technologies, and within individual communities, by two providers: cable modem access provided by the local cable monopoly, and DSL service provided by the local telephone monopoly. This concentration of power does not itself raise constitutional concerns because the relevant parties—cable companies, direct broadcast satellite companies, and telephone companies—are not themselves the government. However, it is easy to see why the government has a legitimate interest, consistent with the First Amendment, in ensuring that the power these companies possess does not lead to a serious reduction in the quantity, breadth, and variety of speech and debate that the public may access and participate in over the Internet. At the same time, however, as the lesson of broadcast teaches, permitting intrusive governmental regulation is a severe mistake and anathema to the purposes of the First Amendment. The conclusion must be that while structural regulation creating greater opportunities for speech and debate should be permissible, the courts must take a close look at any such regulation to ensure that there is no sign of content control, intrusive governmental oversight of the media, or favoritism among media entities (which can easily become a guise for control over content, or otherwise for intimidation). On this measure, the Court's performance in the cable television area has only been middling. On the one hand, the Court has clearly rejected the idea of treating cable like broadcast and permitting intrusive control, which is certainly the correct result. On the other hand, as noted previously the Court has upheld rules (called "must-carry" rules) requiring cable operators to provide free channel space to—in effect, to subsidize—broadcasters. Such favoritism should be highly suspect, and probably should have been struck down. If, however, Congress were to choose to impose neutral access obligations on cable television providers, requiring them to choose which channels to carry on a nondiscriminatory basis (i.e., without favoring channels owned by the operators themselves), and if such rules can be implemented without excessive governmental oversight, that is the sort of neutral, structural regulation that seems consistent with First Amendment policies.

With respect to the Internet, regulation is still in its infancy. Given the enormous variety of private speech communicated over the Internet, there is of course no justification for direct government regulation of content. The above analysis does suggest, however, that because of the market power enjoyed by broadband access providers, the kind of "net neutrality" regulations advocated by such figures as Professor Tim Wu of Columbia University and Professor Lawrence Lessig of Harvard University should be permissible. This is because net neutrality—the requirement that internet service providers do not discriminate among the different types of data and traffic they carry—is precisely the kind of structural regulation, protecting access and diversity without controlling content, that the First Amendment permits. Otherwise, there seems no reason to accord the Internet any less than full First Amendment protection, which would justify little or no targeted regulation (though as noted above, the First

Amendment does not prevent the application of generally applicable laws, such as taxation or fraud rules, to the Internet).

Having considered the scope of permissible government regulation of the media, we should now take a broader perspective regarding the relationship between the media and government. Two particular issues arise here: first, does the media have any special right of access to information and for newsgathering; and second, may the government ever punish the media for releasing confidential or secret information. The first issue, a special right of newsgathering, turns out to be a complex one, raising many subsidiary questions, such as whether reporters may refuse to divulge the identity of their sources (when needed for legitimate, law-enforcement purposes), whether they can be subject to other laws when enforcement interferes with their ability to obtain newsworthy information, and generally whether the government may withhold information or access to information from reporters. At some level, an answer is clearly that the press has no special immunity from the laws—surely reporters have no right to commit trespass or blackmail in gathering information. Harder questions arise, however, when the battle is over the confidentiality of sources, or conversely whether the media can be held liable for breaking a promise *to* keep a source's identity confidential. Over the years, the Supreme Court has been sharply divided on all of these questions, and generally has failed to provide clear answers to the basic, underlying question of whether the media has special rights or privileges.[61] However, it is fair to say that the strong implication and pattern of the Supreme Court's cases over the years is that the institutional media does *not* enjoy any special privileges, or any special rights of access to information, at least as a matter of *constitutional* law. (It should be noted that legislatures can, and do, provide the media with special statutory rights, through laws such as the Freedom of Information Act, which permits the public to access government information, and the laws of many states protecting the confidentiality of reporters' sources.) As a structural matter, this seems correct. As we have noted, the purpose of the free speech and press clauses of the First Amendment is to permit communication free of government interference, which in turn permits citizens to shape values and organize themselves in such a way as to provide a counterpoint to the power of the State. The institutional media is one, admittedly important, player in this process, but it has no unique role to play. The idea here is to create ideological and power centers that are *independent* of the State, not dependent on it for special privileges or access. Thus a special status, linked to the government, seems inconsistent with the structural vision underlying the First Amendment. Indeed, there is a greater problem: to grant special privileges to "the press" or "the institutional media," the *government* must identify and decide who exactly is

---

61. *See, e.g.,* Branzburg v. Hayes, 408 U.S. 665 (1972); Cohen v. Cowles Media Co., 501 U.S. 663 (1991).

entitled to such special privileges, who is "the press." But that step, of creating a special, licensed media chosen by the government, is one fraught with dangers of manipulation and favoritism, and is anathema to the underlying goal of creating institutions *free* of governmental control or manipulation. As such, a structural view of the First Amendment would seem to leave little or no space for special media rights.

The second question, whether the media may be punished for disclosing confidential information, is much more difficult. This question was raised in a very salient way when in 2006, then–Attorney General Alberto Gonzales and other senior Republicans suggested that the New York Times might be criminally prosecuted for publishing articles disclosing the details of a warrantless wiretapping program authorized by President George W. Bush in the aftermath of the 9/11 attacks.[62] A similar question arose, though not in the context of criminal prosecution, when during the Vietnam War the Nixon Administration sought a judicial order preventing the Washington Post and New York Times from publishing a top-secret Pentagon study of the war called the "Pentagon Papers," disclosure of which, the administration claimed, would threaten national security. Ultimately, the Bush Administration did not choose to prosecute the New York Times, and indeed, no American newspaper has ever been prosecuted for disclosing classified information. Moreover, in the Pentagon Papers case the Supreme Court held that the First Amendment prohibited the courts from issuing an order preventing publication of newsworthy information unless a true catastrophe loomed, as it surely did not in that context.[63] The truth is, however, that the exact rule regarding whether the government may punish the press for publishing classified information remains unclear. Indeed, in the Pentagon Papers case some Justices specifically raised the possibility of a criminal prosecution against the newspapers. In a 2001 case the Supreme Court did hold that normally the press may not be punished for publishing confidential information of public concern (there, a cell phone conversation between union officials involved in a labor dispute, which had been illegally intercepted by an unknown third party);[64] but because that case did not involve national security, it does not really resolve the issue.

The question then arises, *should* the Constitution be read to prevent such prosecutions? Two preliminary points should be made. First, the only question here is liability for disclosure; for the reasons discussed above, there is no doubt that newspapers can be punished for illegally *obtaining* information, for example by using an illegal wiretap or by bribing a government official to release

---

62. Devlin Barrett, *Lawmaker Wants Paper Probed Over Stories*, ASSOCIATED PRESS (June 25, 2006), *available at* http://www.breitbart.com/article.php?id=D8IFB4V01&show_article=1. The recent Wikileaks controversy of course raises the same issues.

63. New York Times v. United States, 403 U.S. 713 (1971).

64. Bartnicki v. Vopper, 532 U.S. 514 (2001).

classified information. Second, it should be noted that if immunity is to be provided for publishing classified information, it cannot be limited to the "media" as such, it must be a universal immunity, or else the entire problem discussed above of identifying an officially recognized "media" is raised. Posed as such, the question is a very difficult one, because there are important interests on both sides. On the government's side is, of course, the very real interest in national security and retaining important, state secrets. On the other side is the interest of the public in knowing what their government is doing. One possible solution is to "balance" these two interests, on a case-by-case basis, to try and reconcile the government's interest with the newspaper's "right" to publish. This solution, however, is entirely unsatisfactory, for two different reasons. First, the very possibility of criminal prosecution is likely to deter anyone from publishing classified information, even if they have a reasonable chance of ultimately winning, after judges balance. Second, the balancing test misconceives the relevant inquiry, because it treats the issue as one of reconciling the government's needs with an individual's autonomy interest in speaking. But the First Amendment does not really protect such interests (and if it did, one suspects that individuals would usually lose, when their interests are balanced against national security interests). The concern here is a structural one—can the government be trusted with the power to decide which secrets should, and should not, be available to the public. Stated that way, I believe that the answer must be no, the government cannot be trusted with such power. The problem is that the government has a predictable and common tendency to classify information not because it is dangerous, but because it is embarrassing. And, one suspects, the government will be especially zealous to prosecute the disclosure of information that is politically embarrassing (as both the Pentagon Papers and the Bush wiretapping program undoubtedly were). But the ability of the People to know what their government is doing, to be able to supervise, criticize, and control those activities, lies at the core of representative democracy. For the People to be able to play that role, to maintain ultimate control and power in themselves, they *must* know what their government is up to. That need is so fundamental a structural feature of our system, that it ultimately must prevail here, thereby limiting the government's power to prosecute disclosures even of secrets. It must be conceded that the weakening of the government's ability to keep secrets that this implies *does* have serious social costs; but they are costs that a democracy must bear.

INCIDENTAL BURDENS ON SPEECH AND THE SPEECH/CONDUCT DISTINCTION

Until now, this chapter has focused largely on limitations that the First Amendment, viewed from a structural perspective, *does* impose on government. At this point, there is some value in considering areas where a structural perspective cuts in the opposite direction, toward a narrower view of constitutional rules. We begin with the problem of incidental burdens. An incidental burden on a free speech right occurs when the government passes a law that is not *directed* at speech, but that nonetheless makes it more difficult, expensive, or even impossible for a person or persons to engage in speech (or publication). This topic was discussed in general terms, with some free speech examples, in Chapter 4. As we noted then, a structural analysis of the Bill of Rights leads us to conclude that normally neutral laws with incidental effects on speech should *not* be unconstitutional, even if the consequence is to substantially restrict individual autonomy or liberty, because such governmental action does not raise structural concerns. Leading constitutional scholars, including notably Michael Dorf of Cornell University, have argued to the contrary, that incidental burdens *do* require scrutiny, but Professor Dorf's analysis is based on an autonomy-based view of rights, that I argue we should reject.[65] However, as was also emphasized in Chapter 4, it is critical that courts, when faced with claims of incidental burdens, should take a close look to ensure that the governmental action was not cleverly written in speech-neutral terms, but was in fact intended to suppress speech. As an example, consider a municipal ordinance banning making fires in a particular park, which is enacted immediately before a planned antiwar rally, at which the government knew protestors intended to burn the American flag. The antifire ordinance would normally be a completely unproblematic law, despite its incidental effects on speech; but in the factual context described above, a reviewing court should probably find (absent other explanations) that the purpose of the law was to suppress disfavored speech, which is unconstitutional. With that caveat, however, truly neutral laws normally should not be considered to raise serious constitutional concerns.

The fact that governments may target conduct because of its harmful effects, despite any incidental effects on speech, leads to another conclusion—that sometimes, speech is so closely associated with socially harmful conduct that the government may suppress such speech without constitutional concern. The reason is that when the government narrowly targets speech closely intertwined with conduct, the regulation is best treated as one of conduct, not truly speech, and as such only incidentally related to the purposes of the First Amendment. As examples of such laws, consider statutes forbidding threatening violence to others, soliciting crime, or conspiring with others to commit a crime. In each of these instances, a law on its face prohibits "speech," and so might be viewed as gravely suspect. Furthermore, such speech can sometimes be political in nature—consider as examples a threat against the president accompanied by the recitation of some real or imaginary grievance, or a conspiracy to commit a political crime such as animal rights activists bombing a laboratory. Regardless, however,

---

65. *See* Michael Dorf, *Incidental Burdens on Fundamental Rights*, 109 HARV. L. REV. 1175 (1996).

violent threats, solicitation of murder, and conspiracy are examples of speech that is so closely intertwined with actual, dangerous conduct—actual violence or other crime—that laws banning such speech should properly be viewed as only imposing incidental restrictions on speech, because the government is in fact targeting the unlawful conduct. Once that perspective is taken, such laws are entirely unproblematic from a structural perspective, even if they do have the effect of silencing the speech (including sometimes political speech) of some individuals.

THE GOVERNMENT AS SPEAKER, EMPLOYER, AND OWNER

Another area where the structural approach provides the government greater flexibility than an individual-autonomy perspective is in the government's role as proprietor, which means in its role as an employer, owner, and provider of funding. Let us begin with the related problems of the government as speaker and of the free speech rights of public employees. As a preliminary matter, it should be relatively clear that when the government itself speaks, when it expresses its opinions, it may do so free of any restrictions imposed by the Constitution and the First Amendment, because it is not coercing anyone or otherwise restricting the private sphere of citizens. This simple statement of principle, however, ignores a difficulty, for the idea of the government "speaking," is of course a myth. The "government" is not a person, it is an abstract entity, a concept. As such, government can "speak" only through its employees; but public employees are individual citizens with views and interests of their own. Suppose that senior government policymakers adopt a particular policy regarding what the government should and should not say on a particular topic (say the Iraq war), and require *all* employees to implement that policy by either saying specific things, or remaining silent on a specific topic, in the course of their employment. What if those employees disagree with that policy and so refuse to follow it—can they then be disciplined or fired? From an autonomy perspective, such punishment seems problematic, since it involves effectively coercing what a citizen says or does not say, which surely seems to raise free speech concerns. From a structural perspective, however, it seems clear that such punishment is perfectly permissible because when the government controls what employees say in the course of their jobs, this action has absolutely no impact on the power of private citizens, or groups of citizens, to organize themselves and express their views. Thus controlling what employees say simply does not implicate the purposes of the First Amendment. And in fact, the Supreme Court has held that the First Amendment imposes no limits on the power of government to discipline employees for speech made pursuant to their official duties.[66]

---

66. Garcetti v. Ceballos, 547 U.S. 410 (2006).

It should be emphasized, however, that the conclusion that public employee's speech is unprotected must be strictly limited to speech (or silence) in the course of public employees' job duties. When public employees speak in a private capacity, they remain citizens of our democracy, government coercion of whom raises precisely the same structural concerns raised by coercion of other citizens. Thus it is not that restriction of public employees' speech does not raise constitutional concerns, it is that the structural purposes of the Constitution are implicated only by regulation of their private speech. By the same token, however, it surely is, and should be, unconstitutional for the government to punish, fire, or refuse to hire individuals because of what they said, or because of organizations they joined, independently of their jobs.[67] Among other things, this conclusion means that political patronage—the custom of hiring and firing public employees based on their willingness to support particular politicians or political parties in their private capacity—violates the First Amendment by extending the power of the State into the private sphere in ways that are extremely dangerous to the democratic process.[68] Indeed, recognizing the structural concerns raised by such behavior, the Court has extended its antipatronage rule to protect public contractors as well as employees.[69] Given the sheer size of public payrolls and expenditures in the modern era, any other conclusion would substantially expand the sphere of governmental authority over private association and speech, thereby dramatically shifting the balance of power between citizens and the State and dramatically reducing the accountability of elected officials.

Unfortunately, the distinction between "job-related" and "private" speech of public employees turns out to raise some difficult line-drawing issues. With respect to some very senior employees such as cabinet members, for example, it is probably fair to say that *all* of their speech is "job-related" when they are in office. Moreover, how is one to classify a government employee who speaks or writes during her private time but about her job, using information obtained in the course of employment (for example, by whistle-blowing to the press)? On the one hand, such speech is not literally "in the course of employment," but on the other hand, the government does have legitimate interests in its capacity as an employer in maintaining confidentiality and avoiding disruption to its workplace, which raise no structural concerns. The compromise the Supreme Court has come to in such cases is supposedly to "balance" the "interests" of the government against those of its employees.[70] In fact, however, this balancing seems a bit of a fraud. In practice, when the employee's speech implicates legitimate

---

67. *See* Elfbrandt v. Russell, 384 U.S. 11 (1966); United States v. Robel, 389 U.S. 258 (1967).

68. *See* Elrod v. Burns, 427 U.S. 347 (1976); Branti v. Finkel, 445 U.S. 507 (1980); Rutan v. Republican Party of Illinois, 497 U.S. 62 (1990).

69. O'Hare Truck Service, Inc. v. City of Northlake, 518 U.S. 712 (1996).

70. Pickering v. Board of Education, 391 U.S. 563 (1968).

confidentiality concerns, or threatens real disruption to the workplace, the government tends to win—which is probably the right result given the gap between these cases and the core, structural purposes of the First Amendment. It is only when the employee's speech truly is private, or implicates no serious interests of the of the government as employer, that employees prevail, because in that situation the real purpose of the government's action seems to be the illegitimate one of controlling employees in their private capacity. Of course, the silencing of whistle-blowers *does* have an impact on the functioning of our democracy, by limiting the ability of citizens to oversee their government's activities, suggesting, contrary to the trend of the cases, that whistle-blowers should receive constitutional protection. As noted in the earlier discussion of the media, however, the balance the Constitution and the First Amendment appear to have drawn in this area is to protect the independence of private citizens and groups, including the media, but not to empower them to intrude into the workings of the government itself.

Issues similar to those raised by the regulation of government employees arise when the government provides funding for the speech of private citizens or groups. Generally, of course there is no objection to such funding. However, conflicts can arise when the government limits (as it often does) the content of the speech it is willing to fund, and potential or actual recipients disagree with those limits. Famous examples of such conflicts include *Rust v. Sullivan*,[71] the famous "abortion gag rule" case in which the Reagan Administration adopted regulations forbidding recipients of federal family planning funds from providing referrals for, or even *encouraging the use of* abortions as a method of family planning, and *National Endowment for the Arts v. Finley*,[72] in which artists challenged a congressional statute requiring the National Endowment for the Arts (NEA), a federal agency that funds artists, to consider "general standards of decency" in awarding grants (this law was triggered by NEA grants supporting the homoerotic photography of Robert Mapplethorpe and a photograph called "Piss Christ" showing a crucifix in urine). From an autonomy perspective, such government actions seem highly problematic, since they certainly impinge on the "liberty" of funding recipients. From a structural perspective, however, the government's refusal to *fund* or support views with which it disagrees cannot be equated with governmental interference with citizens' ability to form and express views and associations free of governmental interference. As noted above, the key value advanced by the First Amendment is citizens' independence from government, and funding cannot equate to independence. In fact, in both the *Rust* and *Finley* cases, the government's rules were upheld. A very different question would have been raised if the government, for example, denied social security or unemployment benefits to abortion advocates or controversial artists, because

---

71. 500 U.S. 173 (1991).
72. 524 U.S. 569 (1998).

then the government would be using its financial clout to impinge on the private sphere of citizens. But it is simply unrealistic to describe government-funded speech as "private" for constitutional purposes.

The most difficult free speech problems in the area of government as proprietor arise when the government acts not as an employee, or as a provider of funding, but as a landowner. The question, in short, is whether the government may control what citizens say on its property. Private owners, of course, generally have that power since (with a few exceptions) they can make a speaker they dislike leave their property, so why not the government? After all, in these situations the government is merely controlling what it owns, not intruding directly into the private sphere. And in fact, this is precisely the conclusion the Supreme Court reached when it first considered these questions, at the turn of the twentieth century.[73] In modern times, however, the Court has rejected this simple view, and instead created an extraordinarily complex body of law, called the "public forum" doctrine, to resolve such conflicts. The reason why the Court has concluded that government's power over its property is not unlimited is fairly straightforward and follows from the First Amendment's structure. To understand this point, it is important to comprehend what "government property" encompasses. It includes not just buildings, but also essentially all roads, sidewalks, thoroughfares, parks, and other public spaces. The impact on the *private* sphere of giving government unlimited control over this property would be catastrophic. Think back to the words of the First Amendment, which forbid government from abridging the freedom of speech and the press, and also "the right of the people peaceably to assemble, and to petition the Government for a redress of grievances." In 1789, where could citizens have assembled, if not in public spaces? Even in the modern era of the Internet and electronic communications, *public* assembly (meaning organizational meetings, demonstrations, marches, etc.) would be impossible without access to public property. And without such assembly, how could the private sphere of ideas and associations protected by the First Amendment come into being? It could not, and so for these structural reasons, at least some public property, the public forum, must be open to private speech and assembly free of intrusive governmental restrictions.

As an example of public forum regulation with a devastating impact on political discourse, consider *Bl(a)ck Tea Society v. City of Boston*,[74] a case that arose during the 2004 Democratic Party Convention in Boston. Given the highly contentious political atmosphere during the 2004 election, the convention inevitably attracted a large number of protest groups seeking to express their views to party delegates—precisely the kind of citizen groups whom the First Amendment seeks to protect. The City of Boston (and the federal government), however, had substantial, legitimate concerns about security given that this was

---

73. *See* Davis v. Massachusetts, 167 U.S. 43 (1897).
74. 378 F.3d 8 (1st Cir. 2004).

the first presidential election cycle since the September 11 attacks. The solution the city adopted to resolve its security concerns was to cordon off large areas around the facility where the convention was held from which protestors were excluded. Instead, protestors were all required to remain in a "demonstration zone" (DZ), located underneath railroad tracks, surrounded by fencing and coiled razor wire—a space the demonstrators described as a "pen." The practical effect of this scheme was, of course, largely to eviscerate the impact of the public demonstrations and to make it almost impossible for demonstrators to communicate their views to the delegates. Nonetheless, the U.S. Court of Appeals for the First Circuit upheld the DZ, concluding that it was justified by security concerns. The *Bl(a)ck Tea Society* case demonstrates clearly how devastating an impact even legitimately motivated government restrictions on public access to the public forum can have on the ability of citizens to influence and oppose their government.

At the same time, unlimited public access is not plausible. The reason, simply, is that in its capacity as landowner, the government has legitimate regulatory interests that have nothing to do with interfering with private speech or associations, but that will sometimes come into conflict with such activities. Most obviously, the government cannot permit public assemblies to have unlimited access to streets, without severely compromising their primary purpose to permit transportation. Similarly, parks must be kept clean, maintained, and sometimes preserved for other uses such as soccer or Frisbee. And certain types of government property, such as office buildings, are probably entirely inappropriate places for speech or assembly, if they are to serve their primary function. So some State control over speech on private property is inevitable. On the other hand, such control is of course susceptible to abuse. As a result, when the government regulates its property, the courts must and do often permit such regulation, but must also carefully scrutinize such actions for abuse. Most obviously, when it is clear that the government does not have substantial proprietary interests at issue, such as, for example, when it singles out particular private viewpoints or perspectives for suppression on its property, the courts cannot permit it. But when regulation appears to be motivated by legitimate proprietary interests, courts are generally deferential to the government since such regulations do not intrude directly on the structural purposes of the First Amendment, and in any event courts have little institutional capacity to judge whether the government "needs" to manage its property as it claims it does (or worse yet, to somehow "balance" the government's needs versus private "rights," as an autonomy-based approach would seem to require). Applying this approach, the Supreme Court has upheld a vast array of regulations, including requiring permits before assembling on streets or in parks,[75] forbidding speech and assembly on military bases and

---

75. *See* Cox v. New Hampshire, 312 U.S. 569 (1941); Thomas v. Chicago Park District, 534 U.S. 316 (2002).

outside post offices,[76] and as noted in Chapter 4, preventing demonstrators from sleeping in Lafayette Park in Washington, D.C. The Court's deference to government in public forum cases is thus very real. It is not, however, and cannot be without limit, because of the potentially devastating impact of a flood of purportedly legitimate regulations on the ability of private citizens to speak and assemble. In particular, it would appear that where the Court's deference ends, and government regulation is struck down, is where the practical impact of the regulation is to eliminate the ability of the speakers to effectively gather and communicate their message. Famous examples of this principle include a congressional statute forbidding essentially all demonstrations on the public sidewalk surrounding the Supreme Court building itself,[77] and (as discussed earlier) an ordinance forbidding all leafleting on public streets, both of which the Court invalidated.[78] The *Bl(a)ck Tea Society* case should also probably have been analyzed in this way, though in fact it was not. A more difficult case is the Court's 1949 decision in *Kovacs v. Cooper*,[79] in which the Court upheld a city ordinance banning the use of sound trucks on streets. There is no doubt that the city's regulatory interests in *Kovacs*—to prevent traffic accidents caused by distracted drivers and to protect the ears of pedestrians—were perfectly legitimate. On the other hand, as Justice Hugo Black, one of the great civil libertarians in the history of the Supreme Court, pointed out in dissent, the practical impact of this law was to favor methods of communication available to the wealthy and powerful (who not coincidentally are likely to be most closely associated with the government itself), while substantially limiting the power of the less powerful to organize and communicate their views. All of which suggests that it will not always be easy to decide if a particular regulation does effectively eliminate speech. Still, applied carefully and properly, this approach represents what is probably the most reasonable, albeit imperfect, compromise possible between important, conflicting principles.

In addition to the practical impact of regulation on the private sphere, the other important factor influencing the Court's law regarding the public forum is the nature of the governmental property being regulated. Reliance on this factor is of course inevitable—after all, surely the public's right of access to streets and parks cannot be the same as to office buildings, much less to say the Pentagon—but in fact the Court's jurisprudence in this area has not been as thoughtful, or cognizant of structural considerations, as other aspects of its public forum doctrine. Generally, the Court divides governmental property into two categories: public forums, to which the public enjoys broad rights of access subject to

76. Greer v. Spock, 424 U.S. 828 (1976); United States v. Kokinda, 497 U.S. 720 (1990).
77. United States v. Grace, 461 U.S. 171 (1983).
78. Schneider v. State, 308 U.S. 147 (1939).
79. 336 U.S. 77 (1949).

reasonable regulation; and nonpublic forums, to which the government may freely restrict access to advance its reasonable, proprietary interests so long as it does not discriminate against particular views. This seems reasonable, given the concerns noted above. The problem is how the public forum category is defined. The question of what kinds of governmental property should be categorized as public forums came to a head in a 1992 case in which the issue was whether the public areas of New York City's three airports—i.e., the areas outside of security zones, open to the general public—should be treated as public forums.[80] A majority of the Supreme Court held that airports were not pubic forums, by defining public forums extremely narrowly to include only streets, parks, and property on which the government itself decides to permit speech. A dissenting opinion by Justice Anthony M. Kennedy would have adopted a broader definition, including all property on which speech and assembly are consistent with other uses of the property, but that view has not won the day. Of course, streets and parks remain available for speech and assembly and are utilized for those purposes every day; but given our increasingly mobile, isolated, and suburban society, the practical value of those forums has declined precipitously, and under the modern Court's rules no new forums will become available except through the voluntary generosity of the government. Such generosity, however, is unlikely to be common, and in any event making private citizens' ability to gather, speak, and organize subject to the whims of public officials compromises the central, structural purpose of the First Amendment, which is to ensure a continuing balance of power between the State and its citizens. Thus the value of the public forum in modern society has substantially diminished. It is to be hoped that a future Supreme Court will correct this major flaw in modern First Amendment law.

REGULATING PRIVATE SPEECH

If difficult questions are raised when the government regulates speech while acting in a proprietary capacity, it would seem as if the easiest free speech case would be when the government regulates purely private speech, with no proprietary interests as employer, landowner, or otherwise. After all, what *legitimate* interest does the State have in suppressing the speech of citizens? As it turns out, however, the issue is not that simple. As noted earlier, it is certainly true that when the government is regulating for illegitimate reasons—i.e., with the intent of twisting public debate, or of discouraging citizens from expressing or organizing around ideas of which it disapproves—the Constitution is clearly violated. Furthermore, as also discussed earlier, anytime the government chooses to single out speech for regulation (as opposed to regulating conduct, with a merely

---

80. *See* International Society of Krishna Consciousness v. Lee, 505 U.S. 672 (1992).

incidental effect on speech), there are reasons to be suspicious that the purpose or practical effect of the regulation is to suppress public debate, thereby empowering the government against its citizens. Nonetheless, the reality is that even when regulating purely private speech, the government does sometimes have legitimate regulatory interests unrelated to the purposes of the First Amendment. Such interests might include concerns about noise—it is not just sound trucks on the streets, after all, that can distract and offend—concerns about congestion, or aesthetic concerns (would you want your neighbors to put up a ten-foot-high political billboard on their front lawn?). In general, courts have been fairly receptive to such concerns, upholding for example a city ordinance banning movie theaters from showing movies between 1 and 6 a.m. because of the resulting congestion and noise,[81] and no one seriously doubts that a homeowner who tried to hold a loud, political rally in her backyard in the middle of the night could be prosecuted for disturbing the peace. Thus some regulation of even purely private speech is surely permissible.

At the same time, great caution is necessary here. Especially given the severe limitations of the modern public forum doctrine, a sphere of private speech must be protected if the free speech clause is to have any meaning. The problem is that even when the government is acting for legitimate (or purportedly legitimate) reasons, government officials can be expected to consistently undervalue the social importance of citizens' speech, because such speech represents ideas, and ultimately power centers, which they do not control. As such, the Constitution must be read to limit the discretion of public officials to suppress such speech if the purposes of the First Amendment are to be met. In *City of LaDue v. Gilleo*,[82] the case discussed in Chapter 4 in which the Supreme Court struck down a flat ban on signs located outside of homes, the Court appeared to recognize this point, holding that the city's admittedly legitimate aesthetic concerns could not justify such a broad intrusion on private speech. Unfortunately, not all courts are as sensitive to these concerns. For example, in one case, the U.S. Court of Appeals for the Third Circuit suggested (though it did not ultimately resolve the issue) that a Delaware statute banning all signs on property adjacent to highways, including signs on private property, for aesthetic reasons might well pass constitutional muster, even as applied to political signs supporting a (nonincumbent) candidate for Congress.[83] The impact of such a law is, of course, strongly to favor incumbent or well-financed candidates and causes, since they already have name-recognition and access to the mass media, while making it very difficult for insurgents to communicate or organize, a highly problematic result given the First Amendment's purposes. The court, however, seemed oblivious to these structural concerns.

81. National Amusements v. City of Dedham, 43 F.3d 731 (1st Cir. 1995).
82. 512 U.S. 43 (1994).
83. Rappa v. New Castle County, 18 F.3d 1043 (3rd Cir. 1994).

How exactly to resolve such cases, in which constitutional principles come into conflict with legitimate regulatory interests of the government, is an extremely difficult question. It seems clear, however, that when the government singles private speech out for regulation, courts must at a minimum be highly suspicious and cannot afford the government the sort of deference that they receive in public forum cases. First, courts must be extremely vigilant to smoke out illegitimate governmental motives, by taking a close look at the context and actual impact of the law. Second, courts must insist that the governmental interests are substantial, not trivial, and cannot be advanced through narrower regulations (the *City of LaDue* case is a good example of such a principle in action). Finally, courts must assure themselves that the practical impact of the law will not be to silence *these* speakers or prevent *this* group from organizing and recruiting. In the words of the Supreme Court, it must be clear that these specific speakers have access to "ample alternative channels of communication."[84] Only if all of these requirements are met should a court uphold direct regulation of private speech, because only then can we have assurance that the free speech and assembly clauses of the First Amendment will not be eviscerated through a thousand cuts.

REGULATING THE POLITICAL PROCESS

I will close this chapter by briefly considering one of the most complicated, divisive, and prominent controversies in modern constitutional law—the limitations imposed by the First Amendment on regulation of the political process, including especially campaign finance reform. While it is impossible to consider fully here the multitude of issues and decisions by the Supreme Court in this area, viewing these issues from a structural perspective provides some important insights. In particular, regardless of details, it should generally be clear that viewing the First Amendment through a structural perspective, there are reasons to be *highly* suspicious of any efforts by public officials to closely regulate the electoral process, other than simply organizing elections. The reason for this is that while, as noted earlier, there are many ways in which associations of private citizens can participate in democracy, including the formation of opinion, lobbying, protest, and so forth, there can be no doubt that the *primary* and most direct way in which citizens control the State is by participating in elections, both by voting and (perhaps more significantly) by trying to influence how other citizens vote on particular candidates and issues. Therefore, if the First Amendment is to fulfill its democratic role, that process of citizen participation in electoral politics must be as free of governmental influence or restraint as possible, since it is

---

84. *City of LaDue*, 512 U.S. at 56.

utterly predictable that when public officials do seek to regulate the political process, they will do so in ways that tend to favor themselves, at the expense of the public.

Turning to specific issues now, I will first briefly discuss the power of government to regulate political parties, and then discuss more generally the problem of campaign finance. Political parties are complicated beasts. On the one hand, as (at least nominally) private associations of citizens involved in the political process through speech and organization, political parties seem to be quintessentially the sort of voluntary organizations of citizens that the First Amendment is designed to protect. On the other hand, political parties are generally dominated and run by elected officials, and are deeply entwined in government, especially the legislative process, making them quasipublic entities. Over the years, the Supreme Court has struggled to choose between these two views, but in recent years the former view, under which regulation of parties should be viewed highly suspiciously, seems to be prevailing. Thus the Court has recently struck down laws that prohibit political parties from permitting independent voters to vote in their primary elections,[85] that *require* political parties to permit independents to vote in their primaries,[86] and that forbid political parties from endorsing or supporting candidates during primary elections.[87] The commonality between these seemingly disparate holdings is the belief that political parties must be able to organize themselves and to choose their candidates independently of the State, and of interference from the State, if they are to act as independent sources of influence able to oppose the government. It may seem odd to think of political parties as opposing the government, but of course that is exactly what opposition parties do. Furthermore, when one recognizes that political parties include not only the two major parties, but also the Green, Reform, Libertarian, and myriad other minor parties, the possibility of parties playing this role becomes more clear. It is not a question of the "rights" of parties or even of party members—after all, it can be argued that by choosing to participate in state-funded primary elections, parties give away any such "rights." It is because structurally political parties play a vital role in ensuring against a governmental monopoly on political power that their independence from government must be preserved.

Campaign finance reform poses much more difficult questions than regulation of political parties. The reason is not so much that the structural concerns posed by regulation of campaign finance are less serious, because they are not; it is rather that the government's interest in trying to control political corruption and the influence of money over politics, seems so obviously significant and legitimate.

---

85. Tashjian v. Republican Party, 479 U.S. 208 (1987).
86. California Democratic Party v. Jones, 530 U.S. 567 (2000).
87. Eu v. San Francisco Country Democratic Central Committee, 489 U.S. 214 (1989).

Congress has made two significant efforts to regulate the financing of federal elections, the first being the 1974 amendments to the Federal Election Campaign Act of 1971, and the second being the Bipartisan Campaign Reform Act of 2002, better known as the McCain-Feingold Act. While both laws are highly complex, their most important provisions can be summarized briefly. The 1974 amendments placed limitations on the size of contributions that candidates for federal office could accept and also attempted to place limits on the amount of money that both candidates and others could spend out of their own pockets to advocate for or against a federal candidate. McCain-Feingold sought to close certain loopholes, known as "soft money" loopholes, that had developed in implementing the previous law, by prohibiting national and state political parties from soliciting or expending money to support candidates for federal office through devices such as "issue ads," voter-registration campaigns, and get-out-the-vote drives, uses of money that had not been regulated by the earlier law. McCain-Feingold also prohibited corporations (including nonprofit corporations) and unions from paying for television ads identifying specific federal candidates, within sixty days of a general election and thirty days of a primary. The combined effect of the two laws was to seek to regulate almost every aspect of campaign financing.

The Supreme Court's reaction to these laws has been complex and not altogether consistent. In it first significant decision in this area, the 1976 *Buckley v. Valeo* case,[88] the Court drew a sharp distinction between regulation of contributions to candidates, which it generally upheld, and regulations of independent expenditures, which it struck down, concluding that expenditure limits imposed substantially greater burdens on free speech rights than contribution limits. This distinction, to which the Court still adheres, has formed the basis of all subsequent law in this area. In 2003, in a closely divided 5 to 4 decision, the Supreme Court upheld essentially all of the major provisions of McCain-Feingold, including notably its restrictions on the use of "soft money" by political parties and its ban on election commercials by corporations and unions.[89] In combination, these two decisions establish a regime in which legislatures possess great discretion to regulate campaign contributions to candidates and to political parties, and to regulate expenditures by corporations and unions, but may not generally limit the campaign expenditures of individuals, either candidates or otherwise. More recently, however, the Court has held that the First Amendment imposes greater limits in this area than previously thought. For example, in a 2006 decision the Court invalidated both expenditure *and* contribution limits imposed by a Vermont law on candidates for state office, finding them too stringent.[90] And in the following year, the Court held

---

88. 424 U.S. 1 (1976).
89. McConnell v. Federal Election Commission, 540 U.S. 93 (2003).
90. Randall v. Sorrell, 548 U.S. 230 (2006).

that the provision of McCain-Feingold prohibiting corporations from paying for television advertisements at election time could not constitutionally be applied to a nonprofit corporation, at least when the ads do not expressly advocate for or against a candidate.[91] Finally, in 2010 in *Citizens United v. Federal Election Commission*, the Supreme Court completely invalidated the ban on independent corporate and union expenditures on campaign advertising. Recent opinions in this area have been highly divided however, revealing grave disagreements among the Justices. In particular, a number of Justices including notably Antonin Scalia, Anthony M. Kennedy, and Clarence Thomas, have argued that the Court's distinction between expenditures and contributions is fundamentally misguided, and that *all* direct campaign finance restrictions should be presumptively unconstitutional. On the other hand, another set of Justices have argued that the Court should permit greater limitations on expenditures, with Justice John Paul Stevens going so far as to argue that the Court's entire premise that expenditure limits (and so a fortiori contribution limits) pose First Amendment problems is incorrect, because "it is quite wrong to equate money and speech."[92] It is fair to say, then, that constitutional law in this area has for years been characterized by instability and confusion.

What contributions can a structural perspective make to these debates? To get at this question, it might be useful to start by considering how a personal autonomy approach to free speech rights plays out in this area. From an autonomy perspective, the modern Court's distinction between expenditures and contributions seems sensible. After all, it does seem a stretch to suggest that limiting how much money individuals can give to candidates seriously impinges on their "freedom" to speak. On the other hand, prohibiting individuals from paying for advertisements out of their own pocket does substantially limit their speech. The more stringent (and now invalidated) restrictions on corporations and unions also seem sensible, because these entities are after all artificial and so possess no true autonomy, while individuals involved with corporations and unions remain free to engage in and pay for speech in their individual capacities.

A structural perspective suggests that there are problems with the Court's campaign finance jurisprudence. The fundamental problem is that the effect of the Court's decisions is to prevent citizens from banding together with candidates to influence elections. Instead, they are forced to act individually, through independent expenditures. As Justice Scalia pointed out while dissenting in the 2003 case upholding McCain-Feingold, "freedom to associate with others for the dissemination of ideas—not just by singing or speaking in unison, but by pooling financial resources for

---

91. Federal Election Commission v. Wisconsin Right to Life, 127 S. Ct. 2652 (2007).
92. Randall v. Sorrell, 548 U.S. at 276 (Stevens, J., dissenting).

expressive purposes, is part of the freedom of speech."[93] Indeed, from a structural perspective, protecting citizens' ability to associate with others to disseminate ideas and otherwise influence the government is *the* primary purpose of the First Amendment, not just a minor part of the freedom of speech. Moreover, it should be clear that if the right of association excluded the right to spend money jointly, the right would largely be eviscerated since in the modern era speech without money—i.e., without access to the media—is almost inaudible. All of this strongly suggests that the First Amendment *must* be read to prohibit legislatures from substantially interfering with the ability of citizens to join together, both with candidates and independently, to organize, speak, and expend money as they see fit. This further suggests that substantial restrictions on *either* contributions or expenditures should be deemed unconstitutional (I put aside the extremely troubling question of whether mere disclosure requirements, that would force individuals to reveal their identity when they make contributions or expenditures, are more justifiable). And finally, for all of the reasons discussed in Chapter 1 in discussing corporate rights, expenditures restrictions on corporations and unions are equally suspect since these entities, no less than Political Action Committees, are combinations of citizens existing independently of the State, and the government has no legitimate interest in regulating the forms of associations its citizens use to participate in politics—a point the Court finally recognized in *Citizens United*. The only plausible counterargument is that the government may restrict the rights of corporations and unions as the price of the legal benefits it provides them—notably, limited liability. From a structural perspective, however, this argument seems extremely dangerous, since it would grant the government seemingly unlimited power to strip citizens and organizations of citizens of their ability to participate in politics as the price of receiving unrelated benefits—after all, who in this modern society does not receive significant governmental benefits.

One final point is necessary here. The above conclusion, that campaign finance regulation should be held to generally violate the First Amendment, will strike some as troubling and perhaps naïve. After all, don't we all know that money has deeply undermined American democracy? And given that, isn't it ridiculous to read the Constitution, and in particular a provision such as the First Amendment designed to support self-governance, to forbid regulation of money in politics? In fact, however, it is this line of reasoning that is naïve. The difficulty, as Justice Scalia pointed out in his 2003 dissent, is that the practical effect of modern campaign finance regulation, including especially McCain-Feingold, is to silence precisely those independent, nongovernmental entities—unions, corporations, and nonprofits—who are most likely to criticize incumbent public officials. Moreover, the practical impact of expenditure and contribution limits is to make it ever more difficult to challenge incumbent office holders. Of course,

---

93. McConnell v. Federal Election Commission, 540 U.S. at 255 (Scalia, J., dissenting).

as Justice Scalia says, the legislation is theoretically "evenhanded," in that it limits both incumbents and challengers. But in practice, given incumbents' name recognition, power to deliver pork, and ability to influence the media, it is entirely predictable that such regulation will systematically burden those who wish to challenge those in control of the government.[94] It is truly a strange result to read our First Amendment to condone such a result.

---

94. *Id.* at 248–249.

6. THE RELIGION CLAUSES
Reconciling Accommodation and Separation

In addition to the speech, press, assembly, and petition clauses discussed in the previous chapter, the First Amendment to the U.S. Constitution contains two provisions dealing with the subject of religion: the Establishment Clause and the Free Exercise Clause. They read as follows: "Congress shall make no law respecting an establishment of religion, or prohibiting the free exercise thereof." Clearly, the religion clauses are intended to severely restrain Congress's power to legislate in the area of religion; but are the restrictions on Congress in this area absolute, or limited? More specifically, what restrictions are placed on Congress? When is it that a law can be said to touch on religion—is it only when the law mentions religion, or are there other laws that might fall within the limitations imposed by the religion clauses? And how are the sometimes seemingly contradictory commands of the Establishment and Free Exercise clauses to be reconciled? Finally, and most importantly, how does a structural approach to constitutional interpretation contribute to our understanding of these issues? These are the questions we explore in this chapter.

In thinking about the religion clauses, there is value in first considering the relationship between those clauses and the other provisions of the First Amendment. We noted in the previous chapter that from the framers' perspective, the protections accorded to speech, press, assembly, and petition in the First Amendment are not distinct, unrelated ideas but rather closely interrelated concepts, designed to work together to protect our democratic system of government. That the framers chose to place the religion clauses in the First Amendment as well suggests that they too probably serve functions related to those served by the rest of the First Amendment. Moreover, given the obvious textual parallels between the Free Exercise of Religion and Free Speech clauses, presumably their meaning and application must be linked as well. On the other hand, there are also very substantial differences between the Constitution's treatment of, and the practical nature of, speech and religion. Most obviously, the Establishment Clause places limits on Congress in the area of religion for which there is no parallel in the areas of speech, press, assembly, or petition. In addition, the nature of religion, its pervasiveness in society (both the framers' and ours), and the specific history of religious strife to which the framers were heirs (just as we are today, though perhaps in a more attenuated way) suggests important, practical differences exist in the ways in which government can and should relate to religion as opposed to speech. We will spend some time in this chapter exploring both those similarities, and those differences.

To begin with, there are obvious and fundamental similarities in the basic, structural functions of the constitutional provisions dealing with religion, speech, press, assembly, and petition. Unsurprisingly, those similarities flow from the basic principle that the various provisions of the Bill of Rights are designed to restrain governmental power and maintain an appropriate balance of power between the State and the sovereign People. As we discussed earlier, the First Amendment's free speech and press, assembly, and petition clauses advance these goals by ensuring that within private, civil society sufficient space exists, free of governmental intervention and coercion, within which citizens can speak, organize, and gather together to form and exchange views, exert influence over their government, and ultimately, if necessary, resist an unjust government. In the previous chapter we discussed the role of secular, social, and political organizations in providing vehicles for such activities. But, of course, in both the framers' society and ours, there are few nongovernmental entities better organized, more powerful, and better placed to provide a space for discussion, organization, and value formation than churches and other religious organizations. Indeed, a religious organization is in many ways the epitome of a group of citizens gathered together, free of the State, to share and develop views regarding questions of morality and justice, questions that are at the heart of democratic politics. The close links that exist between religious beliefs, religious organizations, and political activism are, after all, hardly unique to our era. Political messages, and the duty of resistance to unjust government, have been preached from the pulpit throughout our history, beginning with the religious wars of Europe, which contributed to the founding of the original American colonies, through the American Revolution, the Abolitionist movement and the Civil War, up to the Civil Rights movement and the growth of the modern religious right. Churches and other religious groups are, and always have been, deeply involved in political activism in our system of government, and the role they have played has been central to the evolution of our democracy. This is not to say, of course, that political activity is the most important role of religious groups; but it is to recognize that our political history would be unrecognizable without the role that religious groups have played as havens within which citizens could develop ideas, organize, and influence or resist the State.

One immediate conclusion that follows is that if religious groups are to play the role outlined above, they *must* remain free of governmental control, coercion, or undue influence. If the central meaning of the Free Speech and Assembly clauses of the First Amendment is that citizens must be free to speak, and organize, through private civic groups free from the State, the central meaning of the religion clauses is that they must be free to do the same through private religious groups. In this sense, the Free Exercise Clause imposes limits on government in the religious sphere that are precisely parallel to those imposed by the Free Speech and Assembly clauses: citizens must remain free to join churches or other religious groups (or refuse to do so) to form beliefs and values, and to worship, free of state interference. Under this reading of the Free Exercise Clause it is equally impermissible for the government to force an individual to join a religion, or to worship, against his wishes, as it is for the government to forbid particular forms of worship or to ban particular religious groups. Again, the parallels to speech and assembly are obvious. It is no surprise, then, that the famous 1943 flag salute case, *West Virginia Board of Education v. Barnette*,[1] might just as easily have been decided as a free exercise of religion case as a free speech case (since the reason why the Jehovah's Witness children in that case refused to salute the flag was their *religious* beliefs, not their political ones). *Barnette* demonstrates that there are in fact no clear lines between religious, moral, and political beliefs, and for that reason the framers did not even try to draw such distinctions.

In other ways, however, the framers did draw important distinctions between religion and speech, most notably in the Establishment Clause. As discussed in Chapter 5, in the area of speech the framers placed no limitations on the government itself becoming involved in political debate and trying to influence the views of citizens. The only limitation is that the government is not permitted to coerce citizens, or to deny them the right to organize and participate in such debate. The existence of the Establishment Clause, though, suggests that in the religious arena, the framers' views were different, that here the government is *not* allowed even to participate. There is much truth to this reading—though as it turns out, the truth is rather more complicated.

The difficulty lies in the history of the Establishment Clause. As Professor Akhil Amar and others have noted, it is quite clear that the precise language of the Establishment Clause—that "Congress shall make no law *respecting* an establishment of religion"—had two purposes: first, to ensure that no national religion is established; but second, to ensure that Congress did not interfere with existing *State* religious establishments.[2] The simple truth is that in 1791, when the First Amendment was ratified, several of the existing states, including most of the states of New England, did permit or have religious establishments, including in some cases direct government support for particular religions, and the Establishment Clause was designed not to eliminate those establishments, but rather to protect them from the national government. As noted in Chapter 3, such a reading posed no difficulties during the era from the framing to the Civil War, because during this period the Bill of Rights did not limit the power of state governments, only the national government. Since the adoption of the Fourteenth Amendment in 1868, however, almost all of the various provisions of the Bill of Rights have been "incorporated" against the states. With respect to the Free Exercise Clause, as with the Free Speech Clause, this seems unproblematic. But what does it mean to "incorporate"—i.e., to apply against state governments—in

---

1. 319 U.S. 624 (1943).
2. AMAR, THE BILL OF RIGHTS 32–42 (Yale 1998).

a way that bans state establishments of religion, a provision originally designed to *protect* state establishments? This point has been made by no less a figure than Justice Clarence Thomas, writing separately in a case involving an Establishment Clause challenge to the recital of the pledge of allegiance in public schools (a majority of the Court dismissed the case for technical reasons).[3] Nonetheless, as a matter of practice and precedent, the incorporation of the Establishment Clause is now firmly rooted in constitutional law. The principle was announced as early as 1947,[4] and was vigorously reaffirmed by a majority of the Supreme Court in 1963 in one of the earliest and most important of the school prayer cases.[5] Writing separately in that same case, Justice William Brennan (surely one of the most influential Justices of the twentieth century) explicitly rejected the arguments against incorporation set forth above.[6] At this point in our history, then, it is fair to say that whatever the historical questions, the prohibitions of the Establishment Clause have been, and will continue to be, applied against both the national government and state governments.

Moreover, this result (while not inevitable) is probably correct. As noted in previous chapters, the Fourteenth Amendment fundamentally altered the role of the states in our system of government. Prior to the Civil War, the assumption built into the *federal* Constitution was that the national government, not the state governments, posed the greatest risk to the People. The Fourteenth Amendment abandons, and indeed to a great degree reverses that presumption, in particular recognizing the danger that a state government will draw lines among its citizens and oppress minority groups. The primary concern in this regard was, of course, the drawing of racial lines, but surely religious favoritism poses similar threats to the polity. This insight suggests that the Establishment Clause prohibition on religious favoritism is properly extended to the states.

With these preliminary matters out of the way, we turn to specific questions that are raised in applying the Free Exercise and Establishment clauses to modern circumstances. Because of its close relationship to the topic of the previous chapter, we begin with the Free Exercise Clause.

FREE EXERCISE AND THE QUESTION OF MANDATORY ACCOMMODATION

We noted in Chapter 5 that the central purpose of the Free Speech Clause of the First Amendment was to prohibit the government (originally the national government and, since, incorporation state governments as well) from suppressing or otherwise punishing speech because of hostility to the ideas being expressed.

---

3. Elk Grove Unified School Dist. v. Newdow, 542 U.S. 1, 49–51 (2004).
4. Everson v. Board of Education, 330 U.S. 1 (1947).
5. Abington School District v. Schempp, 374 U.S. 203 (1963).
6. *Id.* at 256–258 (Brennan, J., concurring).

When we turn to the Free Exercise Clause, it is reasonable to conclude that a parallel, structural principle emerges: government may not suppress any form of religious exercise, any form of worship, because of hostility to that faith. Moreover, as with free speech, it seems clear that any time the government *singles out* religious worship for unfavorable treatment, either explicitly or intentionally, a strong presumption arises that the government is acting with improper motives—i.e., out of hostility to religion—and so is transgressing constitutional limits. Indeed, the presumption against governmental actions singling out worship should probably be irrebuttable, since it is hard to imagine any valid reason for such action. The reasons for this rule are also straightforward. If religious faith, and religious institutions, are to play the structural, democratic role outlined above, acting as sources of community, organization, and values independent of the State, it is to be expected that at times conflict will arise between religious groups and the State (consider the relationship between Black churches and Southern state governments during the Civil Rights era). Given the coercive power of the State, such conflict will inevitably lead to attempts at harassment and suppression by self-interested public officials, seeking to protect the status quo that favors them, unless strong constitutional restraints exist to prevent such behavior. The Free Exercise Clause, of course, provides precisely such a restraint, just as the rest of the First Amendment restrains the State's power to suppress the media and other secular citizens' groups. Given the lack of any legitimate need to single out religion, therefore, the Free Exercise Clause condemns *any* governmental action ("Congress shall make *no* law") that punishes religious exercise. Note that this unambiguous rule emerges clearly from a structural reading of the Free Exercise Clause, while an autonomy-based approach yields no such clear principle, since the singling out of religious exercise does not necessarily impinge more on individual autonomy than would neutral laws that incidentally burden religious exercise (a topic we will pick up shortly).

While the central principle of the Free Exercise Clause is fairly easily stated, the truth is that unlike in the free speech context, it provides little help in resolving most modern religious freedom controversies. The reason is, simply, that in the modern world it is extremely rare—though not unknown—for government explicitly or intentionally to single out a religious worship for unfavorable treatment. The Supreme Court confronted one such example in its 1993 decision in *Church of the Lukumi Babalu Aye v. City of Hialeh.*[7] The Santeria religion is a faith, with roots in Cuba, which practices animal sacrifice as part of its rituals (the sacrificed animals are then generally cooked and eaten). In 1987, adherents of Santeria leased land in the City of Hialeh, Florida, with the stated intention of establishing a church. In response, the city government obtained an opinion from the Florida Attorney General that Santeria sacrifice would violate state

---

7. 508 U.S. 520 (1993).

animal cruelty laws, which forbade "unnecessary" killing of animals, and later adopted two ordinances prohibiting the killing of animals as part of a "sacrifice" or "ritual," with various exemptions for killing animals primarily for food. Notice that on its face, the state animal cruelty statute does not single out religious exercise, and even the Hialeh ordinances *could* be interpreted as neutral, since not all "sacrifices" and "rituals" are necessarily religious. Nonetheless, given the context of the case, the Supreme Court easily (and unanimously!) concluded that all of these laws were intended to, and did, single out religious practice. With respect to the state statute, the reason was that by treating religious sacrifice as an "unnecessary" killing, but almost all other killings (e.g., for food, hunting, euthanasia, etc.) as necessary, the Attorney General's interpretation effectively singled out religious worship. The city ordinances posed an even easier case, since the practical effect of the ordinances was to ban *only* Santeria sacrifice (indeed, the ordinances had been gerrymandered to permit kosher slaughter), and the context demonstrated that the laws were intended to have precisely this effect. Ultimately, therefore, the Supreme Court concluded that all of the challenged laws violated the Free Exercise Clause.

The notable thing about the Santeria case was not the result, which was surely correct (though shockingly, the Santeria plaintiffs had lost their case in both of the lower federal courts), but the rarity of the kind of governmental action condemned there—a point that Justice Anthony Kennedy, the author of the case, explicitly made in his opinion for the Court.[8] In the modern world, governments generally know better than to persecute religion explicitly. The far more common sort of Free Exercise controversy arises when a law that is *not* targeted at religion, either by its terms or its underlying intent, nonetheless has the *effect* of burdening religious exercise. The problem arises because much religious exercise constitutes not just words (such as prayer), but also often *conduct*. In addition to Santeria animal sacrifice, consider Catholic Communion, which includes the consumption of alcohol (obviously a heavily regulated activity); the consumption of alcohol during the Jewish Passover Seder; Islamic fasting during the month of Ramadan; the lighting of candles during the Hindu festival of Diwali; and the consumption of controlled substances in rituals of the Native American Church (on which more later). Each of these rituals includes conduct that could easily violate religiously neutral laws, adopted for secular reasons with no intention to suppress religion, especially if minors (or those under the age of twenty-one) participate in the ritual. In these situations, would enforcement of the neutral laws raise nontrivial free exercise concerns? Remember that in the free speech context, the speech/conduct distinction has played a critical role in modern constitutional law, and when neutral laws are applied to expressive conduct, while in theory courts engage in some level of scrutiny, in practice the laws are

---

8. *Id.* at 523.

usually upheld. In the free speech context such a result is acceptable because most speech is *not* in practice subject to conduct regulations, and so the rule does not threaten to undermine the purposes of the First Amendment. In the religious context, however, *most* religious exercise includes some aspect of conduct, and so the application of even neutral laws can have a potentially devastating effects on religious worship. Moreover, it is predictable that especially with respect to small or controversial faiths, legislatures will often fail to provide explicit exemptions for religious rituals (we will discuss later whether such an exemption, if provided, would be constitutional). As a practical matter, even absent an exemption large and powerful religions are probably safe—after all, have you ever heard of a Catholic priest being prosecuted for providing alcohol to a minor? But as the Santeria case demonstrates, small religions are not. The question then arises, does the Free Exercise Clause impose an *obligation* on governments to exempt religious rituals from neutral regulations of conduct, absent some strong reason not to (the caveat is necessary—after all, presumably even if such an obligation existed, states would not have to exempt human sacrifice from their murder laws)?

The answer that the modern Supreme Court has given to this question is a simple one—there is no such obligation. This rule was announced in 1990, in the Court's very controversial decision in *Employment Division, Department of Human Resources v. Smith.*[9] Alfred Smith and Galen Black were members of the Native American Church, one of whose rituals involves the ingestion of peyote, a controlled substance whose use or possession is illegal under Oregon law. After Smith and Black were fired from their jobs as drug rehabilitation counselors because of their use of peyote, they applied for state unemployment benefits, but were refused because the state decided that they had been fired for "misconduct." They sued, claiming that application of the Oregon drug laws to their use of peyote as part of a religious ritual violated the Free Exercise Clause. The Oregon Supreme Court accepted their claim, but the U.S. Supreme Court, in an opinion by Justice Antonin Scalia, reversed. In a wide-ranging opinion, Justice Scalia interpreted (or more honestly, reinterpreted) existing Supreme Court precedent to hold that the government has *no* obligation to exempt religiously inspired conduct from its generally applicable laws, no matter how devastating the impact of applying the law on a particular religion or individual's religious beliefs. Since Smith and Black could have been criminally prosecuted for their ingestion of peyote, a fortiori it was permissible to deny them unemployment benefits.

When the *Smith* decision was announced in 1990, it triggered an avalanche of bitter criticism, both in academic and political circles.[10] Indeed, so reviled was

---

9. 494 U.S. 872 (1990).

10. *See, e.g.,* James D. Gordon III, *Free Exercise on the Mountaintop,* 79 CAL. L. REV. 91 (1991); Michael W. McConnell, *Free Exercise Revisionism and the* Smith *Decision,* 57

the decision that within a few years Congress had adopted a statute, by over-whelming votes in both Houses, purporting to reverse *Smith*.[11] The Supreme Court, however, soon struck down this statute as exceeding Congress's legisla-tive authority,[12] and despite continuing criticism, as of this writing *Smith* remains the law of the land. Much of the criticism of *Smith* relies on the argument that despite the reasoning of Justice Scalia's opinion, in fact the law prior to *Smith* had been that the Free Exercise Clause *did* obligate government to permit reli-gious exemptions to any law that substantially burdened religious exercise, absent an extremely powerful reason (what in the jargon of constitutional law is called a "compelling interest") for refusing to do so. In fact, examination of the previous law strongly suggests that the critics are correct, and that Justice Scalia's opinion in *Smith*, in purporting not to change the law, was at best disingenuous. For example, in its important 1963 decision in *Sherbert v. Verner*,[13] the Supreme Court upheld a claim by a Seventh Day Adventist that she was entitled to unem-ployment benefits when she was fired for refusing to work on Saturday, which was her church's Sabbath. Similarly, in *Wisconsin v. Yoder*[14] in 1972, the Court held that the plaintiff, a member of the Old Order Amish, could not be punished for refusing to send his children to high school, because his refusal was a part of his religious faith (in particular, the desire of the Amish to live in a community apart from the world). The *Sherbert* decision in particular had been followed in a number of other cases involving unemployment benefits,[15] and when *Smith* was decided certainly most lawyers believed that the existing law required the gov-ernment to justify refusing to grant religious exemptions.

So was Justice Scalia's position in *Smith* indefensible? In truth, it was not. The difficulty, rarely acknowledged by the critics of *Smith*, was that the Supreme Court had over the years been *highly* inconsistent on the subject of required reli-gious exemptions from neutral laws. As early as 1879, the Court had upheld the application of bigamy laws to a Mormon, on the grounds that religious practices were not immune from neutral laws.[16] In more recent decisions, the Supreme Court has permitted among other things: the application of Sunday closing laws to Orthodox Jews, whose religion required them to close their stores on Saturday as well;[17] requiring a member of the Old Order Amish to pay social security taxes

---

U. Chi. L. Rev. 1109 (1990); *The Supreme Court: 1989 Term: Leading Cases: I. Constitutional Law; C. Free Exercise of Religion*, 104 Harv. L. Rev. 198 (1990).

11. The statute was the Religious Freedom Restoration Act of 1993.

12. *See* City of Boerne v. Flores, 521 U.S. 507 (1997).

13. 374 U.S. 398 (1963).

14. 406 U.S. 205 (1972).

15. *See* Thomas v. Review Board of Indiana Employment Security Div., 450 U.S. 707 (1980); Hobbie v. Unemployment Appeals Commission, 480 U.S. 136 (1987); Frazee v. Illinois Department of Employment Security, 489 U.S. 829 (1989).

16. Reynolds v. United States, 98 U.S. 145 (1879).

17. Braunfeld v. Brown, 366 U.S. 599 (1961).

for his Amish employees;[18] the disciplining by the Air Force of an Orthodox Jewish officer because he wore a yarmulke with his uniform;[19] the refusal to grant welfare benefits to a family who declined to obtain a social security number for their daughter on religious grounds;[20] and the construction by the U.S. Forest Service of roads on land considered sacred by Native American tribes and used for religious rituals.[21] In each of these cases, the Court not only refused to find a religious exemption required, it engaged in no serious scrutiny of the government's actions or the strength of their policies. Thus, the truth is that when *Smith* was decided in 1990, while at times the Supreme Court had purported to state a general rule requiring religious exemptions, the true state of the law was confusion.

Nor was this surprising. As we noted in the previous two chapters, the question of how to reconcile the government's general power to regulate conduct with the fact that such regulation sometimes has the incidental but practical effect of impinging on constitutionally protected areas is an exceedingly difficult one. An autonomy-based approach to free exercise suggests that a strong set of constitutional rules prohibiting such incidental effects is necessary, because as noted earlier, incidental burdens impinge on autonomy no less than laws that single out religious exercise. The problem however, is that such rules place the courts in the very difficult position of having to second-guess legislative judgments regarding the strength of particular public policies, and then somehow to "weigh" those public policies against constitutional rights. In the free exercise context, for example, consider three religions, one of which practices the use of peyote as part of its rituals, one of which practices animal sacrifice, and one of which practices human sacrifice. Suppose that in each case, the religion's practices violate a neutral law, adopted without any intention of harming or singling out religion. If the Constitution required the government to permit religious exemptions to such laws absent a very strong public policy, and if the legislature fails to enact such exemptions, in each case judges would be required to decide if the public policy underlying the challenged law somehow "outweighs" the constitutional interest in religious freedom. The problems here are obvious, for both practical and theoretical reasons. First of all, how is a court to assess the strength of an individual's interest in exercising his or her religion? Does it turn on the strength of the individual's religious faith? Or on the centrality of a particular practice (whether it be taking communion, or ingesting peyote) to the religion's tenets? How are courts to assess such things? As a practical matter, even if we could decide what the strength of the constitutional interest is, how are we to decide the strength of the public policy? Presumably most in our

---

18. United States v. Lee, 455 U.S. 252 (1982).
19. Goldman v. Weinberger, 475 U.S. 503 (1986).
20. Bowen v. Roy, 476 U.S. 693 (1986).
21. Lyng v. Northwest Indian Cemetery Protective Association, 485 U.S. 439 (1988).

society would agree that the policy against the taking of human life outweighs any religious interest in human sacrifice (even if the victim of the sacrifice was a competent, adult volunteer—though I suppose some may differ even on this point). But how is one to judge the strength of the public policy against unnecessary killings of animals (and how is one to define unnecessary)? Similarly, what exactly is the strength of the public policy of banning all hallucinogenic drugs, without exception? On the first question, members of PETA probably have different views from members of the NRA. On the second question, divisions are even deeper. On what basis is an unelected federal judge to make these distinctions, then? The truth is that there is no basis upon which such judgments can be made, other than policy preferences. And that in turn means that when judges do try and make such judgments, the result is generally a chaotically inconsistent body of law—which is precisely what was in place prior to the Supreme Court's decision in *Smith*. These factors clearly demonstrate the futility of an autonomy-based approach in this area.

It should be noted that the difficulties intrinsic in a balancing test are not limited to autonomy-based interpretations of the Constitution. A structural approach also fails to provide much assistance in a weighing process. All the same problems of evaluating the strength of public policy remain. Moreover, as a matter of theory, once one abandons the individual-autonomy approach to rights, it becomes unclear precisely what one is "weighing" against public policy, other than the general constitutional interest in government not interfering with religion. But how are courts to assess the strength of that interest?

All of which suggests that perhaps Justice Scalia and the Supreme Court were correct to conclude in *Smith* that there is no constitutional obligation to create religious exemptions from neutral laws. The difficulty with this solution is that it largely denudes the Free Exercise Clause of meaning, given the rarity in the modern world of laws that actually target, or are intended to target, religious exercise (as we noted earlier, the Santeria case is notable mainly for how unusual it was). Moreover, given the reality that smaller religious groups, as a practical matter, are far less likely to obtain legislative exemptions from neutral statutes, and are far more likely to face prosecution/persecution in any event, Justice Scalia's approach of ending his analysis after determining that a law is formally neutral (indeed, Justice Scalia would not even inquire into the motives behind the law) leaves little of the principle of free exercise of religion. The practical import is that such an approach is very unlikely to achieve the underlying structural purpose of the religion clauses, which is to prevent the social division and strife that ensues when particular religious sects obtain control of, or favorable treatment from, the machinery of the State. Furthermore, an approach to free exercise that systematically disfavors smaller, less orthodox religions substantially undermines the constitutional objective of ensuring that public debate and value formation is engaged in by a *diversity* of private secular and religious groupings of citizens, who can remain free of state interference and persecution.

Something more is needed if the structural goals of the Free Exercise Clause are to be achieved.

How is one to reconcile these competing concerns? For all of the reasons discussed above, it seems clear that there can be no general obligation on the part of government to create religious exemptions from neutral laws. Perhaps, then, the solution lies in expanding the definition of discrimination, and concomitantly narrowing the class of laws that are considered "neutral" if they have the effect of interfering with a particular religion's rituals. One possible such expansion would be to adopt for this area a definition of discrimination proposed by Professor David Strauss of the University of Chicago Law School in the areas of race and gender discrimination. Professor Strauss argues that in defining discrimination, it is not enough to focus only on facial (i.e., explicit) and intentional discrimination. Those approaches are too narrow, since so much discrimination is unconscious or below the surface (we will explore this topic further in the area of race and gender discrimination later). Instead, he argues, the test we should use is what he calls the "Reversing the Groups" test. The question he would have a court ask is: "suppose the adverse effects of the challenged government decision fell on whites instead of blacks, or on men instead of women. Would the decision have been different? If the answer is yes, then the decision was made with discriminatory intent."[22] In the context of religious exemptions, the question we would ask is: suppose this or a similar law impeded the religious rituals of a religion practiced by a substantial fraction of the population—would the government formally, or in practice, permit an exemption? If the answer is yes, then a small religion should get the benefit of an exemption. If, on the other hand, it seems clear that the social policies underlying the law are so strong that no exemption would be granted, then there is no constitutional problem.

Applying this test will, of course, not be easy. Given the crucial educative function of religion, it is unsurprising that the values, and perception of public policy, of most of our citizens, including federal judges, are shaped by the teachings of the major religions of this country. As a result, it will often be hard to determine if an exemption would be granted, because usually a law that interferes with a major religion simply will not pass. Sometimes, however, parallel laws *do* exist, and judges will be able to make reasonable judgments about whether an exemption would be granted. In case of doubt, the rule must be that no exemption is required, but even then many otherwise difficult cases can be resolved under this approach. The most obvious example is the City of Hialeh's approach to animal sacrifice by the Santeria. The fact that Hialeh's laws (and the Florida Attorney General's interpretations) were clearly designed to protect Jewish kosher practices, while condemning Santeria practices, demonstrates

---

22. David Strauss, *Discriminatory Intent and the Taming of* Brown, 56 U. CHI. L. REV. 935, 956–957 (1989).

that under a Reversing the Groups approach, there was clear discrimination afoot (as the Supreme Court concluded). The *Smith* case, involving the use of peyote in rituals of the Native American Church, is also, I think, an easy case—though here the Court got it wrong. While there may not be an exact analogy to the Oregon law upheld in *Smith*, we do know that during the period of Prohibition in this country, there was an explicit exemption in federal law for the sacramental use of wine—an unsurprising thing given the number of Catholics and other Christians in this country who use sacramental wine in their rituals.[23] We also know that even when state law prohibits providing alcohol to those under the age of twenty-one, with no religious exemptions (as does, for example, California law),[24] it is unheard of for prosecutions to be initiated of religious or lay figures who serve alcohol to minors as part of a religious ritual. Surely, though, the public policy against alcohol use during Prohibition (which remember, was implemented by a *constitutional* amendment) and the modern public policy against providing alcohol to minors are as strong as the policy against use of peyote? If so, then the two cases are parallel, and so an exemption for the religious use of peyote should have been required. Human sacrifice, on the other hand, poses the obvious opposite situation. There seems to be no analogy, where a similar law is not enforced against major religions. As such, assuming the unlikely situation of a religion claiming the right to engage in human sacrifice, they should surely lose.

So, under an expanded definition of religious discrimination, and a more nuanced view of neutrality, some cases can be resolved with some ease. Many cases, however, remain very difficult. Consider as an example a case that arose in 1994 in the Livingston Union school district in Merced County, California. Rajinder, Sukhjinder, and Jaspreet Cheema are children (at the time, aged seven, eight, and ten) who are members of the Khalsa Sikh religion (a religion with its roots in the Punjab region of India). Among the tenets of their faith is a requirement that at all times, they wear a "kirpan" or ceremonial knife—apparently the kirpans the Cheema children sought to wear had blades approximately 3.5 inches long, about the size of a Swiss Army knife. The Livington Union School District refused to grant them permission to carry the knives to school under any circumstances, citing a state statute making it a crime to carry any knife with a blade longer than 2.5 inches to school. Unable to obtain any exemption from the school district, the Cheemas sued.[25] Ultimately, because of the way the case was

---

23. For a discussion of this topic, and an analysis of the analogy between sacramental wine and ritual peyote, *see* Douglas Laycock, *Peyote, Wine, and the First Amendment*, available at http://www.religion-online.org/showarticle.asp?title=886 (last visited 9/3/08).

24. *See* Cal. Bus. & Prof. Code, §25658.

25. Cheema v. Thompson, 67 F.3d 883 (9th Cir. 1995). The Cheemas did not sue under the Free Exercise Clause because their dispute arose after the *Smith* case, and so they had no constitutional claim for an exemption, since no one disputed that the state statute was

litigated, the U.S. Court of Appeals for the Ninth Circuit upheld the Cheemas' claim, and issued an order requiring the school district to allow the children to carry the kirpan, with suitable precautions (in particular, the knives were required to have dull blades, be sewn into their sheaths, and to be kept under the children's clothing). The Cheemas, however, had lost their claim before the trial court judge, and on the appeals court, one of the three judges dissented, arguing that the school district's interest in school safety justified its refusal to grant the Cheemas any exemption. Note then that of the four federal judges that heard the case, two sided with the Cheemas, but two sided with the school district—it is only because the Cheemas had the support of two appellate judges that they prevailed. The reason why the courts had so much difficulty deciding this case is that under the prevailing approach, the conflict posed by the Cheemas' case is almost irresolvable. No one doubted the validity and strength of the Cheemas' religious beliefs—Sikhism is an ancient religion, and the requirement of the kirpan is a well-established one. On the other hand, no one doubted the strength of the school district's interest in public safety either, and there were serious doubts raised about whether the restrictions ultimately imposed on the Cheemas would be adequate to protect that interest. The school district legitimately argued that it had strong reasons to enforce a weapons rule with *no* exceptions, to send a strong message, and there was a dispute among the appellate judges about whether the restrictions in fact eliminated the danger of the knife being exposed or wielded during school (remember, the youngest of the children was only seven years old, and so may well have lacked the maturity to realize the consequences of exposing the knife). How is a judge to balance these concerns? Apparently, by instinct (and unsurprisingly, the instincts of the judges varied widely). Justice Scalia's approach in *Smith* suggests that the Cheemas had absolutely no constitutional claim, since there was no allegation that the California statute forbidding weapons in schools was aimed at religion. But for the reasons stated above, that seems too simple a conclusion, since it ignores the plight of small religions. What does a "Reversing the Groups" approach suggest? The answer, unfortunately, is not clear. There is little doubt that some school rules would be relaxed for religious reasons—it is hard to imagine, for example, that a school district would interpret a rule against jewelry or a rule requiring uniforms to forbid the wearing of a cross. On the other hand, a cross is not a weapon, and the policy against weapons in school is surely stronger than most policies regarding clothing or jewelry. I am forced to conclude that given the lack of any truly analogous situation where a major religion was granted an exemption, the Cheemas did not make their case that enforcement of the no-weapons rule

---

"neutral," as defined by the Court in *Smith*. Instead, their claim was based on the statute discussed earlier that Congress passed—and the Supreme Court later overturned—to try and reverse *Smith*. But this point does not reduce the problem the case demonstrates.

constituted discrimination. As such, they were probably not entitled to a constitutional exemption; but under any approach, the case remains a difficult one.

A structural approach to the Bill of Rights thus provides important insights into the proper interpretation of the Free Exercise Clause. In short, it suggests that the traditional "balancing" approach to questions of required religious exemptions is unwise and unworkable, rooted as it is in an autonomy-based approach to rights. At the same time, it is important to provide some protection to religious exercise, if the State is to be constrained as it must be. Professor David Strauss's Reversing the Groups test provides one possible solution to the dilemma of determining when religious exemptions from seemingly neutral laws are required. This analysis, however, deals only with the question of required exemptions. What if, however, a legislature chooses voluntarily to accommodate religious exercise by granting a religious exemption from its laws, in a situation where the Free Exercise Clause would not require one? Does such an action raise nontrivial constitutional concerns? In answering that question, it is important to remember that the Free Exercise Clause is only one of the two great constitutional provisions dealing with religion. The other, of course, is the Establishment Clause. We now turn to the Establishment Clause, and the problem of voluntary accommodation and support of religion by the government.

THE ESTABLISHMENT CLAUSE—VOLUNTARY ACCOMMODATION AND SCHOOL PRAYER

The Establishment Clause of the First amendment states that "Congress shall make no law respecting an establishment of religion." As we noted earlier, originally this Clause had two purposes—first, to ensure that Congress did not establish a national church, but second, also to protect existing *state* religious establishments from interference by Congress. Nonetheless, as we also noted, since World War II it has become widely accepted—though it is still controversial in some circles—that the Establishment Clause is properly "incorporated" against the states, which means that in its modern guise, the Clause prevents *either* the national or state governments from creating an establishment of religion. But what does an "establishment of religion" mean? At a minimum, all agree that the government may not designate a particular religion as the national religion and fund it with taxes. Beyond that, however, there is widespread disagreement. Some Supreme Court Justices, generally conservative ones, have argued that the Establishment Clause only forbids governmental *coercion* of private citizens to engage in religious activities.[26] This is the basis upon which the

---

26. *See* County of Allegheny v. American Civil Liberties Union, 492 U.S. 573, 659–660 (1989) (Kennedy, J., dissenting).

Court has struck down essentially all officially sponsored prayer in public schools and at public school events, including graduations and football games.[27] Others have argued that aside from direct, preferential support, the key prohibition of the Establishment Clause is that government may not *endorse* any particular religion, or religion generally, and on this ground struck down some (but not all) displays of religious symbols such as a crèche or a menorah on government property.[28] Yet others have focused on whether the government is acting with a secular purpose (the lack of such a purpose implied an impermissible purpose of advancing religion)—indeed, this was the basis upon which the Supreme Court struck down a Louisiana statute requiring the teaching of "creation science" in public schools.[29] Each of these approaches, however, is controversial and has been opposed at times by some of the Justices.

Given this legal uncertainty, it is (as always) worthwhile to return to first principles in considering what the Establishment Clause means. The Supreme Court discussed the history and purposes of the Establishment Clause in great detail in the first of its school prayer cases, *Engel v. Vitale*, written in 1962 by the great Justice Hugo Black.[30] Justice Black's opinion begins by recounting the history of religious division, strife, and persecution in the centuries leading up to the framing era that clearly influenced the framers in their decision to adopt a First Amendment, beginning with the religious wars in Europe following the Reformation (including notably the English Civil War of the seventeenth century), and including divisions within the American colonies, many of which had adopted religious establishments prior to the American Revolution. From this history, Justice Black concludes that the framers

> knew, some of them from bitter personal experience, that one of the greatest dangers to the freedom of the individual to worship in his own way lay in the Government's placing its official stamp of approval upon one particular kind of prayer or one particular form of religious services. They knew the anguish, hardship and bitter strife that could come when zealous religious groups struggled with one another to obtain the Government's stamp of approval from each King, Queen, or Protector that came to temporary power.[31]

In short, the purpose of the Establishment Clause was to disable the government from adopting or supporting religion, in order to prevent competition between different religious sects over control of the State, with its great resources

---

27. *See, e.g.*, Engel v. Vitale, 370 U.S. 421, 431 (1962); Lee v. Weisman, 505 U.S. 577 (1992); Santa Fe Independent School District v. Doe, 530 U.S. 290 (2000).

28. Lynch v. Donnelly, 465 U.S. 668, 688 (1984) (O'Connor, J., concurring); County of Allegheny v. American Civil Liberties Union, 492 U.S. 573, 592 (1989).

29. Edwards v. Aguillard, 482 U.S. 578 (1987).

30. 370 U.S. 421 (1962).

31. *Id.* at 429.

and coercive apparatus. Such competition is destructive of democratic government for two different reasons. First, if one sect *does* gain control of the State, this largely undermines the role of religious groups as centers of ideas, values, and power independent of the government, because the winning sect will no longer be independent and is likely to use its new powers to suppress its competitors. Second, however, even if no particular sect wins the fight, the very process of competition and striving is highly divisive of society, and can result in deep, abiding social fissures that make it difficult to maintain a functioning, democratic society. In this key sense, religion is quite different from free speech and politics. Political debate and division are an inevitable part of any democratic society—indeed, they are the essence of the democratic process. Moreover, it is inevitable and unavoidable that the government itself will become involved in such debate, and as we noted previously, governmental speech as such poses no constitutional problems, so long as it does not involve coercion of private citizens. Religious division and competition, however, is *not* a necessary or desirable thing (other than, perhaps, through proselytizing), and insofar as such division exists, the government's involvement in it is a recipe for disaster. The Establishment Clause thus states as deeply structural a principle as any part of the Constitution, and it is with this understanding that we must proceed to consider the practical meaning of the clause.

Needless to say, even with the above in mind, determining what the Establishment Clause should mean under modern circumstances remains a daunting challenge. Some conclusions do, however, follow fairly easily. First, the idea that the Establishment Clause prevents only the official designation of a church, or coercion of religious activities, cannot be correct. Many governmental actions short of actual designation or coercion raise the risks of division and strife starkly, and if the Establishment Clause is to accomplish its goals, such actions must be restrained. Moreover, most actual, governmental coercion of religion would clearly violate the Free Exercise Clause, making the Establishment Clause largely redundant—but in fact, the Establishment Clause has distinct goals from Free Exercise. Second, however, the "endorsement" test probably goes too far in mandating a division of church and state. Not all governmental action that recognizes the value of religion, and the significance of religion in the lives of citizens, or tries to accommodate the religions needs of citizens, poses the threat of division or rivalry, but all such actions at some level "endorse" religion. Indeed, it could be said that the Free Exercise Clause itself, by singling out religious exercise for constitutional protection, endorses religion; yet it would be supremely foolish to argue that the Free Exercise Clause violates the Establishment Clause. Certainly the framers did not see these provisions as adopting opposing principles. Finally, the secular purpose test, while sometimes useful, is also problematic because it fails to specify what constitutes an illegitimate governmental purpose in this context. Any legislative decision to facilitate or accommodate the private religious choices of its citizens, including simply complying with the Free Exercise Clause, can be said to have the "purpose" of advancing religion, but that cannot be enough to invalidate them. It is not that governmental purpose is irrelevant to Establishment Clause analysis—given the structural functions of the clause, purpose is unsurprisingly highly relevant here. The key, however, is to recognize that the purpose forbidden by the Establishment Clause is not "advancing" the religions of its citizens in some abstract sense, but rather a governmental purpose of propagating religion itself or adopting religion as its own.

Given the weaknesses of any single-minded, overarching approach to the Establishment Clause (after all, if the Establishment Clause can be boiled down to one word, surely the word is "establishment"), it is useful to proceed by considering specific Establishment Clause problems and what insight is shed on them by the basic principles outlined above. Consider first the general problem of accommodation. Government, in its many functions and capacities, takes actions that accommodate and facilitate its citizens' ability to practice their religion of choice in many ways. For example, the government hires and provides chaplains to the military and in prisons, so that soldiers and prisoners may practice their faiths despite the constraints placed on them by their circumstances. The government also provides favorable tax treatment to religious institutions, for example making donations to religious groups tax deductible. Zoning laws are often designed to facilitate the construction of houses of worship, and public holidays, when government employees do not have to work, often coincide with major religious holidays, again permitting citizens to practice their religion. Finally, governments often do grant religious exemptions to otherwise neutral laws, even if the Free Exercise Clause does not require an exemption. Many states and the federal government grant an exemption from their laws banning peyote for sacramental use, even though after the *Smith* decision they obviously are not required to do so.[32] Similarly, the federal government exempts conscientious objectors from the draft. Religious institutions are often exempted from nondiscrimination statutes such as Title VII of the Civil Rights Act of 1964, which forbids employment discrimination, because enforcement of such laws could seriously interfere with the religious practices of some institutions (imagine if Title VII were applied to require the Catholic Church to hire female priests, for example).[33] All of these actions have the purpose and effect of facilitating religious practices. As such, they appear to "endorse" religion and have the purpose, in some sense, of "advancing" religion. Do they therefore violate the Establishment Clause? The answer must be, surely not. To read the Constitution in such a way would be to read it as actively hostile to religion, an absurd reading from a historic perspective. More substantively, governmental accommodations

---

32. Employment Division v. Smith, 494 U.S. 872, 906 (1990) (O'Connor, J., concurring).

33. *See* 42 U.S.C. §20003 *et seq.;* 42 U.S.C. §2000e-1(a).

of private religious choices and activities simply do not, as a general matter, create the dangers of divisiveness, or co-optation by the State, that the Establishment Clause is designed to prevent. From a structural perspective, therefore, official accommodation of private religious practice should not normally pose substantial constitutional concerns.

An important caveat is necessary here, however. Accommodation does not pose the risks outlined above *only* so long as citizens perceive the government to be acting neutrally, both between different sects and between believers and nonbelievers. If that perception of neutrality is lost, then in the eyes of citizens government will be acting to favor the exercise of one sect, while acting to suppress others—in other words to be playing favorites. And if that is the belief, then the incentive for religious groups to seize control of the State, and use the government to favor themselves, reappears. The requirement of neutrality is thus crucial; but it is not an easy one to meet. If the Native American Church is granted an exemption for peyote use, for example, does that mean that Rastafarians must receive an exemption for marijuana use? What about the sacramental use of heroin or opium? And yet failing to grant such exemptions certainly creates the impression of favoring some faiths over others (just as did the City of Hialeh's differential treatment of the Santeria and Jewish faiths). There is also the simple problem of legislative ignorance—legislators and other governmental officials are likely to know the religious requirements of faiths shared by substantial numbers of their constituents, and so to accommodate them insofar as possible, but they are not likely to be aware of the tenets of less common faiths. Does this violate the neutrality requirement? On its own, probably not—though if, once made aware of the needs of a particular faith, government officials decline accommodation under circumstances similar to those where other faiths have been accommodated, suspicions should arise that the neutrality requirement of the Establishment Clause is being violated. Finally, as a practical matter some kinds of accommodation *cannot* be offered neutrally. For example, government offices generally close on Saturdays and Sundays, and national holidays tend to be major Christian holidays such as Christmas. Similar accommodation is not provided to Muslims, whose day of rest is Friday, or to the holidays of other religions, such as Islam, Judaism, and Hinduism, with substantial numbers of adherents in the United States. The reason, of course, is that if the government shut down for all religious holidays, it could barely function. Christian practices are favored because Christianity remains by far the largest religion in the United States. Is this favoritism, or is this a legitimate governmental effort to accommodate the religious needs of as many of its citizens as possible? While people may differ in answering this question, given the practicalities of the situation the neutral explanation is probably the better one, suggesting that sometimes, even unequal accommodation can satisfy the neutrality requirement. The Establishment Clause thus provides great scope for governmental accommodation of religion. Neutrality, and the perception of neutrality, however, is critical if accommodation is not to cross the line into favoritism, which is itself a form of establishment. In this regard, Justice Scalia's admonition in the *Smith* case that in a democratic society, the decision on whether and when to accommodate religion must be left entirely to the political process seems surely incorrect.[34] Such an approach would foster precisely the religious divisiveness that the Establishment Clause was intended to end, and so would abandon an important constitutional value. Difficult as it is, therefore, courts must continue to police governmental accommodation to ensure neutrality.

Regardless of the interesting issues of constitutional principle that it raises, governmental accommodation of private religious practices has not raised serious, public controversy in this country. Our next topic, however, the permissibility of voluntary school prayers and the teaching of religiously oriented subjects such as "creation science" in public schools, have raised enormous public controversy, and indeed probably rate with the debate over abortion as the two most divisive questions of constitutional law in the modern era. Indeed, so controversial is this question that despite almost half a century of consistent pronouncements by the Supreme Court holding that voluntary school prayer violates the Establishment Clause, academic research suggests that in many parts of this country, public schools continue to sponsor prayers, thereby defying the Supreme Court,[35] a pattern of behavior that reflects the fact that despite the Supreme Court many if not most Americans continue to support voluntary school prayer. What insights does a structural approach to the school prayer controversy yield? To approach this question, and understand what this debate is about, it is first necessary to understand what the Supreme Court has said about prayer in public schools.

As noted earlier, the first great Supreme Court decision on school prayer was the 1962 decision in *Engel v. Vitale*.[36] The New York State Board of Regents, a government body with authority over public schools in the State of New York, composed a "nondenominational prayer," which it recommended be recited aloud by all students, at the beginning of each school day. The prayer read as follows: "Almighty God, we acknowledge our dependence upon Thee, and we beg Thy blessings upon us, our parents, our teachers and our Country." No student was required to recite the prayer, and the board's rules required that a student's failure to participate would not be punished or singled out. Finally, students were also permitted to leave the room during the recitation, without adverse consequences. The Supreme Court held this practice unconstitutional under the

---

34. Employment Division v. Smith, *supra*, 494 U.S. at 890.

35. Kevin T. McGuire, *Public Schools, Religious Establishments, and the U.S. Supreme Court: An Examination of Policy Compliance*, available at http://www.unc.edu/~kmcguire/papers/prayer.pdf; *see also* Michael Klarman, *Rethinking the Civil Rights and Civil Liberties Revolutions*, 82 Va. L. Rev. 1, 15 & n.69 (1996).

36. 370 U.S. 421 (1962).

Establishment Clause. The Court emphasized in particular the inappropriate-ness of having governmental officials compose an "official" prayer, as the Board of Regents did, but also noted the "indirect, coercive pressure" on students to conform to such officially sanctioned religious activities.[37] The next year, in *Abington School District v. Schempp*,[38] the Court was faced with a challenge to a Pennsylvania statute and a school district's policy stating that at the beginning of every day, students would recite ten verses from the Bible, as well as the Lord's Prayer. Again, no student was required to participate, and again, students had the option of being excused from the reading altogether. Despite the fact that this case did not involve actual governmental composition of prayers, the Court again struck down the policy. After *Engel* and *Schempp* were decided, it seemed well established that any official sponsorship of an overtly religious activity or ceremony such as prayer during the school day was forbidden by the Constitution. The next major test of the Court's school prayer jurisprudence came twenty-two years later, in 1985 when the Court decided *Wallace v. Jaffree*.[39] In *Wallace* the Court struck down an Alabama law that permitted school districts to begin the school day with a "moment of silence." The Court did not hold that such a moment of silence was necessarily unconstitutional under all circumstances, but concluded that the purpose of the Alabama statute was to reintroduce prayer into public schools, which was an illegitimate purpose (five years earlier the Court had struck down a Kentucky statute requiring the posting of the Ten Commandments in all public school classrooms, for similar reasons[40]). Most recently, the Court has considered whether the Establishment Clause bans prayers at public school events outside of the classroom and has generally con-cluded that it does. The leading case on the subject is *Lee v. Weisman*,[41] involving middle school and high school graduation ceremonies. Providence, Rhode Island, had a policy of inviting members of the clergy to deliver "nondenomina-tional" invocation and benediction prayers at its middle and high school gradua-tion ceremonies. In an opinion by Justice Anthony Kennedy, the Supreme Court held that this practice violated the Establishment Clause. Justice Kennedy's opin-ion emphasized the subtle, coercive effect on students of having to sit through an officially sponsored religious exercise and emphasized the unfairness of requiring students to skip their graduations if they did not want to be exposed to such prayers. The Court also expressed concern over the involvement of govern-ment officials (in particular, school principals) in the prayers, including the decisions on whether to invite a member of the clergy, the choice of which clergy, from which sect, to invite, and the decision over what forms of prayer are

---

37. *Id.* at 430–431.
38. 374 U.S. 203 (1963).
39. 472 U.S. 38 (1985).
40. Stone v. Graham, 449 U.S. 39 (1980).
41. 505 U.S. 577 (1992).

permissible (because they are sufficiently nondenominational). Finally, in *Santa Fe Independent School District v. Doe*,[42] the Court held that a school district could not permit students, chosen by the student body, to deliver prayers prior to high school football games.

In short, the Supreme Court has with absolute consistency, since 1962, struck down any and all officially sponsored prayers and other religious activities at public school events. Has the Supreme Court been correct to so consistently condemn even voluntary prayer in public schools? If one approaches this question from the perspective of individual autonomy, there are reasons to be doubtful. After all, the actual burden on the individual autonomy of dissenting students in the school prayer cases is relatively minor, since no student is ever required to participate in such prayers. Certainly in the context of the classroom, group prayer does have some coercive impact, especially on young children; but that must be balanced against the desire of other students, perhaps a majority, who wish to begin their school day with a prayer. Moreover, even if group prayers or Bible readings in the classroom setting are so coercive as to justify the decisions in *Engel* and *Schempp*, that still leaves doubts about the more recent cases. The idea that a "moment of silence" coerces students into praying (as opposed to say gathering their thoughts) seems doubtful; and prayer in settings like graduation ceremonies and football games also seem to have quite a minor impact on individual autonomy. Thus if justified as necessary to protect individual liberty, the Supreme Court's school prayer cases, especially the more recent ones, seem difficult to defend—which is perhaps why they remain so controversial.

The truth is, however, that while an autonomy-based approach to the Bill of Rights is always problematic, it is particularly incoherent with respect to the Establishment Clause. The key point is that the Establishment Clause, by its very terms, is a purely structural provision, which does not even purport to speak in terms of individual freedoms. The original structural purpose was federalism-based: to keep the *national* government out of the sphere of religion. After incorporation, the structural purpose is broader, to draw boundaries between government and religion, but it is still unrelated to individual autonomy. Two examples illustrate this point. First, what if Congress passed a law declaring that Christianity (or some specific Christian sect) was the "official religion of the United States of America? Such a law would *surely* violate the Establishment Clause, despite the fact that such a declaration, standing alone, has no impact on the individual autonomy of anyone. Second, the truth is that in practice individuals are forced to listen to or read religious statements by government leaders all the time, in ways that do arguably invade their "autonomy" but that no one believes raise serious constitutional questions. References to God, including prayers, are a regular part of speeches by political leaders, including presidential

---

42. 530 U.S. 290 (2000).

addresses; God is mentioned in the Declaration of Independence itself; and religious references and iconography permeate public life in any number of other ways. Given this reality, there is obviously no constitutional "right" on the part of citizens to be free of unwanted references to God or religion, as the school prayer cases are sometimes read to suggest.

The key purpose of nonestablishment, then, is not to protect individual liberty or autonomy, it is to maintain a structural barrier between religion and government. Why that barrier is needed we have already discussed. Why officially sponsored prayer, especially in public schools, violates that principle should be equally clear. Any time public officials, especially public school officials who have custody over our children, are enlisted to advance or spread religious faith, conflict will arise not only over whether religion should be propagated, but also over *whose* faith the government should adopt as its own. It is a historical fact, for example, that during the nineteenth century, there was intense conflict between Protestant school officials and Catholic parents over the reading of the King James version of the Bible in school, which Catholics viewed as an attempt to convert their children (because this was prior to incorporation, the conflict did not result in federal, constitutional litigation).[43] In modern times, defenders of school prayer try to downplay this problem by arguing that school prayers would be "nondenominational." This, however, is highly dubious, because truly "nondenominational" prayer is impossible. All prayers must make some religious assumptions—for example, about whether there is one God or many gods—that are themselves highly contested and divisive. To permit the government to take sides in such debates is to introduce the division and strife that the Establishment Clause was adopted to forestall; but anytime the government officially sponsors prayer, it inevitably must make religious choices and take sides in religious divisions. The reason that religious references by political leaders do not raise such problems is because they are understood as personal expressions of belief, not as promises to use the machinery of government to propagate those beliefs. When government officials *do* use the power of their office to further religion or a particular religion, serious concerns are raised—which is why, for example, Thomas Jefferson refused to issue Thanksgiving Day proclamations when he was president, even though he himself was happy to profess faith in a higher being.[44] This same reasoning also explains why the Establishment Clause bars public schools from teaching religiously inspired subjects such as "creation science"—and so, why the Supreme Court's decision striking down Louisiana's attempt to require such teaching was correct. The problem is that once the government starts teaching students religious doctrine, the inevitable question that will arise is *whose* doctrine to teach. There are as many creation stories as there are religions, so

---

43. RODNEY K. SMITH, PUBLIC PRAYER AND THE CONSTITUTION 261–262 (Scholarly Resources 1987).

44. AMAR, *supra*, THE BILL OF RIGHTS at 35.

whose creation story takes precedence? It is noteworthy in this respect that even within the Judeo-Christian tradition, there are obviously wide disagreements on this subject, including on the question of whether the creation story of Genesis should be taken literally. This problem does not arise when schools educate students about what different groups have believed as a historical matter, because such education does not put the government in the role of taking sides. But when the government teaches religious doctrine as *truth*, such preferentialism is unavoidable.

Given the fundamental structural objectives of the Establishment Clause, it is thus clear that officially sponsored prayer, or official propagation of particular religious beliefs, is unconstitutional. Sometimes, however, it is difficult to know when the government is engaging in such conduct, as opposed to merely accommodating its citizens' religious needs as best it can, or acknowledging the social role of religion as a historic or cultural matter. This problem is raised in a particularly stark form when the government places religiously oriented displays, such as holiday displays or the Ten Commandments, on its property. The Supreme Court has struggled with these situations for decades, with no apparent progress in clarifying when the constitutional line is crossed. For example, the Court has upheld a town's Christmas display that included a crèche, because the crèche was part of a larger display including many more secular elements such as reindeer and Santa Clause. The setting, according to the Court, rendered the nativity scene sufficiently secular to eliminate any thought that the government was advocating or endorsing Christianity.[45] The Court has also upheld a holiday display of a menorah next to a Christmas tree, but in the same case struck down the display of a freestanding nativity scene.[46] More recently the Court, when faced with challenges to two displays of the Ten Commandments on public property, upheld one display on the grounds of a county courthouse in Texas, but struck down another display within a county courthouse in Kentucky.[47] Whatever the merits of these individual decisions—and it must be acknowledged that some of the nitpicky distinctions the Court has created seem a bit absurd— these are genuinely difficult cases, because they require judges to draw distinctions between accommodation and acknowledgement of religion, which are permissible, and propagation, which is not. In making such determinations, context and history are everything, and so no easy, general rule can emerge—as Justice Stephen Breyer, the *only* Justice to agree on the result in both Ten Commandments cases, acknowledged.[48] The most that can be said is that when

---

45. Lynch v. Donnelly, 465 U.S. 668 (1984).

46. County of Allegheny v. American Civil Liberties Union, 492 U.S. 573 (1989).

47. Van Orden v. Perry, 545 U.S. 677 (2005); McCreary County v. ACLU of Kentucky, 545 U.S. 844 (2005).

48. Van Orden v. Perry, 545 U.S. at 699–700 (Breyer, J., concurring in the judgment).

a governmental display is purely religious, in that it has no secular or historical significance, there should be at least a strong suspicion raised that the government is engaged in proselytizing; but when a display has mixed significance, normally the government can be given the benefit of the doubt, absent contextual reasons to believe that the government action's true purpose and effect is religious. By this reasoning, displays of the Ten Commandments will often be permissible given that the Ten Commandments have legal as well as religious significance, especially when displayed in a legal context. But even the Ten Commandments are not always permissible—the Court was surely correct, for example, to ban such a display in a *classroom*, where its impact is much more likely to be to proselytize than to educate,[49] and there were special factors in the Kentucky courthouse case that also suggested such a purpose and effect. A nativity scene, on the other hand, is much more problematic, since it has no obvious nonreligious significance, and to suggest otherwise borders on disrespect for Christian beliefs. Indeed, Professor Philip Kurland went so far as to describe the Supreme Court's 1984 decision upholding a crèche display in context as "sleazy," because it "clearly demeans the religion of those who erected it."[50] Aside from such general conclusions, however, it seems that there is no escape but to decide governmental display disputes on a case-by-case basis.

The final Establishment Clause topic that we shall tackle is the vexing question of government aid to religious institutions. This question touches on some of the most fundamental and universally accepted principles regarding the Establishment Clause, and yet at the same time has triggered some of the most bitter modern disputes in the area. What is undisputed is that the Establishment Clause clearly bans, indeed was at its core designed to ban, the government's imposition of taxes on citizens to fund a preferred religion, generally by paying the salary of clergy. This principle emerged from perhaps the most famous religious dispute in the United States prior to the adoption of the Constitution, which occurred in Virginia during 1785 to 1786 (indeed, so fundamental is this dispute to the meaning of the Establishment Clause that it is discussed in great detail in the Supreme Court's first great Establishment Clause case, *Everson v. Board of Education*,[51] decided in 1947). In 1785, Virginia had an established church, the Church of England. That year, a bill came before the state legislature to renew an existing tax for the support of "teachers of the Christian religion." In response, James Madison—the man who later introduced the First Amendment into Congress, and yet later of course became president—authored a "Memorial

---

49. Stone v. Graham, 449 U.S. 39 (1980).

50. Philip Kurland, *The Religion Clauses and the Burger Court*, 34 CATH. U. L. REV. 1, 13 (1984).

51. 330 U.S. 1, 11–13 (1947).

and Remonstrance Against Religious Assessments,"[52] in which he argued passionately against religions establishments in general, and against the use of coerced taxes to support religion in particular. As Madison famously put it, "Who does not see that . . . the same authority which can force a citizen to contribute three pence only of his property for the support of any one establishment, may force him to conform to any other establishment in all cases whatsoever?"[53] Moreover, Madison argued that it was irrelevant that the Virginia bill supported Christianity generally (it was not limited to Anglican clergymen), rather than a specific sect. Ultimately, Madison's arguments were so persuasive that not only did the legislature not renew the tax, the following year it adopted at Madison's behest the "Virginia Bill for Religious Liberty," which had been written earlier by Madison's good friend and mentor Thomas Jefferson, and which once and for all established the principle of religious liberty and noncoercion in Virginia. There can be no doubt that these events were in Madison's mind when, just three years later, he introduced to Congress proposed constitutional amendments, including a prohibition of religious establishment, that would eventually become the Bill of Rights.

While the above history is largely uncontroversial, its implications for modern disputes is not. The difficulty is that unlike the Virginia act that Madison opposed, modern governments typically do *not* directly provide funds to religions *per se*. Instead, the typical modern funding dispute arises when the government adopts a program offering to provide money to private persons or institutions for some secular purpose—most commonly, to support the education of children—and a religious institution that performs that function seeks such funding. The difficulty is that while such programs on their face have nothing to do with religion, in practice the *vast* majority of government aid in such programs, especially in the educational arena, goes to religious schools (most often parochial schools). The question, then, is whether such public financial support for religious institutions violates the Constitution. In the first modern Establishment Clause case *Everson*, for example, the challenge was to a government program that reimbursed parents for money they spent for school buses to private schools, as applied to parents whose children attended religious school. The Court upheld the program. The Court has also upheld a government program loaning secular textbooks to private schools, including religious ones;[54] and a state tax deduction for parents' expenditures on tuition, textbooks, and transportation for schooling, as applied to parents whose children attended religious schools.[55] On the other hand, in the early 1970s the Court decided a series of cases striking down many

---

52. The Memorial and Remonstrance is reprinted in its entirety in the Appendix to the dissenting opinion in *Everson*, 330 U.S. at 63–64 (Rutledge, J., dissenting).

53. *Ibid.*

54. Board of Education v. Allen, 392 U.S. 236 (1968).

55. Mueller v. Allen, 463 U.S. 388 (1983).

forms of governmental aid to religious schools, including statutes reimbursing religious schools for the cost of teachers' salaries and textbooks for secular courses[56] and a law granting tuition reimbursement to parents whose children attend private schools.[57] A particularly confusing dispute has been over a federal program to provide assistance such as remedial education to economically deprived children enrolled in private schools. New York City implemented this program by sending public school teachers—all volunteers—into private schools, including religious schools, to provide remedial services. The teachers were under strict instructions to avoid religious activities, and the schools were required to remove religious symbols from classrooms during such sessions. In 1985, the Supreme Court struck down this program, holding that implementation of the program would result in "excessive entanglement of church and state."[58] Twelve years later, however, the Supreme Court reversed itself *in the same case*, and upheld New York City's program because it found that it did not advance religion.[59]

The Supreme Court's jurisprudence on the topic of government aid to religious institutions can only be described as baffling. There can be no doubt, however, that the trend of recent decades has been a greater tolerance of such aid. The critical turning point was probably a 1993 decision upholding the government's paying the salary of a sign-language interpreter for a deaf student in a parochial school.[60] Then in 1997, as mentioned earlier, the Court reversed itself regarding New York City's program for providing assistance to needy students in religious schools. In the next crucial step, in 2000, the Court upheld a Louisiana program permitting state education agencies to loan instructional materials such as computers, software, and books, to private schools, including parochial schools.[61] Finally, in 2002 in a case called *Zelman v. Simmons-Harris*,[62] which is almost certainly the most significant decision in this area in decades, the Supreme Court by a bare majority upheld Cleveland, Ohio's school voucher program. That program granted parents a voucher, the size of which depended on the parents' financial need, which they could use to send their children to any participating school, including private schools and participating public schools from neighboring jurisdictions. Parents also had the option of remaining in Cleveland's public schools and receiving tutorial aid. As it turned out, 82 percent of the schools who participated in the voucher program were religious (no neighboring public schools participated), and *96 percent* of the students participating

---

56. Lemon v. Kurtzman, 403 U.S. 602 (1971).
57. Committee for Public Education v. Nyquist, 413 U.S. 756 (1973).
58. Aguilar v. Felton, 473 U.S. 402 (1985).
59. Agostini v. Felton, 521 U.S. 203 (1997).
60. Zobrest v. Catalina Foothills School District, 509 U.S. 1 (1993).
61. Mitchell v. Helm, 530 U.S. 793 (2000).
62. 536 U.S. 639 (2002).

in the voucher program attended religious schools. The Court held that because the purpose of Cleveland's program, to provide educational assistance to poor children, was clearly secular and valid and because the program rested entirely on "true private choice in which government aid reaches religious schools only as a result of the genuine and independent choices of private individuals,"[63] the program was valid. According to the majority, the key factor supporting the program's validity was neutrality—i.e., that the program involved private choice, that the program did not in any way favor religious schools over secular ones (or, *a fortiori*, schools of one sect over another), and therefore that the program did not result in *State* support or sponsorship of religion. Given this fact, the Court deemed it irrelevant that the practical effect of Cleveland's program was undoubtedly to expend substantial sums of taxpayers' money on funding religious education, a result that Justice David Souter, dissenting in *Zelman*, argued would never have been permitted under the Court's previous decisions from *Everson* onwards.[64]

Has the Supreme Court, as the dissenters in *Zelman* argued, abandoned the basic meaning of the Establishment Clause in permitting greater state funding of religious institutions? From an individual autonomy perspective, there is much to be said for this argument. If the Establishment Clause creates an individual right, an entitlement, to prevent government from using that individual's tax dollars to support religion, then that right appears to be clearly violated in cases such as *Zelman* and other recent cases upholding "neutral" funding. That the support is provided as part of a broader program seems irrelevant to the individual's rights and concerns, especially in the typical situation where the vast majority of funding is in fact provided to religious institutions, indeed often to one particular sect (typically the Catholic Church). The key is that the support is real, deliberate, and perfectly predictable.

As is so often the case, however, this is another area where an autonomy-based analysis leads one astray. For all of the reasons we have discussed, the Establishment Clause of course does *not* create any sort of right to control the use of one's taxes. Instead it imposes a structural limit on governmental involvement in religion. Do the kind of genuinely neutral programs that in practice substantially support religion, such as Cleveland's voucher program, violate that limitation? While the question is not free of doubt, the best answer is that they do not. The reasons are related, unsurprisingly, to the factors emphasized by the *Zelman* Court: neutrality and private choice. So long as a government program is *truly* neutral, in that it is not intended or designed to favor religion, or any particular religion, and so long as the allocation of governmental funds in such a program is a product of truly voluntary, private choice, it cannot be said that

---

63. *Id.* at 649.
64. *Id.* at 688–689 (Souter, J., dissenting).

such programs involve the *State* supporting religion, in the way that Madison condemned. Put differently, the facts of neutrality and private choice mean that such programs do not create the incentives on the part of religions to seek to gain control of the State, which the Establishment Clause seeks to avoid, nor do they create mechanisms for the State to leverage its financial support to gain control over religious institutions—another result which the First Amendment guards against—because again, the practical power in these situations lies not with the government but with private individuals. Of course, it is incumbent on judges, in assessing funding programs, to ensure that they in fact do satisfy the requirements of neutrality and private choice, both as designed and in practice. Finally, it seems perverse to argue, as the *Zelman* dissent did, that the very fact that the majority of the aid ends up, as a result of private choice, in the hands of religious institutions condemns the program. In effect, that argument places governments in the position of having to ignore, or worse yet actively resist, their citizens' attachments to religion and preferences for religious education, a result that the First Amendment surely did not intend. Seen in this light, the Cleveland voucher program looks much more like permitted accommodation than like forbidden establishment.

There is one significant counterargument here, stemming from the problem of entanglement. The difficulty is that even when a government funding program is "neutral," the very fact of governmental funding, and the inevitable oversight that must go along with it (in a voucher program, for example, the government must ensure that schools who receive vouchers are in fact educating the supported children competently), means that some entanglement between government and religion will follow. This entanglement—the setting of rules by government, that religious institutions must follow on pain of losing funding—poses its own risks to the values of the Establishment Clause. In particular, it gives government a potentially dangerous lever against religious institutions, undermining their autonomy and threatening to co-opt religious institutions into the cultural values that the government favors, thereby again undermining the principle that religious institutions should be *independent*, private sources of social power, cohesion, and values. There is a nontrivial argument that any substantial amounts of governmental funding of religious institutions, on whatever terms, will inevitably result in entanglement that threatens First Amendment values, and so should be understood to violate the Establishment Clause. Ultimately, however, I would argue that this position should be rejected, for practical reasons. The reality is that in our modern society, in which government is ubiquitous and government funding an essential aspect of almost every aspect of our economy and society from healthcare to education to agriculture, the consequence of banning all governmental funding of religious institutions, on whatever terms, is to require religion to absent itself from public life, and in particular from most education. This, however, is surely not what the framers intended. As Professor Akhil Amar has pointed out, during the framing era, religious institutions played a very significant role in society, and in particular dominated education (remember, this is before the time of prevalent, public education).[65] Indeed, it was the very fact that churches controlled almost all education, with its important role in shaping values, that made them such an effective countervailing force to the power of the State. To exile religious institutions from education and public life is to deprive them of that role, and so to expand the already overweening influence of the State. This is not to say that the Constitution requires religious education, or even disapproves of public education—it certainly does not. But it does seem quite perverse to read the Constitution, and the First Amendment in particular, to create rules that have the effect of increasing the State's power in areas such as education and value formation, when the underlying purpose is in fact to restrain the State's authority. Better, probably, to accept some level of state/religious entanglement, with its attendant dangers, than to pursue a path with such perverse consequences.

---

65. *See* AMAR, *supra*, THE BILL OF RIGHTS at 44–45.

7. PROPERTY RIGHTS AND ECONOMIC REGULATION

The protection of private property and the sanctity of contract from governmental overreaching clearly played a crucial role in the framers' thinking about the constitutional structure and the role of the State. In the body of the Constitution itself, the Contracts Clause of Article I, Section 10 specifically forbids *state* governments from "impairing the Obligation of Contracts"—one of the very few limitations imposed on states by the Constitution, it should be noted, and the only one (other than the ban on titles of nobility) that is not understandable as simply preventing state governments from intruding on the powers of the new national government. In the Bill of Rights, two provisions of the Fifth Amendment specifically protect property: the Due Process Clause, which provides that no person shall "be deprived of life, liberty, or property, without due process of law"; and the so-called Takings Clause, which states "nor shall private property be taken for public use without just compensation." Finally, the Fourth Amendment's assurance that the "right of the people to be secure in their persons, houses, papers, and effects, against unreasonable searches and seizures, shall not be violated" also has the effect of protecting private property from governmental intrusions.

THE IMPORTANCE OF ECONOMIC RIGHTS

Why did the framers choose to so limit the power of the government to regulate property and contracts? What role does private property, and its protection, play in the constitutional structure? These are surprisingly difficult questions, associated with some quite ambiguous history. To understand the framers' desires, however, it is important to understand their context. A belief in the importance of property rights was widely shared by legal and political thinkers during the Framing period, who considered property to be one of the most basic and fundamental of natural rights. The famous English legal writer William Blackstone, who had an enormous influence on the framers, called private property an "absolute right, inherent in every Englishman" and described the various legal protections accorded by English law to property. These included the principle that freemen could be divested of property only by "the law of the land" (the principle enshrined in the Due Process Clause), and that when an individual's property was needed for some public purpose, an individual could be compelled to yield his property to the public only by the legislature, and then only if the owner is indemnified for the value of his property (the principle of the Takings Clause).[1] Similarly, several extant state constitutions at the time the Bill of Rights was being adopted also provided that property could not be taken for public use except by legislative action, and at least three (those of Massachusetts, Pennsylvania, and Vermont) included a compensation requirement.[2] Finally, and perhaps most significantly, during the debates over the ratification of the original Constitution in 1787, James Madison argued in the *Federalist Papers*, in particular in the famous Federalist No. 10, that unequal distribution of property was one of the basic sources of conflict in democratic societies and that one of the key roles of good government was to protect property from such "wicked and improper projects" as "an abolition of debts [or] an equal division of property."[3] Clearly, then, protection of property was at the center of at least some of the framing generation's thinking about the role of government.

Nor is this centrality surprising. As we have discussed throughout this book, the overarching concerns of the framers in designing their new, national government revolved around the proper role of government, and the appropriate relationship and balance of power between the People's government and the People themselves. Private property, owned and controlled by citizens free of the State's interference, plays a fundamental role in maintaining that balance. Without property, citizens cannot provide for themselves or their families, and so are at the mercy of the State for their necessities. In this situation, the State inevitably gains autocratic power over citizens, which it will use to its benefit (this is surely one of the lessons of twentieth-century Communism). Give the government unlimited power to deprive citizens of their property, or to control it, and a similar result follows. Sanctity of contract has a similar significance, because without the ability to enter into and enforce contracts, citizens lose the ability to use and exchange their property or to sell their labor, once again depriving them of their livelihoods and independence. Finally, Madison's concerns that the use of governmental power to redistribute property can exacerbate existing social divisions based on wealth also carry some weight and provide an alternative reason to limit the State's power over property (note here the parallel to the reasons why governmental control over religion is limited, which also arise from concerns about social division). It would seem, therefore, that in a free society with a limited government, private property and the sanctity of contract must be preserved.

---

1. WILLIAM BLACKSTONE, COMMENTARIES ON THE LAWS OF ENGLAND, bk. 1, ch. 1; vol. 1 at 134–135 (Oxford, 1765), *reprinted in* Neil H. Cogan ed., THE COMPLETE BILL OF RIGHTS 376–377 (Oxford 1997).

2. COGAN, *supra*, THE COMPLETE BILL OF RIGHTS at 372–374.

3. ALEXANDER HAMILTON, JAMES MADISON, AND JOHN JAY, THE FEDERALIST PAPERS (Garry Wills ed., Bantam 1982), FEDERALIST No. 10 at 42–49.

Appealing as this story is, however, there are limits to it. In particular, absolute autonomy with respect to property or contract has *never* been possible or even desirable, for two separate reasons. First, there is the problem that the unequal division of property that Madison extols in *Federalist* No. 10 does not ensure independence for all citizens, only those who own property. For the poor, dependence is inevitable. Of course (absent a welfare state), that dependence is not on the government, but rather on the propertied classes, and so the dependence does not raise the concern about governmental power. There was a strong strain of thought during the framing era, however, associated with classical republican thinking (and to which Thomas Jefferson was sympathetic) that such uneven divisions of property created a divided society in which effective democracy was impossible and government would likely be corrupted by wealth.[4] This perspective was, unsurprisingly, more sympathetic to government regulation or redistribution of property to achieve equity; and while it is true that classical republican thought is generally associated more with the anti-federalist opponents of the new Constitution than with its supporters, many of those same anti-federalists were among the primary proponents of the Bill of Rights, making it less likely that the Bill of Rights would incorporate exceedingly stringent limitations on governmental power to control property.

Second, even among those who did support strong property rights, there was always an essentially universal recognition that in any complex, interdependent society, the holding and use of private property must be subject to reasonable legal restrictions. Blackstone himself recognized that the traditional English right of property was subject to "control and diminution [by] the laws of the land," though he emphasized that property could be limited *only* by law.[5] It was also universally understood that on occasion, important governmental projects such as road-building would require access to private property, sometimes against the will of the owner. Needless to say, these implicit limits on property, the need for which was recognized in the framing era, are that much more essential in our modern, postindustrial society.

The starting point in our consideration of property and contract rights, then, is a mixed one. On the one hand, the framing generation clearly recognized the importance of limiting state power over private property and contractual liberty, as a critical aspect of a free society. On the other hand, the framers knew that some substantial governmental power over property was necessary in a functioning society, and also recognized that the nature of regulation might change with changing circumstances (though, of course, it is hard to imagine that they could

---

4. *See* Cass Sunstein, *Beyond the Republican Revival*, 97 YALE L. J. 1539, 1552–1553 (1988).

5. WILLIAM BLACKSTONE, COMMENTARIES ON THE LAWS OF ENGLAND, bk. 1, ch. 1; vol. 1 at 134–135 (Oxford, 1765), *reprinted in* Neil H. Cogan ed., THE COMPLETE BILL OF RIGHTS 376 (Oxford 1997).

have foreseen modern conditions). One implication of this multifaceted history is that a strong autonomy-based approach to property and contractual rights is implausible because it has been acknowledged throughout our history that individual autonomy in these areas is subject to substantial, open-ended governmental controls. Of course, this reality does not eliminate the possibility of weaker protections for autonomy in this area, based on some sort of balancing between individual property interests and governmental needs. But as we shall see, balancing poses its own, irresolvable dilemmas.

Unlike the inherent uncertainty of autonomy-based analysis, there are as we have discussed clear, structural purposes served by the Constitution's protections for property and contract. But as we have also seen, those purposes are to some extent conflicting. As a result, strong, substantive rules regarding what the role of government should be are lacking in this area, other than the broad principle of compensation for property actually taken by the government (on which more later). Instead, as we shall see, the nature of protection accorded to property by the Constitution, and the limits imposed on state action in this area, are more limited and more procedural than the strong substantive limitations in the area of speech and religion. This is most obvious with the Due Process Clause of the Fifth Amendment (and, of course, the Due Process Clause of the Fourteenth Amendment, which extended the same limits originally imposed on the national government to state governments). The Due Process Clause does *not* state that the government may not deprive individuals of property, it only states that such a deprivation must be according to due process of law, meaning that it must occur pursuant to a valid law enacted by the legislature, and must be carried out using legally adequate procedures such as a hearing in court. This clause by its terms provides no substantive protection to property at all (indeed, the clause does not even single out property for protection, it protects life, liberty, *and* property). It is true, as we noted in Chapter 3, that there was a period during the first half of the twentieth century—the so-called "*Lochner*" era from 1905 to 1937— during which the Supreme Court did interpret the Due Process clauses of the Fifth and Fourteenth Amendments through the lens of an autonomy-based approach to rights, and read it to impose substantive limits on governmental power to regulate property and contract. It is also true, however, that this line of cases was definitively abandoned in 1937 and has since then been almost universally vilified as an illegitimate expansion by the Supreme Court of its own power, an intellectual and historical aberration from our constitutional traditions.[6]

---

6. Outside of the area of property and contract, the Due Process Clause continues to be invoked substantively for two purposes: to "incorporate" the original Bill of Rights against state governments, and to protect "privacy" rights such as contraception and abortion. Incorporation remains defensible, though as discussed in Chapter 3, it probably should have proceeded through the Privileges and Immunities Clause of the Fourteenth Amendment rather than the Due Process Clause. Privacy rights we will pick up in Chapter 10.

SEARCHES AND SEIZURES

Consider now the Fourth Amendment to the Constitution. This provision, with its protection for "houses, papers, and effects" against unreasonable searches and seizures clearly is more directly focused on private property than the Due Process Clause—though note that the Fourth Amendment also protects "persons," so its interest is not limited to property. In his insightful, eye-opening, and thoroughly convincing recounting of the history and purposes of the Fourth Amendment, Professor Akhil Amar demonstrates that the underlying motivation for the Fourth Amendment's limitation on searches and seizures (as well as its limits on the issuance of general warrants, a topic beyond the scope of our discussion) was to disable the government from using its powers of search and seizure to harass its political opponents among the People, a core structural principle.[7] Amar recounts the story of John Wilkes, an English critic of King George III (and member of Parliament), who was imprisoned, and whose home and papers were searched in retaliation for his political activities. Wilkes successfully sued the royal officials who perpetrated these actions,[8] and his case became a cause célèbre in the American colonies (which thirteen years later became the United States). Crucially, however, the protection accorded against such official behavior, both under English law and by the Bill of Rights, is at its core procedural, not substantive. The amendment does not bar *all* searches or seizures, only unreasonable ones—necessarily, since without searches and seizures, the law could not be enforced. If a government official searches or seizes a citizen's person or property without a warrant, the citizen can sue the official for damages in court (the amendment also imposes strict limits on the issuance of warrants, to close that loophole). At this point, English law entitled the citizen to a trial before a jury of his peers—a right that is enshrined in the Seventh Amendment to the U.S. Constitution. The question of the reasonableness of the search would then be decided by a civil jury of citizens, *not* by officials of the State. Again, it is not that individual autonomy with respect to property (or person) is fully protected, because it is not; it is that an outside, structural check, drawn from the People themselves, is placed on the government to minimize abuse of this necessary power.

A final, necessary point here is that while the above appears to be an accurate description of how the framers viewed the protections of the Fourth Amendment, and of the way those protections worked in practice in the early period of our history, it does not accurately describe modern practice. Today, the rule is that absent special circumstances, searches and seizures must be conducted pursuant to a warrant (which, Amar convincingly argues, is almost certainly a misreading by

---

7. AMAR, *supra*, THE BILL OF RIGHTS at 64–77.
8. Wilkes v. Wood, 98 Eng. Rep. 489 (C.P. 1763), 19 Howell's State Trials 1153.

the Supreme Court of the Fourth Amendment), and if a valid warrant has issued, officials are immune from damages. The role of the jury has thus been eliminated, and the protection that exists is provided by the federal and state magistrates and judges who issue warrants—government officials in whom the framers would have had little confidence, but whose role in enforcing constitutional limits is today widely accepted. Moreover, even today the limits imposed by the Fourth Amendment are riddled with judicially created exceptions, and so the protections afforded by the Fourth Amendment are far from absolute.

THE CONTRACTS CLAUSE

That leaves for our consideration the Contracts Clause of Article I, Section 10, and the Takings Clause of the Fifth Amendment, the two most apparently substantive constitutional provisions dealing with contract and property. The Contracts Clause appears, by its terms, to provide extremely broad protection to the sanctity of contract; it states flatly that "[n]o State shall . . . pass any . . . Law impairing the Obligation of Contracts." In practice, however, the protections it provides are quite limited. First and foremost, the Contracts Clause, as noted above, limits the power *only* of state governments, not the national government. This in itself makes it highly unusual, and means that the clause does not fit well with the general constitutional structure, with its focus on the powers and limits of the national government. In fact, the history suggests that the specific concerns driving the Contracts Clause arose from the perception that during the decade prior to the ratification of the new Constitution, many state governments had been interfering in contracts between debtors and creditors, to try and provide relief to poor debtors during a period of economic upheaval. Many of the framers, however, believed that such policies threatened economic stability (remember James Madison's horror in *Federalist* No. 10 over the "abolition of debts") and were the product of the capture of the legislative process by the "masses" against the public interest. Their response was the Contracts Clause, which forbade such laws. (Anti-federalist Luther Martin, one of Maryland's representatives at the Constitutional Convention in Philadelphia, argued against the ratification of the Constitution in part because of its inclusion of the Contracts Clause, which he felt disempowered the states from helping the deserving poor![9]) The national government was not seen to be prone to such capture, and so was not subject to the same limitations. The Contracts Clause is thus probably best understood not as a wholesale defense of contract, but as a reflection of distrust in state politics of the time.

---

9. Luther Martin, *Genuine Information*, No. 8, January 22, 1788, reprinted in COGAN, *supra*, THE COMPLETE BILL OF RIGHTS at 376.

The other crucial limitation of the Contracts Clause is that it has always been understood to prevent only laws that abridge or modify *existing* contracts, those entered into beforehand. It does not limit the power of state governments to forbid or regulate particular contracts prospectively. In other words, what the Contracts Clause says is that once two people enter into a contract (which is a legally binding agreement), state governments may not, after that, pass a law excusing one of the parties from the obligation to carry out their part of the agreement (e.g., pay a debt on time). However, governments remain free to pass a law stating that henceforth all future contracts must satisfy certain conditions (e.g., that interest above a certain level may not be charged, or debtors must be given a minimum amount of time to pay a debt, etc.). Thus the actual protection to economic autonomy accorded by the Contracts Clause is quite limited since it places no limits on future action. A contrary reading of the Contracts Clause would have an extraordinary impact on modern regulation because it would call into doubt the constitutionality of a whole host of laws limiting the terms of contracts, including minimum wage laws, maximum hours laws, laws protecting the right to form unions, and most consumer protection laws. In the modern world, such a result seems unthinkable. It is true that early in our history an argument was made that the Contracts Clause should forbid even prospective legislation that interfered with the "natural right" to enter into contracts, but that argument was rejected by a majority of the Supreme Court (over a dissent by the great Chief Justice John Marshall) and has not since been revived.[10] Of course, during the *Lochner* era the Supreme Court did strike down even purely prospective limits on contractual freedom, under the rubric of "substantive due process"; but as we noted earlier, that period was an aberration.

Even as a historical matter, therefore, the protection accorded to economic "liberty" as such by the Contracts Clause was quite limited, though at least with respect to truly retroactive state legislation, the clause did act as an effective bar. In the modern era, however, even that limitation has not survived. The key change occurred in 1934, when the Supreme Court decided the famous (or infamous) decision in *Home Building & Loan Association v. Blaisdell.*[11] The State of Minnesota passed a law in 1933, providing that at least temporarily, when a homeowner faced foreclosure because he could not meet his mortgage payments, courts were authorized to postpone foreclosure and extend the period in which the homeowner could repay his debt. The context, of course, was the Great Depression, during which vast numbers of homeowners faced devastation due to high unemployment and a massive economic downturn, as well as the collapse of capital markets (*plus ça change, plus c'est la même chose*). The Supreme

---

10. Ogden v. Saunders, 25 U.S. (12 Wheat.) 213 (1827).
11. 290 U.S. 398 (1934).

Court, by a closely divided 5–4 vote, upheld the law. Four dissenting Justices pointed out that the Minnesota law was *precisely* the sort of law that the framers intended the Contracts Clause to prohibit. The majority did not deny this point, but rather responded as follows:

> It is no answer to say that this public need was not apprehended a century ago, or to insist that what the provision of the Constitution meant to the vision of that day it must mean to the vision of our time. If by the statement that what the Constitution meant at the time of its adoption it means today, it is intended to say that the great clauses of the Constitution must be confined to the interpretation which the framers, with conditions and outlook of their time, would have placed upon them, the statement carries its own refutation.[12]

Ultimately, the majority concluded that given the special circumstances of the Great Depression, the state possessed power to take action for the public good, including modifying the terms of existing contracts, so long as contractual rights are not completely destroyed.

In the more than half a century since *Blaisdell* was decided, the Supreme Court has essentially abandoned enforcement of the Contracts Clause, consistently finding that state legislation modifying contractual obligations is justified by public necessity. In short, the Contracts Clause has been rendered effectively dead letter. What explains this surprising development? Basically, the problem the Court has faced in this area is the problem we noted earlier, that while there are strong structural reasons to restrict the government's power to interfere with property and contract, it is equally clear that some State authority in this area is essential. In particular, in the devastating circumstances of the Depression, the Court simply could not stomach any more the simplistic refrain that all rights under existing contracts must be sacrosanct. Once the concession is made, though, that some governmental intervention is justified, depending on the need, the problem becomes one of balancing and line-drawing. Judges, however, are extraordinarily poorly placed to make such judgments, or to second-guess the preferences of elected legislators. After all, on what basis is a judge to say that the economic emergency of 1934 was greater, or less, than the emergency of the 1780s? And how is a judge to assess the impact on the national economy of granting, or refusing to grant, relief to debtors? Faced with such questions, judges inevitably deferred to elected and accountable officials; but that spelled the end of the Contracts Clause (as we shall see, the Court has faced a similar conundrum in interpreting the Takings Clause).

The inevitable failure of balancing meant that an autonomy-based approach to the Contracts Clause is doomed. But does it also, necessarily, spell the end for

---

12. *Id.* at 442–443.

a structural approach? In practice it has, but is that inevitable? Put differently, if a serious effort were made to read the Contracts Clause from a structural perspective, is a revival of the Contracts Clause under modern circumstances plausible?

The argument *against* a revival is straightforward. While the Contracts Clause had an important structural role to play during the framing era, to limit divisive, class-based politics within state governments, that role is no longer necessary or plausible, for two reasons. First, class-based politics are much less of an issue in our modern, far more egalitarian society. But second, even if such divisive politics were still a concern, given the complexity and economic interdependence of modern, postindustrial society, the need for governmental power to regulate even existing contracts is so strong and so well-established that it trumps any such concerns. This is a powerful, perhaps decisive point.

The retort, the argument *for* a limited revival of the Contracts Clause starts with the presumption that *all* structural principles written into the Constitution have value, and so as with the Second Amendment, we should not casually abandon the Contracts Clause. Modern circumstances might mean (as they surely do) that the scope of the clause will be more limited today than in the past, but that does not mean that the clause should be completely interred, as the post-1934 Supreme Court has done. The underlying, structural presumption of the Contracts Clause, remember, is that redistributive policies based on class-based politics are destructive of free societies. The insight that has been achieved since the framing era is that not all governmental policies that interfere with existing contracts, and have redistributive consequences, necessarily constitute class-based politics. Instead, some such policies, such as the mortgage foreclosure moratorium upheld in *Blaisdell*, have broader social purposes—in that case, to break the downward spiral of prices and spending power that characterized the Great Depression of the 1930s (as well as the Great Recession that began in 2008). However, the underlying structural presumption that class-based politics *alone* (at least at the state level) are to be avoided still stands, and is still a part of our Constitution. The job of the courts in any Contracts Clause dispute, then, is to determine whether a particular governmental regulation of contracts in fact has a broader public purpose, or whether it is purely redistributive. Admittedly, this is not an easy line to draw, not least because there is a plausible argument, rooted in anti-federalist thinking, that pure redistribution designed to achieve economic equality is itself in the public interest. However, at least with respect to state laws impairing existing contracts, it seems necessary to read the Contracts Clause as rejecting that argument. Thus courts must undertake this inquiry, and enforce this distinction between class-based and public-minded contractual impairments, in a serious fashion. Of course, courts will inevitably have to defer to some extent to legislative judgments regarding the purposes and need for particular laws, but if the Contracts Clause is to be revived, that deference cannot be unlimited, as it has been since 1934.

TAKINGS: THE *KELO* CASE AND THE PROBLEM OF PUBLIC USE

We now turn to the most important, and most troubling, of the constitutional provisions dealing with private property, the Takings Clause of the Fifth Amendment. Recall what the Takings Clause says: "nor shall private property be taken for public use without just compensation." By its terms, this is a narrow restriction. It merely says that the federal government (and after incorporation, the states) must pay property owners if the government chooses to seize their property by exercising its power of eminent domain (which is the power to force property owners to sell their property to the government). The State clearly retains the power of eminent domain, and no obvious limits are placed on when that power may be exercised, except that any taking be for public use (in fact, even that limit is not obvious from the text of the clause). Furthermore, the Takings Clause does not appear to place any limit on the government's power to *regulate* the use of private property, short of actual dispossession—though as we shall see, the modern Supreme Court has interpreted the Takings Clause to impose some such limits. In short, the Takings Clause, by its terms and original meaning, provided little or no protection for the autonomy of property holders. In that sense, it fits in well with the rest of the Bill of Rights.

If the purpose of the Takings Clause is not to protect property as a right of personal autonomy, presumably it has some structural function, similar to the other provisions of the Bill of Rights. At first blush, such a function is not hard to imagine. After all, if the government had the power to take property from citizens without compensation, that would be a powerful weapon to use against its opponents among the citizenry at large and would represent a substantial imbalance in power between the State and the People. This explanation of the Takings Clause, however, is a bit dissatisfying. For one thing, the Due Process Clause assured that any deprivation of property could occur only according to law, which already provided substantial protection for property. Second, the threat of legislative dispossession of property, as a way of harassing political critics, seems rather unlikely because of the compensation requirement, and in any event the Takings Clause does not prevent dispossession, it merely requires payment. Another clue that the Takings Clause was not widely perceived to respond to the same structural concerns as the rest of the Bill of Rights is that the Takings Clause, uniquely among the provisions of the Bill of Rights, was not included in *any* of the proposals for constitutional amendments that emerged from the state ratifying conventions during the debate over ratification[13] and was not a part of the "Master Draft of the Bill of Rights" created by Virginian George Mason, which provided the blueprint for the proposals of many of the state conventions as well as for

---

13. *See* AMAR, *supra*, THE BILL OF RIGHTS at 78.

James Madison's eventual proposals to Congress for a Bill of Rights.[14] The inclusion of the Takings Clause appears to have been a product purely of James Madison's conviction that such a provision belonged in the Bill of Rights—though as we noted at the beginning of this chapter, Madison was not operating in a vacuum, since several state constitutions of the time did contain similar provisions. Nonetheless, the Takings Clause is probably best understood as Madison's brainchild. This is significant because, as we discussed in Chapter 3, Madison appears to have held somewhat idiosyncratic views for his time. In particular, his distrust of popular government, his fears that democratic majorities would use their electoral power to attack the propertied classes, and his commitment to preserving private property as the touchstone of liberty were not entirely typical of his time, and modern scholarship suggests that his views appear not to have had much influence on his contemporaries, no matter how powerful the influence on future generations.[15]

In any event, regardless of the uncertain intellectual pedigree of the Takings Clause, the truth is that the clause's basic requirement, that the government compensate owners for property that it seizes, appears not to have been controversial then, or now (though of course differences might arise regarding how seized property should be valued). Regarding its original application to the power of eminent domain, the only issue that has raised any serious controversy has been whether the "public use" requirement imposes any serious limits on *when* eminent domain may be used. This debate came to a head in the Supreme Court in the highly controversial decision in *Kelo v. City of New London*.[16] New London is a city on the southern coast of Connecticut, which has been suffering substantial economic decline because of lost manufacturing and military jobs. In the late 1990s, the city government created a redevelopment plan designed to create a development area, occupied by a combination of industrial and research facilities (including a large facility owned by the pharmaceutical giant Pfizer), businesses (including a new hotel/conference center and restaurants and shops), residences, and recreational facilities, which would hopefully revitalize the city's waterfront and downtown areas. Most of the land to be used for this plan was already owned by the government (much of it had been part of a closed military base), but there were one hundred fifteen private residences that the city needed to acquire to carry out its plans. Most of the owners of those residences sold out voluntarily, but some did not, and when the city instituted eminent domain condemnation proceedings to seize their property (with compensation, of course), they brought suit challenging the constitutionality of the city's actions (among

---

14. George Mason's Master Draft is available at http://www.constitution.org/gmason/ amd_gmas.htm.

15. *See, e.g.,* Larry Kramer, *Madison's Audience*, 112 HARV. L. REV. 611 (1999); AMAR, *supra*, THE BILL OF RIGHTS at 78–79.

16. 545 U.S. 469 (2005).

the challengers were two dream plaintiffs, a woman named Wilhelmina Dery, who had been living in her home since she had been born in it in 1918, and her husband Charles, who had been living in the home since marrying Wilhelmina sixty years previously). Their claim was that because the city intended not to keep their property for the use of the public, but rather to sell or lease it to private owners who in many cases would not open the land to the public, the condemnation did not satisfy the "public use" requirement of the Takings Clause. The Supreme Court, in a closely divided opinion, upheld New London's plan. It held that while the Takings Clause did forbid uses of the eminent domain power purely for the benefit of private persons (i.e., taking property from A and giving it to B, simply to benefit B), it did not require that condemned land be literally open to the public. Instead, it sufficed if the condemnation advanced a "public purpose," and on the question of whether such a purpose existed, courts should generally defer to legislative judgments. Here, the redevelopment plan easily satisfied the public purpose requirement. Four Justices joined a powerful dissenting opinion that argued that permitting condemnation under the circumstance of this case violates the fundamental purposes of the Takings Clause, because the taking here involved neither use of land by the public, nor land that was imposing affirmative harm on the public, and therefore constituted nothing more than a private benefit.

The response to the *Kelo* decision was extraordinary. It was met with widespread condemnation in both the press and by political leaders and has triggered something of a backlash throughout this country against the eminent domain power. This backlash, however, is frankly quite peculiar from a *constitutional* perspective (there is certainly nothing peculiar about a political backlash against legislatures who adopt plans such as New London's). The fact is that when *Kelo* was decided in 2005, it was already well accepted that governments had broad discretion regarding the uses of eminent domain, as a result of two earlier decisions: *Berman v. Parker*,[17] in which the Court had upheld a redevelopment plan for "blighted areas" of Washington, D.C.; and *Hawaii Housing Authority v. Midkiff*,[18] in which the Court upheld Hawaii's use of eminent domain to force landowners to sell to renters, in order to break up an exceedingly concentrated housing market, where a handful of families owned the lion's share of the land in the state (the *Kelo* dissent sought to distinguish these cases, but its efforts were not very convincing). Moreover, as a matter of constitutional principle, *Kelo* seems an easy case. The underlying question, remember, is how the government may use its eminent domain power. There may have been a time when the literal language of the Takings Clause was read to require a very narrow power—that land could be seized *only* if it was to be used for the benefit of the public, i.e., by

17. 348 U.S. 26 (1954).
18. 465 U.S. 1097 (1984).

the government. In the industrial era, however, that reading had to be abandoned because there were times when private entities, such as railroads (most importantly), telephone companies, or power companies, needed to be able to take control of private land (with legislative authorization, of course), in order to provide essential services to the public. Once that step had been taken, of effectively redefining public use as public benefit (a step that only one member of the Supreme Court, Justice Clarence Thomas, today contests[19]), the question of what constitutes a public use (or more accurately, a public purpose) becomes a matter of judgment. For all of the reasons we have already discussed, this is the sort of judgment that judges are exceptionally ill-placed to make or to second-guess. Moreover, it is a judgment that must be permitted, even if it impinges on some individuals. *All* laws, whether they be tax laws, spending decisions, environmental regulations, or criminal laws, harm some people and benefit others (the law of theft, for example, harms thieves); but no one thinks that fact alone makes these laws constitutionally suspect. The use of the eminent domain power for economic redevelopment is no different, especially because the requirement of just compensation ensures that the sort of class politics that Madison feared is unlikely to be the basis for the government's actions. In this situation, there seems little basis for thinking that the constitutional structure requires this authority to be removed from the legislature, and placed in the hands of the courts, as an aggressive reading of the "public use" requirement would do. *Kelo*, then, was correctly decided. It bears emphasizing that this is not to say that the use of eminent domain for economic development purposes is wise or good policy—Justice Thomas in his *Kelo* dissent quotes academic analysis pointing out that "[i]n cities across the country, urban renewal came to be known as 'Negro removal,'"[20] and he has a point. The critical point, however, is that the decision on whether to pursue such policies is a *legislative* judgment, and if the People do not like what their legislatures choose to do, they can always respond at the next election (it should be noted that in New London itself, political pressure led to at least delay and reconsideration of the condemnations[21]).

There is, however, one wrinkle to this seemingly simple result. It is the possibility that the eminent domain power will be employed to harass political opponents of the government and benefit supporters, which is of course a core, structural concern. Earlier, I suggested that the just compensation requirement alleviates this concern, but that may be a bit too facile. Dispossession from one's property, especially one's home, *is* a traumatic experience, even if one is

---

19. *Kelo*, 545 U.S. at 505–523 (Thomas, J., dissenting).

20. *Id.* at 52, *quoting* Pritchett, *The "Public Menace" of Blight: Urban Renewal and the Private Uses of Eminent Domain*, 21 Yale L. & Pol'y Rev. 1, 47 (2003).

21. William Yardley, *Eminent Domain Project at Standstill Despite Ruling*, New York Times, Nov. 21, 2005, available at http://www.nytimes.com/2005/11/21/nyregion/21domain.html?scp=7&sq=New%20London,%20redevelopment&st=cse.

compensated for the value of the property, and so such use of the power is not impossible to imagine. Thus courts may well still have some role to play in this area, similar to the Contracts Clause, in ensuring that uses of eminent domain do serve *some* broader public purpose, and are not merely a way of benefiting some individuals at the expense of others. Again, as with the Contracts Clause, some level of deference is inevitable here, but it should not be absolute—some judicial scrutiny remains necessary. Justice Anthony M. Kennedy made precisely this point in a separate opinion he penned in *Kelo*,[22] and there is much to be said for his argument, which would entail a narrow, but significant revival of judicial scrutiny under the Public Use Clause.

REGULATORY TAKINGS

Until the early twentieth century, the scope of the Takings Clause of the Fifth Amendment was to limit governmental uses of the eminent domain power, or other actions that were the equivalent of eminent domain because they effectively dispossessed owners of their property (an example of such physical dispossession was creating an airplane flight path directly over property, in a way as to make it unusable[23]). The major controversies over application of the clause therefore were those discussed above. In particular, the Takings Clause was not understood to limit the government's power to regulate the *use* of property in ways that fell short of effective dispossession. As a consequence, the Takings Clause was of limited social significance since in the modern industrial and postindustrial eras economic regulation, not eminent domain, has been the subject of most controversies regarding governmental power over property. All of this changed, however, with the Supreme Court's landmark decision in 1922 in *Pennsylvania Coal v. Mahon*,[24] authored by Justice Oliver Wendell Holmes, Jr., perhaps the greatest Justice to sit on the Supreme Court.

The *Pennsylvania Coal* case arose as a dispute between a coal company, which owned the right to mine coal under certain land, and the owners of the surface over the coal, who had built homes and other buildings above the coal deposits. The surface owners sued the coal company, seeking a judicial order forbidding the coal company to mine coal to the point where support for the surface was eliminated, causing the surface to subside—i.e., the surface owners' homes to fall into the ground. The difficulty the surface owners faced with this seemingly reasonable request was that the coal company had originally owned the land outright, and when it had sold the surface to the owners (or their predecessors as owners), the company had specifically retained the right to mine all of the coal,

---

22. *Kelo*, 545 U.S. at 490–493 (Kennedy, J., concurring).
23. United States v. Causby, 328 U.S. 256 (1946).
24. 260 U.S. 393 (1922).

and the buyers had by contract agreed to take the risk of any damages from the mining. So, seemingly, the homeowners had no case. However, their claim was based on the fact that the State of Pennsylvania had passed a law forbidding coal companies from mining coal in such a way as to cause subsidence of homes. The coal company's response was to claim that the Pennsylvania law was unconstitutional, because it deprived them of rights of property and contract. The Supreme Court agreed with the coal company. Justice Holmes recognized that not all regulation of property that reduced its uses or value violated the Constitution—indeed, he specifically said that "[g]overnment hardly could go on if to some extent values incident to property could not be diminished without paying for every such change in the general law."[25] He also recognized that there could be no clear line between permissible regulations and impermissible ones (or more accurately, regulations requiring compensation, because remember, the Takings Clause does not forbid the government seizures of property, it merely requires payment). He argued, however, that at some point regulation must be considered to have crossed the line into a taking, if property rights were to have any meaning. "The general rule," he said, is "that while property may be regulated to a certain extent, if regulation goes too far it will be recognized as a taking."[26] In this case, he concluded that the combination of the facts that the coal company had specifically retained the right to mine coal, and that the law imposed heavy financial losses on it, compelled the conclusion that compensation was required here. Justice Louis Brandeis, another giant in the history of the Supreme Court, dissented from Holmes's opinion (even though Holmes and Brandeis were usually allies on the Court). Brandeis argued that so long as a regulation can be said to serve the public interest, and does not dispossess an owner entirely, it does not violate the Takings Clause.

The Court's decision in *Pennsylvania Coal* seemed to open up a hornet's nest of problems. The 1920s was an era of rapid industrialization and urbanization, and concomitantly a period when the role of the government in managing property and the economy was expanding, especially at the state and local level (the explosion of federal authority was to come in the next decade, during the Great Depression and the presidency of Franklin Delano Roosevelt). Because *all* governmental regulation can reduce the value of property to some extent, the Court's decision seemed to cast doubt on the ability of governments to pursue needed regulation for the public welfare—because in practice, a compensation requirement would doom most regulation, given limited budgets. Soon thereafter, however, the Court alleviated these concerns by recognizing that most day-to-day regulation was permissible. In particular, in 1926 the Court upheld a zoning law that zoned an area for residential use, as applied to a particular property, vacant

---

25. *Id.* at 413.
26. *Id.* at 415.

but intended for industrial use, whose value was reduced from $10,000 to $2500 per acre because of the zoning rule. The Court explained that under modern, urban circumstances it was highly beneficial to all citizens for the government to separate industrial and residential neighborhoods, and that so long as a zoning scheme was evenhanded, courts should not second-guess legislative judgments, despite heavy burdens on individuals.[27] Two years later, the Court upheld a Virginia law requiring owners of cedar trees that had been infected by "cedar rust," a fungal disease highly harmful to apple trees (but not to cedars), to cut down the trees at their own expense (talk about adding insult to injury!), in order to protect nearby apple orchards.[28] Again, the Court emphasized that the law advanced the public interest (because apples were more economically valuable to the state than cedars) and so was presumptively valid.

These decisions, and others like them, seemed to curb the threat posed by *Pennsylvania Coal*, and in subsequent decades most economic regulation was upheld as valid regulation serving the public interest. This trend reached its apotheosis in *Penn Central Transportation Co. v. New York City*,[29] a Supreme Court case decided in 1978. The plaintiff in the case, Penn Central Railroad, was the owner of Grand Central Terminal in New York City, a famous beaux-arts building that opened in 1913. Because of economic difficulties, the railroad wanted to construct a modern office tower on top of Grand Central, to earn additional rental revenues on the order of $2 million per year. Unfortunately for the railroad, however, Grand Central had been designated a historic landmark by New York City, and the city's Landmarks Preservation Commission had unsurprisingly declined to grant permission for the construction. The railroad therefore sued. The Supreme Court, in an opinion by Justice William Brennan, leader of the liberal wing of the Court during the 1970s and 1980s, rejected the railroad's claim. The Court stated that the question of whether a regulation constituted a taking was an "ad hoc, factual inquir[y]"[30] (not much progress from Holmes's "goes to far" test), and here, the Court concluded that because the regulation did not eliminate the existing use of the terminal (as a railroad station) and because preserving historic landmarks was a valid public purpose, no compensation was required.

The *Penn Central* case seemed to spell the effective end of the Takings Clause as a meaningful restraint on economic regulation. In fact, however, reports of the clause's demise were highly exaggerated. Since the late 1980s, the Takings Clause, and in particular the regulatory takings doctrine, has enjoyed a renaissance on an increasingly conservative Supreme Court. The trend began with two decisions, soon after *Penn Central*, holding that when the government physically

---

27. Euclid v. Amber Reality Co., 272 U.S. 365 (1926).
28. Miller v. Schoene, 276 U.S. 272 (1928).
29. 438 U.S. 104 (1978).
30. *Id.* at 124.

intrudes on property, by permitting itself or others to permanently physically occupy the property, even in the most trivial way (the lead case involved a New York City law requiring apartment building owners to permit cable television companies to install cable equipment on their buildings), an automatic taking occurs.[31] More importantly, however, were two decisions authored by Justice Antonin Scalia, the undoubted leader of the conservative wing of the modern Court. The first, in 1987, struck down a decision of the California Coastal Commission that required owners of beachfront property to grant the public the right to cross their property, as a condition of rebuilding homes.[32] Then, in 1992, the Court held that a South Carolina law that, because of fears of erosion, effectively forbade a developer named David Lucas from developing in any way two beachfront parcels he owned and wished to build on for his private use also constituted a taking. (Lucas had been permitted to develop and sell adjoining parcels of land before the new South Carolina law had been passed, which must have made the situation particularly frustrating for him.) The *Lucas* case was particularly significant because it held that a taking occurs anytime a "regulation denies all economically beneficial or productive use of land,"[33] thereby raising the risk that some environmental regulations might be found to take property and so require compensation (Justice Scalia recognized an exception from his rule in *Lucas* for harmful uses of land, but that exception would not apply to many types of environmental regulation such as application of the Endangered Species Act). The full implications of *Lucas* remain unclear because of the rarity of economic regulation that denies a private landowner of *all* economically beneficial uses.

The long and short of it is that the law of regulatory takings is, and has been since its inception in 1922, a confusing muddle. While a few clear rules have emerged—in particular, that permanent physical occupations require compensation, as do regulations that eliminate all economic value of land—most controversies are resolved on an ad hoc, inevitably unpredictable basis. This uncertainty, however, should not be surprising. The underlying problem here is the same underlying problem we have seen throughout this chapter: while the protection of private property (and contract) represents an important constitutional value, absolute protection is impossible. The framers recognized, and Justice Holmes recognized in creating regulatory takings law, that in a complex, interdependent society, some regulation of private property is unavoidable, including regulation with sometimes dramatic impacts on property values (remember the zoning and *Penn Central* cases). Faced with a perceived need to reconcile strong public policies with individuals' autonomy "right" to control their own property (remember that when *Mahon* created regulatory takings law in 1922, the Supreme Court was

31. Loretto v. Teleprompter Manhattan CATV Corp., 458 U.S. 419 (1982); Kaiser Aetna v. United States, 444 U.S. 164 (1979).

32. Nollan v. California Coastal Commission, 483 U.S. 825 (1987).

33. Lucas v. South Carolina Coastal Council, 505 U.S. 1003, 1015 (1992).

still in the midst of the *Lochner* era, with its autonomy-based approach to rights), the Court concluded that the Constitution required courts to balance the societal need for particular regulation against the impact of the regulation on the owner.[34] This, however, seems another one of those tasks that is beyond the competence of unelected federal judges. How is a judge to decide how important a particular social policy is? Is the preservation of historic landmarks a valuable enterprise? How about preventing the erosion of coastlines, or the subsidence of houses? And how is a court to decide if the burden imposed on an individual owner is "worth" the social gain? Indeed, this kind of inquiry, "balancing" the burden on individual constitutional "rights" against social policies, is precisely the kind of autonomy-based approach to constitutionalism which, we have seen, is unworkable, and contrary to the design of the Constitution and the Bill of Rights. Insofar as regulatory takings law requires courts to undertake such a task, it is intellectually bankrupt, and has no place in constitutional law.

Indeed, at some level, the whole idea of a law of takings that protects individual autonomy is incoherent. After all, autonomy means an entitlement to be free from governmental interference, but the Takings Clause gives property owners no such entitlement—all it does is to ensure financial compensation, if a taking has occurred. Nor does this compensation always provide the owner with much satisfaction. In *Loretto v. Teleprompter Manhattan CATV Corp.*, the cable television case discussed above, the apartment building owner was apparently awarded compensation of $1 per year for being required to permit cable equipment on her property.[35] Contrasting *Loretto*, where the Court found a taking worth $1 per year, with *Penn Central*, where the Court found no taking despite lost income of $2 million per year, demonstrates thoroughly that if the purpose of the law of regulatory takings is to protect individuals from financial harm, or to protect their "right" to use their property as they please, this body of law is an incoherent failure.

Does this mean that there is nothing to be salvaged from the law of regulatory takings? Perhaps so—given the lack of any historical basis for the application of the Takings Clause to *regulations* (as opposed to eminent domain or dispossession), and the incoherence of the law here, there is much to be said for abandoning the entire enterprise. But then again, perhaps not. Till now, all that our analysis has established is that to the extent that regulatory takings law seeks to protect the "right" of individuals to hold and use property, as a matter of personal autonomy, it must fail. This does not mean, however, that limiting governmental power over property or contracts is pointless; to the contrary, as we noted earlier,

---

34. The *Penn Central* case asks us to look at "[t]he economic impact of the regulation . . . and, particularly, the extent to which the regulation has interfered with distinct, investment-backed expectations . . . [as well as] the character of the governmental action." *Penn Central*, 438 U.S. at 124.

35. *See* http://en.wikipedia.org/wiki/Loretto_v._Teleprompter_Manhattan_CATV_Corp.

such limitations are an important element of the Constitution's objective of maintaining a healthy balance between state and private power, minimizing the vulnerability and dependence of citizens vis-à-vis the State, and avoiding the exacerbation of class divisions among the People. If regulatory takings law is to be resuscitated and revitalized meaningfully, it must reflect these underlying purposes, while also recognizing the institutional limitations on what judges can reasonably do. In thinking about this problem, it is important to recall that the key underlying concern here is that the State will misuse its inevitable power to regulate property, in order to punish its opponents and make them dependent upon the government. Particularly dangerous are governmental actions that seem to simply transfer benefits from one easily identifiable person or group (whom the government presumably disfavors) to another person or group (whom the government favors), both because such action might be motivated by spite, and because it might increase social divisions. From this vantage point, laws that regulate property broadly and evenhandedly, spreading costs and benefits widely and unpredictably, seem to raise no special concerns, because such laws are extremely unlikely to be a tool for self-dealing government officials to harm their opponents. The very fact that the impact of such laws is widespread means that they are unlikely to be targeted, and in addition, the saliency of such laws to the mass of the People means that political checks are likely to be sufficient to prevent misuse of power. Moreover, this conclusion remains true even if, as it turns out, a particular owner or owners suffer substantial losses—that is an autonomy-based concern that should have no place in constitutional law. This is why in *Euclid v. Amber Realty Co.*, the 1926 zoning case discussed above, the Supreme Court upheld the zoning law in question despite the devastating impact on one owner; and this is also why, at least according to the Court, Penn Central's claim for compensation for regulation of the Grand Central Terminal was rejected (though as we shall see, that decision might be questioned on these grounds). This reasoning also suggests that broadly written environmental laws, whose impact cannot be predicted ahead of time, should not raise serious concerns under the Takings Clause.

The converse of this conclusion is that when regulation of property is *not* even-handed, when it seems to impose substantial economic burdens on a selected few, then real concerns arise that the State is punishing its enemies. Even in this situation, of course, we permit regulation to proceed so long as compensation is paid, but as we discussed in the context of eminent domain, the requirement of compensation makes such regulation a much less dangerous weapon. Such a concern might well explain the result in the granddaddy of all regulatory takings cases, *Pennsylvania Coal*, where the State of Pennsylvania appeared to have singled out a handful of coal companies for highly unfavorable and financially harmful regulatory treatment—though it should be noted that in 1987, on facts essentially identical to *Pennsylvania Coal*, the Supreme Court (albeit by a bare 5–4 majority) upheld an antisubsidence law, suggesting that it had reevaluated the situation as involving not singling out, but a general safety regulation.[36] In both *Nollan v. California Coastal Commission* and *Lucas v. South Carolina Coastal Council* as well (the two beachfront property cases authored by Justice Scalia), the Court appears to have been influenced to some degree by the appearance of singling out, where big burdens were being placed on landowners that had not been imposed on identically situated neighbors—in the Nollans' case, because they were rebuilding their home and so required a new building permit, in Lucas's case because his property was undeveloped when the new law came into effect, unlike his neighbors' property.[37] Finally, the concern about singling out may also explain the Court's unyielding treatment of regulations that result in permanent physical occupations or loss of all value. Such results are sufficiently rare, and sufficiently intrusive in most cases (albeit not all, as *Loretto* demonstrates), that a presumption that such laws involve the singling out of property owners for unfavorable treatment, and so require compensation, may well be justified.

There is thus much to be said for an approach to regulatory takings that focuses on whether a particular regulation, which imposes substantial losses on property owners, appears to regulate broadly and evenhandedly, or whether it imposes selective, unequal burdens. This is not to say, however, that such a rule is easy to apply, as the facts of the *Penn Central* case demonstrate. In *Penn Central*, a majority of the Supreme Court concluded that designation of Grand Central Terminal as a historic landmark by New York City did not constitute a taking, even though the consequence was to deprive the owner of $2 million a year in lost revenues, in significant part because the designation was part of a "comprehensive" landmark preservation plan that placed restrictions on "all the structures contained in the 31 historic districts and over 400 individual landmarks, many of which are close to the Terminal."[38] In other words, the majority emphasized that Grand Central had not been singled out by the city for unfavorable treatment. The three dissenting Justices in the case, however, fundamentally disagreed. They pointed out that "[o]f the over one million buildings and structures in the city of New York, [the government has] singled out 400 for designation as official landmarks," so that in practice in this case, "a relatively few individual buildings, all separated from one another, [have been] singled out and treated differently from surrounding buildings."[39] The dissent would therefore have found a taking. So who was correct? The answer depends on one's starting point. Four hundred designated landmarks is certainly a substantial number, alleviating fears of unfair singling out; but at the same time, it is a trivial fraction of the buildings in New York City, raising fears of arbitrariness which, the

---

36. *See* Keystone Bituminous Coal Association v. DeBenedictis, 480 U.S. 470 (1987).

37. *Nollan*, 483 U.S. at 835 n.4; *Lucas*, 505 U.S. at 1008.

38. *Penn Central, supra*, 438 U.S. at 109, 134 & n.32.

39. *Id.* at 138, 140 (Rehnquist, J., dissenting).

dissent also points out, do not exist with truly general zoning rules.[40] My own view is that because the designation of landmarks in New York was governed by an open, neutral, and professional process (the landmark commission included three architects and a historian among its eleven members[41]), the danger of political manipulation was probably sufficiently mitigated to justify the majority's decision to uphold the system. Reasonable people, however, can certainly disagree about that conclusion.

In closing our discussion of economic rights, it is important to acknowledge the vagueness and ambiguities that pervade this area of constitutional law. Of course, many areas of constitutional law are characterized by some lack of clarity, but the problem is especially prevalent in the economic arena because of the grave uncertainties that persist regarding the underlying purposes of the Contracts and Takings clauses, and the difficulty of translating what we know about those provisions into the modern industrial and postindustrial world, with its vastly more complex economic system than existed during the framing era. The result is a body of law whose fundamental legitimacy can be questioned. This is true of the Contracts Clause, where the Supreme Court has abandoned fairly plain restrictions on governmental power for pragmatic reasons since the 1934 *Blaisdell* decision; but it is equally true of the law of regulatory takings, which has essentially been made up out of whole cloth in the past century (lest there be any doubt of this fact, it should be noted that Justice Scalia himself, the primary modern proponent of regulatory takings law, has acknowledged that "early constitutional theorists did not believe that the Takings Clause embraced regulations of property at all"[42]). Nevertheless, limiting governmental power over property and contract is an important element of our system of government, and in any event, the basic structure of modern law in this area is probably here to stay. Given that, the best we can hope for is that over time, the law evolves to reflect the structural concerns that drove the framers to include the Contracts and Takings clauses in the Constitution.

---

40. *Id.* at 139–140 (Rehnquist, J., dissenting).

41. *Id.* at 110 n.8.

42. *Lucas, supra,* 505 U.S. at 1028 n.15; *see also* William Michael Treanor, *The Original Understanding of the Takings Clause and the Political Process,* 95 COLUM. L. REV. 782, 782 (1995).

8. RACIAL DISCRIMINATION AND AFFIRMATIVE ACTION
The Meaning of Equal Protection

Between 1861 and 1865, the United States fought the Civil War, the most brutal, devastating, and significant conflict in our history. Following the Northern victory, the country adopted three new amendments to the Constitution of the United States. The Thirteenth Amendment, ratified in 1865, ended slavery, thereby finishing the work begun by President Abraham Lincoln's Emancipation Proclamation. The Fifteenth Amendment, ratified in 1870, forbade the national government and the states from depriving U.S. citizens of the right to vote because of their race. Both of these are incredibly important provisions, of course, but they are narrow in scope and not part of our central story. The Fourteenth Amendment, however, ratified in 1868, is central to our story and indeed has transformed the American constitutional structure. It undoubtedly represents the most important change to our Constitution since the ratification of the Bill of Rights in 1791.

To understand the purpose and meaning of the Fourteenth Amendment, it is important to understand its context. In order for an amendment to become part of the Constitution, it must first be proposed by a two-thirds vote of each House of Congress. It must then be ratified by the legislatures of three-quarters of the states.[1] Congress proposed the Fourteenth Amendment in 1866, in order to provide a firm constitutional basis for its program of Reconstruction in the South following the Civil War. Congress was faced by recalcitrant, White-dominated governments in the Southern States that had lost the war but were seeking to undo its results by stripping their newly emancipated African American citizens of essentially all civil rights through pieces of legislation known as "Black Codes." Congress was also faced with a president, Andrew Johnson (who took office upon Abraham Lincoln's assassination), who seemed sympathetic to these Southern efforts and was using his powers to obstruct Reconstruction however he could. The Fourteenth Amendment was designed to end these practices, both directly and by empowering Congress to pass legislation prohibiting such state actions (Section 5 of the Fourteenth Amendment states that "Congress shall have power to enforce, by appropriate legislation, the provisions of [the Fourteenth Amendment]"). The amendment, which is quite lengthy, contains several provisions dealing with issues of the day that have little modern relevance, such as whether former officials of the Confederacy could serve as government officials

---

1. The Constitution also permits ratification by state conventions, but that method has never been employed.

and the validity of debt issued by the Confederacy. Section 1 of the Fourteenth Amendment, however, contains provisions that are central to modern constitutionalism. In Chapter 3, we have already discussed the importance of some of those provisions, including the first sentence granting *all* persons born in the United States citizenship (thereby reversing the Supreme Court's racist *Dred Scott* decision, which held that African Americans, even if free, were not U.S. citizens[2]); the Privileges or Immunities Clause, which the Court denuded in its *Slaughter-House Cases* decision; and the Due Process Clause, which has become the vehicle for incorporation of the Bill of Rights against the States. In this chapter and the next we examine the last provision of Section 1, the Equal Protection Clause, which states that "[n]o State shall . . . deny to any person within its jurisdiction the equal protection of the laws."

The Equal Protection Clause is, in modern constitutional law, the primary vehicle for combating governmental discrimination. It provided the legal basis for the Supreme Court's decision in *Brown v. Board of Education*[3] in 1954 ending racial segregation in the South; and it was later invoked by the Court to combat sex-based and other forms of invidious discrimination. Notice that the Equal Protection Clause is in some sense a procedural, rather than a substantive provision. Unlike the Free Speech Clause or the Free Exercise Clause, it does not restrict governmental power in any particular, substantively defined area. Instead, it is a guarantee of *equality*. When the government acts evenly toward all citizens, no equal protection question arises, no matter how seemingly unfair the treatment. It is only when people are treated unequally—in other words, when the government discriminates among citizens—that equality concerns are triggered.

What is the underlying purpose, the principle enacted by the Equal Protection Clause? It is tempting to respond that the principle is simply one of nondiscrimination—that states should not discriminate among their citizens. That answer, however, is both incomplete and unsatisfying. The difficulty is that the word "discrimination" is not self-defining. It cannot mean treating people differently, because *all* legislation does that. For example, speed limits "discriminate" against people who like to drive fast, and bans on smoking in restaurants "discriminate" against smokers. More broadly, as we noted in the last chapter, it is the norm for government regulation to create winners and losers, yet that alone cannot violate the equal protection principle (or any other constitutional rule). The context of the adoption of the Fourteenth Amendment makes it clear that the framers were focused on differential mistreatment of coherent *groups*, not simply individuals who happen to be disadvantaged by a law. In other words, the evil that the authors of the Fourteenth Amendment sought to combat was that a group within the

---

2. Dred Scott v. Sandford, 60 U.S. (19 How.) 393 (1857).
3. 347 U.S. 453 (1954).

People as a whole, constituting a majority, might use its control over the government to oppress other, minority groups, to strip them of rights, power, and participation in government. It should be noted that this particular concern, that divisions *within* the People would lead to misuse of governmental power, was not a prominent one during the framing era. Other than James Madison's personal and not widely shared concerns on behalf of the propertied classes, the framers' primary focus, as we have discussed, was on conflict between the State and the People as a whole—in other words, it was to protect the People from self-serving representatives and other government officials. Given the context of the American Revolution and the struggle against a distant monarchy, it must have seemed a fanciful fear that the People would turn on themselves. Moreover, as we know, the Bill of Rights was designed to restrict the powers of the *national* government, which was feared because of its remoteness and power. State governments, to the contrary, were seen as defenders of the People against the national government.

By 1866, however, perspectives had changed. The realities of slavery, the Civil War, and Reconstruction had made it clear that at least for some citizens, state governments were most definitely not a source of protection. Instead, the Black Codes demonstrated that the states had become vehicles for oppression by some citizens over others. More basically, the very juxtaposition of large African-American populations in the South, living amongst their former owners and oppressors, made the very idea of a unified "People" seem naïve at best. For Congress to ignore these divisions would effectively permit the South to undo the achievements of the North in winning a long and bloody war, a result that no Northern member of Congress could tolerate. Seen in this light, it is clear that the primary purpose of the Fourteenth Amendment was to prohibit racial discrimination, and in particular, racial discrimination by White Southern governments against Blacks. Indeed, it is tempting to conclude that this is the *only* purpose and function of the Equal Protection Clause. The Supreme Court suggested such a reading in its poorly reasoned *Slaughter-House* decision,[4] and more recently Justice Antonin Scalia has also pushed in this direction (though he inexplicably expands his definition to cover all racial discrimination, against other minority groups and even against Whites).[5] This temptation, however, should be resisted. For one thing, it has never truly held sway—as early as 1886, the Supreme Court invoked the Equal Protection Clause to strike down discrimination against Chinese laundry owners in the city of San Francisco.[6] There is also evidence that at least some of the authors of the Fourteenth Amendment had a

---

4. *The Slaughter-House Cases, supra*, 83 U.S. at 81.

5. Tennessee v. Lane, 541 U.S. 509, 56–564 (2004) (Scalia, J., dissenting).

6. Yick Wo v. Hopkins, 118 U.S. 351 (1886).

broader view of its purposes,[7] and in particular that the Fourteenth Amendment was designed to protect not only freed slaves, but also White Northerners who had moved to the South, as well as other Republicans in the South (during this period, the Republican Party, the party of Lincoln, was the party of Reconstruction; the Democratic Party tended to be more sympathetic to the South, and dominated Southern politics). Most importantly, however, the Equal Protection Clause is not *written* in terms so narrow. The Reconstruction Congress knew how to write a prohibition of race discrimination alone—it did so, soon after the Fourteenth Amendment, in the Fifteenth Amendment—but in the Equal Protection Clause a broader principle was enacted.

If one accepts the proposition that the Equal Protection Clause establishes the rule that the states may not permit a part of their citizenry to use the powers of government to oppress or dispossess another part, the difficult question that then arises is how one is to define, precisely, the behavior that the clause prohibits. In other words, how is one to distinguish unconstitutional discrimination from the usual give and take of democratic politics, with its inevitable winners and losers? In drawing this line, the natural starting point is to consider the character of the discrimination that the authors of the Fourteenth Amendment would certainly have considered the epitome of a denial of equal protection—legislation by White-dominated Southern state governments, denying Black citizens their basic civil rights. What is it about such discrimination that offends constitutional standards? Contrary to some modern intimations, it cannot be merely the fact that racial discrimination is unfair to its victims—though unfair it undoubtedly is. When the State of Louisiana gave a monopoly to a single company to operate slaughterhouses in a large part of the state, including all of the City of New Orleans, this was undoubtedly an unfair discrimination against existing butchers, who were deprived of their livelihood. Yet in the *Slaughter-House Cases*, the Supreme Court quite correctly rejected constitutional challenges to this action, including one based on the Equal Protection Clause.[8] It was probably equally unfair for the New York City Transit Authority to refuse to hire anyone currently receiving methadone as a treatment for heroin addiction, including those who had successfully completed one year of treatment and so posed little risk of relapse; yet once again, the Supreme Court easily rejected an equal protection challenge to this policy.[9] More generally, many government regulations treat some professions or economic actors more favorably than

---

7. *See* Aaron J. Walker, *"No Distinction Would Be Tolerated": Thaddeus Stevens, Disability, and the Original Intent of the Equal Protection Clause*, 19 YALE LAW & POL'Y REV. 265, 283–284 & n.158 (2000).

8. *The Slaughter-House Cases, supra*, 83 U.S. at 81.

9. New York City Transit Authority v. Beaser, 440 U.S. 568 (1979).

others, and such favoritism is often unfair, but modern law generally does not consider such actions to raise serious equal protection issues.[10]

Where are the key distinctions between the types of permissible discriminations described above, and the paradigmatic example of unconstitutional discrimination, the Black Codes following the Civil War? First, Blacks in the South constituted a coherent, distinct group in society, in a way that butchers, and even methadone users, do not. Second, the discrimination being practiced against Blacks in the South was not an isolated legislative victory by one group over another, it was part of a systematic effort to suppress and disempower an identifiable group of citizens. And third, the impact of the system of discrimination being practiced against Southern Blacks was likely to be to create a long-term division in society, between haves and have-nots, as opposed to merely a one-time redistribution of resources. It is the combination of these factors—group coherence, systematic discrimination, and pervasive and lasting social divisions and hierarchies—that epitomize the kind of official discrimination forbidden by the Equal Protection Clause. In the famous footnote 4 of the 1938 *Carolene Products* opinion (which we examine in more detail in Chapter 10) Justice (later Chief Justice) Harlan Fiske Stone made this point by suggesting that special constitutional scrutiny is required when laws are "directed at particular religious . . . or national . . . or racial minorities," because "prejudice against discrete and insular minorities may be a special condition, which tends seriously to curtail the operation of those political processes ordinarily to be relied upon to protect minorities, and which may call for a correspondingly more searching judicial inquiry."[11]

There are sound, structural reasons why the Equal Protection Clause is best read as targeting systematic discrimination against coherent groups, and not merely "unfair" discrimination as such. Unfair discrimination might be defined as any governmental policy that economically favors one group of citizens over another, without a rational, public interest–oriented reason. The difficulty is that such "discrimination" is pervasive in modern government. Once the State becomes actively involved in regulating the economy, economic and social groups will inevitably seek to influence government to adopt policies favoring them, thereby leaving others at a relative disadvantage. That is an inevitable part of democratic politics (though hopefully that is not all that democratic politics is). To read the Equal Protection Clause to bring all such laws into question would

---

10. *See, e.g.,* Railway Express Agency v. New York, 336 U.S. 106 (1949) (upholding law banning commercial advertising vehicles, but permitting delivery trucks to carry advertising); Williamson v. Lee Optical, 348 U.S. 483 (1955) (upholding law forbidding opticians to even duplicate glasses, without a prescription from an optometrist or ophthalmologist); Fitzgerald v. Facing Association of Central Iowa, 539 U.S. 103 (2003) (upholding law taxing slot machines at racetracks more heavily than slot machines on riverboats).

11. United States v. Carolene Products, 304 U.S. 144, 152 n.4 (1938).

require the judiciary, in the guise of enforcing the Fourteenth Amendment, to test almost every act of legislation for "fairness," and so to have judges second-guess almost all legislative judgments. There is absolutely no reason to believe that the authors of the Fourteenth Amendment intended such an antidemocratic result. Moreover, so long as the winners and losers in this political context even out over time, there is no systematic reason for the courts to get involved. In other words, the simple fact of winners and losers in legislative battles does not pose a *structural* threat to our system of government, the kind of threat that constitutional provisions are intended to forestall. Systematic discrimination against coherent groups, however, does pose such a threat. Such discrimination threatens to create a permanently divided society, split between resentful outsiders and self-serving insiders. This is, of course, the same sort of threat posed by an establishment of religion, the very existence of which can be seen as a form of discrimination against members of nonestablished churches—in this sense, the Establishment Clause might be thought of as a narrow precursor to the Equal Protection Clause. Such a divided society is intrinsically weak, since its energies are wasted on internal squabbles (it is surely no coincidence that until Southern states abandoned racial segregation, they were among the most economically depressed in the country). In addition, and perhaps more to the point, divisions among the People tend to shift power greatly toward the State and public officials, since the groups in control of the government tend to forgive abuses of power by officials because of the benefits they receive, and disempowered groups, by definition, are marginalized and so cannot check the abuses of the State (it is also surely no coincidence that governments in racially divided communities, both in the United States and abroad, have a reputation for brutality, corruption, and incompetence). Finally, from the perspective of the classical republican strain that continues to exist in American constitutional thought (as discussed in the previous chapter), a tiered and permanently divided society is utterly corrosive of republican and democratic ideals.

The Equal Protection Clause is thus best read as designed to prevent the creation of a tiered society, or as Professor Cass Sunstein put it, to implement an "anticaste principle."[12] One clear implication of this analysis is that for governmental discrimination to raise equal protection concerns, it must be *group*-based. Unfairness toward individuals, while certainly troubling, simply does not pose the sort of structural, constitutional concern that the Equal Protection Clause is addressed to. This is not to say that individuals cannot raise equal protection claims if they are discriminated against. Of course they can, but such a claim must assert that he or she was discriminated against because of membership in a coherent group. Arguments have been made that the Equal Protection Clause is violated even when the government treats an individual differently from other

---

12. Cass Sunstein, *The Anticaste Principle*, 92 MICH. L. REV. 2410 (1994).

citizens in an unfair manner, and surprisingly, the Supreme Court seemed to accept such an argument in a case decided in the year 2000.[13] Such a claim, however, makes no sense in light of the structural purposes of the Equal Protection Clause, and more recently the Court appears to be backing away from its willingness to accept so-called "class of one" discrimination claims.[14]

One final point needs to be made about the coverage of the Equal Protection Clause. It is clear from the historical context and language of the Fourteenth Amendment that the Equal Protection Clause limits only the power of *state* governments, not the national government (the same is true of the Due Process Clause of the Fourteenth Amendment, but because the Fifth Amendment imposes an identical limit in national power, that matters less). This is in contradistinction to the various provisions of the Bill of Rights, which as we've discussed applied only to the national, not state governments until incorporation occurred during the twentieth century. The Fourteenth Amendment generally, and the Equal Protection Clause in particular, thus represents a dramatic shift in perceptions about the dangers posed by the different levels of government in our country. While during the founding period the greatest danger to the People was posed by a distant, national government (a reasonable fear, given that the framers had just finished a war of independence against a distant government in Great Britain), to the Reconstruction Congress of the 1860s, who had just finished fighting a war against rebel state governments, it was the states that could not be trusted. This was especially true with respect to equal protection, given the treatment of African Americans by the Southern states, both during the slave era and (through the Black Codes) immediately after the Civil War. The national government, on the other hand, was not under the control of tyrannical local majorities, and in fact had been acting in recent years as the defender of the rights of minority groups (notably, emancipated slaves). Thus, there was no perceived need to limit national power in this area—to the contrary, the Fourteenth Amendment *increases* national power, by authorizing Congress to enforce its provisions. By the middle of the twentieth century, however, it became clear that the Reconstruction Congress had been overly optimistic in thinking that the national government was free from prejudicial feelings, as instances of federal discrimination were challenged, and the Supreme Court began applying equal protection limitations on federal as well as state power through the Due Process Clause of the Fifth Amendment (the key cases applying such a principle involved challenges to the internment of Japanese American citizens during World War II, and to racial segregation of public schools in Washington, D.C. by Congress).[15] This process of "reverse incorporation" of equal protection principles against the

---

13. Village of Willowbrook v. Olech, 528 U.S. 562 (2000).

14. Engquist v. Oregon Dept. of Agriculture, 128 S. Ct. 2146 (2008).

15. Korematsu v. United States, 323 U.S. 214 (1944); Bolling v. Sharpe, 347 U.S. 497 (1954).

national government is of dubious legitimacy as a matter of text and history (though Professor Akhil Amar defends it[16]), but is now a well accepted part of constitutional law. Today, the assumption is that the "equal protection component" of the Fifth Amendment's Due Process Clause imposes exactly the same limits on national power as the Equal Protection Clause imposes on state governments.[17]

We now turn to a study of how equal protection principles have played out in practice, in the modern era. In this chapter, we begin by examining issues of race discrimination, starting with the paradigmatic example of discrimination against racial minorities, and then turning to the problem of affirmative action. In the next chapter, we explore the question of what other groups, and what other forms of discrimination, might pose equal protection concerns under the structural approach laid out above.

SEGREGATION AND RACIAL DISCRIMINATION

Brown v. Board of Education,[18] decided in 1954, was almost certainly the Supreme Court's most important constitutional law decision of the twentieth century (the only serious competitor is the 1973 abortion decision, *Roe v. Wade*[19]) and may well be the most significant constitutional decision in our history. In *Brown*, the Supreme Court held that officially imposed racial segregation of public schools in the South violated the Equal Protection Clause. In so holding, the Court rejected its own rulings in earlier cases, including notably its infamous 1896 decision in *Plessy v. Ferguson*,[20] that racial segregation was permissible so long as "separate but equal" facilities were provided to the different races. As Chief Justice Earl Warren, the author of *Brown*, put it, "in the field of public education the doctrine of 'separate but equal' has no place."[21] In subsequent years, the Supreme Court relied upon *Brown* to hold unconstitutional every aspect of the system of racial segregation, called Jim Crow, which dominated Southern society between Reconstruction and the modern era. The story of the epic, and ultimately successful struggle of the NAACP, under the leadership of the great Thurgood Marshall (who himself was later appointed to the Supreme Court), to fight racial discrimination in the courts has been extensively recounted

---

16. AMAR, *supra*, THE BILL OF RIGHTS at 281–283.
17. *See* Adarand Constructors, Inc. v. Pena, 515 U.S. 200 (1995).
18. 347 U.S. 483 (1954).
19. 410 U.S. 113 (1973).
20. 163 U.S. 537 (1896).
21. *Brown*, 347 U.S. at 495.

elsewhere, and I do not propose to rehash it.[22] Given the importance of the *Brown* decision to modern constitutionalism, however, we should consider what the decision means, and what insight it provides into the meaning of the Equal Protection Clause.

Despite the fact that no one today seriously questions the validity of *Brown* (undoubtedly in part because of its obvious, moral rightness), the *Brown* decision turns out to be surprisingly difficult to explain from the perspective of constitutional theory. The most fundamental difficulty is that the Supreme Court has been remarkably unclear about exactly *why* racial segregation violates equality principles, if equal facilities are provided. After all, in this situation no individual suffers any material inequality or deprivation, so where is the lack of equality? In *Brown* itself, the Court relied heavily on social science data suggesting that racial segregation generated "a feeling of inferiority" among Black school children, which impaired their ability to learn.[23] It turns out, however, that the social science data upon which the Court relied was highly questionable,[24] and in any event, such data cannot explain the Court's extension of its ruling against segregation to contexts such as buses[25] and golf courses.[26] If one tries to escape this conundrum by positing a constitutional "right" to associate with whomever one pleases, including members of other races, one is faced with the response, originally posed by Professor Herbert Wechsler, as to why the associational rights of those favoring integration should trump the associational rights of segregationists, who *don't* want to associate with people of other races.[27]

A second problem with understanding *Brown* has to do with the nature of the "right" recognized in *Brown*, and the nature of the remedy. When *Brown* was decided, the Supreme Court did not immediately order Southern states to integrate their public schools. Instead, the Court ordered the lawyers to reargue the case the following year and address the question of how desegregation should be implemented. This resulted in a second opinion by the Court, addressing remedies in which it held that Southern school districts should be accorded flexibility in how to implement desegregation, given the logistical difficulties involved,

---

22. *See, e.g.,* RICHARD KLUGER, SIMPLE JUSTICE: THE HISTORY OF BROWN V. BOARD OF EDUCATION AND BLACK AMERICA'S STRUGGLE FOR EQUALITY (Vintage 2004) (originally published 1976); MARK TUSHNET, THE NAACP'S LEGAL STRATEGY AGAINST SEGREGATED EDUCATION, 1925–1950 (University of North Carolina 2005); MICHAEL KLARMAN, FROM JIM CROW TO CIVIL RIGHTS: THE SUPREME COURT AND THE STRUGGLE FOR RACIAL EQUALITY (Oxford 2006).

23. *Id.* at 494.

24. Mark Yudof, *School Desegregation: Legal Realism, Reasoned Elaboration, and Social Science Research in the Supreme Court,* 42 LAW & CONTEMP. PROBS. 57, 70 (1978).

25. Gayle v. Browder, 352 U.S. 903 (1956) (per curiam).

26. Holmes v. City of Atlanta, 350 U.S. 879 (1955) (per curiam).

27. Herbert Wechsler, *Toward Neutral Principles of Constitutional Law,* 73 HARV. L. REV. 1, 34 (1959).

so long as they implemented desegregation "with all deliberate speed."[28] The result of this flexible standard, and of the policy of Southern states of offering "massive resistance" to the implementation of *Brown*, was that by 1964, ten years after *Brown* was decided, only 2.25 percent of Black school children in the eleven Southern states attended desegregated schools![29] Of course, there were important moments and civil rights victories during this period. For example, when in September 1957 Governor Orville Faubus of Arkansas deployed the Arkansas National Guard to block the racial integration of Central High School in Little Rock, Arkansas, President Dwight Eisenhower used U.S. military troops, including the 101st Airborne and a federalized National Guard, to force compliance with the judicial order requiring integration.[30] A year later, the Supreme Court unanimously affirmed that state officials had a constitutional obligation to follow the U.S. Constitution, as interpreted by the Supreme Court, thereby establishing the primacy of federal law.[31] The truth is, however, events such as those in Little Rock were minor victories in the grand scheme, with little effect on most African American children, who continued to attend segregated schools. Desegregation did not truly get implemented in the South until the late 1960s and early 1970s, as a result of aggressive enforcement of civil rights laws by the administration of President Lyndon Johnson, and the Supreme Court's authorization of extensive busing programs.[32] While an important chapter in American history, and ultimately a great victory for principles of equality, the story of the implementation of *Brown v. Board of Education* poses a dilemma for constitutional theory. The problem is that according to an individual rights/nondiscrimination reading of the Equal Protection Clause, when the Supreme Court decided *Brown* in 1954 it recognized a right, belonging to all Black school children, to attend public schools that were not racially segregated. In fact, however, actual racial integration did not occur until fifteen to twenty years later. By that time, *all* of the children whose "right" had been recognized in 1954 would have completed high school, essentially all of them in segregated schools throughout their school careers. This makes an utter mockery of the "right" to a desegregated education.

The two conundrums described above can be resolved only if we recognized that the Supreme Court's desegregation decisions have nothing to do with individual "rights" as such. Rather, these decisions have to do with constitutional

---

28. Brown v. Board of Education *(Brown II)*, 349 U.S. 294, 301 (1955).

29. James R. Dunn, *Title VI, the Guidelines and School Desegregation in the South*, 53 Va. L. Rev. 42, 44 n.9 (1967).

30. The events of the Little Rock Crisis are described in Keith E. Whittington, *The Court as the Final Arbiter of the Constitution:* Cooper v. Aaron (1958), *in* Creating Constitutional Change 9–21 (Gregg Ivers and Kevin T. McGuire eds., 2004); *see also* Ashutosh Bhagwat, Cooper v. Aaron *and the Faces of Federalism*, 52 St. Louis U. L. J. 1087 (2008).

31. Cooper v. Aaron, 358 U.S. 1 (1958).

32. *See* Swann v. Charlotte-Mecklenburg Board of Education, 402 U.S. 1 (1971).

limitations on the nature of decisions that may legitimately be implemented by government, and in particular, on the structure of permissible group dynamics within the democratic process. Most obviously, this perspective makes it abundantly clear why racial segregation in the South in the 1950s, both in public schools and elsewhere, violated the Equal Protection Clause. The reason, quite simply, is that the entire concept of "separate but equal" was a farce. Even if segregated facilities in the South had been materially equal—which they most decidedly were not—it was absolutely obvious that the whole point of the Southern system of racial segregation was to suppress, subordinate, and deny political power to African Americans as a group. Once one acknowledges this fact, the conclusion that racial segregation, as it existed in twentieth-century America, violates equality principles becomes not only logical but unavoidable. As Professor Charles Black of the Yale Law School (who was writing in response to the article by Professor Herbert Wechsler cited earlier) put it, "if a whole race of people finds itself confined within a system which is set up and continued for the very purpose of keeping it in an inferior station, and if the question is then solemnly propounded whether such a race is being treated 'equally,' I think we ought to exercise one of the sovereign prerogatives of philosophers—that of laughter."[33] Moreover, as Black points out, the history of segregation, and the details of its practice in the South, leave absolutely no doubt that this was in fact the purpose and function of the Southern system of racial segregation. In short, "separate but equal" was unconstitutional not because racial separation is always unequal, or because the system unfairly discriminated against individuals (though it surely did), it was because the system was intended and functioned to make one social group fundamentally unequal to another. Segregation was thus the paradigmatic example of a government policy, or set of policies, that was directed at a coherent group, imposed pervasive and systematic discrimination, and created lasting social divisions and hierarchies. Thus, it violated the basic, structural principle represented by the Equal Protection Clause.

A structural, group-based perspective on equal protection also illuminates the seeming mismatch between the rights and remedies announced by the Supreme Court in *Brown*. As noted above, if considered in individual terms, the Court's tolerance of over a decade of delay in implementing *Brown* makes no sense. If one reconceives the Court's task in the 1950s as correcting a systematic breakdown in democratic politics in the South, which had resulted in the complete political and social disempowerment of a large social group, the delay begins to make some sense. Racial segregation was an intrinsic part of the entire political and social structure of the South when *Brown* was decided. It was simply impossible to dismantle that system overnight, or even promptly, especially because in

---

33. Charles L. Black, Jr., *The Lawfulness of the Segregation Decisions*, 69 YALE L. J. 421, 424 (1960).

the 1950s the courts were engaging in this task essentially alone, with no support from Congress and almost none from the Eisenhower Administration (except for the dramatic intervention in Little Rock). The truth is that the courts on their own were never going to be able to do much more than chip away at the edifice of segregation, especially because much of it was private, and so not subject to constitutional control. It was only when the Civil Rights Movement under the leadership of Dr. Martin Luther King, Jr., and others, and especially the brutal response of White, Southern governments to that movement, galvanized Northern public opinion that real progress could be made, through passage of legislation such as the 1964 Civil Rights Act and the 1965 Voting Rights Act, which ended the complete exclusion of Southern Blacks from political power. Once those doors had been opened, courts were in turn able to step in more aggressively, authorizing broad remedies such as busing and redistricting, which could effectively dismantle officially imposed segregation.

Another good example of how a structural perspective clarifies the meaning of equal protection is miscegenation. During the Jim Crow segregation era, Southern states enacted "antimiscegenation" laws, which prohibited marriage between Whites and non-Whites (indeed, it was not just Southern states that adopted such laws; California prohibited miscegenation until its antimiscegenation statute was struck down by the California Supreme Court in 1948[34]). The constitutionality of these laws was challenged by Mildred and Richard Loving, an interracial couple living in rural Virginia (Mildred was of mixed African American and Native American heritage, while Richard was White). The Lovings had been dating for several years and got married in June 1958 after Mildred became pregnant. (They were of necessity married in Washington, D.C., because Virginia did not issue marriage licenses to mixed race couples.) In July 1958, the Lovings woke up to find law enforcement officials from Caroline County, Virginia, in their home, surrounding their bed.[35] When they told the local sheriff they were married, the Lovings were tried and convicted for violating Virginia's antimiscegenation statute, which made it a felony for any "white person" to marry any "colored person," punishable by a sentence of one to five years in prison for both parties. The Lovings were sentenced to one year in prison each, but the sentence was suspended on the condition that they leave the State of Virginia, which they did, moving to Washington, D.C. In 1964, the Lovings instituted a lawsuit challenging the constitutionality of Virginia's miscegenation laws, which eventually wound its way to the U.S. Supreme Court. Before the Supreme Court, Virginia argued that miscegenation laws did not violate the Equal Protection Clause because they treated the races equally—by definition, after all, in any miscegenation

---

34. Perez v. Sharp, 32 Cal.2d 711 (1948).

35. The Lovings' story is recounted in Mildred Loving's obituary in THE ECONOMIST. *See Mildred Loving,* THE ECONOMIST, May 15, 2008, *available at* http://www.economist. com/obituary/displaystory.cfm?story_id=11367685 (last visited Sept. 24, 2008).

prosecution there would be two defendants, one White and one non-White, so where was the inequality? The Supreme Court, in an opinion by Chief Justice Earl Warren, quite properly rejected this argument. "The fact that Virginia prohibits only interracial marriages involving white persons," Warren pointed out, "demonstrates that the racial classifications must stand on their own justification, as measures designed to maintain White Supremacy." This, he said, "violates the central meaning of the Equal Protection Clause."[36] As a postscript, after their legal victory, the Lovings returned to Caroline County with their children. Richard died in a car accident in 1975, but Mildred never remarried and passed away in 2008.[37]

While racial segregation is the most famous and historically significant example of the kind of government policy forbidden by the Equal Protection Clause, it does not of course represent the limits of what the Equal Protection Clause prohibits. It is thus generally accepted that governmental discrimination against racial minorities, including against individuals, violates equal protection principles. This is not surprising, since such discrimination does not occur in a vacuum, it is typically a part of a social system of subordination, akin to segregation. Sometimes, however, governmental discrimination raises more difficult questions, which can be illuminated by recourse to structural principles. Consider, for example, a historical episode we touched upon earlier, the mass internment of the Japanese American population of the West Coast during World War II. In the wake of the Japanese attack on Pearl Harbor on December 7, 1941, concerns arose that the West Coast of the United States was threatened by a Japanese attack. In response, military governors were appointed to coordinate defense of the area. On February 19, 1942, President Franklin Delano Roosevelt issued Executive Order 9066, which authorized military commanders to exclude "any or all persons" from prescribed military areas, and a month later Congress passed legislation making it a crime to disobey military orders issued pursuant to this authority. Soon thereafter, General John L. DeWitt, the military commander of the Western region, issued an order establishing a curfew on the West Coast for all persons of Japanese ancestry (the Supreme Court later upheld this curfew, in a narrowly written opinion[38]). In May, General DeWitt issued new orders, which required all persons of Japanese ancestry, including U.S. citizens, to leave the West Coast and report to inland "assembly centers," from which most were moved to "relocation centers." Pursuant to these orders, over 100,000 people, a majority of them U.S. citizens of unquestioned loyalty, were forced to leave their homes and spend years in what were in truth, despite the government's euphemisms, concentration camps. Most Japanese Americans obeyed

---

36. Loving v. Virginia, 388 U.S. 1, 11 (1967).

37. *Mildred Loving*, THE ECONOMIST, May 15, 2008, *available at* http://www.economist.com/obituary/displaystory.cfm?story_id=11367685 (last visited Sept. 24, 2008).

38. Hirabayashi v. United States, 320 U.S. 81 (1943).

these orders, fearful of the consequences of resistance given world events. Fred Korematsu did not. Korematsu was a natural-born U.S. citizen, born and raised in Oakland, California. He was a welder by trade and had worked in shipyards until he lost his job after Pearl Harbor, when the local union expelled all Japanese American workers. When the exclusion orders were issued, Korematsu's family reported to an Assembly Center, but Fred decided to remain behind, not because he wanted to make a political statement, but because he wished to remain with his fiancée, who was White. Korematsu was arrested on May 30, 1942, and eventually convicted of disobeying the exclusion orders.[39] With the assistance of the local ACLU office, Korematsu decided to fight his conviction, appealing it all the way to the U.S. Supreme Court.

On December 18, 1944, the Court issued an opinion authored by Justice Hugo Black, otherwise known as a great civil libertarian, affirming Korematsu's conviction.[40] The opinion begins by conceding that the government's actions here were "immediately suspect" because they "curtail the civil rights of a single racial group."[41] Ultimately, however, the Court concluded that given the military threat the nation faced in the spring of 1942, it was not unreasonable for military authorities to take the steps they did, and that the burden imposed upon Japanese American citizens was justified because "hardships are a part of war."[42] Along the way Justice Black specifically rejected the claim that "this [is] a case involving the imprisonment of a loyal citizen in a concentration camp because of racial prejudice."[43] Three Justices dissented and one of them, Justice Frank Murphy, went so far as to argue that the exclusion "falls into the ugly abyss of racism."[44] In subsequent years, Justice Murphy's opinion has prevailed. In 1984, Fred Korematsu's conviction was reversed by a federal district court, based on evidence that the government had withheld important information from the courts during the original litigation.[45] Four years later, Congress enacted legislation repudiating the Internment and granting compensation to surviving internees.[46] It is tempting therefore, to conclude, that *Korematsu* was simply a mistake, a product of wartime hysteria, with no consequences for "normal" constitutional law. In fact, however, *Korematsu* reflects a basic fissure in constitutional law. If the Equal Protection Clause (or more accurately in *Korematsu*, the "equal protection component" of the Fifth Amendment's Due Process Clause, since the Internment

---

39. *See* Neil Gotanda, *The Story of* Korematsu: *The Japanese-American Cases* 267–268 in CONSTITUTIONAL LAW STORIES (Michael C. Dorf ed., 2004).

40. Korematsu v. United States, 323 U.S. 214 (1944).

41. *Id.* at 216.

42. *Id.* at 219.

43. *Id.* at 223.

44. *Id.* at 233 (Murphy, J., dissenting).

45. Korematsu v. United States, 584 F.Supp. 1406 (N.D. Cal. 1984).

46. Gotanda, *supra, The Story of* Korematsu: *The Japanese-American Cases* at 283.

was a federal not a state policy) is seen as creating a personal right against racial discrimination, then clearly what happened to Fred Korematsu was constitutionally troubling. Personal rights, however, are never absolute—they must always yield to pressing public necessity. And in *Korematsu*, the Court perceived the Internment to be justified by precisely such a necessity, to wit, a dangerous threat to national security during wartime. This argument is sufficiently persuasive that even today, there are respected voices, including that of Richard Posner, a federal appellate judge and leading legal intellectual, who argue that the Internment was justified by military necessity.[47] From a structural perspective, however, this argument will not wash. The whole point of structural limitations on state power is to prohibit certain kinds of government action because they are destructive of our system of government. It is no answer, when the government is violating a *structural* prohibition, for it to say "yes, but we have a really good reason for doing what we did," as essentially the government did in *Korematsu*. Given that during the Internment, the government singled out a distinct, coherent group of citizens based on their race, imposed massive disabilities on them, and so created lasting social and economic divisions, this seems another clear example of the sort of group-based discrimination that the Equal Protection Clause forbids. This conclusion is buttressed by strong evidence, cited by Justice Murphy in his dissenting opinion, that much of the political support for the Internment came from White farmers on the West Coast, competitors of Japanese American farmers, who were not only racially prejudiced, but also stood to gain economically from the Internment.[48] Such action is a clear example of the systematic misuse of government power by one majoritarian group at the expense of a minority group, the very thing the Equal Protection Clause forbids.

The final question we will consider before turning to modern debates over so-called "affirmative action" is the meaning of the word "discrimination" in the context of equal protection law. This question was posed starkly by the facts of a famous 1976 Supreme Court decision called *Washington v. Davis*.[49] The government of Washington, D.C. used a written test of verbal and reading skills to screen applicants for jobs as police officers. The plaintiffs in the case, Black applicants for police jobs who had been rejected because of their test scores, produced evidence showing that a higher percentage of Black applicants failed the test than White applicants, and on that basis argued that use of the test violated equal protection principles. There was no evidence, however, that the test

---

47. RICHARD A. POSNER, LAW, PRAGMATISM, AND DEMOCRACY 293–295 (Harvard 2003).

48. *Korematsu, supra*, 323 U.S. at 239–240 & n.12. *See also* Andrew E. Taslitz, *Stories of Fourth Amendment Disrespect: From Elian to Internment*, 70 FORDHAM L. REV. 2257, 2307 & n.317 (2002).

49. 426 U.S. 229 (1976).

had been adopted for the purposes of excluding minority candidates. Based on these facts, the Supreme Court rejected the plaintiffs' claim, finding no constitutional violation. Crucial to this result was the Court's holding that in order to prove a violation of the Equal Protection Clause, one must demonstrate that the government has acted with "a racially discriminatory purpose"; "a racially disproportionate impact" is not enough.[50] Let us consider the implications of this holding. At some level, the *Washington v. Davis* Court's equation of discrimination with discriminatory purpose, or intent, seems to accord with common sense—after all, isn't that what discrimination means? Furthermore, the Court surely was correct that racially disproportionate impact alone cannot violate the Constitution. In our complex, diverse society, composed of myriad racial, ethnic, and other groups, it will be inevitable that innocently intended decisions will have disproportionate effects. Imagine, for example, that a diverse, urban public school district, faced with tight funding and perhaps a growing obesity problem among students, decides to reallocate some resources from its music programs to its athletic programs. Might it be that such a decision might disproportionately harm certain ethnic or religious groups (perhaps Asian Americans, or Jewish Americans)? Yet surely that does not make the decision constitutionally suspect. Or imagine that the government decides to raise income tax rates on high-income individuals. Given the distribution of income across racial groups in this country,[51] such a decision is likely to disproportionately impact White and Asian Americans; yet once again, surely that is not a constitutional problem.

The above considerations suggest that the Supreme Court clearly got it right in *Washington v. Davis*. Take a closer look, however, and this conclusion is far less obviously correct. The question one should ask is, why did Black candidates have more trouble passing the D.C. police department's written test than White candidates? The answer, at least in part, must of course be past discrimination. Remember, Washington, D.C. is a Southern city, which practiced legal, racial segregation of its public schools (and other aspects of public life) until the 1950s. The Court's decision in *Brown v. Board of Education* obviously did not miraculously end all societal discrimination in 1954, and such discrimination surely plays a part in continuing achievement gaps between Blacks and Whites in this country (especially in 1976, when actual integration was just being achieved). Seen in this light, the effect of the written test was to continue, and indeed exacerbate, the effects of past discrimination on Blacks, and the Court's holding that use of the test was permissible was effectively a statement that the Equal Protection Clause permits the government to act in this manner. Put differently,

---

50. *Id.* at 239.

51. *See* Carmen DeNavas-Wait, Bernadette D. Proctor, and Jessica C. Smith, *Income, Poverty, and Health Insurance Coverage in the United States: 2007* at 6 (U.S. Census Bureau 2008), *available at* http://www.census.gov/prod/2008pubs/p60-235.pdf (last visited Sept. 25, 2008).

the claim made by the plaintiffs in *Washington v. Davis* might be stated thusly: "We, and other Black candidates for police jobs, are at a disadvantage because of past discrimination against African Americans by the government and by others. In that context, achieving real equality requires that the government take steps to ensure that we are substantively equal, that we are not punished for the effects of past discrimination. At a minimum, if the Equal Protection Clause requires the government to treat people equally, it cannot take actions that actually make African Americans worse off by exaggerating the lingering effects of discrimination, as the written test that we challenge does." This is a quite a powerful argument, and one to which the Court does not really respond in *Washington v. Davis*. And indeed, from an individual rights perspective, it is not clear what the correct response here is. After all, to say to the Black candidates that they are being treated "equally" despite the fact that they are disproportionately being refused jobs due to factors beyond their control and linked to past discrimination seems sophistic. Indeed, even if the Equal Protection Clause is seen as conferring "group rights" on racial minorities, it is hard to see how to respond to the plaintiffs' argument, since government policies such as the written test used by the D.C. police department most definitely do not contribute to equality between racial groups; to the contrary, they increase inequality.

The response to this argument must come out of a recognition of the limited function and purposes of the Equal Protection Clause. In fact, the Equal Protection Clause does *not* create a "right" to equality, either for individuals or even for racial groups. The authors of the amendment did not see its function as such (it is hard to imagine that even the most enlightened of members of the Reconstruction Congress who proposed the Fourteenth Amendment supported true racial equality, given the pervasive racism of the time), and that is not how the clause has operated since. Instead, the purpose of the clause is to prevent misuse of governmental power, where subsections of society use the government to suppress other subsections. The clause is not designed to ensure equality of outcomes, or indeed, even to require the government to act to undo the consequences of past social divisions. The truth is that a judicially enforced constitutional requirement of equality of outcomes across races, or even of compensation for past wrongs, is far beyond the institutional ability of judges to implement. The kinds of difficult policy decisions, about how to allocate resources, how to judge when current, unequal outcomes are a product of past discrimination, and how to balance these interests against the need for governmental efficiency, are simply not the kinds of things that judges do well. Rather, they are quintessentially the sorts of decisions we leave to our elected representatives. The judicially enforced Equal Protection Clause has the much more modest goal of preventing *current* misuses of State power. Seen in this light the written test in *Washington v. Davis* was constitutional. Absent discriminatory intent, it is hard to see how the test could be characterized as a *current* abuse of power by a White majority against Blacks. Indeed, all the evidence in the case suggested that the D.C. government had been making extensive efforts to recruit Black officers, and that in the period that the litigation covered, 44 percent of new police recruits had been Black.[52] Unwise, and perhaps even unfair, the test may have been, but given this factual background, it cannot be fairly characterized as an abuse of governmental power.

The practical implication of the *Washington v. Davis* "discriminatory intent" requirement, then, is that the government has no *constitutional* obligation to compensate for past societal discrimination against minorities, nor does it have an obligation to avoid exacerbating the impact of such past discrimination (of course, it may well have *moral* obligation in this regard, but that is a different matter). More broadly, the Constitution does not require the government to take steps to create a substantively equal society.

The next question we turn to is the more difficult one of whether the Constitution even *permits* the government to take such actions, in particular if the government's actions take account of race.

AFFIRMATIVE ACTION

"Affirmative action" is a generic term referring to governmental or private policies (though we will focus here only on the government) that distribute benefits such as jobs, government contracts, or admissions to educational institutions, to individuals based on their membership in some group that has faced prior discrimination. Affirmative action, albeit under different names, is practiced in many parts of the world with histories of discrimination, including South Africa (in favor of non-Whites), India (in favor of historically disadvantaged castes), Malaysia (in favor of native Malaysians), and parts of Scandinavia (in favor of women). In the United States, affirmative action policies generally favor racial minorities, especially disadvantaged minorities such as African Americans, Hispanic Americans, and Native Americans, and sometimes women. Such policies have proven to be highly controversial, both politically and as a matter of constitutional law. At the political level, California, Washington State, and Michigan have all passed popular initiatives banning their state governments from implementing affirmative action policies,[53] and the issue continues to be the subject of political battles in other states.[54] At the constitutional level, the key point of contention has been whether affirmative action policies violate the Equal

---

52. Washington v. Davis, 426 U.S. at 235.

53. California banned affirmative action in Proposition 209, adopted in 1996. Washington State followed suit with Initiative 200 in 1998, and Michigan passed Proposal 2 in 2006.

54. Linda Royce, *Affirmative Action Ban Heads for Ballot in 5 States* (March 5, 2008), *available at* http://www.cnn.com/2008/POLITICS/03/07/affirmative.action/.

Protection Clause. We will focus here on the constitutionality of race-based affirmative action. Gender-based policies raise similar questions, but are best discussed in the next chapter, when we will address gender-based discrimination more generally.

To understand the constitutional debate surrounding affirmative action, it is necessary to have a sense of the objectives that such policies seek to advance. Affirmative action is often justified as compensation for past discrimination, but at the most literal level that cannot be quite correct, because beneficiaries of affirmative action have no obligation to prove that they themselves were subject to past discrimination. When an actual victim of discrimination is provided compensation, either financial or by reinstatement to a job, for example, that is not affirmative action, that is simple justice. Moreover, while there is of course no doubt that racial minorities have suffered often grievous discrimination in the past, absent some highly contentious (and morally dubious) theory of racial obligations and entitlements, that cannot explain current preferences. Nonetheless, the compensation rationale can be revived with one of two arguments. First, affirmative action is sometimes justified as necessary to undo the specific effects of past governmental discrimination, such as an absence of minority police officers because of a previous refusal to hire minorities. Second, it might be that because of prevalent, past and continuing racial discrimination, all or almost all members of minority groups begin unfairly disadvantaged vis-à-vis Whites, in competing for jobs, contracts, college slots, etc. If so, then racial preferences merely even the playing field, restoring fairness. While both of these arguments have some force, they are also controversial. Regarding the first argument, undoing the effects of past discrimination, it might be questioned why it is important or socially valuable to undo those effects at a group-based level when current beneficiaries have no clear connection, other than their race, with past victims. Regarding the second argument, there is obviously disagreement in our society over how prevalent current discrimination, and the effects of past discrimination, really are. Because of these divisions, in recent years defenders of affirmative action have migrated toward another set of justifications for racial preferences, which go under the rubric of diversity, integration, or ending racial isolation. In effect, proponents of affirmative action argue that regardless of past injustices, it is a positive good for our society, looking forward, to ensure that different racial groups mix in order to improve understanding, achieve social peace, and obtain the benefits of different perspectives. Opponents, unsurprisingly, argue that it is not fair to pursue these social goals at the expense of excluding innocent White (or other nonbeneficiary race) applicants who would have received a benefit, absent racial preferences.

Ultimately, the bottom line is that affirmative action is likely to remain a contentious issue in our society, so long as basic disagreements persist about both the need for such policies, and their moral implications. At the level of constitutional law, we can see the same divisions dividing the Justices of the Supreme

Court since they first addressed these issues in 1978, in *Regents of the University of California v. Bakke.*[55] *Bakke* involved a challenge to the admissions policies at the medical school of the University of California at Davis. The medical school admitted a class of one hundred students every year, and reserved sixteen of those slots for minority applicants, who were admitted through a separate admissions process from the general one. Allen Bakke, a White man, applied to the medical school in both 1973 and 1974, but was rejected both times, despite fairly high scores which were well above the scores of most students admitted through the special process. Bakke sued the university and won before the California Supreme Court. The U.S. Supreme Court then took his case and divided sharply on the result. Four Justices (William Brennan, Byron White, Thurgood Marshall, and Harry Blackmun, the more liberal wing of the Court at the time) would have ruled for the university, on the grounds that affirmative action policies did not pose the same constitutional problems as discrimination against minorities. Four Justices (Chief Justice Burger, John Paul Stevens, Potter Stewart, and William Rehnquist) would have ruled for Bakke on narrow, statutory grounds, holding that federal law prohibited taking account of race in university admissions (at least if the university received federal funding). The case was resolved by the vote of the one swing Justice, Lewis Powell. Justice Powell concluded that any governmental use of a racial classification, including in an affirmative action program, was highly troubling, and required close judicial scrutiny (in the parlance, it required "strict" scrutiny). However, he also concluded that a public university has a strong, legitimate ("compelling," again in the parlance) interest in achieving racial diversity within its student body, and may take account of race in admission to achieve that diversity. However, he concluded that race can be used only as a "plus factor" in an otherwise open admissions process. Davis's quota was too blunt an instrument and so was held unconstitutional. Bakke thus won admission to the medical school, but the Court did not ban all uses of race in public university admissions.

In the ten years following *Bakke*, the Court continued to be highly divided on affirmative action issues, deciding many cases but failing to reach agreement on the proper legal standard. In the late 1980s, however, a new, more conservative majority had arisen on the Supreme Court, thanks to the appointments of President Ronald Reagan. (It is worth noting that between 1968, when Richard Nixon was elected president, and 1993, when Bill Clinton took office, there was not a single Democratic appointment to the Supreme Court, because the only Democratic president during that time, Jimmy Carter, faced no vacancies during his four years in office). Since that time, a majority of the Court (albeit a narrow, 5–4 majority) has consistently held that *all* governmental uses of race, including affirmative action, are highly suspicious under the Equal

---

55. 438 U.S. 265 (1978).

Protection Clause and require "strict scrutiny."[56] Furthermore, there was language in at least some opinions from this era, both in the Supreme Court and in the lower courts, suggesting that the *only* justification for affirmative action was to undo the effects of specific, past discrimination.[57] Indeed, two Justices, Antonin Scalia and Clarence Thomas, have gone so far as to argue that affirmative action as such is *never* justified, other than as compensation to the actual victims of discrimination, because (in Justice Scalia's words) "under our Constitution there can be no such thing as a creditor or a debtor race. . . . In the eyes of the government, we are just one race here. It is American."[58] In the decade of the 1990s, therefore, a growing consensus appeared to be emerging in the federal courts that governmental affirmative action was permissible only for narrow, remedial purposes.

Then, in 2003, the Supreme Court handed down a surprise. The University of Michigan Law School granted racial preferences in its admissions policy to members of minority groups who had been historically discriminated against, such as African Americans, Hispanics, and Native Americans. The stated goal of this policy was to create "diversity" among its students, and the specific admissions process used by the law school was to use race as a "plus factor" in an otherwise open process that took account of many factors, including academic indicators and diversity factors other than race—i.e., exactly the sort of policy endorsed by Justice Powell in his opinion in *Bakke*. Barbara Grutter, a forty-nine-year-old mother of two and owner of her own consulting firm (she was forty-three when she first applied to the law school),[59] sued the law school when she was denied admission, claiming that if she had been a member of a favored minority group her scores would have entitled her to admission, and so her rejection constituted racial discrimination in violation of the Equal Protection Clause. The Supreme Court, in another 5–4 decision, rejected her claim.[60] In an opinion authored by Justice Sandra Day O'Connor, the first woman to serve on the Court and a Reagan appointee who had previously voted with the conservative bloc of the Court on affirmative action issues, the Court rejected Grutter's argument that affirmative action was limited to remedial purposes. Instead, the Court reaffirmed Justice Powell's conclusion that student body

---

56. See City of Richmond v. J.A. Croson Co., 488 U.S. 469 (1989); Adarand Constructors, Inc. v. Pena, 515 U.S. 200 (1995).

57. City of Richmond v. J.A. Croson Co., *supra*, 488 U.S. at 493–494; Hopwood v. Texas, 78 F.3d 932, 944–945 (5th Cir. 1996).

58. Adarand Constructors, Inc. v. Pena, *supra*, 515 U.S. at 239 (Scalia, J., concurring in part and concurring in the judgment); *see also id.* at 240–241 (Thomas, J., concurring in part and concurring in the judgment); City of Richmond v. J.A. Croson Co., *supra*, 488 U.S. at 524 (Scalia, J., concurring in the judgment).

59. Bill Mears, *Supreme Court Hears Affirmative Action Argument* (April 2, 2003), *available at* http://www.cnn.com/2003/LAW/04/01/scotus.affirmative.action/.

60. Grutter v. Bollinger, 539 U.S. 306 (2003).

diversity, at least in higher education, was a social interest of sufficient importance to justify race-based affirmative action policies. The Court also concluded that the law school's "plus factor" approach to admissions was a permissible way to implement such a policy, because it was flexible and permitted all students to compete for all seats, so it was not unfair to White applicants. The same day, however, the Court by a 6–3 vote struck down a race-based admissions process for undergraduates at the University of Michigan, because it resembled the quota system struck down in *Bakke*.[61] Despite this mixed result, however, the University of Michigan cases clearly opened the door to the use of race as a factor in public university admissions and seemed to step back from the increasingly stringent approach to affirmative action of the previous decade.

Four years later, however, the Court changed course once again. This time, the challenge was to the use of race not in university admissions but in public schools. Two companion cases were before the Court.[62] In one, White students were challenging admissions practices for high schools in Seattle, Washington. The Seattle School District permitted students entering ninth grade to select which of the ten regular high schools in the system they wished to attend. If any of the schools were oversubscribed, the district used a series of tie-breakers to admit students, the second of which was the race of the student (the first was whether a sibling already attended the school). The racial tie-breaker was triggered if the desired high school had a student body whose White/non-White racial balance was substantially different from that of the district as a whole (the balance in the system as a whole was 41 percent White, 59 percent non-White), in which case preference was given to students who would bring the racial balance closer to the district average. Parents of students who had been denied admission to high schools because of their race challenged the system. One of the lead plaintiffs in the case was a woman named Jill Kurfirst whose son, Andy Meeks, suffered from hyperactivity and dyslexia. Andy's mother and teachers thought Andy would benefit from a small biotechnology program at one of the oversubscribed high schools, but he was denied admission because he was White. The second case involved a challenge to student assignment policies at the elementary school level in Jefferson County, Kentucky, which encompasses Louisville. Like Seattle, Jefferson County considered race in assigning students to elementary schools, again with the purpose of ensuring that individual schools did not deviate too broadly from the school district's racial balance (which was 34 percent Black and 66 percent White). This system was challenged by a mother whose kindergarten-aged son was assigned to a school ten miles from his house, because admitting him to a closer school, only one mile away, would have moved the school further away from the district's racial balance.

---

61. Gratz v. Bollinger, 539 U.S. 244 (2003).

62. Parents Involved in Community Schools v. Seattle School District No. 1 and Meredith v. Jefferson County Board of Education, 127 S. Ct. 2738 (2007).

In both cases, the school districts defended their programs on the grounds that school districts have a strong interest in increasing racial diversity and integration and avoiding racial isolation. Neither claimed that the use of race in school assignment was necessary to cure the effects of prior segregation—in the case of Seattle, because its schools had never been legally segregated, and in the case of Louisville, because the effects of segregation had already been found to have been eliminated by a prior desegregation plan.

The Supreme Court, again by a vote of 5–4, held that both of the school districts' plans violated the Equal Protection Clause. The main difference in votes between the *Grutter* decision in 2003 and this case was that in the interim Justice O'Connor, the author of *Grutter*, had retired and been replaced by Justice Samuel Alito, who voted against the school districts. The result in the *Seattle School District* decision (as these cases are known) was more nuanced than one would think. The leading opinion in the case, written by Chief Justice John Roberts (who was appointed to the Court in September 2005, after the passing of Chief Justice William Rehnquist, for whom Roberts had clerked), took a very harsh line, concluding that *Grutter*'s holding about diversity was limited to the context of higher education, and that school districts had absolutely no constitutional interest in "racial balancing"[63] as such. Interestingly, however, only four Justices (including Roberts) joined the crucial parts of this opinion, and since four is less than half of nine (the number of Justices on the Supreme Court), those parts of the opinion did not establish binding law. The crucial fifth vote for the result was provided by Justice Anthony M. Kennedy, who wrote a much more modest opinion. Contrary to Chief Justice Roberts, Justice Kennedy explicitly stated that school districts have an interest in eliminating racial isolation and may sometimes take account of the race of their students in doing so.[64] Ultimately, however, he concluded that in both cases before the Court, the school districts' use of what he called "a crude system of individual racial classifications"[65] was too burdensome on excluded students and should be reserved for situations where it was absolutely clear that no less burdensome policies, such as redistricting or the like, could achieve the school districts' goals. As a result, he found equal protection violations in both cases. Four Justices dissented, arguing that under *Grutter* school districts were permitted to take race into account to achieve diversity.

The divisions among the Justices in the *Seattle School District* case provide a powerful opportunity to explore some of the deeper uncertainties regarding the application of the Equal Protection Clause to affirmative action. Consider first the approach of Chief Justice Roberts, joined by Justices Antonin Scalia, Clarence

---

63. *Id.* at 2757–2758.

64. *Id.* at 2791–2792 (Kennedy, J., concurring in part and concurring in the judgment).

65. *Id.* at 2792 (Kennedy, J., concurring in part and concurring in the judgment).

Thomas, and Samuel Alito. Roberts argued, following other recent decisions, that serious constitutional concerns arise anytime a government entity classifies individuals based on their race. He also rejected the idea that the government had a legitimate interest in racial diversity, or in racial integration for its own sake, as opposed to as part of a more broad program of diversity such as that upheld in *Grutter*. The reason for this, he said, was that "[a]t the heart of the Constitution's guarantee of equal protection lies the simple command that the Government must treat citizens as individuals, not as simply components of a racial, religious, sexual or national class."[66] He concluded with the remarkable argument that the questions at stake in the *Seattle School District* case were essentially the same as the fundamental problem in *Brown v. Board of Education*, which he said was that "schoolchildren were told where they could and could not go to school based on the color of their skin."[67] Justice Clarence Thomas, going even further, equated the dissenting Justices' defense of the school districts' assignment policies to the arguments made by segregationists in *Brown*, because both ignored what Thomas described as "the color-blind Constitution."[68] In contrast to these views, Justice Kennedy and the four dissenting Justices had very different understandings of the relationship between this case and *Brown*. Justice Kennedy explicitly rejected the simple equation of segregationist policies with race-conscious policies designed to increase integration, recognizing rather that the goal the Court endorsed in *Brown* was "equal educational opportunity," including racial integration, not just color-blindness.[69] The dissenting Justices went even further. Justice John Paul Stevens, for example, described Chief Justice Roberts's invocation of *Brown* as a "cruel irony" because it ignored the power dynamics of Southern segregation,[70] and Justice Stephen Breyer, joined by Justices Stevens, David Souter, and Ruth Bader Ginsburg stated explicitly that the school district policies that Court had struck down were not only not inconsistent with *Brown*, they constituted "local efforts to bring about the kind of racially integrated education that [*Brown*] long ago promised—efforts that this Court has repeatedly required, permitted, and encouraged local authorities to undertake."[71]

Examined closely, the key division that emerges among the Justices goes to the basic question of what *Brown v. Board of Education*, and by extension the Equal Protection Clause, is about. The key principle that Chief Justice Roberts and his allies endorse is individual fairness, which in their view generally

---

66. *Id.* at 2757 (*quoting* Miller v. Johnson, 515 U.S. 900, 911 (1995).

67. *Id.* at 2768.

68. *Id.* at 2782–2788 (Thomas, J., concurring).

69. *Id.* at 2791–2792 (Kennedy, J., concurring in part and concurring in the judgment).

70. *Id.* at 2797 (Stevens, J., dissenting).

71. *Id.* at 2800 (Breyer, J., dissenting).

requires color blindness. They see it as an injustice of constitutional magnitude whenever the government denies an individual a benefit because of his or her race, which the Equal Protection Clause generally forbids. Justice Kennedy, in contrast, places greater emphasis on equality of opportunity as the core principle underlying the Equal Protection Clause, and so rejects the view that any governmental use of race is, ipso facto, constitutionally suspect. His response to Chief Justice Roberts's and Justice Thomas's endorsement of a firm color-blindness principle is that "[f]ifty years of experience since [Brown], should teach us that the problem before us defies so easy a solution."[72] Nonetheless, Kennedy remains suspicious of racial classifications because of the harm that he perceives as arising from them: "Reduction of an individual to an assigned racial identity for differential treatment is among the most pernicious actions our government can undertake. The allocation of governmental burdens and benefits, contentious under any circumstances, is even more divisive when allocations are made on the basis of individual racial classifications."[73] Ultimately, therefore, he rejects what he perceives as the blunderbuss approach of the defendant school districts. Finally, the dissenting Justices see racial integration as the key value underlying Brown and the Fourteenth Amendment. Justice Stevens emphasizes the importance of racial hierarchies, while Justice Breyer's opinion treats racial integration itself as the paramount constitutional value at stake in these cases, because of the importance of racial integration in the quest for true equality.

It is time now to return to first principles. Recall our discussion of the structural function of the Equal Protection Clause, which is to prevent majorities from seizing state power to oppress identifiable minority groups among the People. This reading is consonant with the history of the Fourteenth Amendment, rooted as it was in the Reconstruction and with broader constitutional structures. Chief Justice Roberts's opinion appears to completely miss this point. All of his emphasis is on individual fairness and the injustice to individuals of government-imposed racial classifications. The idea, however, that the authors and ratifiers of the Fourteenth Amendment in the 1860s, faced as they were with the massive task of, as Justice Breyer puts it, of "mak[ing] citizens of slaves,"[74] intended to enact as their key principle a rule of color-blindness, with no attention to underlying power arrangements, beggars belief. In effect, what Chief Justice Roberts and Justice Thomas do, in emphasizing color-blindness, is to try to convert the Equal Protection Clause's structural limitation on misuse of governmental power into an individual entitlement to be free of racial classifications. But that cannot be right. Individual fairness never was and cannot be the primary concern of the Equal Protection Clause. As we have seen, all of the major rights-granting provisions of the Constitution ultimately have a structural

---

72. *Id.* at 2791 (Kennedy, J., concurring in part and concurring in the judgment).
73. *Id.* at 2796 (Kennedy, J., concurring in part and concurring in the judgment).
74. *Id.* at 2836 (Breyer, J., dissenting).

rather than an individualistic focus, and that is even more true of the Fourteenth Amendment, born as it was in a time of enormous social division among the People, and indeed, a redefinition of who constituted the sovereign People through the inclusion of a previously excluded group.

On the other hand, Justice Breyer's emphasis on racial integration as itself the ultimate constitutional touchstone is also not entirely convincing. The concern addressed by the Equal Protection Clause is the misuse of governmental power, not private discrimination, and so it is hard to see how racial isolation alone, absent government action, poses serious constitutional concerns (this conclusion is implicit in the Supreme Court's consistent position that only state-imposed, or "*de jure*" segregation violates the Equal Protection Clause; private or "*de facto*" segregation does not). More plausible are Justice Kennedy's emphasis on equality of opportunity and Justice Stevens's discussion of the racial hierarchies. Equality of opportunity is indeed an attractive vision of the ultimate goal of the Fourteenth Amendment and is certainly consistent with the constitutional vision of the Equal Protection Clause. Again, however, Justice Kennedy's approach focuses too much on individuals and not enough on misuse of power, a mistake he compounds to the extent that his suspiciousness of explicit racial classifications is based on concern for "innocent victims." Ultimately, as we have seen, it is group dynamics and its impact on the political process that is the concern of the Equal Protection Clause, and it would appear that Justice Stevens's focus on hierarchical nature of racial segregation in the Jim Crow era, a hierarchy completely absent in the Seattle and Louisville situations, that best captures this idea.

At first glance, based on this reasoning it would seem that the Supreme Court was clearly incorrect to invalidate the student assignment policies in Seattle and Louisville, since it is clear that in neither city was there present the sort of systematic racial subordination characteristic of Southern segregation. As always, however, things are somewhat more complicated. What is clear is that the approach taken by Chief Justice Roberts and his allies, with its emphasis on formal race neutrality and individual fairness, is not supported by the Equal Protection Clause as properly understood. However, that does not mean that dissenting Justices' approach is correct either. In discussing the validity of the race-based student assignment policies, Justice Breyer and his allies are extraordinarily deferential to the choices of local governments to use race-based policies to achieve racial integration, because they perceive no constitutional concerns absent evidence of racial hierarchies. This, however, may move too fast. In his separate opinion, Justice Kennedy points to an independent reason to fear government policies that classify individuals, and distribute benefits, based on race, which is that such policies may themselves feed the sort of racial divisions, and disintegration of democratic politics, that the Equal Protection Clause is designed to prevent. As he puts it, "[g]overnmental classifications that command people to march in different directions based on racial typologies can cause a new divisiveness.

The practice can lead to corrosive discourse, where race serves not as an element of our diverse heritage but instead as a bargaining chip in the political process."[75] In other words, ill-considered use of official racial classifications can exaggerate rather than reduce racial divisions in our society. Of course, these concerns are less serious when an electoral majority adopts race-based policies that burden itself, as in Seattle, because then presumably the legislature is able to weigh these concerns, without bias, when it decides that race-based policies are called for. Nonetheless, because of the possibility of divisions within a racial "majority" (for example, on the basis of class), the possibility that racial classifications will increase racial divisions cannot be ignored. If, as Justice Kennedy argues, this is a serious possibility, it argues for a much more careful and skeptical approach to official uses of racial classifications, even for purposes such as increasing racial integration.

More generally, Justice Breyer's deferential approach fails to take account of the fact that in the modern world, not all misuse of governmental power in a racial context will be by Whites, even if historically that was the primary concern. While it remains true that (President Barack Obama notwithstanding) at the national level, and at the level of most (but not all) state politics, Whites continue to predominate, that is not true at the local level, where it is entirely possible to envision non-White groups, either separately or in coalition with each other or with Whites, implementing government policies to divert resources to themselves, at the expense of racial groups outside the power structure. Such misuse of governmental power, however, is as much a violation of equal protection principles as the discrimination practiced by Southern Whites during the first half of the twentieth century. The Supreme Court, unsurprisingly, has demonstrated an awareness of this possibility. In one of the first of its decisions elevating the level of constitutional scrutiny given to affirmative action programs, for example, the Court noted that when the City of Richmond, Virginia, enacted a set-aside program favoring minority-owned contractor firms (which the Court struck down), five of the nine members of the Richmond City Council were Black.[76] Of course, minority control over government does not compel the conclusion that an official policy of racial preferences constitutes an illegitimate use of power; but it certainly creates grounds for skepticism, just as courts would surely be skeptical, in most situations, of racially based policies that favored Whites.

The bottom line, then, appears to be—no surprises here—that the proper treatment of affirmative action type policies under the Equal Protection Clause is complicated. The extreme hostility to such policies evinced by Chief Justice Roberts and Justices Scalia, Thomas, and (apparently) Alito does not appear to be justified by the history or purposes of the Fourteenth Amendment. On the

---

75. *Id.* at 2797 (Kennedy, J., concurring in part and concurring in the judgment).
76. City of Richmond v. J.A. Croson Co., *supra*, 488 U.S. at 495–496.

other hand, race-based allocations of benefits always raise the risk of creating social divisions and so must be closely scrutinized to ensure that they constitute a use of race for constitutionally acceptable purposes, such as fostering racial integration and equality, and not simply as a means of using governmental power to seize resources. This skepticism means that courts must take a close look at any government program that allocates benefits based on race to ensure that a real problem exists and that the program is designed so that it addresses the problem directly, in such a way as to minimize the risk of creating resentment among those burdened by the program. Finally, courts must assure themselves that the reason for the government policy, the problem it is seeking to resolve, is a serious one, justifying the risks posed by race-based policies. It is tempting to go further and adopt a "limited purpose" analysis of the sort discussed earlier, in chapters 4 and 5, under which racial classifications will be permitted *only* for equality-enhancing purposes, such as facilitating integration or compensating for past discrimination. That, however, may go too far, by assuming unnecessarily that any use of race must be presumed to violate equal protection principles. It is in fact not hard to imagine the government using racial classifications, for example in medical or other forms of research,[77] which pose no risk of the sort of power abuse the Equal Protection Clause seeks to limit, and it seems silly to read the Fourteenth Amendment to prohibit such programs. In short, while skepticism toward race-based government classifications is clearly warranted, neither the history nor the structural functions of the Equal Protection Clause compel such a degree of hostility to such policies as to condemn them out of hand in all, or even most, cases.

Let us close our consideration of affirmative action by considering what such a skeptical but open approach to affirmative action implies for some of the real-world disputes we have touched upon, starting with the Seattle and Louisville student placement policies.

To begin with, it is obvious that in neither Seattle nor Louisville were the student placement policies a product of the sort of systematic, majoritarian abuse of power that characterizes a classic equal protection violation. In both school districts, the race-based policies did not have the effect of systematically subjugating one race, and indeed, did not predictably harm any particular race, since depending on the demographics of a particular school, any student of any race might have found himself or herself preferred or excluded. Moreover, insofar as the practical effect of the policies was to burden more White students, it is worth

---

77. For an example of such a research program, upheld by the courts, see *Hunter ex re. Brandt v. Regents of the University of California*, 190 F.3d 1061 (9th Cir. 1999), cert. denied 531 U.S. 877 (2000), in which the U.S. Court of Appeals for the Ninth Circuit upheld the use of race in granting admission to an elementary school run by the Graduate School of Education at the University of California at Los Angeles, because the school asserted that it required a racially balanced student body in order to pursue its educational research.

noting that in neither city do minorities make up anything close to a majority of the population (Seattle's population is seventy percent White,[78] while that of Louisville/Jefferson County is over seventy-seven percent White).[79] In that regard, the efforts of some of the Justices to analogize those policies to school segregation in the South border on the absurd. The fact that these programs appear to primarily burden members of the majority race appears to be a powerful argument for deference to legislative choices, because such choices do not implicate structural principles.

On the other hand, divisiveness is a serious structural concern, which as noted earlier may not be fully alleviated by the fact that a program burdens the majority. In Louisville in particular, the inflexibility of the school district's placement program, and its application to very young students, as early as kindergarten, suggests a lack of legislative attention to the risks posed by race-based policies that might well justify invalidating the program. Seattle, however, poses a much closer case. In Seattle, race was used for admission only at the high school level and was limited to racially imbalanced *and* oversubscribed schools, so that the effects of the policy were unlikely to be widespread or terribly controversial. The most troubling aspect of the Seattle program was its exclusive focus on "White" and "non-White" students, without any attempt to seek diversity among different groups of non-White students such as Asians, Blacks, and Hispanics (remember that 59 percent of the students in Seattle's school system were non-White). This singling out of one racial group, albeit a group constituting an electoral majority, is somewhat troubling, but given the overall circumstances, probably not troubling enough to warrant invalidating Seattle's program. This is not to say that Seattle's program is not troubling in some ways—Andy Meeks' exclusion from the high school of his choice certainly strikes one as unfair, for one, and one aspect of Seattle's policy identified by Chief Justice Roberts, which required all students, including mixed-race students, to identify themselves as members of a single race, and permitted school district employees to select a race for a student if none is selected, also seems quite demeaning.[80] But it is not troubling in ways that violate the Equal Protection Clause.

Race-based admissions policies at the university level, such as those challenged in the *Bakke* and *Grutter* cases, pose somewhat different issues than Seattle and Louisville, though there are also similarities. The basic similarity is, of course, that it is simply not plausible to portray minority preferences in university admissions as a form of discrimination against coherent groups, though some opponents of affirmative action seek to portray it as such, citing the fact

---

78. *See* http://www.ofm.wa.gov/census2000/profiles/place/1605363000.pdf.

79. *See* http://factfinder.census.gov/servlet/GCTTable?_bm=n&_lang=en&mt_name= DEC_2000_PL_U_GCTPL_ST2&format=ST-2&_box_head_nbr=GCT-PL&ds_ name=DEC_2000_PL_U&geo_id=04000US21.

80. *Seattle School District, supra*, 127 S. Ct. at 2754 n.11.

that affirmative action programs often end up disfavoring working-class Whites. The reason that this characterization is unconvincing is that the impact of affirmative action on Whites is incidental, a by-product of pursuing other policies, not intentional in the way that segregation was *intended* to subjugate Blacks. Racial preferences at the university level, however, appear to have a greater potential to create resentment and divisiveness than the programs in Seattle and Louisville, since their effect is not simply to move a student to another school, but to completely deny admission. Even here, though, the story is complicated. The fact that such policies apply to older students, generally adults (both *Bakke* and *Grutter* involved graduate school admissions, so the affected students were all adult, college graduates), and are implemented in a context where no one is assured of admission because of a competitive admissions process, suggests that they may cause less resentment. On the other hand, the stakes are much higher at the university level, because exclusion of particular students can deprive them of access to an affordable (remember, these are all public universities), elite education, with all of the ramifications that has for future life prospects. Moreover, the sense that one is competing for a small number of highly valued slots tends to heighten the sense of resentment when the competitive process is skewed. These considerations suggest that the type of absolute set-aside of minority slots employed by the University of California at Davis, and invalidated in *Bakke*, has too strong a potential to create resent and division and should be invalidated. On the other hand, a more nuanced program of racial plus factors such as that upheld in *Grutter*, which excludes no one from competing for slots, and which grants only small preferences for race, alongside other diversity factors, does not raise serious equal protection concerns. (It must be acknowledged that there were serious disputes among the Justices in *Grutter* over whether the University of Michigan Law School really was running such a nuanced program, as opposed to a simple set-aside disguised in those terms, but for the purposes of our discussion I assume the university's good faith.)

Outside of education, the most important context in which governments have implemented affirmative action is in hiring public employees and in awarding contracts to provide services to the government, such as construction or consulting contracts. The contexts in which such programs are implemented are so varied, and the issues often so complex, that across-the-board conclusions are hard to reach here. Some guidelines, however, do emerge. First, in reviewing such programs courts must be extremely diligent in assuring themselves that the programs serve some genuine, neutral government policy and are not simply a way to reward political allies in racial coalitions. This requires a close look both at the politics that produced the program and at the practical implementation of the program: Is it a vehicle for rewarding cronies? Does it focus closely on groups who need its assistance? Does it minimize the burden on disfavored groups? Second, courts must recognize that implementing preferences in the context of competitive processes such as hiring and contract awarding is likely to be highly controversial and divisive. As such, they must require governments to demonstrate that any racial preference policy is written narrowly and designed so that it will not result in gross disparities in result relative to a racially neutral process (i.e., individuals or firms who prevail as a result of preferences must possess qualifications in the same range as rejected candidates). Finally, racial preferences must not effectively exclude Whites and other disfavored races from the competitive process, because such a result is almost assured to breed massive resentment. Assuming these requirements are satisfied, however, there is no reason to think that the Equal Protection Clause imposes an insurmountable barrier to such policies.

It is worthwhile to consider one final thought, before we leave the topic of affirmative action. The above analysis suggests that so long as affirmative action policies are carefully designed and implemented, and motivated by a good faith desire to address a serious social problem, the Equal Protection Clause should not be considered a major barrier to such policies. This is not, however, to say that affirmative action policies are necessarily either desirable or socially beneficial. There are many perfectly valid reasons to oppose affirmative action policies, including the demeaning effect of racially typecasting individuals and the potential for such policies to stigmatize their beneficiaries. These objections, however, are rooted in policy concerns, not constitutional principles, and they are best addressed through the democratic process. The Constitution, after all, may not generally forbid affirmative action, but nor does it in most circumstances mandate it.

9. DISCRIMINATION ON THE BASIS OF SEX ORIENTATION, AND OTHER CHARACTERIST
Translating[1] Equal Protection

In the previous chapter, we examined the history and structural purposes of the Equal Protection Clause of the Fourteenth Amendment (as well as its judge-made twin, applying to the federal government), and we considered how the clause limited the government's power to discriminate on the basis of race, including both discrimination against racial minorities and affirmative action. Race discrimination was, of course, the original target of the Equal Protection Clause and remains in modern times the archetypal example of the type of discrimination the clause was designed to forbid. The nondiscrimination principle implicit in equal protection, however, has never been limited to race. Nowhere in the clause is race mentioned (unlike in the Fifteenth Amendment, which forbids discrimination in voting *only* on the basis of race), and there is no reason that the broad structural principle of equal protection has application only to groups defined by race. It is true that early in its history, the Supreme Court did suggest that the Equal Protection Clause should be so limited—indeed, the Court suggested that the clause prohibited *only* discrimination against African Americans, not even any other racial group.[2] That position, however, was rejected soon thereafter, when the Supreme Court applied the Equal Protection Clause to protect Chinese laundry owners against racial discrimination,[3] and by the time of the World War II Internment cases, the Court was able to invoke equal protection principles in evaluating (though upholding) discrimination on the basis of national origin against Japanese Americans, without dissent on this point.[4] Today, moreover, it is well accepted that neither the text nor the purposes of the Equal Protection Clause limit its scope to race discrimination alone. In this chapter, we consider what other forms of discrimination are sufficiently similar to race discrimination so as to fall within the purview of the Equal Protection Clause.

---

1. The idea of translation as a method of constitutional interpretation was developed first by Professor Lawrence Lessig of the Harvard Law School. *See* Lawrence Lessig, *Fidelity in Translation*, 71 Tex. L. Rev. 1165 (1993).

2. *See, e.g., The Slaughter-House Cases*, 83 U.S. (16 Wall.) 36, 81 (1873) (opinion for the Court by Justice Miller).

3. Yick Wo v. Hopkins, 118 U.S. 356 (1886).

4. Korematsu v. United States, 323 U.S. 214 (1944).

SEX DISCRIMINATION

We begin with what has undoubtedly been the most significant application of equal protection principles other than race, which is sex discrimination, an area of enormous importance both intrinsically and because of the light it sheds on constitutional analysis in this area. We can begin with a straightforward historical point—it is absolutely clear, as clear as such things can be, that the authors of the Fourteenth Amendment and its ratifiers had no desire to limit discrimination against women when they enacted the Equal Protection Clause. Indeed, because the Equal Protection Clause actually contained a provision that appeared to ratify restricting the vote to men (for the first time in our constitutional history), many leading feminists of the era opposed ratification of the Fourteenth Amendment.[5] Given this history, how then are we to justify employing the Equal Protection Clause to restrict sex discrimination, as the Supreme Court has consistently done since the early 1970s? The answer must be found in a return to first principles.

In the previous chapter, recall, we concluded that there were three key characteristics that exemplified the sort of discrimination forbidden by the Equal Protection Clause: the discrimination must be targeted at a coherent, social group, generally a minority group; it must be systematic, not merely a one-time phenomenon; and it must threaten to create lasting social divisions. By these standards, discrimination against women appears to be a peculiar target for equal protection law. After all, while women are an easily defined group, they are hardly socially separated out in the way that racial minorities traditionally have been. Women are not even a minority—they have constituted a majority of qualified voters since the Nineteenth Amendment was ratified in 1920. Finally, while discrimination against women certainly has been systematic in our society historically, it is not at all clear that such discrimination has produced the sorts of social divisions that race discrimination yields. More basically, sex discrimination is fundamentally different from race discrimination, and so the problems it causes are different, too. As historically practiced, race discrimination in this country is rooted in a desire to subjugate, and in emotions of outright animus and hatred. While there is no doubt that misogyny plays an important role in our society, it is hard to characterize the sorts of *legal* sex discriminations that our nation has historically practiced, such as the exclusion of women from voting until 1920 (upheld by the Supreme Court in 1874[6]), the exclusion of women from professions such as the practice of law (upheld by the Supreme Court in 1873[7]), the exclusion of women from certain types of jobs such as bartending

---

5. *See* ELEANOR FLEXNER, CENTURY OF STRUGGLE 146–148 (1975).

6. Minor v. Happersett, 88 U.S. (21 Wall.) 162 (1874).

7. Bradwell v. Illinois, 83 U.S. (16 Wall.) 130 (1873); *see also In re* Lockwood, 154 U.S. 116 (1894).

(upheld by the Supreme Court in 1948[8]), and as late as the 1960s the exclusion of women from jury service unless they specifically requested otherwise (upheld by the Supreme Court in 1961[9]), as being motivated by simple animus or a simple desire to subjugate. After all, given the structure of traditional society, when men succeeded in acquiring money and social power, their wives and daughters enjoyed the fruits of that success also, in a way that was antithetical to race relations during the segregation era. Instead, legal sex discrimination was designed to maintain social roles, and in particular, to ensure that women continued, in the words of Supreme Court Justice Joseph Bradley, "to fulfil the noble and benign offices of wife and mother," which were their "paramount destiny and mission."[10] Forcing women into that narrow social role of course had the consequence of economically disempowering women and so making them dependent on men, which was perhaps the whole point; but that dependence was not the equivalent of the economic and political subjugation of African Americans during the segregation era, not least because defenders of that social system at least claimed to admire and respect the social roles accorded to women.

One possible conclusion from the above analysis is that the sex discrimination in fact does *not* raise serious equal protection concerns because while it is undoubtedly unjust to individuals to force them into social roles they do not desire, such action does not threaten the *structural* values protected by the Equal Protection Clause—and, concomitantly, that the Supreme Court was simply wrong to conclude otherwise. This argument is buttressed by the fact that over the past several decades women have made enormous strides in the economic and political spheres, progress that (critically) has largely been a product of social and legislative reform, *not* judicial intervention. There is no judicial decision close to an equivalent to *Brown v. Board of Education* for women. This argument is frankly a plausible one, and may well be correct. I should note at this juncture that even if official sex discrimination does not violate the Equal Protection Clause, this does not mean that sex discrimination poses no constitutional problems. In particular, an argument can be constructed that the forms of sex discrimination targeted by the Supreme Court's modern cases in fact pose serious concerns under the *Due Process Clause* of the Fourteenth Amendment, a point discussed in Chapter 10.

Even in equal protection terms, an argument can be constructed that sex discrimination can, contrary to the suggestions above, create lasting social divisions. The reason is that women as a group are not, of course, homogeneous. While the traditional social system restricting female roles, implemented by law,

---

8. Goesaert v. Cleary, 335 U.S. 464 (1948).

9. Hoyt v. Florida, 368 U.S. 57 (1961), *overruled by* Taylor v. Louisiana, 419 U.S. 522 (1975).

10. Bradwell v. Illinois, *supra*, 83 U.S. (16 Wall.) at 142 (Bradley, J., concurring).

may have been supported by some women, others objected vehemently. (Of course, racial groups such as African Americans are also not homogeneous, but opposition to Southern segregation was surely close to universal among African Americans.) Moreover, when the Nineteenth Amendment granted women the vote in 1920, women became constitutionally recognized as full citizens, members of the sovereign People (if they were not so before). While it may not make sense to treat all women as a coherent group, women who resisted traditional social roles, and sought to achieve economic independence, might be described in these terms. Feminism has been an important, coherent political movement in this country since the middle of the nineteenth century,[11] and discrimination against this group of women has in fact been systematic and has created lasting social divisions, reflected in the "culture wars" of our modern politics. This then is the form of sex discrimination that the Equal Protection Clause arguably forbids—discrimination designed to retain and reinforce traditional gender roles, whether they be familial, social, or economic, because this is the kind of discrimination that triggers equal protection concerns. Admittedly, this argument is not without its weaknesses. In particular, it is not clear that women who oppose traditional social roles really are the sort of coherent social group protected by the Equal Protection Clause. After all, ideology changes over time, and this group expanded dramatically over the course of the twentieth century, as a percentage of American women. Furthermore, many men of course are also sympathetic to feminism and oppose the imposition of traditional social roles on women, again suggesting a lack of coherence to the protected "group." Finally, under modern circumstances, even if this posited, coherent group exists, it is far from clear that it constitutes a politically powerless minority of the sort requiring judicial protection if social divisions are to be avoided. In short, the theoretical roots of the Supreme Court's jurisprudence in this area are shallow. As noted earlier, however, there are alternative constitutional theories (notably the Supreme Court's "privacy" doctrine, rooted in the Due Process clauses of the Fifth and Fourteenth Amendments and discussed in Chapter 10) that might justify the Court's activism in this area. For the balance of this discussion, I will assume that there is some constitutional basis for the Court's decisions invalidating sex discrimination, which I will call "equal protection" for the purposes of simplicity.

The types of laws that the Supreme Court's cases dealing with sex discrimination have tended to invalidate tend to be ones that reinforce traditional gender roles. For example, in the first case in which it found sex discrimination to violate the Equal Protection Clause (decided in 1971), the Court invalidated an Idaho law that granted men a preference over women in serving as an administrator

---

11. *See* Sandra Day O'Connor, *The History of the Women's Suffrage Movement*, 49 VAND. L. REV. 657 (1996).

for an estate, thereby clearly reinforcing the social stereotype of financial affairs being a "man's job." Two years later, in the very important decision in *Frontiero v. Richardson*,[12] the Supreme Court held unconstitutional a federal law providing that in the military, a male service member could claim his wife as a dependent automatically, but a female member could claim her husband as a dependent only if she could demonstrate that she actually provided him with over half of his support. Such a law obviously disadvantaged working women vis-à-vis working men by paying an identically situated woman (i.e., one with a nondependent spouse) less than a man, and so reinforced the social role of women as economic dependents. Thus it clearly violated equal protection principles. In subsequent years, the Court invalidated two similar laws, one a provision of the Social Security Act, which disfavored working women by granting widowed mothers social security benefits based on their spouse's earnings, but not widowed fathers (thereby reducing the value of the deceased wife's earnings),[13] and the other a provision of another federal program that again made it easier for wives than for husbands to receive survivor benefits (in this case, as in *Frontiero*, by requiring husbands to prove dependency).[14] Around the same time, the Court invalidated a Utah law requiring parents to support their male children until they turned twenty-one, but requiring support of daughters only until eighteen. Again, such a law clearly was based on, and reinforced, the stereotype that men, but not women, needed to pursue higher education to support a family. Finally, the Supreme Court has also invalidated laws that punish *men* for undertaking non-traditional gender roles—for example, an Alabama law authorizing Alabama courts to require husbands, but never wives, to pay alimony upon divorce, thereby punishing financially dependent men;[15] and a state-run nursing school in Mississippi's policy of admitting only women, thereby burdening men who sought admission to what was traditionally considered a "woman's job."[16]

The cases discussed above (which represent a large fraction, but certainly not all of the Court's decisions finding unconstitutional sex discrimination) clearly demonstrate the power of the Equal Protection Clause's condemnation of laws that reinforce gender roles and stereotypes. The converse, however, is also true. When laws distinguish between men and women in ways that in the view of a majority of the Justices do not reinforce traditional roles, the Court has been much more tolerant. Thus, the Court has consistently upheld laws that seek to

---

12. 411 U.S. 677 (1973).

13. Weinberger v. Wiesenfeld, 420 U.S. 636 (1975).

14. Califano v. Goldfarb, 430 U.S. 199 (1977); *see also* Wengler v. Druggists Mutual Insurance Company, 446 U.S. 142 (1980).

15. Orr v. Orr, 440 U.S. 268 (1979); *see also* Kirchberg v. Feenstra, 450 U.S. 455 (1981) (invalidating Louisiana law giving husband sole control over property held jointly with his wife).

16. Mississippi University for Women v. Hogan, 458 U.S. 718 (1982).

compensate women for past social and economic discrimination against women as a group, even if such laws sometimes end up disfavoring nontraditional men, because such laws are not seen to reinforce social stereotypes. On this reasoning, the Court has upheld a Florida law that granted a property tax exemption to widows but not widowers;[17] a federal law granting female naval officers a longer time to earn promotions than male officers, compensating for the fact that women were not eligible for combat and many sea duty jobs (on which more later);[18] and a provision of the Social Security Act that (before 1972) calculated retirement benefits for women using a more generous formula than that for men.[19]

The Supreme Court has thus firmly embraced the principle that laws that impose or reinforce traditional gender roles violate the Equal Protection Clause, but that otherwise sex-based classifications are not always constitutionally suspect. This is not to say, however, that this distinction is always easy to apply, or that the Court has always applied it properly. One example of this difficulty can be found in one of the Supreme Court's most significant sex discrimination decisions, *Craig v. Boren*.[20] (The case is important primarily because in that case, a majority of the Court for the first time held that sex discrimination posed constitutional concerns at a similar level with race discrimination.) Oklahoma had a law permitting eighteen-to–twenty-one-year-old women, but not men, to buy 3.2 percent alcohol level beer (which the state considered "nonintoxicating"). The Supreme Court struck down this statute on the grounds that it reinforced the "stereotype" of young men as being reckless and wild and of women as being demure. The difficulty with this easy conclusion was that there was evidence before the Court (cited by then-Justice, later Chief Justice, William Rehnquist in dissent) that young men in the relevant age group were *eighteen times* more likely to be arrested for drunk driving than women, and ten times more likely to be arrested for drunkenness.[21] In other words, there were serious grounds for wondering whether Oklahoma was really acting in a way to reinforce social roles, or was reacting to real differences in behavior between men and women. Of course, the underlying issue in the litigation was a trivial one (especially because Oklahoma law forbade young men from buying 3.2 percent beer, but not from drinking it if provided by their female friends), but the underlying legal question was not. On balance, the majority's conclusion is probably defensible, but I find the case to be an extremely close one.

If sex-differentiated drinking ages provide a difficult question in this area of law, the problem is vastly intensified in considering situations where the government

---

17. Kahn v. Shevin, 416 U.S. 351 (1974).
18. Schlesinger v. Ballard, 419 U.S. 498 (1975).
19. Califano v. Webster, 430 U.S. 313 (1977).
20. 429 U.S. 190 (1976).
21. *Id.* at 223 (Rehnquist, J., dissenting).

treats men and women differently based on purportedly "real" biological differences. The underlying difficulty here is that there are, of course, real biological differences between men and women, most significantly the fact that women can become pregnant and give birth while men cannot, and it seems absurd to require the government to ignore this fact. On the other hand, it is often hard to tell whether in any particular situation the government is acting on the basis of need to recognize biological differences or on the basis of stereotypes about social roles. Most obviously, the Court has sustained laws that tend to grant mothers greater rights than fathers over nonmarital children, in particular in consenting to adoption, based on the reality that the father of a nonmarital child may not be present and indeed may not even be known.[22] A more difficult case is *Michael M. v. Superior Court*.[23] Michael M. was a seventeen-and-a-half-year-old teenager, living in Sonoma County, California. One night, Michael and a group of his friends came up to Sharon, a sixteen-and-a-half-year-old, and her sister at a bus stop. Michael and Sharon walked away and began to kiss. At some point, Michael struck Sharon in the face when she refused to consent to sex. Eventually, she and Michael had sex. Michael was then charged with violating California's statutory rape law, which made it a crime to have sex with any female under the age of eighteen, unless the female was your wife. Note that the California statute forbade all sex, not just forcible sex, but at the time penalized only men, since it did not prohibit having sex with underage men (the law has since been changed to make it gender neutral). Given the above facts, there is a decent argument to be made that Michael M. should have been charged with forcible rape, but he was not (perhaps because of the difficulty of proving lack of consent), and so he challenged the statutory rape law as a form of sex discrimination. The Supreme Court rejected his claim, concluding that the law was valid because the law merely reflected a true, biological difference between men and women, which was that only women became pregnant. The purpose of the law, the Court said, was to prevent underage pregnancy, and since only women become pregnant, it made perfect sense to forbid only sex with underage females. The obvious counterargument, of course, is that the real bases for the California law were the stereotypical beliefs that men are always the sexual aggressors and that there is value in female chastity but not male chastity, so that the law should protect only the former. Which is the correct characterization is hard to tell, but one does wonder whether the Court was unconsciously influenced by its views about male and female sex roles—views that might certainly have been reinforced by the disturbing facts of the case. Again, the correct answer is hard to definitively identify, though one does suspect that in this case the Court got it wrong.

---

22. Lehr v. Robertson, 463 U.S. 248 (1983); Parham v. Hughes, 441 U.S. 347 (1979); *but see* Caban v. Mohammed, 441 U.S. 380 (1979) (invalidating state law which flatly denied fathers of nonmarital children the right to object to adoption).

23. 450 U.S. 464 (1981).

There is simply too much cultural baggage in this area to believe that the California legislature was not significantly influenced by beliefs about female chastity and male aggression. The effect of the California statute, by making it perfectly legal for adult females to have sex with underage men but not vice versa, was of course to reinforce those views, making it highly problematic as a matter of equal protection law—but a majority of the Justices, given their cultural moorings, could not see this point.

The *Michael M.* case and the adoption cases are now somewhat dated, having been decided in the late 1970s and early 1980s. The problem of how to treat "real" differences, however, has not gone away. Notably, in 2001 the Supreme Court upheld the constitutionality of a federal law that made it much easier for U.S. citizen women than U.S. citizen men to pass on their citizenship to nonmarital children.[24] The case involved Tuan Ahn Nguyen, who was born in Vietnam in 1969 to a U.S. citizen father, Joseph Boulais, and a Vietnamese mother, who were not married. Under federal law, if Nguyen had been born abroad to a U.S. citizen mother, he would automatically have been a citizen. U.S. citizen fathers, however, passed on their citizenship to out-of-wedlock children born abroad only if they formally established paternity before the child turned eighteen. Nguyen was raised from the age of six by his father in Texas, but he never obtained citizenship, and his father never formally established paternity. In 1992, Nguyen was convicted of two counts of sexual assault on a child and faced deportation. At this point, his father sought to establish Nguyen's citizenship by proving paternity through a DNA test, but because Nguyen was now past the age of eighteen, his request was rejected. Nguyen and his father challenged the constitutionality of the citizenship statute, as sex discrimination. A bare majority of the Supreme Court rejected his claim, concluding that the law permissibly recognized a key, biological difference between men and women, which is that because women are necessarily present at the birth of a child, they are able to demonstrate their parenthood and have an opportunity to form a bond with the child, which may be missing with fathers. Hence differential treatment of fathers is justified by biology. Four dissenting Justices (interestingly including the only two women, and mothers, on the Court, at the time, Sandra Day O'Connor and Ruth Bader Ginsburg) wrote a vehement dissent, pointing out that given the accuracy of modern DNA tests, the government's argument regarding proof of parenthood is nonsense; and furthermore, that the government's argument that mothers have a greater opportunity to form a bond with the child was based "not in biological differences but instead in a stereotype—i.e., 'the generalization that mothers are significantly more likely than fathers . . . to develop caring relationships with their children.'"[25] As with the *Michael M.* case, while the issue is not

---

24. Nguyen v. INS, 533 U.S. 53 (2001).

25. *Id.* at 89 (O'Connor, J., dissenting) (*quoting* Miller v. Albright, 523 U.S. 420, 482–483 (1998) (Breyer, J., dissenting)).

free of doubt, one suspects that the Court got it wrong, allowing the majority Justices' own stereotypes to trump serious concerns about the use of the law to reinforce gender roles. On the facts of this case, the practical effect of this law was to punish a father, Joseph Boulais, who broke gender stereotypes in caring for his nonmarital son by treating him differently, and worse, than a mother who took the same steps.

The broader lesson from all of this is that the Equal Protection Clause does not impose the same limits in the gender context as it does with respect to race, though the precise lines are sometimes hard to identify. This is most obvious in the area of "segregation." Our society, including public institutions and universities, continue to segregate the sexes in a variety of ways, most notably in providing separate restroom facilities, housing (i.e., single-sex dormitories), and athletic programs. Such separation would surely be impermissible if done on the basis of race, but it is widely perceived that gender is different. Why? It is tempting to argue that the reason is "real differences"—i.e., that men and women have real, physical differences, but different races do not. On closer examination, however, this turns out to be an inadequate answer. First of all, the fact that men and women are biologically different, as of course they are, does not necessarily lead to a need for separation and privacy with respect to those physical differences. That is a social construct, which is not universal. However, because most people in our society do not currently believe that the purpose and effect of protecting privacy between the sexes with respect to their sexual organs is to reinforce traditional social roles, such segregation does not pose constitutional problems. Second, physical differences are not necessarily limited to sex. Suppose that we had statistical evidence that there were systematic differences, among different races, in their average size, strength, or what have you. Surely we would not think that this justified single-race sporting events! Yet in the case of sex, that is exactly what we do, even though many women, especially female athletes, are surely bigger and stronger than many men. Why this difference? It must be because the historical dynamic of racial segregation in this country is such that it is *closely* associated with division, strife, and subjugation. Separate sports programs for men and women simply do not have that connotation—indeed, if anything they have the reverse connotation, since they tend to break down traditional female social stereotypes of physical weakness and lack of competitiveness.

This is not to say, however, that sex segregation never poses constitutional problems. Consider in this respect the saga of the Virginia Military Institute (VMI). VMI is a state-run military college in Virginia that seeks to train "citizen-soldiers" for leadership positions in the military and in civilian society using an "adversarial method" of education on the lines of traditional military schools. From its founding in 1839 until the 1990s, VMI admitted only male cadets, and Virginia provided no comparable institution for women. In 1990, the U.S. government sued Virginia, asserting that VMI's male-only admissions policy violated the Equal Protection Clause. After losing in the lower courts, Virginia chose not to admit women to VMI, but rather to establish a separate school for women called the Virginia Women's Institute for Leadership (VWIL). VWIL, like VMI, was designed to produce leaders, but it had far fewer resources and it did not use an "adversative" military-style of education, instead emphasizing "a cooperative method which reinforces self-esteem," because Virginia asserted that such a system would be better for most women. On appeal, the U.S. Supreme Court held that VMI's admissions policy was unconstitutional and that the creation of VWIL as a separate institution for women did not cure the problem—in other words, that the Equal Protection Clause required Virginia to admit women to VMI.[26] Crucially, the Court's opinion by Justice Ruth Bader Ginsburg, herself a former litigator on behalf of feminist causes, held that VWIL did not constitute an adequate substitute for admission to VMI because it denied the admittedly few women (and men) who desired it access to VMI's adversative method. In other words, Virginia's assumption that men, but not women, would desire a military-style education was itself based on social stereotypes about sex roles, which Virginia was reinforcing.[27] The Court was surely correct in reaching this conclusion (as reflected by the fact that only one Justice, Antonin Scalia, dissented from the Court's conclusion, in an exceedingly poorly reasoned opinion from an otherwise highly eloquent justice), but the underlying issues here are difficult. In particular, the *VMI* Court emphasized that it was not condemning *all* state-sponsored single-sex education. But, it did seem to suggest that if single-sex education is pursued, the government cannot deny members of one sex access to education provided to the other, based on overbroad generalizations about what men or women desire. Given this standard, it is hard to see why a state could or would pursue single-sex higher education, since the Court's reasoning appears to forbid any *differences* between all-male and all-female programs, seemingly making the whole thing pointless (though admittedly under *VMI* a government might pursue single-sex schools at the middle or high school level, where truly equal facilities are plausible, and there may be good, biologically based and nonstereotyping reasons for segregating boys and girls).

If *VMI* is a relatively easy case, the same cannot be said of the other major area of dispute regarding separation of men and women, which is the exclusion of women from direct combat positions in the armed services. The Supreme Court has never directly addressed this issue—the closest it came was in 1981 when the Court upheld a law requiring only men to register for the draft, on the grounds that this made sense given the combat exclusion rule, but the Court did not consider the constitutionality of the exclusion rule itself.[28] The truth is, also, that the courts have generally been hesitant to intervene in military affairs, so that the constitutionality of the exclusion rule is unlikely to be resolved by a court.

---

26. United States v. Virginia, 518 U.S. 515 (1996).

27. *Id.* at 549–550.

28. Rostker v. Goldberg, 453 U.S. 57 (1981).

Nonetheless, it is legitimate to ask whether, as a matter of principle, this rule is permissible. The answer, however, is difficult. On the one hand, to the extent that the combat exclusion rule is based on traditional social notions of the role of men and women (i.e., that fighting wars is men's work), it clearly unconstitutional. On the other hand, modern defenders of the rule say that today the rule is justified not by stereotypes, but by the very real danger that female prisoners of war will be mistreated by captors, capture being an inevitable risk of warfare. This concern in turn is driven by a fact—that women are far more likely to be sexually abused than men—which, whether rooted in biology or in social customs, is a reality. Determining which of these explanations is more convincing requires knowledge about the true danger of capture, and of abuse, which is exceedingly difficult to determine in the abstract. It is, however, a question to which Congress and our military leadership should pay close attention in determining whether the combat exclusion rule should continue in place, if they are to meet their own obligations to uphold the Constitution.

SEXUAL ORIENTATION

Homosexuals, like women, are a group for whom there is no plausible argument that the authors of the Fourteenth Amendment intended to protect them from discrimination. Indeed, as Justice Anthony M. Kennedy pointed out in his opinion for the Court in *Lawrence v. Texas*,[29] a case involving a challenge to the constitutionality of sodomy laws, many scholars believe that the very "concept of the homosexual as a distinct category of person did not emerge until the late nineteenth century."[30] Nevertheless, can an argument be developed that proper translation of equal protection principles into the modern world requires the extension of the Equal Protection Clause's protections to this group? As it turns out, the answer to that question turns heavily on how one defines and understands the relevant group, a question that has already divided the Supreme Court.

The Supreme Court has addressed the question of whether, and how, the Equal Protection Clause protects homosexuals in only one case, *Romer v. Evans* decided in 1996.[31] *Romer* involved the constitutionality of Colorado's "Amendment 2," a voter-approved amendment to the Colorado state constitution that forbade Colorado's state government, and local governments within Colorado, from adopting rules protecting homosexuals against discrimination. (Note that because the U.S. Constitution trumps all state rules, a provision of a

---

29. 539 U.S. 558 (2003).

30. *Id.* at 568 (*citing* J. KATZ, THE INVENTION OF HETEROSEXUALITY 10 (1995); J. D'EMILIO AND E. FREEDMAN, INTIMATE MATTERS: A HISTORY OF SEXUALITY IN AMERICA 121 (2d ed. 1997)).

31. 517 U.S. 620 (1996).

state constitution can be invalidated if it violates any part of the federal Constitution.) Colorado adopted this measure after several cities in Colorado, including Boulder, Aspen, and Denver, had adopted local ordinances protecting homosexuals from discrimination. Conservative groups, opposed to such protections but unable to secure electoral majorities within these cities, turned to the state-wide referendum process to reverse these policies and succeeded in enacting Amendment 2. After several years of litigation, the Supreme Court ultimately held by a 6–3 vote that Amendment 2 violated the Equal Protection Clause. The majority opinion, written by Justice Anthony M. Kennedy, held that the fundamental problem with Amendment 2 was that it was motivated by simple "animus," dislike of homosexuals, and that laws that are motivated by nothing more than dislike of a class of citizens almost by definition violate equal protection.[32] A sharp dissenting opinion by Justice Antonin Scalia (joined by Chief Justice William Rehnquist and Justice Clarence Thomas) disagreed with several aspects of the majority opinion. For example, Justice Scalia argued (rather weakly) that Amendment 2 should not be construed as discrimination because it did nothing more than deny homosexuals "special treatment"—an argument that Justice Kennedy easily refused by pointing out that in the modern world, we all expect to be free of arbitrary discrimination as a matter of course.[33] The most fundamental disagreement between the two sets of Justices, however, goes to the heart of the matter here—it concerns the nature of animus toward, and discrimination against, homosexuals. In the central portion of his dissent, Justice Scalia argued that what Coloradans were expressing animus toward, in adopting Amendment 2, was homosexual *conduct*, and that they were fully entitled to express such animus. (At the time, the Supreme Court had not yet held that the government could not criminalize sodomy—it reached that conclusion seven years later, in *Lawrence v. Texas*.[34]) The majority, on the other hand, described the effect of Amendment 2 as discriminating against a "class of persons" or a "group of citizens."[35] In other words, the fundamental disagreement between the majority and dissent was whether homosexuals, defined by Amendment 2 as persons with a "homosexual, lesbian, or bisexual orientation," constitute a coherent group of citizens. For Justice Scalia, they do not, and animus toward homosexuals is best understood as dislike of particular conduct, which the State may legitimately criminalize if it wants to and so may certainly discourage with less severe sanctions. For Justice Kennedy and the majority, homosexuals are a coherent, defined group of citizens, constituting a cognizable minority, and so deserving of protection under the Equal Protection Clause.

---

32. *Id*. at 632–634.
33. *Id*. at 638 (Scalia, J., dissenting); *id*. at 631.
34. *Id*. at 640–644 (Scalia, J., dissenting).
35. *Id*. at 633.

That this is the key difference between the Justices in this area is not surprising. If, as we have discussed, the central purpose of the Equal Protection Clause is to prevent systematic discrimination against coherent groups of citizens because of the social divisions and political failures that such discrimination engenders, then the starting point of analysis in this area must be to define coherent groups. It must be understood, however, that while the underlying principle of equal protection remains stable, application of that principle will shift over time, as new understandings grow of what constitute legitimate, coherent groups of citizens. Note that under this definition, the question of whether homosexual orientation is genetic or otherwise immutable is perhaps relevant but is not critical—the central issue is group coherence. There is little doubt that in 1868, homosexuals would not have been considered such a group—even if homosexuals were recognized as a distinct category, which is doubtful, they would not have been considered a legitimate group of citizens, being defined rather by conduct that was unlawful at the time. Even today, of course, our society remains somewhat divided over this question, but it seems quite clear to me that at this point in our social evolution, even more so than when *Romer* was decided in 1996, we have evolved toward a fairly broad consensus that homosexuals *are* a legitimate, definable group of citizens, and that simple discrimination and animus against them is wrong. Given that social understanding, the Equal Protection Clause should be read to forbid discrimination against homosexuals, which is to say that *Romer* was correctly decided.

The question that remains is whether, given this conclusion, the Constitution prohibits *all* differential treatment of homosexuals. The truth is that in general, the question barely arises, because in most social contexts it is hard to think of *any* reason to distinguish between people based on sexual orientation, except animus. Sexual orientation, like race, is simply irrelevant to most social interactions, and so discrimination against homosexuals will inevitably fall because it has no reason other than to create social division. (I leave aside the rather politically unlikely scenario of affirmative action in favor of homosexuals.) As an example of this, consider modern sodomy statutes. Historically, the crime of sodomy, also called "deviant sexual conduct" or the "crime against nature," was defined as any contact between the genitals of one person, and the mouth or anus of another. Note that this definition did *not* limit itself to homosexuals; rather, it clearly applied against opposite-sex couples as well—for example, traditional sodomy laws would have forbidden all oral sex, including between married, heterosexual couples. Needless to say, in modern times such laws have become entirely unenforceable dead letter, with little or no popular support. As a result, in modern times, sodomy laws have been enforced solely against homosexuals, and indeed several states (including Texas) amended their sodomy laws to limit their application to homosexuals. Such a limitation, however, has *no* historical precedent or basis, and largely undermines the original purpose of the law, which was to channel *all* sex into procreative paths (in this sense, sodomy laws were part of a larger legal system that also prohibited masturbation and limited access to birth control). Such a limitation of sodomy statutes is therefore comprehensible only in terms of animus toward homosexuals, a desire to single them out and ostracize them from society (since single-sex sodomy laws make criminal behavior by homosexuals that is legal if engaged in by heterosexuals). For this reason, single-sex sodomy laws, and sodomy laws that while written generally are enforced only against homosexuals, are clearly unconstitutional—which means in effect that *all* sodomy laws in the modern United States are unconstitutional. Indeed, in *Lawrence v. Texas* in 2003, Justice Sandra Day O'Connor made precisely this argument in favor of striking down Texas's sodomy statute, which forbade only same-sex sodomy (the majority struck the statute down on other grounds, which we will discuss in the next chapter).[36] More generally, laws that explicitly treat homosexuals differently from heterosexuals must usually be considered unconstitutional, because they have no legitimate basis. Indeed, it is probably because of the lack of any such basis that such laws are in fact so rare.

There are two contexts where the above conclusion may not hold and where society continues to treat homosexuals differently—military service and marriage. Consider first military service, which is frankly the easier issue. Historically, the U.S. military discharged service members who were discovered to be homosexual (the policy is in flux as of this writing, with legislation passed by Congress authorizing the admission of homosexuals into the military, but not yet fully implemented). The general defense of this policy is "unit cohesion," the idea that acceptance of homosexuals into the military will create sexual tension or hostility within military units, especially because of the lack of privacy attendant to much military life, which will reduce combat effectiveness. The difficulties with this argument are manifold. First, it assumes hostility by service members toward homosexuals, an assumption that seems increasingly out of date given the evolution of social attitudes over recent decades and the increasingly widespread acceptance in the general public of the idea that homosexuals should be permitted to serve.[37] Second, even if such hostility existed, using it as a justification for exclusion of a group of citizens seems utterly perverse, permitting government to effectuate private prejudice—after all, using such an argument one could cite racism as a justification for racial segregation of the military, a policy that in fact existed until after World War II. The justification given for the exclusion of homosexuals from military service is thus unconvincing. Moreover, the policy

---

36. Lawrence v. Texas, *supra*, 539 U.S. at 579–585 (O'Connor, J., concurring in the judgment).

37. *See* Kyle Dropp and Jon Cohen, *Acceptance of Gay People in Military Grows Dramatically*, WASHINGTON POST A03 (July 19, 2008), *available at* http://www.washingtonpost.com/wp-dyn/content/story/2008/07/18/ST2008071802580.html (last visited 10/13/2008).

continues to be a highly contentious, socially divisive issue, because of its tendency to treat homosexuals as second-class citizens—precisely the kind of result the Equal Protection Clause was designed to avert. There is little doubt, therefore, that the exclusion of homosexuals from military service violates equal protection principles. This is not to say that courts of law should invalidate the policy, given the tradition of judicial deference to the military. However, it does mean that military and political leaders have an obligation to reconsider U.S. policy in this area, as a result of their independent obligation to obey the Constitution.

If the question of gays in the military poses a fairly straightforward equal protection issue, same-sex marriage is somewhat more difficult. The fundamental, constitutional question raised in the same-sex marriage debate is, of course, whether state laws that restrict marriage to a man and a woman discriminate against homosexuals in violation of the Equal Protection Clause. To date, only one court (a trial court in California) has held that same-sex marriage restrictions violate the federal Equal Protection Clause. Several state Supreme Courts have held that such bans violate the Equal Protection Clause or other equality provisions of their *state* constitutions,[38] and several other states have rejected such arguments,[39] but the federal question remains decidedly open—the only time the U.S. Supreme Court touched on the issue, it explicitly declined to address it.[40] As it turns out, constitutional analysis of same-sex marriage is complex because there is a fundamental difference between laws defining marriage as a union of a man and a woman and other instances of discrimination, which is simply that marriage laws do not explicitly target homosexuals. Unlike Colorado's Amendment 2, or the military's ban on gay soldiers, marriage laws do not exclude homosexuals from marriage as such, or otherwise single them out by name. Of course, to say that homosexuals remain free to marry people of the other sex is in practical terms absurd, since surely in the modern world access to the institution of marriage implies the ability to marry the person *of your choice*, a choice denied homosexuals by restrictive marriage laws. The significance of the lack of explicit exclusion, however, is that traditional marriage laws were not intended, or designed, to exclude homosexuals, or any other group, because at the time they were written, the idea of same-sex marriage was simply not conceivable to most people. This fact might mitigate the divisive impact of

---

38. *See, e.g.,* Baehr v. Lewin, 80 Haw. 341, 910 P.2d 112 (1996) (Hawaii—this holding was overturned by a state constitutional amendment); Goodridge v. Department of Public Health, 440 Mass. 309, 798 N.E.2d 941 (2003) (Massachusetts); *In re Marriage Cases,* 43 Cal. 4th 757, 183 P.3d 384 (2008) (California); Kerrigan v. Commissioner of Public Health, No. 17716 (Ct. S. Ct. Oct. 28, 2008) (Connecticut).

39. *See, e.g.,* Hernandez v. Robles, 7 N.Y.3d 338, 855 N.E.2d 1 (2006) (New York); Anderson v. King County, 158 Wn.2d 1, 138 P.3d 963 (Wa. 2006) (Washington State); Citizens for Equal Protection v. Bruning, 455 F.3d 859 (8th Cir. 2006) (Nebraska); Morrison v. Sadler, 821 N.E.2d 15 (Ind. Ct. App. 2005) (Indiana).

40. Lawrence v. Texas, *supra,* 539 U.S. at 578; *Id.* at 585 (O'Connor, J., concurring in the judgment).

traditional marriage laws, by alleviating feelings of exclusion. It is also true that, in principle, advocates of restricting marriage to opposite-sex couples can point to a neutral justification, which is the idea that marriage as an institution is designed to create and sustain a procreative unit, and that only opposite-sex couples can procreate biologically. Thus again, limiting marriage to a man and a woman, the argument goes, should not be seen as intended to harm or exclude homosexuals, but rather to pursue completely neutral social goals.

Of course, there are strong, indeed overwhelming responses to these arguments. First, the argument that traditional marriage laws were not intended to exclude homosexuals is belied by the fact that in truth, many traditional statutes made no explicit mention of the genders of marrying couples. Laws explicitly restricting marriage to one man and one woman are a modern phenomenon, almost all of them having been adopted since the mid-1990s (since that time, twenty-six states have adopted state constitutional amendments restricting marriage to a man and a woman).[41] There can be no doubt that *these* laws were indeed explicitly intended and written to exclude homosexual couples, because they were a response to court decisions extending marriage rights to same-sex couples. As such, they are indeed explicitly discriminatory and exclusionary. Second, the argument regarding procreation also seems a poor fit with modern marriage laws. After all, we permit many opposite-sex couples who cannot procreate to marry, including older couples and infertile couples. Furthermore, while it is true that same-sex couples cannot procreate biologically on their own, many same-sex couples can and do raise children, through adoption, with technological assistance (such as artificial insemination), or in other ways (as do, of course, many different-sex couples). Given the reality of families headed by same-sex couples, the exclusion of such couples from the legal rights and protections of marriage cannot be explained by a policy favoring procreation (unless we justified restrictive marriage laws as motivated by hostility to adoption and reproductive technologies, which seems insane). One is left then with the unavoidable conclusion that whatever its history, in the modern context the exclusion of same-sex couples from the institution of marriage is in fact a form of systematic, intentional discrimination. It is a discrimination that is rooted in genuine, deeply held beliefs, no doubt, but it is nonetheless a form of state-sponsored discrimination. The question is not whether religious institutions can exclude same-sex couples from their marriage rituals—of course they can. Nor is it a question of whether private citizens have an obligation to accept same-sex marriage as legitimate or appropriate—of course, they do not. The question is whether the *government* can be used as a tool to enforce those beliefs, by excluding a group of people from the benefits of a valuable institution created and maintained by the State. The logic of equal protection analysis suggests that it cannot.

---

41. Http://www.hrc.org/documents/marriage_prohibitions.pdf.

Ultimately, much of the anguish and divisiveness that arises over the question of same-sex marriage can probably be traced to one phenomenon, which is the merger in modern society of the government-sponsored institution of legal marriage, with all of its attendant benefits and obligations, with the private, religious institution of marriage. This is a relatively modern development, driven by the growth of a more regulatory and ubiquitous government.[42] The difficulty is, however, that the State-sponsored institution of marriage is, in the minds of most people, thoroughly intermingled with religious marriage, since state governments typically grant religious figures such as priests, rabbis, and ministers the power to perform legally binding marriage ceremonies. This mental conflation of distinct ideas may also explain why many strong opponents of same-sex marriage argue that such marriages threaten "traditional" marriage—an idea that is otherwise difficult to comprehend. The Constitution, of course, places no restrictions on what religious institutions do, but it does restrict State power, because of the dangers posed by the State. Once marriage became a State-sponsored institution, therefore, constitutional restrictions kicked in with important consequences. In 1967 this resulted in the invalidation of state laws forbidding interracial marriage, despite the long history of such laws and continuing hostility at that time among many Americans to such marriages (such hostility appears to have abated since then).[43] Today, the same process is gradually leading us to the elimination of state laws that forbid same-sex marriage. It must be remembered, however, that these constitutional developments affect only the government in its dispensing of benefits and obligations; they do not affect either private beliefs, or religious institutions, both areas where neither the government nor the Constitution treads.

AGE, DISABILITY, AND OTHER IRRELEVANT CHARACTERISTICS

Having examined the three most prominent and controversial areas of modern discrimination law—race, sex, and sexual orientation—we will close our discussion of equal protection by considering other types of discrimination that might implicate the Constitution. In approaching this question, it is important to begin by distinguishing between *constitutional* limits on government discrimination, imposed by the Equal Protection Clause, and statutory prohibitions on discrimination. There are many laws, both federal and state, that prohibit discrimination. The most important federal antidiscrimination provision, Title VII of the Civil Rights Act of 1964, prohibits discrimination in employment on the basis of "race,

---

42. *See generally* LAWRENCE M. FRIEDMAN, A HISTORY OF AMERICAN LAW 495–497 (2nd ed. 1985).

43. See Loving v. Virginia, 388 U.S. 1 (1967).

color, religion, sex, or national origin."[44] In addition, the Age Discrimination in Employment Act (ADEA) prohibits discrimination in employment on the basis of age (the protected class is employees older than forty), and the Americans with Disabilities Act (ADA) prohibits many forms of discrimination against the disabled. Furthermore, states and local governments have adopted a wide range of statutes and ordinances forbidding discrimination on any number of grounds, including but not limited to those identified by federal law. These statutory provisions typically limit both governmental and private discrimination, and are not necessarily linked to any constitutional prohibition. The underlying basis for them is a legislative conclusion that the protected criterion, whether it be age, race, disability, or what have you, is fundamentally a morally irrelevant characteristic, which should not be the basis for exclusion of individuals. In short, it is a conclusion that such discrimination is unfair.

Statutory protections against discrimination play an extraordinarily important role in modern society, and as a practical matter are far more significant than the Constitution, because they restrict private as well as governmental discrimination. Being legislative enactments, however, they are of course repealable. Given this fact, should the Constitution be read to prohibit governmental discrimination on the basis of age, disability, or other irrelevant characteristics such as marital status, etc.? It is tempting to think that they should. After all, discrimination or exclusion of individuals on the basis of characteristics such as age or disability, which are irrelevant and over which the individual has no control, seems fundamentally unfair, and un-American. In fact, however, over the years the Supreme Court has consistently rejected the idea that the Equal Protection Clause imposes significant limits on the government's power to discriminate on the basis of irrelevant characteristics such as age,[45] disability,[46] or poverty.[47] The reason, quite simply, is that—as we noted in the previous chapter—the Equal Protection Clause is not primarily concerned with fairness. Instead, it is concerned with averting the social divisions and ensuing consequences resulting from systematic discrimination against coherent groups. Seen in this light, it seems clear that neither the elderly nor the poor count as such a group. Age is particularly easy to reject—after all, how would one even define older Americans as a coherent group? What ages would we include? And is it plausible to argue that this group, even if it could be defined, suffers from systematic discrimination, given that almost all political and economic power in

---

44. 42 U.S.C. § 2000e-2.

45. Massachusetts Board of Retirement v. Murgia, 427 U.S. 307 (1976); Kimel v. Florida Board of Regents, 528 U.S. 62 (2000).

46. City of Cleburne v. Cleburne Living Center, 473 U.S. 432 (1985) (mental retardation); Board of Trustees of the Univ. of Alabama v. Garrett, 531 U.S. 356 (2001) (disability).

47. San Antonio School District v. Rodriguez, 411 U.S. 1 (1973).

this country is wielded by relatively older Americans? Similarly, it is hard to conceive of the poor as a coherent group, subject to systematic, intentional exclusion and discrimination. Who are "the poor"? How would one define them? Given the possibility of social mobility, are the poor a coherent group at all?[48] And is it really plausible to say that they suffer from systematic discrimination by the government, as opposed to neglect and indifference? There is no doubt, of course, that differences in wealth can be an important source of social division—indeed, many of the framers were deeply concerned about such divisions. But in modern society, it does not appear that governments systematically mistreat the poor in a way that implicates equal protection principles.

Disability poses a somewhat more difficult question than age or poverty. The disabled probably are a coherent group, in that they are easily identifiable and share common features and interests (though obviously there are wide variations among the disabled as well, but that is true of all significantly sized groups). Moreover, there is a history of often systematic and sometimes grotesque discrimination against the disabled, which in turn can create resentments and divisions. There are thus powerful arguments in favor of reading the Equal Protection Clause to impose strict limits on differential treatment of the disabled. There are also, however, difficulties that counsel caution. First, with respect to certain groups within the general class of disabled, notably the mentally retarded and to some extent the mentally ill, some differential treatment is necessary and inevitable, and it is probably beyond the competence of the courts to police when such treatment crosses the line into discrimination. Nor does this seem an area where substantial social divisions are likely, so equal protection concerns are not truly implicated, though fairness and decency certainly are. With respect to the physically disabled, there seems no doubt that gratuitous exclusion of such citizens from government services or benefits is dangerous and illegitimate, and quite plausibly does violate equal protection. The difficulty is that today, such express exclusion is rare. The real problem is failure to accommodate government programs to facilitate access by the disabled, for example by physically altering buildings to permit access (in a recent case, the Supreme Court recounted a particularly disturbing story of a paraplegic who was forced to crawl up two

---

48. Admittedly, in our increasingly multiracial society, it could be argued that race, too, is incapable of definition, like age and poverty. The truth is, however, that even though the concept of race lacks any scientific basis, and becomes more difficult to identify as interracial marriage increases, our *society* still maintains fairly clear and observable rules regarding racial identity—consider as an example the fact that President Barack Obama is almost universally described as African American, even though he is half White. If in fact our society reaches a point where assimilation and toleration have progressed to the point where rules imposing racial identity wither away, then racial groups, too, may lose the coherence necessary to trigger equal protection concerns—but of course, at that point the structural concerns regarding social division that necessitate equal protection scrutiny will also have disappeared.

flights of stairs to answer criminal charges against him, because the courthouse lacked an elevator[49]), or to adjust work responsibilities for disabled employees. That governments have a moral obligation, and sometimes because of the ADA a statutory obligation, to provide such accommodations seems right and just. But it is hard to translate this into a *constitutional* obligation. As we noted in the context of racial discrimination, the Equal Protection Clause does not generally oblige the government to take positive steps to assist or benefit citizens, even when the citizens' disadvantaged position is a product of past discrimination. With respect to the disabled, where the government is not generally the source of their disadvantage, such an obligation seems even more clearly to be absent.

In short, while the Equal Protection Clause is an important part of our modern constitutional system, it is also a distinctly limited provision. The clause (and its judge-made federal counterpart) has a distinct, structural function, which it can and should be aggressively interpreted and enforced to fulfill. It is not, however, a solution to all governmental injustices, nor is it even a bar to all unfair discrimination. As is so often the case, those are problems that the Constitution does not address, and so must be attacked through the democratic process, as we have increasingly done in recent years.

---

49. Tennessee v. Lane, 541 U.S. 509, 513 (2004).

10. THE NONTEXTUAL CONSTITUTION
Privacy and Other Unenumerated Rights

Up to this point in our discussion, we have focused our attention on various specific provisions in the Constitution, such as the First Amendment or the Equal Protection Clause of the Fourteenth Amendment, that impose explicit limits on governmental power. We now turn to another, even more controversial topic: whether the Constitution should be read to create "rights," or impose limits on state authority (as we will see, even the proper characterization is controversial), that are *not* derivable from specific constitutional text. Put differently, the dispute centers over whether judges are empowered to find/recognize/create (again, the characterization is controversial) constitutional rights, constitutional limits on governmental power, and constitutional principles more generally, that are largely disassociated from specific constitutional text; and if they are so empowered, how judges are to go about this task. This general topic encompasses what are undoubtedly the most politically divisive constitutional debates of the past half century, including the abortion debate, the debate over homosexuality, and the debate over assisted suicide. It is thus well worth our careful attention.

At first glance, it would seem as if the question we are asking here is a trivial one. After all, if the Constitution does not speak specifically to an issue, such as abortion (as it does not), how can judges possibly be authorized to enforce constitutional rules on such a topic? Isn't that just a power grab by judges? Many commentators (especially politically conservative ones, in modern times) argue precisely that. The truth, however, is more subtle. The difficulty is that while the Constitution does not speak specifically to the subject matters at issue in these cases, it does speak in general terms on the topic of "rights" not mentioned in the constitutional text. In particular, the Ninth Amendment to the Constitution, an important part of the original Bill of Rights, states that "[t]he enumeration in the Constitution of certain rights shall not be construed to deny or disparage others retained by the people." The obvious, literal meaning of this provision is that "the people" *do* possess what are called "unenumerated rights," other than those enumerated, or listed, in the Bill of Rights. Moreover, in James Madison's speech introducing the predecessor to this provision to the Congress as a proposed amendment, he specifically stated that it was included in order to counter the "plausible" argument that a Bill of Rights, "by enumerating particular exceptions to the grant of power, . . . would disparage those rights which are not placed in that enumeration; and it might follow by implication, that those rights which were not singled out, were intended to be assigned into the hand of the General

Government, and were consequently insecure."[1] Over the years any number of commentators, including notably Robert Bork, have sought to avoid the plain and obvious meaning of the Ninth Amendment through either denial or elaborate reinterpretations.[2] Recently, however, scholars such as Professor Randy Barnett and my Calvin Massey have thoroughly debunked such efforts, leading to the unsurprisingly conclusion that the Ninth Amendment means what it says—that the list of "rights" in the Constitution is not exclusive.[3] Of course, this conclusion only begins the debate, because it provides little assistance in figuring out *which* unenumerated rights to recognize; but it does go far toward answering the argument that judges act illegitimately when they move beyond the literal, constitutional text.

The Ninth Amendment does suffer from one serious limitation as a source of nontextual principles. Like the rest of the Bill of Rights as we know, it is directed only against the federal government not state governments, and it has never been formally "incorporated." As it turns out, however, this limitation is more fanciful than real. The reason is the "Privileges or Immunities" Clause of the Fourteenth Amendment. As we discussed in Chapter 3, this provision was enacted by the Reconstruction era Congress in order to impose significant limitations on the power of *state* governments. It seems fairly clear from modern scholarship that the limits on state power the authors of this clause had in mind included probably the original Bill of Rights, "incorporated" against the states, and also *other* "fundamental" limitations as well. The key language defining what kinds of things the authors had in mind appears in an opinion written by Justice Bushrod Washington of the Supreme Court in 1823, interpreting a parallel provision of the original Constitution, the "Privileges and Immunities" Clause of Article IV: "We feel no hesitation in confining these expressions to those privileges and immunities which are, in their nature, fundamental; which belong, of right, to the citizens of all free governments. . . . They may . . . be all comprehended under the following general heads: Protection, by the government; the enjoyment of life and liberty, with the right to acquire and possess property of every kind, and to pursue and obtain happiness and safety. . . ."[4] This opinion appears to have heavily shaped the views of the Fourteenth Amendment's authors regarding the meaning of what they were enacting, and again, it clearly envisions protection of liberties beyond the Bill of Rights (though it probably was meant to include much, if not all, of the

---

1. *Annals of Congress* 424–450 (statement of Rep. Madison on June 8, 1789), *available at* http://www.constitution.org/ac/001/r01-1/bill_of_rights_hr1789.htm.

2. For a summary of the views of such "Skeptics," *see* RANDY E. BARNETT, RESTORING THE LOST CONSTITUTION: THE PRESUMPTION OF LIBERTY at 242–252 (Princeton 2004).

3. *Id.* at 234–242; CALVIN R. MASSEY, SILENT RIGHTS: THE NINTH AMENDMENT AND THE CONSTITUTION'S UNENUMERATED RIGHTS at 53–94 (Temple 1995).

4. Corfield v. Coryell, 6 F. Cas. 546 (C.C.E.D. Pa. 1823).

original Bill of Rights as well).[5] Of course, the Supreme Court ended up emasculating the Privileges or Immunities Clause in the *Slaughter-House Cases*, but that does not undermine the point that the constitutional text, and its fairly understood meaning, themselves seem to authorize nontextual constitutional principles, thereby legitimating judicial efforts to discover and enforce such principles.

The above argument fairly responds to the fundamental critique regarding the legitimacy of the entire enterprise of enforcing constitutional principles not traceable to specific text, directly on point. It does not, however, provide much guidance regarding how such principles are to be identified, and relatedly, exactly what those principles *are*. We turn now to these questions. We begin with a brief overview of how the Supreme Court has handled this issue over the years, including a summary of its important, recent decisions in areas of nontextual constitutionalism such as abortion. We then consider what light a structural approach to the Constitution might shed on these difficult and divisive questions.

THE HISTORIC EVOLUTION OF THE NONTEXTUAL CONSTITUTION

The problem of nontextual constitutional principles is not a new one. As early as 1798, in a case called *Calder v. Bull*,[6] Justices Samuel Chase and James Iredell had a pointed exchange in this subject, with Justice Chase arguing that:

> There are acts which the Federal, or State, Legislature cannot do, without exceeding their authority. There are certain vital principles in our free Republican governments, which will determine and over-rule an apparent and flagrant abuse of legislative power; as to authorize manifest injustice by positive law; or to take away that security for personal liberty, or private property, for the protection whereof the government was established. An ACT of the Legislature (for I cannot call it a law) contrary to the great first principles of the social compact, cannot be considered a rightful exercise of legislative authority. . . . To maintain that our Federal, or State, Legislature possesses such powers, if they had not been expressly restrained; would, in my opinion, be a political heresy, altogether inadmissible in our free republican governments.[7]

Justice Iredell responded as follows:

> If . . . the Legislature of the Union, or the Legislature of any member of the Union, shall pass a law, within the general scope of their constitutional power, the Court cannot pronounce it to be void, merely because it is, in their judgment,

---

5. *See generally* BARNETT, *supra*, RESTORING THE LOST CONSTITUTION at 60–68; Steven G. Calabresi, *Substantive Due Process after* Gonzales v. Carhart, 106 MICH. L. REV. 1517, 1532–1536 (2008).

6. 3 U.S. (3 Dall.) 386 (1798).

7. *Id.* at 388–389.

contrary to the principles of natural justice. The ideas of natural justice are regulated by no fixed standard: the ablest and the purest men have differed upon the subject; and all that the Court could properly say, in such an event, would be, that the Legislature (possessed of an equal right of opinion) had passed an act which, in the opinion of the judges, was inconsistent with the abstract principles of natural justice.[8]

In other words, Justice Chase defended judicial enforcement of nontextual constitutional principles on the grounds that such principles are inherent in "our free Republican governments," and so inherent in our constitutions. Justice Iredell, however, argued that judges cannot enforce such principles of "natural justice" because they are undiscoverable, and so judges have no right to impose their views on legislatures. That disagreement, expressed less than a decade after the ratification of the Constitution, has been echoed repeatedly, and passionately, in the more than two centuries since then, with no clearer resolution than Chase and Iredell were able to achieve.

A caveat is necessary here. The debate between Justices Chase and Iredell reflects very different views about the appropriate role of the judiciary. What it does *not* reflect, however, is disagreement about the *existence* of natural rights, or what Iredell calls "natural justice." As we noted in Chapter 2, during the Framing era there was widespread agreement about the existence of natural law generally, and legal thinkers of that era, Iredell included, would certainly have agreed that as a matter of principle legislatures and government generally should conform to such concepts. The difficulty, however, is that determining the contours of natural rights, and the limits they pose on organized government, is exceedingly difficulty—in Iredell's view sufficiently so to make judicial enforcement impossible. Iredell's view, however, was clearly not universally held. Modern scholars such as Susanna Sherry and Thomas Grey argue that during the Framing era natural law was generally viewed to be legally enforceable,[9] though Professor Sherry acknowledges that this approach largely withered and died by the 1820s.[10] No less a figure than Chief Justice John Marshall, probably the most important figure ever to sit on the Supreme Court, relied partially on natural law principles in an 1810 decision, *Fletcher v. Peck*,[11] in which Marshall held that a state legislature lacked the power to rescind title in land that had been purchased in good faith by an owner, from someone who had previously been granted the land by the state. And most infamously, in its 1857 decision in *Dred Scott v. Sandford*,[12]

---

8. *Id.* at 399 (Iredell, J., dissenting).

9. *See* Suzanna Sherry, *The Founders' Unwritten Constitution*, 54 U. CHI. L. REV. 1127 (1987); Thomas Grey, *Do We Have an Unwritten Constitution?*, 27 STAN. L. REV. 703 (1975).

10. Sherry, *supra*, 54 U. Chi. L. Rev. at 1175–1176.

11. 10 U.S. (6 Cranch.) 87 (1810).

12. 60 U.S. (19 How.) 393 (1857).

the Supreme Court relied upon what were recognizable natural law principles (though not described as such by the Court) in holding unconstitutional a congressional statute, the Missouri Compromise, which forbade the institution of slavery in the northern sections of the Louisiana Purchase. Despite these appearances, however, it is fair to say that natural rights, and the nontextual Constitution generally, played only a limited role in the constitutional law during the first century of the Constitution's existence.

The great renaissance of nontextual constitutional law, and of a natural-rights-based jurisprudence (though it was not described in those terms) occurred not in the Founding era, and not even in the post–Civil War era, but rather in the very late nineteenth and early twentieth centuries. This was an era of rapid industrialization and urbanization and fundamental societal changes as more and more wealth and means of production came to be concentrated in the hands of a new, capitalist elite. The result was fierce, sometimes violent confrontations between workers and employers, and strong political pressure to enact legislation protecting workers from dangerous working conditions, long hours, and employer hostility to unions—all a product of the great mismatch in bargaining power between employers and workers. Progressive era legislatures began enacting laws protecting workers by regulating workplace safety, limiting working hours, and forbidding employers from preventing unionization. The Supreme Court's response was the so-called *Lochner* doctrine, named after the 1905 *Lochner v. New York* decision discussed in Chapter 3. In essence, this doctrine held that the Due Process clauses of the Fifth and Fourteenth Amendments (directed against the federal and state governments, respectively) were not only procedural, but had a "substantive" component, preventing arbitrary state interferences with life, liberty, or property; and that the "freedom of contract" was one of the fundamental liberties protected by the Due Process clauses. In a series of cases during the *Lochner* era, from 1905 to 1937, the Court invoked this principle to strike down many state regulations on the grounds that they denied both workers and employers contractual freedom, including laws limiting workers' hours,[13] setting minimum wages,[14] and forbidding employers from refusing to hire union members.[15] Indeed, during this era the Court generally was highly skeptical of business regulation, striking down many different kinds of restrictions on business, including price regulation and entry regulations,[16] as well as

---

13. Lochner v. New York, 198 U.S. 405 (1905).

14. Adkins v. Children's Hospital, 261 U.S. 525 (1923); Moorehead v. New York *ex rel.* Tipaldo, 298 U.S. 587 (1936).

15. Coppage v. Kansas, 236 U.S. 1 (1915).

16. *See, e.g.,* Williams v. Standard Oil Co., 278 U.S. 235 (1929); New State Ice Co. v. Liebmann, 285 U.S. 262 (1932).

consumer protection legislation,[17] all on freedom-of-contracts grounds. The cases of the *Lochner* era did not speak in terms of "natural rights" or nontextual constitutional principles, instead claiming merely to be protecting "liberty" as described in the Due Process Clause. In practice, however, the Court's practice of identifying certain types of liberty as fundamental—primarily, though not exclusively as we shall see, contractual liberty—clearly constitutes a form of nontextual analysis, since it cannot be derived in any way from the text of the Constitution.

The advent of the Great Depression in the early 1930s created social and political conditions, not least the election of Franklin Delano Roosevelt as president in 1932, that spelled the end of the *Lochner* era. After some resistance, in 1937 in *West Coast Hotel Co. v. Parrish*,[18] another case discussed in Chapter 3, the Supreme Court abandoned the *Lochner* approach, rejecting the view that "freedom of contract" deserved any special constitutional protection. The following year, in *United States v. Carolene Products*,[19] the Court confirmed and clarified this view, explaining that when legislatures adopt economic regulations, courts must presume that the regulations are factually justified and may strike down regulations only if they lack a "rational basis"—a standard that the Supreme Court has *never* found to be violated since then in a case challenging economic regulation. At this point in the opinion Justice Harlan Fiske Stone dropped a footnote—the famous "footnote four," which Supreme Court Justice Lewis Powell called "the most celebrated footnote in constitutional law"—explaining when this presumption of constitutionality might not be appropriate, i.e., when searching judicial review might be required. Stone identifies three such circumstances: first, "when legislation appears on its face to be within a specific prohibition of the Constitution, such as those of the first ten amendments"; second, if the legislation "restricts those political processes which can ordinarily be expected to bring about the repeal of undesirable legislation"; and third, if legislation is directed against particular religious or national or racial minorities, and so reflects "prejudice against discrete and insular minorities" (we discussed this last part of footnote four in Chapter 8).[20] Notice that nowhere in this list does there seem to be any scope for nontextual constitutional law. Instead, the Court focuses on the textual Bill of Rights, on political processes (the cases the Court cites on this point involve racial discrimination in voting, covered by the Fifteenth Amendment, and interference with free speech and assembly, covered by the First Amendment), and on discrimination (covered by the Equal Protection Clause). Nor is this gap surprising, given that the Court of this period was self-consciously trying to distance itself from the nontextual jurisprudence of the

---

17. Weaver v. Palmer Bros., 270 U.S. 402 (1926); Jay Burns Baking Co. v. Bryan, 264 U.S. 504 (1924).

18. 300 U.S. 379 (1937).

19. 304 U.S. 144 (1938).

20. *Id.* at 152 n.4.

Lochner era. And indeed, for almost thirty years following the 1937 constitutional revolution, the Court adhered to this approach.

The post-*Lochner* era came to an end in 1965, when the Supreme Court decided *Griswold v. Connecticut*.[21] *Griswold* involved a challenge to a Connecticut statute that flatly banned the use of contraceptives (the case was brought by the Executive Director of Planned Parenthood in Connecticut, and by a doctor and Yale Medical School professor, both of whom had been arrested and fined $100 for operating a clinic providing advice about contraceptives to married couples). In an opinion authored by the brilliant but erratic Justice William O. Douglas, which was notable for its high-flown language and intellectual confusion, the Supreme Court held that this provision violated the Constitution, without ever clarifying exactly what *part* of the Constitution it violated. Instead, Douglas argued that textual constitutional provisions "have penumbras, formed by emanations" that extend their reach, and that one such penumbra was a "zone of privacy." In particular, the Court held that this penumbra protected a right of *marital* privacy, making it unconstitutional to apply the Connecticut statute to married couples. In reaching this conclusion, the Court relied on two *Lochner* era cases—*Meyer v. Nebraska*[22] and *Pierce v. Society of Sisters*[23]—in which the Court had struck down on substantive due process grounds laws that interfered with parents' abilities to control their children's educations (*Meyer* involved a law banning the teaching of modern languages in schools, and *Pierce* a law requiring children to attend public, not private schools), but explicitly distanced itself from the substantive due process reasoning of those cases. In short, the majority opinion in *Griswold* is a hash, a decision that quite plainly is reviving a form of nontextual constitutionalism, but denies doing so and thus fails to explain its reasoning at all. Two Justices, Arthur Goldberg and the great second Justice John Marshall Harlan (Harlan was the grandson of the equally great first Justice John Marshall Harlan, who sat on the Supreme Court in the late nineteenth and early twentieth centuries, and dissented from both the *Plessy v. Ferguson* "separate but equal" and *Lochner* decisions) wrote separate opinions that were more forthright, explicitly relying on principles of substantive due process (Goldberg also relied heavily upon the Ninth Amendment).[24] Both of these opinions have been highly influential in subsequent cases. Goldberg argued that in identifying which nontextual liberties deserve constitutional protection, judges should "look to the 'traditions and [collective] conscience of our people' to determine whether

---

21. 381 U.S. 479 (1965).

22. 262 U.S. 390 (1923).

23. 268 U.S. 510 (1925).

24. *Id.* at 486–499 (Goldberg, J., concurring); *id.* at 499–502 (Harlan, J., concurring). Justice Harlan primarily incorporates by reference an earlier dissenting opinion he had authored in *Poe v. Ullman*, 367 U.S. 497, 522 (1961) (Harlan, J., dissenting).

a principle is 'so rooted [there] . . . as to be ranked as fundamental.''[25] In similar terms, Harlan suggested that the content of substantive due process, as established by the Supreme Court

> has represented the balance which our Nation, built upon postulates of respect for the liberty of the individual, has struck between that liberty and the demands of organized society. If the supplying of content to this Constitutional concept has of necessity been a rational process, it certainly has not been one where judges have felt free to roam where unguided speculation might take them. The balance of which I speak is the balance struck by this country, having regard to what history teaches are the traditions from which it developed as well as the traditions from which it broke. That tradition is a living thing.[26]

In short, the Goldberg and Harlan opinions, which as noted above have strongly influenced the development of future law in this area, represent a decisive rebirth and redefinition of nontextual constitutionalism.

Despite its jurisprudential adventurousness, *Griswold* has not proven to be an especially controversial decision. Seven years after *Griswold*, the Court extended the reach of *Griswold* (in an opinion particularly noteworthy for its incoherence) to the distribution of contraceptives to unmarried couples,[27] but that too did not generate much outcry. One year later, however, the Court extended *Griswold* again, in a decision that has elicited more controversy, and more vitriol, than almost any decision in the history of the U.S. Supreme Court. That decision was, of course, *Roe v. Wade*.[28] In *Roe*, the Court held that the privacy right recognized in *Griswold*—which the Court now firmly located in the Due Process Clause—"was broad enough to encompass a woman's decision whether or not to terminate her pregnancy."[29] Exactly why this was so the Court did not explain, but what was clear was that the privacy right now included a right to choose an abortion. The Court went on to balance this right against the government's legitimate interests in protecting potential life and the health of the mother, and came up with a complex framework for assessing abortion regulations, the details of which we need not dwell on (especially because the Court subsequently abandoned that framework). Nontextual constitutionalism was back with a vengeance.

The political and legal response to *Roe* was unprecedented—at least since the Court's 1857 decision in *Dred Scott*, which may have helped bring on the Civil War.

---

25. *Id.* at 493 (Goldberg, J., concurring) (*quoting* Snyder v. Massachusetts, 291 U.S. 97, 105 (1934).

26. Poe v. Ullman, 367 U.S. at 542 (Harlan, J., dissenting).

27. Eisenstadt v. Baird, 405 U.S. 438 (1972).

28. 410 U.S. 113 (1973).

29. *Id.* at 153.

The decision was celebrated by some scholars while condemned by others, and it was a critical factor in the growth of the religious right in American politics, which in turn contributed to the election of President Ronald Reagan in 1980. These events in turn contributed to a dramatic change in the makeup of the Supreme Court, as a result of conservative appointments by Republican presidents—between 1968 and 1992, *every single* Justice appointed to the Supreme Court was appointed by a Republican president. By the end of the first Bush presidency, in 1992, these developments seemed to have put the future of *Roe v. Wade* in doubt, as several Justices, including notably Chief Justice William Rehnquist and Justice Antonin Scalia, were writing opinions vocally criticizing *Roe*. Nonetheless, in 1992 in *Planned Parenthood of Southeastern Pennsylvania v. Casey*, five Justices of the Supreme Court, all Republican appointees including two Reagan appointees (Sandra Day O'Connor and Anthony M. Kennedy) and one Bush appointee (David Souter), voted to uphold "the essential holding of *Roe v. Wade*."[30] The lead opinion in the case, jointly authored by Justices O'Connor, Kennedy, and Souter—a rare practice intended to emphasize the significance of the decision—relied explicitly on both substantive due process principles and the Ninth Amendment, and quoted heavily from Justice Harlan's *Griswold* opinion[31] in reaffirming both the existence of nontextual constitutional principles and the inclusion of the abortion right in the list of "fundamental rights" protected therein. Since *Casey*, while the abortion right remains the subject of intense political debate, the Court has not directly considered the continuing vitality of the abortion cases.

The contraception/abortion line of cases undoubtedly represents the most prominent and important strain of modern nontextual, "substantive due process" jurisprudence. It is not, however, the only manifestation of modern "privacy" law. Another important principle that the Supreme Court has enforced in this area is that the Constitution restricts the government's power to interfere in the organization of families (these cases are of course related to the procreation cases, in that they involve state regulation of the family unit, but they nonetheless raise some distinct questions). As noted above, the roots of this aspect of "privacy" law can be traced back to the *Meyer* and *Pierce* cases from the 1920s, holding that the government may not strip parents of their control over their children's education. In two cases in the 1970s the Court extended these rulings

---

30. 505 U.S. 833, 846 (1992).

31. Or more accurately, Justice Harlan's *Poe v. Ullman* dissent, incorporated into his *Griswold* opinion.

to grant families greater protection against state interference. First, in *Stanley v. Illinois* the Court struck down an Illinois law holding that the children of unwed fathers, but not mothers, automatically became wards of the state (i.e., the father's parental rights were terminated) upon the death of the mother.[32] The case was brought by Peter Stanley, a father of three children who lived off and on with their mother, Joan Stanley, for eighteen years, without ever getting married, and who lost his children upon Joan's death. The Court held that Peter was at a minimum entitled to a hearing regarding his fitness as a parent, before his children could be taken from him. In the second case, *Moore v. City of East Cleveland*, the Court was faced with a municipal ordinance that prohibited anyone not belonging to a single "family" from cohabitating in a house or apartment, and that defined "family" narrowly in such a way as to exclude cousins, in effect. The law was challenged by a woman, Inez Moore, who was living in her house with her son, his son, and another grandson who was the child of another son (who had come to live with them when his mother died). Because the two grandsons were cousins, the law forbade them from living in the same home. The Supreme Court (or more accurately, four Justices—the fifth vote was provided by Justice John Paul Stevens on idiosyncratic grounds) held that such a law interfered with the "sanctity of the [Moores'] family" and therefore violated the Due Process Clause.[33] It should be noted that the *Moore* case is centrally a case about family, albeit extended rather than nuclear family, and not a case about controlling one's property, because just three years earlier the Court had *upheld* a law prohibiting unrelated persons from living together,[34] and *Moore* reaffirmed that decision.

The Supreme Court's protection of parental rights and family sanctity is not without limit. In an important decision in 1989, *Michael H. v. Gerald D.*,[35] the Court limited constitutional protection for parental rights. The facts of the case are dizzying (involving a mother who was a model, the French businessmen she married, multiple affairs, breakups, and reconciliations), but to summarize and simplify, the father in question had had an affair with the child's mother while she was married to another man, as a result of which she became pregnant and bore a child named Victoria while still living with her husband. The married couple separated after the child's birth, but then reconciled and decided to raise the child as their own. Under California law, where Victoria was born, a child born to a woman living with her husband is *conclusively* presumed to be the husband's child, regardless of genetics. So, under California law the husband was the father, and the natural father had no parental rights. This, the Court held, was permissible because American traditions do *not* protect the rights of "an adulterous, natural father." *Michael H.*, however, should not be read to spell the

---

32. 405 U.S. 645 (1972).
33. 431 U.S. 494, 503 (1977).
34. Village of Belle Terre v. Boraas, 416 U.S. 1 (1974).
35. 491 U.S. 505 (1989).

demise of this strand of law. As recently as 2000, the Court invoked the family rights line of cases to hold unconstitutional a Washington State statute authorizing courts to grant visitation rights, over parents' objections, to any person if it was in the "best interests of the child." The case involved a conflict between a mother and a child's grandparents on the father's side—the father had earlier committed suicide—over the extent of the grandparents' visitation rights. The state courts, relying on the above statute, had granted extended visitation, but the Court held that this result violated the "fundamental right of parents to make decisions concerning the care, custody, and control of their children."[36] In short, this nontextual restriction on government power remains alive and potent.

Two further strands of the Court's privacy jurisprudence require quick discussion. The first is marriage. Unsurprisingly, in addition to reproduction and family sanctity, the Supreme Court has held that the Constitution, as an aspect of privacy, protects a fundamental right to marry. The Court invoked this principle in *Loving v. Virginia* in 1967 as an alternative ground for striking down for Virginia's "antimiscegenation" statute forbidding interracial marriage;[37] and it later applied the principle to strike down a Wisconsin statute that flatly forbade any person to marry if he had existing children to whom he owed child support, which he either had not paid or a court determined was likely not to be able to pay.[38] This "right to marry" thus has teeth; but it should be recognized that the constitutional rule regarding marriage is complex, because marriage is unusual. The difficulty is this: as we have repeatedly noted, in general constitutional "rights" do not protect autonomy, they restrict governmental power in a particular area, disempowering the government from acting. Modern marriage, however, is a government-created institution, which by its nature comes into being only because of government action. As such, the government necessarily *must* regulate it, including restricting it (e.g., not permitting children or close relatives to marry). It is meaningless, therefore, to say that this is an area where the government lacks the power to act, and the Court has never so claimed. It has only said that when the government interferes "directly and substantially with the right to marry" a constitutional problem arises. Unsurprisingly, the Court has failed to provide much explanation about what kinds of restrictions interfere in this way with marriage and which don't (for example, why doesn't a ban on siblings marrying interfere with the right, in the same way as the ban on interracial marriage?). Given the obvious significance of this question in the modern debate over same-sex marriage, we will return to it later in this chapter.

---

36. Troxel v. Granville, 530 U.S. 57, 66 (2000).

37. 388 U.S. 1 (1967).

38. Zablocki v. Redhail, 434 U.S. 374 (1978). *Zablocki* technically relied on the Equal Protection rather than the Due Process Clause, based on an aspect of equal protection law, the "fundamental interests" prong, which is discussed below; but it is considered to rest within the general "right to marry" jurisprudence.

The final (though again, as we shall see, closely related) strand of modern privacy doctrine came into being in the Supreme Court's very important 2003 decision in *Lawrence v. Texas*. Given its significance, both the facts and the holding of *Lawrence* are worthy of close attention. The facts themselves are tangled and confusing. The official facts, as reported by the Supreme Court, are simple. One evening in 1998, the Houston police were called to an apartment in response to a reported weapons disturbance (which as it turns out was a false report). When they entered the apartment, they found two men, John Lawrence and Tyron Garner, having sex. The two men were charged with "deviant sexual intercourse" under Texas law. The men plead no contest (reserving their right to challenge the constitutionality of their prosecution) and were fined $200 each.[39] They then appealed their convictions all the way to the U.S. Supreme Court, where they won a great victory for gay rights. Professor Dale Carpenter has conducted a careful investigation into the background in this case and provides many more details, as well as raising questions about the accuracy of the official facts.[40] Some undisputed additional facts: John Lawrence is White and was fifty-five years old at the time of the arrest, while Tyron Garner is Black and was thirty-one at the time, raising questions about whether there was a racial element to their arrest and prosecution (prosecutions for consensual sodomy being bizarre and almost unknown in the modern age). Lawrence and Garner had known each other for some time, and while they were occasional sexual partners, they do not appear to have been in a long-term, committed relationship.[41] Finally, Professor Carpenter has raised serious doubts about whether Lawrence and Garner actually *were* having sex when the police entered the apartment (which was Lawrence's).[42] Because Lawrence and Garner did not challenge the factual claims made by the police, none of these facts or doubts were brought to the attention of the Supreme Court; but they do raise interesting questions about how and why this case came about.

Turning now to the law, the Texas statute under which Lawrence and Garner were tried criminalized "deviant sexual intercourse *with another individual of the same sex*," and defined deviant sexual intercourse as contact between the genitals of one person and the mouth or anus of another. This definition tracks the usual definition of the traditional crime of sodomy, except, crucially, that traditional sodomy was *not* limited to persons of the same sex—it criminalized anal and (sometimes) oral sex between different-sex couples as well. Indeed, even in Texas the crime of sodomy historically was not limited to homosexual couples. It was only in 1973 that the Texas legislature amended its sodomy law, renaming it

---

39. Lawrence v. Texas, 539 U.S. 558, 562–564 (2003).

40. Dale Carpenter, *The Unknown Past of* Lawrence v. Texas, 102 MICH. L. REV. 1464 (2004).

41. *Id.* at 1478.

42. *Id.* at 1499.

"homosexual sodomy" and limiting it to same-sex couples.[43] Notice that (as we noted in the previous chapter) given this history, there is a strong argument to be made that the Texas statute, by singling out homosexuals for differential treatment, discriminated on the basis of sexual orientation and so violated the Equal Protection Clause—indeed, Justice Sandra Day O'Connor made precisely this argument in a separate opinion in *Lawrence*.[44] This was not the path, however, that the majority chose to take. Instead, the majority, in an opinion by Justice Anthony M. Kennedy, invoked the line of privacy cases beginning with *Griswold*, and going through *Eisenstadt*, *Roe*, and *Casey*. The Court acknowledged that in 1986, in its *Bowers v. Hardwick* decision,[45] it had considered and rejected a claim that privacy protected a right to "homosexual sodomy," but it concluded that *Bowers* was incorrectly decided and so overruled it. Substantively, the Court engaged in a thorough historical review of sodomy laws, noting that such laws had traditionally *not* been directed at homosexual conduct as such, but rather at all nonprocreative sex (notice here the link to the anticontraceptives law struck down in *Griswold*), and that the practice of limiting sodomy laws to homosexuals was a modern one. The Court also noted that over the past half century, many American states and most other Western countries have eliminated criminal penalties for sodomy and that actual enforcement of sodomy laws, even in states where they still existed, was almost unknown. Along the way, the Court emphasized that what was problematic about sodomy laws was that they seek to control

> the most private human conduct, sexual behavior, and in the most private of places, the home. The statutes do seek to control a personal relationship that, whether or not entitled to formal recognition in the law, is within the liberty of persons to choose without being punished as criminals. This, as a general rule, should counsel against attempts by the State, or a court, to define the meaning of the relationship or to set its boundaries absent injury to a person or abuse of an institution the law protects. It suffices for us to acknowledge that adults may choose to enter upon this relationship in the confines of their homes and their own private lives and still retain their dignity as free persons. When sexuality finds overt expression in intimate conduct with another person, the conduct can be but one element in a personal bond that is more enduring. The liberty protected by the Constitution allows homosexual persons the right to make this choice.[46]

The Court concluded with a ringing conclusion that individuals are entitled to engage in "sexual practices common to a homosexual lifestyle" and that the

---

43. *Id.* at 1471–1472.
44. *Lawrence, supra*, 539 U.S. at 579–585 (O'Connor, J., concurring in the judgment).
45. 478 U.S. 186 (1986).
46. *Lawrence, supra*, 539 U.S. at 567.

"State cannot demean their existence or control their destiny by making their private sexual conduct a crime."[47]

There are several noteworthy points about these passages. First, it is interesting, indeed I will argue critical, that in finding a constitutional violation here, the Court focused not so much on a "right" to engage on sodomy or any other sexual act; it instead focused on the *relationship* between individuals engaged in sexual acts and condemned the efforts of the State to control, or intrude into, that relationship. Second, it is significant that in exploring the "traditions" and "collective conscience" of our people that help define unenumerated rights under the separate opinions in *Griswold*, the Court focused on recent history, and on events outside the United States as well as within, creating a more evolutionary jurisprudence, as opposed to the narrowly historical approach favored by Justices such as Antonin Scalia and Clarence Thomas. This acceptance of a "living tradition" is entirely consistent with Justice Harlan's separate opinion in *Griswold*, but it too is highly controversial. Finally, the aggressive and expansive language of the *Lawrence* opinion suggests that the Supreme Court remains, even in the twenty-first century, open to the prospect of expanding the nontextual Constitution.

Two caveats are in order here. First, the above discussion should not be read to suggest that the Court's willingness to enforce the nontextual Constitution is without limits. One such limit was identified in the 1989 *Michael H.* decision, denying protection to "an adulterous, natural father." More significantly, in 1997 in *Washington v. Glucksberg*,[48] the Supreme Court unanimously rejected a claim that its privacy jurisprudence prevented states from prohibiting doctors from assisting terminally ill patients in committing suicide. The Court concluded that the nation's long history of forbidding suicide, and the continued enforcement in most states of laws forbidding assisted suicide, required the conclusion that the nation's traditions did not support a claim to a "right to die," even for terminally ill patients, especially given the strong countervailing governmental interests in protecting patients against abuse and pressure. The *Glucksberg* decision identifies an important, and as we shall see telling, limitation on the privacy jurisprudence.

The second caveat is this. Our discussion in this chapter has focused on the Supreme Court's modern "privacy" or "substantive due process" jurisprudence. While this line of cases undoubtedly represents the most important area of nontextual constitutionalism, it is not the only one. In particular, in a series of cases beginning in 1942 but really taking hold and accelerating in the mid 1960s (i.e., around the same time that *Griswold* was decided), the Supreme Court began holding, under the rubric of the Equal Protection Clause, that when states

---

47. *Id*. at 578.
48. Washington v. Glucksberg, 521 U.S. 707 (1997).

regulated unevenly—i.e., discriminated among citizens—with respect to certain nontextual "fundamental interests," special constitutional concerns were raised, requiring careful judicial scrutiny.[49] Undoubtedly, the most significant of the interests protected by the Court is the right to vote,[50] which will be our focus (other interests the Court has recognized include the right to travel interstate,[51] the right to procreate,[52] and certain criminal procedure rights[53]).

The Court's "right to vote" jurisprudence is an independent, nontextual body of constitutional law—there is no general "right to vote" mentioned in the Constitution, though the Constitution does prohibit *discrimination* among voters on the basis of race, sex, and age (for those eighteen and older).[54] Moreover, unlike most of the other "fundamental interests" jurisprudence, this body of law is neither narrow nor moribund, as illustrated by the Court's decision in *Bush v. Gore.*[55] Most importantly, the basic rule that has emerged from the cases in this area—that when the state grants citizens the right to vote, it must treat them equally, meaning that it may not deprive citizens of their vote on arbitrary grounds such as failure to pay a poll tax or to own property, and may not dilute their vote by creating electoral districts with vastly different populations—have become fundamental tenets of our modern democracy. Interestingly, however, the principle here is quite limited. States have no general obligation to grant the right to vote for any specific office, including, as the *Bush v. Gore* Court noted, for even the president of the United States[56] (though the Constitution does require direct elections for members of Congress).[57] Nor can the "right to vote" plausibly be described as a "natural right" since it can have no existence outside of a system of organized government, in which the government permits and arranges for elections to select its officials. There is thus no "right to vote" as such. Instead, the law in this area, much like in the criminal procedure area,

---

49. *See, e.g.,* Skinner v. Oklahoma, 316 U.S. 535 (1942); Griffin v. Illinois, 351 U.S. 12 (1956); Reynolds v. Simms, 377 U.S. 533 (1964); Shapiro v. Thompson, 394 U.S. 618 (1969).

50. *See, e.g.,* Reynolds v. Simms, 377 U.S. 533 (1964); Harper v. Virginia State Board of Elections, 383 U.S. 663 (1966); Kramer v. Union Free School District, 395 U.S. 626 (1969).

51. Shapiro v. Thompson, 394 U.S. 618 (1969).

52. Skinner v. Oklahoma, 316 U.S. 535 (1942).

53. Griffin v. Illinois, 351 U.S. 12 (1956); Douglas v. California, 372 U.S. 353 (1963).

54. *See* U.S. Const., Amendments XV, XIX, XXVI.

55. 531 U.S. 98 (2000).

56. *Id.* at 104. The Court noted that the Constitution permits state legislatures to provide for the appointment of presidential electors (members of the Electoral College) in whatever way they choose. For most of our history, state legislatures have for political reasons chosen to appoint electors through popular elections.

57. Article I provides for direct election of the House of Representatives, while the Seventeenth Amendment requires direct election of Senators.

dictates rules regarding what a *fair* system of elections must look like. Thus the Court has held that excluding voters for reasons we consider irrelevant, such as poverty, is unfair, and diluting urban votes by creating unequal electoral districts is unfair. Following this lead, *Bush v. Gore* held that it is unfair to count physically identical ballots differently, and so the Florida recount process following the disputed 2000 election was unconstitutional since it did not provide for uniform rules for recounting "dimpled" and "hanging" chads.

THE DEATH OF NATURAL LAW AND THE FAILURE OF CONSENSUS

What are we to make of the Supreme Court's nontextual constitutional jurisprudence, and in particular its modern enforcement of "privacy rights"? Is it a legitimate part of our constitutional law or an unauthorized power grab by the Court? If there is one thing that the above discussion should make clear, it is that no easy answers to these questions emerge. History and theory do, however, suggest several possible paths one might take in approaching this question and in trying to justify the law in this area. We begin with the two justifications, natural law and collective traditions, that most commentators and the Supreme Court itself have tended to invoke.

As a starting point, natural law principles appear to provide the most promising justification for the Supreme Court's privacy jurisprudence, from *Griswold* through *Lawrence*. After all, as we noted, it seems clear that at least *some* of the Framers, and *some* of the authors of the Fourteenth Amendment, believed that courts do have the power to enforce natural law against unjust legislatures, either intrinsically or pursuant to the Ninth Amendment and the Privileges or Immunities Clause of the Fourteenth Amendment. Of course, there was disagreement on this question from the beginning (recall the Chase/Iredell debate of 1798), but the existence of a clear strain of thought justifying such action can certainly be invoked as a defense for the modern Court's decisions. Two serious difficulties, however, arise here. The first is that a pure natural-rights jurisprudence, unconnected from any other part of the Constitution, sits oddly with both the fundamentally *structural* nature of our Constitution and with democratic government more broadly. The Constitution, remember, was created to design and enable democratic government of the People, while at the same time protecting the People from the excesses of that government. A broad, untethered jurisprudence of natural rights certainly does protect *individuals* from governmental excess, but it does so at a severe cost to democracy because it removes from democratic dialogue many issues of critical moral significance, whether it be the morality of slavery (which *Dred Scott* purported to remove from politics), the morality of workplace regulation (which *Lochner* constitutionalized), or the morality of abortion (for which *Roe v. Wade* did the same). More generally, it is hard to conceive of how a pure natural-rights jurisprudence protects the People as a whole against government, since its effect is to disable the People from acting through their elected representatives in specific areas of policy, even when there is no conflict between the People as a whole and their elected leaders. Of course, if we truly have a libertarian Constitution, as scholars such as Professor Randy Barnett argue,[58] then this objection evaporates. However, it is the thesis of this book that we do not have such a Constitution; instead we have a structural Constitution. And in such a Constitution, a purely liberty-enhancing jurisprudence of natural rights simply does not fit.

There is a second and even more profound objection to a natural-rights based jurisprudence of nontextual rights. Even if we concede that during the Framing era and the Reconstruction era, there *did* exist a broad consensus that natural rights did exist and that judges should enforce them, that does not provide much help today. The reason is that today, any such consensus has vanished, even on the crucial question of whether natural rights as such even *exist*. The reasons for this are twofold. One, perhaps resolvable one, is that in the more than two centuries since the Framing, and the almost century and a half since Reconstruction, the degree of intellectual and cultural diversity in our nation has exploded. The result is that basic agreement on what kinds of values, what kinds of rights are "natural," meaning universally valued, is much harder to achieve. This, however, is a less significant point. More basically, many (though by no means all) modern legal thinkers—including myself—simply do not believe any more that natural law as such exists. Because of this lack of agreement, modern law is generally viewed and discussed in positive terms, as law that is enacted by sovereign power. Speaking of the common law, Justice Oliver Wendell Holmes put it thus: "The common law is not a brooding omnipresence in the sky but the articulate voice of some sovereign or quasi sovereign that can be identified."[59] The Constitution, by virtue of its ratification by the People, is valid positive law, as are statutes enacted by duly elected legislatures. But there is no room in such a perspective for "natural law." Where does such law come from? And how are judges to identify it? If these basic questions cannot be answered—as today many would agree they cannot—then the very foundation of a jurisprudence of natural rights disappears.

The modern Supreme Court has, of course, recognized modern doubts and uncertainties regarding natural law. That is why in the modern era, it has not explicitly invoked natural law to justify its nontextual decisions. Instead, as discussed earlier, the dominant framework that the Supreme Court has invoked in elucidating the nontextual Constitution is the one set forth in the separate opinions of Justices Goldberg and Harlan in the *Griswold* case. This approach requires

---

58. *See generally* RANDY E. BARNETT, RESTORING THE LOST CONSTITUTION THE PRESUMPTION OF LIBERTY (Princeton 2004).

59. Southern Pacific Company v. Jensen, 244 U.S. 205, 222 (1917) (Holmes, J., dissenting).

judges to look to the "traditions" and "collective conscience" of the American People and tease out the core, "fundamental" values implicit in our history and shared understandings. This approach has the important advantage over a natural-law-based analysis that the inquiry it requires is an objective one, looking at something real—history and tradition—rather than at some ephemeral concept of natural law. In addition, by focusing on shared values and *living* traditions, as Justice Harlan urged and as the Court did in *Lawrence*, this approach permits the nontextual Constitution to adjust to changing circumstances and a changing nation, in a way that a static concept of "natural law" does not necessarily permit. There are also, however, some serious difficulties with this form of analysis.

One of the basic objections to a tradition-based or "collective values" based methodology for identifying nontextual constitutional principles is an institutional one. The key problem here is that the Harlan approach to "fundamental rights" asks *judges* to identify the traditions and collective values of the American People, and then enforce those values *against* legislatures, the elected representatives of the People, because of course these issues arise only in the context of a constitutional challenge to legislation (or sometimes to the actions of an executive officer such as a governor or president, who are also elected officials). Why, one might ask, are unelected federal judges, who are chosen for their legal training and skills, not their political savvy, at all qualified to make such judgments, and more profoundly, why are they *better* qualified to make such judgments than the People's chosen, elected representatives? One possible answer to this question, offered by Professor Alexander Bickel, is that because of their training and political insulation, judges have the luxury to pursue "the ways of the scholar" and identify society's deeper values, which the hustle and bustle of daily politics does not permit.[60] This, however, is a troubling line of thought. For one thing, it is far from clear that a legal education trains one particularly well to explore either history or collective values. Wouldn't historians or philosophers do a better job? Bickel's argument also rests on a form of elitism and a lack of respect for democratic politics, which seems at odds with a system of government that prides itself on its republican principles. Might it be that when the Supreme Court elucidates the Constitution in ways that stretch beyond its specific text and structure, it is enforcing not the collective values of the People, but rather, as Justice Scalia has put it, "the views and values of the lawyer class from which the Court's Members are drawn?"[61] Unless one is able to answer this question in the negative with some confidence, it is difficult to avoid the conclusion that judicial enforcement of "collective values" is fundamentally undemocratic.

Institutional concerns aside, there is a practical problem, in the modern era, with a jurisprudence based on shared traditions and values. When judges look to

---

60. ALEXANDER BICKEL, THE LEAST DANGEROUS BRANCH: THE SUPREME COURT AT THE BAR OF POLITICS 25–26 (1962).

61. Romer v. Evans, 517 U.S. 620, 652 (1996) (Scalia, J., dissenting).

traditions and collective values in explicating the nontextual Constitution, presumably they are looking at the traditions and values of *We* the People, meaning the current People of the United States, not merely the People as of 1789 or 1868. Historically minded Justices such as Antonin Scalia and Clarence Thomas may disagree with this view, but it seems to be what Justice Harlan had in mind with his reference to "living" traditions, and it is clearly the approach endorsed by the *Lawrence* Court. Moreover, if the Ninth and Fourteenth Amendments are best read as grants of power to judges to elucidate nontextual constitutional principles over time, it seems sensible to assume that judges should be expected to look at the values of *their* society in exercising those powers, as opposed to the unknown and largely unknowable values of bygone generations. The difficulty is, however, that while it is plausible that the American People of 1789, or the People of 1868, were sufficiently homogeneous to have meaningful, shared traditions and values (though even that might be doubted, given the enormous divisions in the Framing era over issues such as slavery and church/state relations), in our enormously heterogeneous society, consisting of citizens whose ancestors immigrated to the United States from all over the world and with vastly different cultural and religious traditions, the quest for such shared values *today* is an extraordinarily challenging one. This is not to say that the modern American People have no shared values. Just by the dint of being, or becoming Americans, We the People largely accept the basic values of democracy, popular sovereignty, and limited government that are the bases of our constitutional system. But once we move beyond those areas, our diversity seems to overwhelm any chance of real consensus. That diversity encompasses not only racial and ethnic differences, but also religious differences, both among sects and between religious and secular elements in our society, political differences reflected in the modern Red State/Blue State rhetoric, and cultural differences, for example between coastal and central states. Moreover, in recent decades these differences appear to have widened, not narrowed.[62] In this situation, the idea that the sorts of serious, morally charged issues that tend to be at the center of nontextual constitutional claims can be resolved based on shared traditions and values seems utopian. Certainly the vociferous, ongoing debate triggered by *Roe v. Wade* belies any such notion, as does the ferocity of the modern debate over gay rights and same-sex marriage.

---

62. It should be acknowledged that there are those who question whether social divisions in the U.S. have truly widened in recent years. *See* Morris P. Fiorina, Samuel J. Abrams, and Jeremy C. Pope, Culture War? The Myth of a Polarized America (3rd ed. 2010). However, the vociferous and vitriolic nature of political debate during the George W. Bush and Obama Administrations suggests that these divisions have indeed widened; and in any event, there seems little doubt that we are a less homogeneous country than during the Framing era.

In short, neither natural rights nor reference to traditions and collective values seem to provide a very solid foundation for a jurisprudence of nontextual constitutional principles. One possible conclusion one could draw from all of this is that at least under modern circumstances, this entire area of law lacks objectivity and legitimacy, and so should be abandoned. There is something to be said for this argument, and certainly reasonable people might adopt it. It is, however, troubling, for two independent reasons. First, taking this position would require abandoning enormous swathes of modern constitutional law, including not only the privacy cases, but also the law of voting rights, aspects of the right to travel, and important parts of the Court's criminal procedure jurisprudence. Such disruptive change should be troubling to anyone who values stability in law, and in fact no Justice of the Supreme Court appears to advocate such a seismic rethinking. Second, limiting the Constitution to specific, textual provisions ignores the plain language and command of both the Ninth Amendment and the Privileges or Immunities Clause of the Fourteenth Amendment. These provisions mean *something*, and it seems illegitimate to ignore them simply because they pose difficult problems. By that logic, why not abandon the First Amendment as well?

What then is the solution? Perhaps the solution is to recognize that the Ninth and Fourteenth Amendments do not exist in a vacuum. They are an intrinsic part of a broader Constitution and a broader constitutional structure. There is no evidence, and no reason to think, that the authors of either the Ninth Amendment or the Privileges or Immunities Clause thought that their *basic* function was different from that of the rest of the Constitution, though they had distinct specific purposes (notably, in the case of the Fourteenth Amendment, placing significant restrictions on state governments for the first time). In particular, there is no reason to doubt that the basic purpose of the Ninth Amendment, like that of the rest of the Bill of Rights, was to maintain the balance of power between the federal government and the People, though while the first eight amendments identify specific areas where government needs to be restrained, the ninth authorizes courts to impose further, as yet unidentified, restraints as needed. Similarly, it seems reasonable to read the Fourteenth Amendment to impose the same balance between the citizens and the government of the various states, as well as (through the action of the Equal Protection Clause) between different groups of citizens. After all, the historical evidence that authors of the Fourteenth Amendment intended to do for the states what the Bill of Rights did for the national government is overwhelming.[63] Let us assume, then, that the nontextual Constitution, like the textual Constitution, is a structural Constitution, with structural purposes, the primary difference being that the textual Constitution defines the means by which it is pursuing its structural ends, while the

---

63. The evidence is summarized in AKHIL REED AMAR, THE BILL OF RIGHTS ch. 9 (Yale 1998).

nontextual Constitution is open-ended in this regard, requiring judges to give it specificity.

The question we turn to now is how to translate, continuing to use Lawrence Lessig's metaphor,[64] this insight into the modern era, which is to say, how judges might approach the problem of providing specificity to the nontextual Constitution in ways that will advance the structural goals of the Constitution under current conditions.

A STRUCTURAL APPROACH TO THE UNWRITTEN CONSTITUTION

Let us then recast our thinking about the nontextual Constitution. Instead of looking for "fundamental rights" or natural-law principles, let us instead ask, how might the specific text of the Constitution be supplemented, in ways that strengthen and protect our constitutional system of democratic government. In particular, what additional constitutional principles, what additional constraints on government power, are necessary to ensure that it is the People who control the government, not vice versa? As we have seen, much of the textual Bill of Rights, and of the Fourteenth Amendment, restrains government power in order to maintain a private sphere within which the People can organize and develop their values and beliefs, free from state coercion. As we shall see, many aspects of the nontextual Constitution, including notably the privacy and voting cases, can be read as advancing this goal as well.

Let us begin with voting. The structural nature of this "right" is clear—voting does not in any way directly enhance individual liberty or autonomy; it rather is the primary mechanism through which the People *directly* exercise control over their government. That much is obvious and critical. An equally important point, however, is that the "right to vote" enforced by the Supreme Court since the 1960s, and now firmly a part of our democratic culture, is a completely modern creation. The Framers of the Constitution said very little about voting, and certainly did not grant anyone a direct right to vote. The Constitution is completely silent about how to select state officials (aside from a vague, unenforceable provision stating that the "United States shall guarantee to every State . . . a Republican Form of Government"[65]), so obviously no "right to vote" existed there, at least as a matter of *federal* constitutional law (state Constitutions of course are a different matter); and even regarding federal offices, very little was said. Senators and the president were not elected at all—senators were chosen by state legislatures, and the choice of how to select presidential electors was also delegated to

---

64. *See* Lawrence Lessig, *Fidelity in Translation*, 71 Tex. L. Rev. 1165 (1993).

65. U.S. Const., Art. IV, § 4; *see* Luther v. Borden, 48 U.S. (7 How.) 1 (1849); Pacific Telephone Co. v. Oregon, 223 U.S. 118 (1912) (both holding "Republican Form of Government" Clause to be nonjusticiable).

state legislatures. The Constitution did provide for direct election of the House of Representatives, but it did *not* assure any citizen the franchise. Instead, the Constitution authorizes state legislatures to set the qualifications for voters, only requiring that those qualifications be the same as those for voters selecting the "most numerous" part of the state's legislature.[66] Nor was it the norm for states to grant the franchise to everyone—restrictions on voting based on factors such as property ownership and the payment of poll taxes were commonplace during the Framing era, and indeed continued through much of American history.[67] Even when the Seventeenth Amendment was added in 1913, providing for direct election of senators, states retained the power to set qualifications for voters, subject to the same limit imposed originally with respect to elections to the House. In other words, the cases discussed earlier, striking down limitations on who may vote, have no historical basis. Nor indeed does the Supreme Court's famous "one man, one vote" rule, prohibiting vote dilution through creation of legislative districts with substantially uneven populations.[68] Even at the time of the ratification of the Fourteenth Amendment, unevenly sized legislative districts were commonplace, and no one thought that the new Amendment raised doubts about their validity.[69]

Does this mean that the Court's voting rights jurisprudence is illegitimate? Perhaps—certainly that point has been argued, most forcefully by the second Justice Harlan, dissenting in the key voting cases. But there is another tack one might take here. The truth is that since the Framing era, and especially since the beginning of the twentieth century, the structure of American democracy, the nature of our constitutional government, has fundamentally changed. It has become more inclusive, more egalitarian, and frankly more democratic. These changes are reflected in some constitutional amendments—such as the Nineteenth Amendment, granting women the right to vote, the Twenty-third Amendment, permitting citizens of Washington, D.C. to vote for the president, the Twenty-fourth Amendment, barring poll taxes in federal elections, and the Twenty-sixth Amendment, granting eighteen-year-olds the right to vote—but the cultural changes we are discussing go far beyond these specific provisions. In combination, they have transformed the *meaning* of popular sovereignty and the concept that the People control the government. In the modern era, concepts such as indirect election, virtual representation (the idea that nonvoters are represented by voters), and political insulation for representatives, all common in the Framing period and after, have lost their cachet. Instead, our democracy is characterized by universal adult suffrage and highly responsive representatives

---

66. U.S. Const., Art. I, § 2, cl. 1.

67. *See* Harper v. Virginia State Board of Elections, *supra*, 383 U.S. at 684–685 (Harlan, J., dissenting) (discussing history).

68. Reynolds v. Simms, *supra*, 377 U.S. 533.

69. *Id*. at 602–607 (Harlan, J., dissenting).

(at least that is the theory). The Supreme Court's voting jurisprudence reflects these changes, in effect constitutionalizing them. Of course, for those who oppose a nontextual Constitution, or who take a narrowly historical approach to it, this is all entirely improper because it is not the Court's role. If, however, one believes that the Constitution does authorize courts to create and enforce new constitutional principles, and one believes that those principles should reinforce the structure of our democratic governments, it seems entirely reasonable that the Court should reinforce *our* system of democratic government, as it exists today, as opposed to the very different, far more exclusionary model of democracy of the Framing era.

Fitting the voting cases into a structural model is fairly trivial. Doing the same for the privacy cases is not. What, one might ask, is the link between issues such as contraception, abortion, or sodomy, and constitutional government? Certainly it is nowhere near as direct as with voting. Nonetheless, it is possible to identify several ways in which the Supreme Court's "substantive due process," privacy cases might advance structural goals.

One possibility is that like the First Amendment's religion clauses, the effect of the privacy jurisprudence is to remove certain intensely personal and highly divisive issues from the political sphere, because the impact of such issues on politics is corrosive. This argument posits that certain kinds of issues such as contraception, abortion, euthanasia, and homosexuality, issues that deal with personhood and which trigger strong, often religiously rooted feelings, are incapable of resolution through rational, political debate. As a result, attempting to resolve such issues through electoral politics creates deep, lasting political fissures that do not fade with time, because of the intensity of feeling attached to them, and so poison democracy at its roots, by turning the People on themselves. Put more bluntly, the argument is that democracy is simply incompetent to deal with such questions, and so they must be removed from democratic politics by the courts, in order to preserve democracy. There is something attractive, even compelling, about this position. Regardless of one's position on these issues, few would gainsay, I think, that debates over issues such as abortion and homosexuality have poisoned and corroded our politics over the past several decades, creating rancor and bitterness that inevitably leaks over into all other areas of disagreement.

There are, however, also profound problems with this justification for the privacy cases. Most obviously, it seems clear that if the purpose of the Supreme Court's intervention was to prevent political divisions, it has failed utterly. More than three decades after *Roe v. Wade*, the divisive, bitter political struggles over abortion continue. There is also something deeply disturbing, and frankly counterintuitive, about the proposition that democracy "cannot handle" difficult and divisive issues. Unlike religious differences, which are not susceptible to legislative "settlement" and which have a long history of triggering political violence, our state governments and nations around the world *have* managed to resolve even the sorts of issues at stake in the privacy cases through the political process. After all, before *Roe v. Wade* was decided, legislatures *did* consider how to best regulate abortion, and as the *Roe* Court itself noted, several states had liberalized their abortion laws in the years preceding that decision.[70] Similarly, state legislatures have not proven incapable of legislating regarding homosexuality—indeed, by the time the *Lawrence* case was decided in 2003, most American states had repealed, or no longer enforced, their sodomy laws.[71] Even euthanasia and assisted suicide have been addressed democratically without untoward political repercussions, most notably in Oregon and Washington states, both of which have legalized some forms of assisted suicide.[72] Not only is it doubtful that democratic politics are incapable of resolving these types of issues, there is a real question of why, even if democratic government struggles in this area, it is legitimate for the views of nine, or even five (a bare majority) Supreme Court Justices to prevail on these types of issues. After all, even if there may be structural reasons to remove these issues from politics, this tells us nothing (on its own) about what the "correct" resolution of them should be. Thus, any particular decision, favoring or disfavoring abortion rights for example, cannot be said to reinforce democracy any more than the opposite conclusion. Given this, making the country abide by the Court's diktat seems profoundly undemocratic. Finally, it is far from clear how the Court is to identify which issues are sufficiently "personal" or "divisive" to justify their removal from the political process. Why, for example, abortion but not euthanasia and assisted suicide? Why contraception, but not tax policy? Absent some solid basis for making these distinctions, there is a grave danger that the Court will slide down a slippery slope of constitutionalizing ever more politically significant issues, at the expense of the democratic process. The result would likely be a highly libertarian Constitution, of the sort championed by among others Randy Barnett.[73] While for many, including myself, this is a tempting and attractive prospect as a matter of policy, the reality is that it is not faithful to the Constitution that we have. For all of these reasons, absent some *substantive* ground for resolving these kinds of disputes, the desire to remove them from the democratic process cannot alone justify the Court's privacy jurisprudence.

Can the privacy cases then be fit into a structural constitutional framework in some other way? And if so, how? The beginnings of an answer to these questions

---

70. Roe v. Wade, *supra*, 410 U.S. at 140 & n.37.

71. Lawrence v. Texas, *supra*, 539 U.S. at 573.

72. *See* Gonzales v. Oregon, 546 U.S. 243 (2006) (discussing Oregon Death with Dignity Act); Curt Woodward, *Wash. Voters Approve Assisted Suicide Initiative*, SEATTLE TIMES, Nov. 4, 2008, *available at* http://seattletimes.nwsource.com/html/localnews/2008352565_apwaassistedsuicide2ndldwritethru.html.

73. *See generally* RANDY E. BARNETT, *supra*, RESTORING THE LOST CONSTITUTION: THE PRESUMPTION OF LIBERTY.

can be found in the Supreme Court's decision in *Lawrence v. Texas*. In *Lawrence*, recall, the Court struck down a Texas statute banning "homosexual sodomy" and tied its ruling to its line of privacy cases dealing with contraception and abortion, including *Griswold, Roe,* and *Casey*.[74] Importantly, however, the *Lawrence* Court did *not* suggest that this series of cases establishes some sort of a general right to sexual autonomy, as a matter of "fundamental rights" or "natural law" (note that in the earlier cases, *reproductive* autonomy might be considered the common theme, but reproduction obviously was not at issue in *Lawrence*). Instead, as discussed above, Justice Kennedy's opinion in *Lawrence* emphasized the private "personal relationship" between John Lawrence and Tyron Garner, and condemned the State's efforts to control and interfere with that relationship.[75] Why emphasize the private relationship, rather than sexuality? For one, this emphasis places important limitations on the holding in *Lawrence*, clarifying that regulation of either prostitution or public sexual acts does not raise serious constitutional questions, since neither are central to an intimate relationship.[76] More broadly, however, the reasoning in *Lawrence* suggests how this and other privacy decisions relate to each other and fit within the broader constitutional framework.

As we discussed in earlier chapters, one of the core purposes of the Bill of Rights, and of the Constitution generally, is to maintain a proper balance of power between the government and citizens, to ensure that the People ultimately retain control over their government. One key technique for accomplishing this is to shield from governmental control or excessive regulation private institutions and associations, which permit citizens to collectively think, organize, and shape their values independently of the State. The First Amendment in particular singles out political and religious associations and institutions for protection. I would argue that the privacy cases can be read to protect another such set of social institutions: the family and family-like relationships. There can be no doubt that family relationships, and the network of connections, emotions, and shared values that they encompass, have throughout our history played a central role in defining the relationship of individual citizens to society, and more to the point, have provided a critical bulwark against the influence of the State. Family ties strengthen individuals and provide spheres of privacy within which values are inculcated, support is provided, and if necessary shelter is provided, independent of the government. Especially with respect to children, and especially in the era of public schools run by the government, the role of the family in creating citizens whose values and beliefs are not under the complete control of the State is critical. Nor is the importance of the family limited to the raising of children. For adults as well, intimate relationships with one's spouse or partner, children,

---

74. Lawrence v. Texas, *supra*, 539 U.S. at 564–565.
75. *Id.* at 567.
76. *Id.* at 578.

siblings, and parents, provide a crucial sanctuary within which discussions can happen and values and beliefs can be formed in *private*, outside the public sphere. Of course, providing a refuge against the State is not the *only* or even the most important role that family plays, any more than providing a bulwark against the State is the most important role of religious institutions; but it is *a* role, and one that is an important, albeit rarely consciously considered, part of the balance in our political and social system.[77]

That this is the best reading of the Court's privacy cases finds strong support in the language of the Supreme Court's 1984 decision in *Roberts v. United States Jaycees*.[78] The issue in the *Roberts* case was whether the United States Jaycees, a large, national organization dedicated to providing young people (at the time, young men) with training and connections in the business world,[79] could constitutionally be required, pursuant to a state antidiscrimination statute, to admit women as members. The Jaycees argued that their rights of privacy and of political association (under the First Amendment) shielded the organization from such regulation. Discussing the privacy claim, which the Court tellingly described as a claim to "intimate association," the Court noted that its decisions in this area "afford the formation and preservation of certain kinds of highly personal relationships a substantial measure of sanctuary from unjustified interference by the State." The reason for this, it added, was "that certain kinds of personal bonds have played a critical role in the culture and traditions of the Nation by cultivating and transmitting shared ideals and beliefs; they thereby foster diversity and act as critical buffers between the individual and the power of the State. . . . Moreover, the constitutional shelter afforded such relationships reflects the realization that individuals draw much of their emotional enrichment from close ties with others. Protecting these relationships from unwarranted state interference therefore safeguards the ability independently to define one's identity."[80] Ultimately, the Court concluded—clearly correctly—that given its size and anonymity, the Jaycees did not constitute an "intimate association."[81]

---

77. For a similar explication of the privacy cases, *see* Philip B. Heymann and Douglas B. Barzelay, *The Forest and the Trees: Roe v. Wade and Its Critics*, 53 B.U.L. Rev. 765, 772–775 (1973).

78. 468 U.S. 609 (1984).

79. *See* http://www.usjaycees.org/.

80. Roberts v. United States Jaycees, *supra*, 468 U.S. at 618–619.

81. The Court did conclude that the First Amendment provided the Jaycees with some protection, but found that the State's compelling interest in prohibiting gender discrimination trumped those interests. This latter conclusion, rooted in "balancing" as it is, seems somewhat dubious, and it should be noted that sixteen years later the Court did *not* follow the reasoning of the *Roberts* opinion, when it held that the First Amendment prevented the State of New Jersey from requiring the Boy Scouts of America to retain a gay scoutmaster. See *Boy Scouts of America v. Dale*, 530 U.S. 640 (2000).

The understanding of privacy cases as shielding intimate associations, such as family, from the control and influence of the State, is supported not only by the language of opinions such as *Lawrence* and *Roberts*, but also by the shape of the Court's privacy cases more generally. Most obviously, the Supreme Court's earliest decisions in this area, *Meyer v. Nebraska*[82] and *Pierce v. Society of Sisters*,[83] involved State efforts to remove from parents their authority to control their children's education, a step that would have profoundly upset the balance between private spheres and the State. Cases involving family definition, such as *Moore v. City of East Cleveland*,[84] ensure that it is individuals, not the State, that get to define the contours and membership of their most important, intimate associations, and cases such as *Loving v. Virginia*[85] protecting the right to marry similarly ensure that it is the individual, not the State, who is empowered to decide *whether*, and with *whom*, to form such associations—the miscegenation statute invalidated in *Loving* constituted a particularly biased, and politically charged, effort by the State to control the formation of families. Finally, in *Griswold v. Connecticut*[86] the Court, by striking down laws prohibiting the use of contraceptives, ensured that just as citizens cannot be prohibited by the State from forming intimate associations, they also cannot be required by the State to form families with particular structures or of a particular nature—i.e., families with children—with all of the constraints and obligations that that implies. Indeed, even the abortion cases can be read as supporting the same principle, though as we shall see, that description is more controversial and open to question. Ultimately, therefore, both the case law and specific language from some cases support the idea that the privacy cases are best read to defend from undue State interference an area of private, intimate association, which provides an important counterbalance to the power of the State.

This reading of the privacy cases also helps to explain some of the limitations of the law in this area. Most obviously, it establishes an important limitation on the scope of the *Lawrence* decision. *Lawrence* did not, as some have suggested, create a general "right" to autonomy in the area of sexuality, it only prohibited the State from interfering with sexual conduct in the context of intimate relationships. Casual sex remains subject to governmental control. Similar reasoning suggests that the Alabama Supreme Court was correct to reject a constitutional challenge to an Alabama statute banning the sale of sex toys.[87] Silly as such a law may be, it is highly unlikely that it significantly interferes with intimate relationships in a way

---

82. 262 U.S. 390 (1923).
83. 268 U.S. 510 (1925).
84. 431 U.S. 494 (1977).
85. 388 U.S. 1 (1967).
86. 381 U.S. 479 (1965).
87. *1568 Montgomery Highway, Inc. v. City of Hoover*, 2009 Ala. LEXIS 209 (Ala. September 11, 2009).

likely to affect the ability of such relationships to shield individuals from the power of the State. And a focus on relationships also explains why, when in *Moore v. City of East Cleveland* the Supreme Court struck down a law forbidding members of extended families from living together, it expressly reaffirmed its earlier decision in *Village of Belle Terre v. Boraas*[88] upholding a law prohibiting unrelated persons from living together.

Consider also *Washington v. Glucksberg*,[89] in which the Court declined to extend its privacy jurisprudence to encompass a "right to die." This decision seems difficult to understand if the substantive due process cases are read to protect spheres of "fundamental" autonomy rights, areas of particular importance to individuals—after all, surely controlling the manner of one's death is as important to individuals as controlling one's procreation or one's living arrangements. A "right to die," however, has little to do with intimate association, as defined above. Recognizing a right to assisted suicide would not in any way strengthen private associations and relationships against State interference, and would not seriously contribute to maintaining the ongoing balance of power between the People and the State. As such, such a "right" has no place in the privacy jurisprudence. Similarly, when in *Michael H. v. Gerald D.*[90] the Court declined to recognize the rights of "an adulterous, natural father," this holding seemed irreconcilable with earlier decisions enforcing parental rights. Crucially, however, the natural father in *Michael H.* was *not* truly a member of an intimate association, and indeed, was arguably trying to insert himself into such a relationship, against the will of that family. One can see why in that situation the Court rejected his claim as unsupported by previous cases—though it must be conceded that there are counterarguments here, including notably the argument that Michael H. did not seek to undermine an existing family, he wished to form a separate intimate relationship with his child. Be that as it may, a focus on intimate associations seems to help explain the overall shape of the law of "substantive due process" better than any of the alternatives, albeit it is not perfect.

Finally, understanding the Court's privacy cases as protecting intimate associations from the power of the State also has important implications for the constitutionality of sex discrimination. As noted in Chapter 9, since the early 1970s, the Supreme Court has struck down a wide variety of laws that discriminate on the basis of sex, on the grounds that such laws violate the Equal Protection Clause of the Fourteenth Amendment. In particular, the Court has held unconstitutional laws that reinforce traditional gender roles, while upholding laws that use sex-based categories to compensate women for past discrimination, or that draw gender distinctions based on perceived "real" biological differences between the sexes. As also noted in that chapter, however, there are serious, perhaps

---

88. 416 U.S. 1 (1974).
89. Washington v. Glucksberg, 521 U.S. 707 (1997).
90. 491 U.S. 505 (1989).

insurmountable flaws with the Court's conclusion that sex discrimination contravenes the structural principles underlying the Equal Protection Clause. The Supreme Court's sex discrimination jurisprudence might, however, find a more stable footing in the law of privacy. The difficulty with official sex discrimination, from the privacy perspective, is that by legalizing traditional gender roles, and forcing women to live their lives according to those roles, the government is effectively forcing families into particular, State-sanctioned patterns—to wit, a male wage earner, married to a female who is economically dependent and primarily responsible for child rearing. That is the clear impact of laws that ban women from particular professions or pay them less for equal work. Discriminatory laws often also have the purpose and effect of reinforcing the notion of male primacy within the family, by denying women political and economic equality and excluding them from pursuits and careers (such as military service) that are associated in our society with prestige and power. In short, laws that reinforce traditional gender roles are deeply and inevitably intertwined with the traditional family structure and represent governmental efforts to force all families into that structure. But this direct intrusion into and interference with the private sphere of the family is precisely the sort of state action that is condemned by modern privacy jurisprudence because it represents an effort by the State to homogenize and control the family, forcing individuals into particular sorts of intimate associations favored by the government. All of the decisions discussed in Chapter 9 striking down laws that discriminated on the basis of sex can be read to implement this principle, from the early cases such as *Frontiero* requiring equal pay for equal work, to the *Hogan* case requiring Mississippi to admit men to a state nursing school, to the *VMI* case forbidding the government from excluding women from a prestigious educational opportunity. The commonality is that in each of them, the Court was faced with official efforts to force men and women into particular social roles, social roles that have meaning only within the context of the traditional family, and so into specific, government-approved forms of intimate association. But that is unconstitutional under the privacy cases. Thus insofar as the Court's sex discrimination decisions cannot be supported by equal protection principles, the structural privacy principle provides an alternate basis to sustain them.

EVOLVING PRIVACY AND DUE PROCESS

An important point to recognize about the Court's privacy jurisprudence, and the concept of intimate association as a constitutionally protected sphere, is that like the rest of the nontextual Constitution, it is an area of law that has evolved, and continues to evolve, in the course of applying broad constitutional principles to contemporary, social realities. During the Framing era, the idea that the family unit required protection from government interference would probably have seemed strange, if not bizarre. After all, this was a time before ubiquitous public schooling and when questions such as marriage and child rearing were left largely in the private and religious spheres, with little State regulation.[91] By the twentieth century, however, the growing power of the State in every field of life, including the education of children most especially, began to create clashes between the private sphere of family and the State, thereby producing the Supreme Court's first cases protecting intimate association, *Meyer* and *Pierce*. At this point, however, given social mores, it would never have occurred to most people, and certainly not to the judges responsible for expounding the nontextual Constitution, that nontraditional relationships outside the traditional family might play a similar social role to the traditional family and so warrant constitutional protection. Even when *Griswold* was decided in 1965, the Court was careful to limit its ruling to *married* couples, emphasizing that it was the marital relationship which, because of its long history and central role in our society, needed to be shielded from State interference in the form of Connecticut's ban on contraceptives. In subsequent years, however, the Supreme Court has demonstrated a growing willingness to protect intimate relationships outside of marriage or the traditional, nuclear family, a willingness that reflects the massive changes that our society has undergone since the mid-1960s. Thus in the *Eisenstadt* case in 1972, the Court extended the holding of *Griswold* to *unmarried* couples, even though traditionally such couples had no legal protection, and indeed would have been considered highly immoral. Around the same time, in *Stanley v. Illinois*, the Court granted protection to the relationship between an unmarried father and his children, and in *Moore v. City of East Cleveland* the Court shielded a nonnuclear family from State interference. Finally, and most significantly, in 2003 the Court, in *Lawrence v. Texas*, extended its protective shield to homosexual couples, despite the obvious lack of historical protection for such relationships.[92] These decisions appear to reflect a growing understanding that in *our* society, with its vastly changed social and sexual mores, the role that the traditional, nuclear family has played historically as a private sphere, independent of the government, in which individuals can be nurtured and values formed, is increasingly played by other relationships as well, including nontraditional families and unmarried couples, both heterosexual and homosexual

---

91. *See generally* LAWRENCE FRIEDMAN, A HISTORY OF AMERICAN LAW 202–204, 496–497 (2nd ed. 1985); MICHAEL GROSSBERG, GOVERNING THE HEARTH: LAW AND THE FAMILY IN NINETEENTH-CENTURY AMERICA ch. 3 (1985).

92. Of course, there is some irony here since, as we discussed earlier, on the facts of the *Lawrence* case itself, there are real doubts if John Lawrence and Tyrone Garner shared the sort of intimate relationship that the Court's jurisprudence seeks to protect. The Court, however, was unaware of that fact, explaining its failure to refer to it. And in any event, the decision might be justified on the true facts as protecting not only existing, intimate relationships, but also the potential development of such relationships.

(the implications of this logic for the question of same-sex marriage is a question to which we turn shortly). Given this social evolution, for the privacy right to perform its structural function, it must be expanded to encompass such nontraditional relationships. In cases such as *Eisenstadt* and *Lawrence*, the Court has done just that—it has kept the privacy jurisprudence relevant to the modern world.

The evolution of the nontextual Constitution, it should be noted, is not a one-way ratchet, expanding constitutional protections only. There are times when social changes require the Constitution to contract, because protections that once made sense no longer do. Consider in this respect the *Lochner* era, and the economic substantive due process line of cases. The premise of the Justices of the *Lochner* era was that it was vital to the constitutional government that economic freedom be protected from excessive State interference, with a particular emphasis on freedom of contract with respect to labor. At some level, this reasoning makes some sense. After all, the ability to earn a livelihood, to feed and support oneself and one's family, is extraordinarily important to all people, and it is easy to see how governmental control over citizens' livelihoods could be abused in dangerous ways, as a means of punishing dissent and undermining the People's independence from the State. There is, after all, a reason why communist countries tend to be totalitarian. As discussed in Chapter 7, there is certainly evidence that the Framers felt this way, going out of their way as they did to protect certain kinds of property and contractual rights from State interference. It is also true that the concept of freedom of labor, the right to sell one's labor freely as an important aspect of personal liberty, was an important element of abolitionist thinking in the antebellum era and would certainly have influenced the authors of the Fourteenth Amendment. During an era when the economy was dominated by agriculture and small enterprises, often of an artisanal nature, these sorts of concerns made some sense because government regulation of economic relationships probably was more of a threat to the People than of much use. All of this changed, however, with the accelerating industrialization of the United States in the late nineteenth and twentieth centuries. In these new circumstances, where businesses evolved into massive corporations and the balance of negotiating power tilted sharply in favor of employers, the idea that lack of government regulation equated with individual control over their economic destiny became at best dubious, and indeed in practice simply untrue. The tragedy of the Supreme Court during the *Lochner* era was not that their ideas and assumptions were nonsensical, but that they failed to adjust their thinking to changing circumstances. Products of the preindustrial era themselves, they (or most of them) simply could not see that lack of government regulation of labor did not mean, any more, that individual citizens controlled their own economic destiny. Instead, such a policy left workers at the mercy of employers, with no economic security at all, and so more vulnerable to all sorts of coercive influence, from both private and public sources. It was only in 1937, seeing the effects of the Great Depression, that a majority of the Supreme Court was able to perceive this changed reality and so turn its back on a jurisprudence that no longer made any sense.

SAME-SEX MARRIAGE AND ABORTION

We close our discussion of the nontextual Constitution by reconsidering, from a structural perspective, the two most controversial topics in the general privacy area: same-sex marriage and abortion. We begin with the newer topic, same-sex marriage,[93] and then turn to the never-ending abortion debate. As a starting point, it is now uncontroversial that the nontextual Constitution places some restrictions on the State's power to regulate marriage. From a structural perspective, this makes perfect sense. After all, despite all of the social changes of the past half century, it remains true that the most common form of intimate association in our society, and the bedrock of the private sphere, remains marriage. To grant the government unlimited power to decide who may marry, and who may marry whom, is to permit State intrusion into this sphere in unacceptable ways. This reasoning suggests that the privacy jurisprudence *must* be extended to prevent the government from limiting marriage to couples of opposite sexes. After all, same-sex marriages and families are no less a private sphere, a bulwark against the normalizing power of the State, than traditional marriages, and as the *Lawrence* case recognizes, the fact that such relationships were not traditionally protected is, under modern circumstances, irrelevant. The difficulty here is that marriage is not quite like other areas of "privacy," in that it is not a purely private institution. Marriage, at least in the modern world, is a government-sanctioned and government-created institution, a state license, as it were (I speak here of legal marriage, not religious marriage, to which the Constitution does not speak). As such, some governmental regulation of, and limitations upon, marriage are inevitable. No one doubts, for example, that the government can enforce incest limits on marriage, and other requirements such as blood tests also seem to be uncontroversial. So, why isn't a rule limiting marriage to "one man and one woman" a similar, reasonable restriction? The answer, I think, can be found in the government's *reason* for imposing the restriction—as noted in Chapter 4, a structural approach to constitutionalism pushes toward a focus on governmental motives in difficult cases. When the government prohibits incest

---

93. As discussed in Chapter 8, modern restrictions on same-sex marriage almost certainly violate the Equal Protection Clause of the Fourteenth Amendment, as read through a structural lens. The analysis provided here, under the Due Process Clause, provides a potential, alternative grounds to invalidate such restrictions. It should be noted that same-sex marriage restrictions are unconstitutional if they violate *either* the Equal Protection or the Due Process clauses.

or imposes blood test requirements, it is seeking to protect individuals entering into marriage from real harms, such as genetic problems in offspring or venereal diseases. No such claim, however, can be made about bans on same-sex marriages. Such bans obviously do not seek to protect those entering into marriage, nor do they otherwise stabilize the institution of marriage (unless one accepts the claim that permitting homosexuals to marry somehow undermines the marriages of heterosexuals, which as discussed in Chapter 9 is probably based on the incorrect conflation in people's minds of the civil, government-controlled and religious institutions of marriage). The sole purpose of same-sex marriage bans is to impose a State-blessed orthodoxy regarding the structure of a "family." Preventing such state control over intimate associations is, however, the very purpose of the modern privacy jurisprudence. To allow the State to decide what sorts of intimate associations, what sorts of families, it will permit to come into existence is to permit the State to intrude directly into the private sphere of intimate association, and thereby to undermine the independence of one of the crucial, social institutions that keeps the power of the State in check. Moreover, this remains true even if a majority of citizens, at any particular time or in any particular place, support the government's policies in this regard. One of the reasons to constitutionalize structural principles of government is to prevent transitory majorities of citizens from undermining the long-term stability of democratic self-government. Of course, denying the benefit of marriage to same-sex couples and families does not mean that such relationships will not exist. But it does undermine them by denying them legal protections and benefits, and given the absence of any neutral reason for the State to act in this way, it seems the better view that such policies violate the "right to marriage" that forms a part of the Supreme Court's modern privacy jurisprudence.

We turn, finally, to the vexing question of abortion. The question we consider, in short, is whether the Supreme Court's decisions such as *Roe v. Wade* and *Planned Parenthood v. Casey*, holding unconstitutional state restrictions on the availability of abortion, can be reconciled with a structural approach to the nontextual Constitution. The argument in favor of the Court's resolution of the abortion problem builds on the same argument that justified the *Griswold* decision. After all, there is an obvious relationship between a state law banning contraceptives and a state law banning abortions—both force individuals to bring children into the world against their will. Therefore, it can be argued, broad prohibitions on abortion, of the sort struck down in *Roe v. Wade*, intrude on individuals' control over their intimate associations by forcing individuals to enter into associations by the will of the State rather than by their own will, just as do laws banning contraception. Indeed, on this understanding abortion laws are particularly problematic because they specifically regulate *women*, often single women, in a way that physically takes over a woman's body for nine months, and then imposes enormous personal and financial burdens for years thereafter. Thus, prohibitions on abortion constitute a particularly pervasive instance of state intrusion into the private sphere, and a socially and politically tilted one, which systematically disadvantages women, especially single women and increasingly women of color,[94] vis-à-vis the rest of society. Abortion regulation, like sodomy laws and bans on same-sex marriage, thus represent the kind of systematically skewed intervention by the State into intimate relationships that is constitutionally problematic, because it involves the government in the shaping of private society, thereby seriously upsetting the balance of power between citizens and the State. Indeed, this argument suggests that abortion regulation is particularly troublesome because it involves state interference with intimate relationships both by controlling the creation of such relationships (parallel to the contraception cases) and by disempowering women, thereby controlling their role in such relationships (parallel to the sex discrimination cases).

The above represents probably the most compelling case that can be made that the Court's abortion decisions fit squarely into its general privacy jurisprudence, as viewed from a structural perspective. The argument is, however, seriously incomplete and therefore potentially vulnerable. The difficulty is that the argument relies critically on characterizing laws prohibiting most or all abortions as State action that is directed toward forcing women to have unwanted children and so occupying their lives. That is of course one understanding of these laws, the one favored by proponents of abortion choice.[95] But it is not the only possible characterization. What it ignores is the other side of the coin. Opponents of abortion would argue that the true *purpose* of abortion laws is not to coerce women, it is to protect the lives of fetuses, which they would value as fully human lives; and that the impact of abortion laws on the lives of women is an unintended consequence only. They would further argue that the desire to protect human, or even potential human, life is a perfectly legitimate governmental policy, that raises no constitutional concerns, even under the broadest reading of the nontextual Constitution, because it has nothing to do with the State intruding into private spheres in which it has no business. This is an argument that cannot really be gainsaid on its own turns, although it rests on highly controversial and unprovable (on both sides) assumptions about the moral status of the fetus. So which is the proper characterization of abortion bans, as laws forcing women to have children, or as laws protecting human or potential human life? The answer is, of course, that both descriptions have some truth to them, because both reflect realities regarding the impact of abortion laws and the motivations of different actors in this drama. It is this uncertainty that is precisely the

---

94. *See* Rob Stein, *Study Finds Major Shift in Abortion Demographics*, WASHINGTON POST A03, Sept. 23, 2008, *available at* http://www.washingtonpost.com/wp-dyn/content/article/2008/09/22/AR2008092202831.html.

95. *See* Lucinda M. Finley, *Contested Ground: The Story of* Roe v. Wade *and its Impact on American Society* in CONSTITUTIONAL LAW STORIES 381–382 (Michael C. Dorf ed., 2nd ed. 2009).

source of the intense controversy over the legitimacy of the Court's abortion decisions.

How then should a Court respond to this uncertainty? As a matter of first principles, I am forced to conclude, extremely reluctantly and with grave doubts it must be said, that in the face of this uncertainty, when a legitimate legislative purpose remains perfectly plausible and likely honestly held, courts generally should defer to legislatures. The reason is that absent a clear basis for concluding that an elected legislature is acting illegitimately, on what grounds is a Court to overturn a democratic judgment? If there is none, then as an original matter, *Roe v. Wade* was incorrectly decided. Of course, if it can be convincingly demonstrated that a desire to push women into traditional gender roles *is* a major force behind abortion regulation, then the privacy argument regains force. Furthermore, the weaknesses in the privacy argument do *not* necessarily mean that the Court should completely abandon its abortion jurisprudence today. In addition to principle, there are of course other values in the legal system, including notably the value of stability and following past precedents, which is called the principle of *stare decisis*.[96] A long time has passed since *Roe* was decided in 1973, and that passage of time alone counsels against a radical reworking of the law—indeed, the Court in *Planned Parenthood v. Casey* relied on precisely this argument in declining to overrule *Roe*.[97] Ultimately, the question of how to balance interpretational consistency and adherence to first principles against the interests in stability and repose is an extremely difficult one, requiring a difficult judicial judgment, and one on which theory sheds little practical light.

---

96. *But see* Gary Lawson, *The Constitutional Case Against Precedent*, 17 HARV. J. L. & PUB. POL'Y 23 (1994); Gary Lawson, *Mostly Unconstitutional: The Case Against Precedent Revisited* 5 AVE MARIA L. REV. 1 (2007) (arguing against following precedent in constitutional cases).

97. Planned Parenthood v. Casey, *supra*, 505 U.S. at 854–869.

11. STRUCTURAL RIGHTS AND THE WAR ON TERROR

Guantanamo Bay. Extraordinary rendition. Enemy combatant. Waterboarding. Warrantless surveillance. Military commissions. Suspension of habeas corpus. The eight long years of the second Bush Administration and the War on Terror that it prosecuted have generated an extraordinary number of complex and divisive questions of constitutional law.[1] Notably, however, most of the constitutional disputes arising out of the War on Terror have *not* primarily implicated the main topic of this book, the Bill of Rights and the Fourteenth Amendment. Instead, they have tended to relate to topics such as the separation of powers, the scope of and limits on executive power, and the role of international law. This is not to say that the Bill of Rights is completely irrelevant to these disputes—in particular, the detention of enemy combatants clearly implicates the Due Process Clause of the Fifth Amendment, and the National Security Agency's (NSA's) program of warrantless wiretapping potentially violates the Search and Seizure Clause of the Fourth Amendment. On the whole, however, the role of the Bill of Rights has certainly been peripheral in recent disputes, and even when clearly implicated, their application to these disputes has been far from clear. Why that is so, but why the insights we have developed up to this point nonetheless shed important light on the constitutionality of certain aspects of the War on Terror, is the subject of this chapter.

We should begin with first principles, clarifying the nature of the *constitutional* questions raised by the War on Terror (the far greater number of moral and policy questions raised are beyond the scope of our discussion). In response to the attacks of September 11, 2001, the administration of President George W. Bush took a number of steps and adopted a number of policies. Some of those steps, such as the invasion of Afghanistan, were explicitly authorized by the Congress.[2] Others, such as the imprisonment without trial of enemy combatants within the United States, were taken in the face of congressional silence or ambiguity. And yet others, such as the NSA's warrantless wiretapping program, quite clearly violated extant congressional statutes.[3] With respect to each of these steps

---

1. This chapter was completed at the dawn of the Obama Administration, and so will focus on the Bush Administration's policies. Obviously, however, the analysis is equally applicable to the Obama Administration's policies.

2. *See Authorization for Use of Military Force*, Pub. L. No. 107-40 (Sept. 18, 2001), *available at* http://www.thomas.gov/cgi-bin/query/D?c107:1:./temp/~mdbsJ25hr3::.

3. *See* Evan Tsen Lee, *The Legality of the NSA Wiretapping Program*, 12 Tex. J. Civ. Lib. & Civ. Rts. 1, 3–5 (2006) (demonstrating that NSA wiretapping program violates the Foreign Intelligence Surveillance Act of 1978, as it then existed).

or policies, the first, crucial constitutional question that arises is whether the Constitution grants the president the *power* to do what he did. With respect to congressionally authorized actions, this question reduces to whether the U.S. government, as a whole, possesses that power, a question to which the answer is almost inevitably yes. With respect to actions taken without congressional permission, however, and even more so with actions taken in the face of a statutory ban, the issues of constitutional authority become far more difficult, and it is around these questions that most recent constitutional disputes have revolved. Even if the president is found to possess the constitutional power to act as he did, however, a separate question can still be raised as to whether his actions violate the restrictions on governmental power created by the Bill of Rights (the Fourteenth Amendment does not pose a problem, since it limits only state governments, not the national government). As noted above, such questions were raised regarding the detainment of enemy combatants and warrantless wiretapping; but in many instances, the Bill of Rights has not played a significant role in resolving constitutional disputes, for what, as we shall see, are good reasons.

That then is the outline, in broadest terms, of the interaction between the Constitution and the War on Terror. Before turning to some specific disputes, however, two important, preliminary points need to be recognized. First, it is important to note that whether or not the War on Terror technically qualifies as a "war" for constitutional and international-law purposes (a question on which reasonable people surely differ), there is no doubt that the U.S. government's actions in the War on Terror implicate the national government's powers in the area of military and foreign affairs, because they generally involve both protecting the United States from attacks commenced and directed from abroad and interacting with foreign governments, organizations, and nationals. This is significant because while the powers of the national government in our system of federalism are quite limited in the domestic sphere, in the international sphere they are both broad and generally exclusive.[4] As a consequence, when Congress and the president act in concert on foreign and military issues, there are few doubts that the Constitution empowers their actions (though the Bill of Rights may impose external constraints). Not only does the national government as a whole possess broad powers in this area, it is also generally acknowledged that the president enjoys unusually broad, unilateral powers over foreign and military affairs, both because of specific powers delegated to him in Article II of the Constitution such as the power to act as "Commander in Chief" of the U.S. military and to "receive Ambassadors and other public Ministers,"[5] and the general

---

4. The classic exposition of this point by the Supreme Court is *United States v. Curtiss-Wright Corp.*, 299 U.S. 304 (1936).

5. U.S. Const., Art. II, §§2, 3.

"executive power" vested in the president.[6] There are, of course, sharp differences among scholars (and politicians) regarding the *scope* of the president's powers in this area, including notably over whether the Constitution authorizes him to commence military hostilities without prior congressional approval,[7] but most observers seem to agree on the existence of at least some, significant presidential powers.[8] As a consequence, as we shall see, even when the president acts unilaterally, in the face of congressional silence, he is often able to advance very plausible arguments that his actions are constitutionally authorized. Of course, this background does little to resolve situations when the president acts *contrary* to congressional will, which as we shall see remain hotly disputed.

The second preliminary point is an even more fundamental one. Let us begin, again, with first principles. The fundamental function of the Bill of Rights in our system of government is to maintain critical limits on the power of the federal government, in order to ensure that a proper balance of power is maintained between the People of the United States and their government. The Bill of Rights is designed, in short, to maintain ultimate sovereignty, and ultimate political authority, in the People. Of course, it is not just the Bill of Rights that serves this function. The carefully designed system of democratic accountability, checks and balances, and limitations on power set forth in the main body of the Constitution have the same, basic aim. At the same time, of course, the framers intended to create a government that actually worked, that could take actions as needed to serve the interests of the People of the United States—as the Preamble to the Constitution states, to "establish Justice, insure domestic Tranquility, provide for the common defence, promote the general Welfare, and secure the Blessings of Liberty to ourselves and our Posterity."[9] As we shall see, because of this commonality of purpose, there are important similarities, and important interactions, between the Bill of Rights and the main body of the Constitution. Before exploring these details, however, a more basic question must be answered, which turns out to be critical in resolving many of the disputes surrounding the War on Terror: Who precisely are the "People of the United States" whom the Constitution and the Bill of Rights serve?

The importance of this question cannot be overlooked, because the concept of the People pervades the Constitution. The very first words of that document state

---

6. U.S. Const., Art. II, § 1, cl. 2. For discussions of the nature and scope of the executive power vested in the president, *see* Steven G. Calabresi and Kevin H. Rhodes, *The Structural Constitution: Unitary Executive, Plural Judiciary*, 105 Harv. L. Rev. 1153 (1992); Saikrishna B. Prakash and Michael D. Ramsey, *The Executive Power Over Foreign Affairs*, 111 Yale L. J. 231 (2001).

7. The debate is summarized in Lee, *supra*, 12 Tex. J. Civ. Lib. & Civ. Rts. at 22–23.

8. The primary naysayers to this thesis appear to be Curtis A. Bradley and Martin S. Flaherty, *Executive Power Essentialism and Foreign Affairs*, 102 Mich. L. Rev. 545 (2004).

9. U.S. Const., Preamble.

that "*We the People* of the United States" are creating the Constitution, establishing the primacy of that concept. In addition, no fewer than five of the ten amendments constituting the Bill of Rights specifically refer to "the People—the First Amendment ("right of the people peaceably to assemble, and to petition the Government for a redress of grievances"), the Second ("right of the people to keep and bear Arms"), the Fourth ("right of the people to be secure in their persons, houses, papers, and effects, against unreasonable searches and seizures"), the Ninth ("others [rights] retained by the people"), and the Tenth ("powers not delegated to the United States . . . are reserved to the States respectively, or to the people"). So again, who are these "People"? The basic answer should be clear—at a minimum, the People are composed of *all* citizens of the United States. It is citizens, after all, who constitute the body politic of the United States, possessing sovereign power, electing representatives to exercise that power on their behalf, and through the ratification and amendment process creating the Constitution in the first place. Of course, in the early days of the Republic there was some ambiguity about who precisely the word "citizen" included—women, after all, may have been "citizens" but they were denied all political rights, and in the *Dred Scott* case the Supreme Court infamously held that African Americans were not citizens of the United States.[10] Subsequent amendments, however, have resolved that problem. Notably the very first words of the Fourteenth Amendment are that "[a]ll persons born or naturalized in the United States and subject to the jurisdiction thereof, are citizens of the United States" (thereby reversing *Dred Scott*), and the Nineteenth Amendment, ratified in 1920, extended political rights to women. So, as of today it seems clear that "the People of the United States" constitutes all citizens, as currently understood, regardless of race, sex, or creed, and regardless of where they happen to be at any time.

The corollary of the conclusion that "the People" include all citizens is that it does not include anyone else—noncitizens simply are not part of "the People" who possess sovereignty.[11] The People who created the Constitution were the individuals who acted in a political capacity to ratify the document. In the framing era, that included voters who chose the members of the state ratifying conventions, as well as those who could not vote (because of limits on the franchise) but were considered to be virtually represented. But it did not include those— i.e., noncitizens—who could not act in a political capacity. Today, the People who possess sovereignty under the Constitution once again constitute those who can act in a political capacity by voting—i.e., almost all adult citizens—plus those who are virtually represented, which is primarily children, but also some adults

---

10. Dred Scott v. Sandford, 60 U.S. (19 How.) 393 (1857).

11. It should be acknowledged that there are hints in the Supreme Court's opinion in *United States v. Verdugo-Urquidez*, 494 U.S. 259 (1990) that noncitizen legal residents of the United States are a part of "the People" referred to in the Bill of Rights. These suggestions, however, are not supported by any analysis and seem clearly incorrect.

(such as felons) who continue to be denied the franchise. But noncitizens simply do not partake of this sovereignty, because they are not yet a part of this nation's body politic. Of course, noncitizens can *become* part of the sovereign People through the process of naturalization, but until that time, they are not the primary focus of the protections afforded by the Constitution.

The question that remains is whether the Constitution limits the power of the U.S. government to act on noncitizens, persons who by definition are not part of the sovereign People. On this point, the text of the Constitution is somewhat unclear (to put it mildly). On the one hand, as noted above, several provisions of the Bill of Rights restrict the government only with respect to rights "of the People," suggesting that noncitizens are not protected. Furthermore, the historically critical (albeit judicially nullified) Privileges or Immunities Clause of the Fourteenth Amendment forbids states from abridging only the "privileges or immunities *of citizens of the United States*," again suggesting a restrictive view. On the other hand, other provisions of the Bill of Rights and the Fourteenth Amendment seem broader. For example, the first part of the First Amendment protects "free exercise" of religion and "freedom of speech, or of the press" without limit. Similarly, the key criminal procedure provisions of the Bill of Rights, including the Due Process Clause of the Fifth Amendment, refer to "persons" or "the accused," and both the Due Process and Equal Protection clauses of the Fourteenth Amendment limit state power over "any person." Noncitizens are, of course persons. However, note that there is strong historical evidence (as discussed in Chapter 3) that the provisions of the Bill of Rights were intended to be applied against state governments through the auspices of the Privileges or Immunities Clause of the Fourteenth Amendment, which clearly refers to citizens—suggesting in turn that the Bill of Rights does not constrain the actions of state governments vis-à-vis noncitizens. Furthermore, this line of analysis would suggest that the Constitution imposes greater limitations on the *federal* government than on state governments in dealing with noncitizens, a result that makes absolutely no sense as a structural matter given the federal government's historical primacy in areas of immigration and naturalization.

Despite these textual ambiguities, as a practical matter the Supreme Court generally has *not* limited application of the Bill of Rights to citizens, but rather has consistently permitted at least legally admitted noncitizens to invoke its protections.[12] It is true that the Constitution appears to grant the national government fairly unconstrained powers to decide who may or may not enter the United States, and to set rules regarding naturalization—and indeed, the Supreme Court has held that the Bill of Rights is not fully applicable in the context of

---

12. *See* United States v. Verdugo-Urquidez, 494 U.S. 259, 270–271 (1990) (and cases cited therein).

immigration and deportation.[13] There are good, structural reasons to believe, however, that once noncitizens have been legally admitted to the United States as residents, and are on the path to citizenship, neither the national nor state governments should have completely constitutionally unconstrained power over noncitizens. After all, by definition, such persons will soon be eligible to become, and many will choose to become, citizens and so members of the sovereign People. To say that the government may exercise coercive power over the speech, beliefs, and personal and political relationships of such persons, without constraint, up to the actual date of citizenship, is to grant the government very troubling powers indeed. For one thing, use of such coercive powers permits the government to shape the future identity and beliefs of the People who in principle should command the government. In addition, noncitizens often actively participate in the civic and political life of our nation, though they cannot actually vote, and it is hard to see what legitimate interest the government has in controlling that participation. Finally, if the government were permitted to control the speech, religion, or political and personal associations of noncitizens in this way, this would permit the government to develop a set of powers and institutions (domestic spying institutions, etc.) that could easily be turned against citizens as well. For all of these reasons, the Supreme Court's basic conclusion that the Constitution limits government power over noncitizens as well as citizens, is probably correct, though it is undoubtedly an extension of basic constitutional principles.

The above conclusions have one important limitation—they apply only to noncitizens within the territory of the United States (and perhaps territory controlled by the United States, on which more later). With respect to interactions between the U.S. government and noncitizens *outside the United States*, the Supreme Court has clearly held that the Bill of Rights does not apply.[14] Moreover, even though the text of some of the Bill of Rights (e.g., the First Amendment's flat ban on laws abridging the freedom of speech) might be read to limit the government's power under all circumstances, the Court's conclusion is surely correct. When the government acts in an unfair or autocratic manner against noncitizens abroad, this simply does not implicate the core purpose of the Bill of Rights, which is to ensure that the power of the People of the United States over their government is not undermined. Noncitizens abroad do not participate in the civic life of *this* country, as noncitizen residents do, nor is there much danger that powers exercised abroad, often in a military context, can be translated into the domestic sphere. Of course, there is always *some* risk that coercive powers exercised abroad could be imported into the United States; but given the

---

13. *See* Reno v. American-Arab Anti-Discrimination Comm., 525 U.S. 471, 487–492 (1999); *see also* Mathews v. Diaz, 426 U.S. 67 (1976).

14. *See* United States v. Verdugo-Urquidez, 494 U.S. 259 (1990); Johnson v. Eisentrager, 339 U.S. 763 (1950).

existence of stringent judicial checks on domestic actions by the government, that risk seems attenuated. As such, from a structural perspective it makes no sense to read the provisions of the Bill of Rights and the Fourteenth Amendment to restrict governmental power over noncitizens abroad. Once again, a structural approach to constitutional interpretation yields a straightforward answer to a basic interpretational question that cannot be resolved through purely textual or historical analysis.

There are two possible counterarguments to the seemingly straightforward conclusion stated above. The first, originally advanced by Justice Hugo Black in a 1957 case called *Reid v. Covert*, is that constitutional restrictions do apply abroad because "[t]he United States is entirely a creature of the Constitution. Its power and authority have no other source. It can only act in accordance with all of the limitations imposed by the Constitution."[15] The short answer to this assertion is that read properly, the Constitution does *not* impose "limitations" on the U.S. government when it acts on noncitizens outside of the United States. (It should be noted that the facts of *Reid* involved prosecution of U.S. citizens—specifically, the wives of military service members posted abroad—and so did not technically implicate the question of power over noncitizens.) Building on Justice Black's argument, Justice William Brennan argued (in dissent) in a 1994 case that the Fourth Amendment's proscription on unreasonable searches and seizures should apply to a search by U.S. government officials of the home in Mexico of a Mexican citizen (an alleged drug kingpin named Rene Martin Verdugo-Urquidez). The core of Brennan's argument was that as a result of the U.S. government investigating and prosecuting Verdugo-Urquidez, "[h]e has become, quite literally, one of the governed."[16] Again, however, this argument is not convincing. Certainly, for the reasons stated above, when Verdugo-Urquidez was actually tried in the United States, the Bill of Rights applied. But that does not mean that the Constitution restricted the government's actions outside of the United States, or that Verdugo-Urquidez somehow became one of "the People" as a consequence of his prosecution. As a structural matter, Brennan's argument makes no sense.

The implications of the conclusion that the Constitution does not restrict the U.S. government's actions against noncitizens abroad are straightforward but profound. Many of the most morally troubling actions taken by the U.S. government in the War on Terror were in fact engaged in abroad and directed at noncitizens. Examples of such practices include:

- "extraordinary rendition," the practice of apprehending/kidnapping terrorist suspects in foreign countries and transporting them to other

---

15. Reid v. Covert, 354 U.S. 1, 5–6 (1957).
16. United States v. Verdugo-Urquidez, 494 U.S. 259, 284 (1990) (Brennan, J., dissenting).

countries where they might be subject to coercive interrogation or even torture;

- the imprisonment of noncitizen terrorism suspects in "black sites," CIA prisons located in other countries, incommunicado and without access to any legal process; and

- the use of highly coercive interrogation techniques, including waterboarding and other similar methods that may well amount to torture, against terrorism suspects at CIA "black sites" (or, for that matter, at Abu Ghraib prison in Iraq, though those events had little to do with the War on Terror).

In each of these situations, the government is engaging in actions that would almost certainly violate the Bill of Rights if directed at U.S. citizens, or even at noncitizens within the United States. Absent either factor, however, the Bill of Rights does not apply.

Two important caveats are necessary here. First, it is important to note that the lines here are not always completely clear. In particular, while the distinction between citizens and noncitizens is straightforward, it is not always clear whether a particular action is occurring "within the United States." As we shall see, it is precisely this line-drawing problem that makes the imprisonment and treatment of "enemy combatants" at the U.S. naval base in Guantanamo Bay, Cuba, such a difficult case. Another close case involved the "extraordinary rendition" of Maher Arar, a Canadian citizen who was detained by the U.S. government while he was changing planes at John F. Kennedy airport in New York City and then transported to Syria, where he was tortured. Arar was eventually released when it became clear that he had no involvement with terrorism. The Arar case is close because while he was seized at JFK Airport, obviously a part of the United States, he was merely passing through and had not been admitted into the United States.[17] As such, it is debatable whether, horrifying as his story might be as a moral matter, his mistreatment had sufficient connection with the United States to trigger constitutional concerns.

The other important caveat is that while governmental actions abroad against noncitizens do not typically implicate the Bill of Rights, this is not to say that no constitutional issues are raised. The problem of constitutional *authority* remains. In particular, actions taken by the executive branch of our government that do not violate the Bill of Rights (or, for that matter, actions that arguably *do* violate the Bill of Rights) might still exceed the executive authority granted to the president by Article II of the Constitution. It is that question to which we now turn.

---

17. *See generally* http://topics.nytimes.com/top/reference/timestopics/people/a/maher_arar/index.html.

THE PROBLEM OF PRESIDENTIAL POWER—TORTURE AND WIRETAPPING

In thinking about the problem of the scope of executive authority to pursue the War on Terror, it is valuable to start with the basics. The first three articles of the Constitution create and define the institutions that constitute the government of the United States. Article I defines the institutional structure of Congress (a House and a Senate, two-year terms for the former, six-year for the latter, etc.) and assigns certain legislative powers to the Congress. Article II defines the nature of the presidency (a single person, elected to four year terms by the Electoral College, etc.) and assigns executive powers to the president. Finally, Article III defines the structure of the federal judiciary (one Supreme Court, as well as lower courts created by Congress) and assigns judicial powers to it. Part of the job of these provisions is to create a functional, efficient governmental structure. But another part is to create a *limited* government, one that is republican in character and will not oppress its citizens or threaten their ultimate sovereignty. For this reason, even the main text of the Constitution restricts the power of the government it creates in myriad ways. So, each branch is given limited powers, and in addition is subject to various checks by other branches, the better to protect citizens from oppressive government. In the case of the executive, such checks include Congress's exclusive power to appropriate funds (it is hard to do much without money), Congress's power of impeachment, and the judiciary's power to order the executive to comply with the law.[18] The key point is that these constitutional limits and provisions have *exactly* the same function as the Bill of Rights, which is to protect popular sovereignty by insisting on a limited government. The mechanism they use is less specific, and more institutional, but it is no less fundamental to our system of government. The Bill of Rights was added to the Constitution two years after ratification not because the original Constitution imposed no limits on the power of the federal government but because, in the views of many, those limits were insufficient. But when the government, or a branch of government, acts in excess of its constitutional powers, that is no less a threat, and at a fundamental level no different a threat, to the People than a violation of the Bill of Rights.

If governmental actions in excess of constitutional authority are generally of serious concern, that is especially the case with extra-constitutional *executive* actions. It is a commonplace that framers had good, historical reasons to fear executive power. The most prominent example of such power they had before them was that of King George III, whose tyrannical actions are the main subject of the Declaration of Independence. It is true that some of the framers, including notably James Madison, expressed particular concerns during the ratification debates about the abuse of legislative power by Congress, suggesting that in a

---

18. *See* Marbury v. Madison, 5 U.S. (1 Cranch.) 137 (1803).

republic legislative usurpations were particularly to be feared.[19] But such sentiments surely did not mean that executive usurpations of power, beyond that granted by the People in the Constitution, were of no concern. After all, ultimately it is the executive, in our system the president, who controls soldiers and guns and so has the means to undermine democracy. *Especially* in times of war, therefore, the framers understood the dangers posed by executive power. To suggest otherwise would be to suggest the framers had somehow forgotten the historical examples before them, such as Oliver Cromwell and Julius Caesar. The bottom line, then, is that when any one of the branches of government, but most especially the executive, threatens the careful balance of powers created by the Constitution, the constitutional concerns raised are of the same order and same magnitude as those raised by a government that gratuitously violates the Bill of Rights. To suggest otherwise, as recent presidential administrations sometimes have, is constitutional illiteracy.

Of course, while these thoughts demonstrate the severity of the problem, they tell us little about what in practice are the constitutional limits on presidential power. As discussed briefly earlier, one of the most heated academic debates in recent years has been over the scope of presidential power to engage in military activities without congressional approval. That debate, while important, is beyond the primary scope of our discussion, because in fact the War on Terror *was* specifically authorized by Congress, in a Joint Resolution passed one week after the September 11 attacks[20] (as indeed was the separate invasion of Iraq).[21] Our primary concern, therefore, is not with wholly unilateral presidential actions, but rather presidential actions taken pursuant to a general congressional authorization to use military force. Here, the situation gets very murky. There is no serious doubt—and the Supreme Court has recognized—that a congressional authorization to use military force triggers the president's powers as Commander in Chief, and authorizes him to take normal military steps, including such incidental steps as capturing and holding prisoners of war on the battlefield (i.e., enemy combatants).[22] Other such incidental powers would also include interrogation and intelligence gathering. Indeed, the president's powers must include foreign intelligence gathering even in times of peace, for obvious reasons (such as self-defense and diplomacy). Finally, while certain kinds of presidential use of such powers, such as coercive interrogation or extraordinary rendition, might

---

19. ALEXANDER HAMILTON, JAMES MADISON, AND JOHN JAY, THE FEDERALIST PAPERS (Garry Wills ed., Bantam 1982), Federalist No. 48 at 250–251.

20. *See Authorization for Use of Military Force*, Pub. L. No. 107-40 (Sept. 18, 2001), *available at* http://www.thomas.gov/cgi-bin/query/D?c107:1:./temp/~mdbsJ25hr3::.

21. *See Authorization for Use of Military Force Against Iraq Resolution of 2002*, Pub. L. No. 107-243 (Oct. 16, 2002), *available at* http://frwebgate.access.gpo.gov/cgi-bin/getdoc.cgi?dbname=107_cong_public_laws&docid=f:publ243.107.pdf.

22. Hamdi v. Rumsfeld, 542 U.S. 507, 518–519 (2004).

raise issues under *international law*, they do not pose serious constitutional concerns unless Congress has forbidden such actions.

The last, it turns out, is the crux of the matter. What if Congress *has* forbidden particular kinds of presidential actions, but he (or she) proceeds to act anyway? It turns out that this is not a hypothetical question. In 2006, under the leadership of Senator John McCain, Congress passed the Detainee Treatment Act, which provided in relevant part that "[n]o individual in the custody or under the physical control of the United States Government, regardless of nationality of physical location, shall be subject to cruel, unusual, or degrading treatment or punishment."[23] When he signed this piece of legislation, however, President Bush issued a statement that he would "construe" its requirements "in a manner consistent with the constitutional authority of the President to supervise the unitary executive branch and as Commander in Chief. . . ."[24] In other words, the president reserved the option of ignoring the congressional statute if he felt it was necessary to perform his duties as Commander in Chief. Is this defensible? Perhaps surprisingly at this late date in our nation's history, the answer is not clear. On the one hand, defenders of presidential authority argue that the Constitution assigns the power of Commander in Chief—i.e., the power to prosecute wars—to the president, *not* Congress, and so any congressional interference with the president in this regard violates the constitutional separation of powers. On the other hand, defenders of legislative authority argue that all of the powers of the president, including his military powers, are subject to the requirement, set out in Article II of the Constitution, that the president "shall take Care that the Laws be faithfully executed,"[25] meaning that the president must at all times follow the laws enacted by Congress. Of course, comes the riposte, the president has no obligation to follow *unconstitutional* laws, and a law interfering with his powers is unconstitutional. Fascinating as this Socratic dialogue is, it is ultimately unresolvable by reference to either history or constitutional text. As is often the case, however, a return to first principles can help clarify an otherwise opaque topic.

The basic purpose of our system of separated, and balanced, powers is to ensure that our government, and its various branches, remains under the control of, and accountable to, *We*, the People of the United States. Of course, the most important mechanism for maintaining popular control is the election of public officials; but because elections occur only irregularly, and because the

---

23. Department of Defense, Emergency Supplemental Appropriations to Address Hurricanes in the Gulf of Mexico, and Pandemic Influenza Act, 2006, Pub. L. 109-148, Sec. 1003, 119 Stat. 2739, *available at* http://frwebgate.access.gpo.gov/cgi-bin/getdoc.cgi?dbname=109_cong_public_laws&docid=f:publ148.109.pdf.

24. President's Statement on Signing of H.R. 2863, *available at* http://www.whitehouse.gov/news/releases/2005/12/20051230-8.html.

25. U.S. Const., Art. II, Sec. 3.

election of individuals can turn on any number of factors aside from specific policy issues, elections alone clearly are not sufficient to maintain a republican government. It is for that reason that the Constitution limits the powers of the different branches of the national government and hedges them in by granting the other branches constitutional checks. The abiding principle here is that no single branch of government can *ever* be said to speak truly for the People—it is only when the branches act in coordination that this can be said to be true. Now, consider the claims of President George W. Bush (and, it must be acknowledged, some of his predecessors) to be able to act unilaterally, even in the face of express opposition from one or perhaps both of the other branches of government (because enforcement of a congressional statute will presumably require judicial involvement as well). Such behavior, completely free of interbranch checks, undermines the principle of popular control, because it posits a president who can exercise unilateral, sovereign power on behalf of the People, even against the will of the other branches. But it is precisely the *point* of the separation of powers to preclude such a claim, to ensure that no single person, or single branch of government, can speak definitively "for the People," because such a claim threatens to undermine the constitutional means by which the People in practice maintain control over their government. The point should not be overstated— there are certainly some powers, such as the president's pardon power and Congress's impeachment powers, that the Constitution necessarily grants one branch to exercise alone, and interference by other branches would be problematic—though, it should be noted, those unilateral powers tend to be narrow, clearly defined, carefully delimited, and generally unthreatening to the People. But it should be relatively clear that we should be *extremely* suspicious of claims by any of the branches of unilateral authority absent clear constitutional authorization, especially the kinds of broad, seemingly unlimited unilateral powers claimed by President Bush in the course of waging the War on Terror.

If torture represents a rather distant (albeit deeply troubling) example of a clash between executive and legislative authority in the War on Terror, a much closer-to-home example can be found in the Bush Administration's warrantless wiretapping program. In the wake of the attacks of September 11, 2001, President Bush instructed the National Security Agency (NSA) to institute a program of warrantless wiretapping of electronic communications, including telephone calls, between people inside and outside the United States, when one of the communicating parties was believed to have connections to terrorists. This program remained in effect until it was publicly disclosed in a New York Times article published on December 16, 2005.[26] Crucially, it is quite clear that the NSA program violated provisions of the Foreign Intelligence Surveillance Act of 1978,

---

26. James Risen and Eric Lichtblau, *Bush Lets U.S. Spy on Callers Without Courts*, NEW YORK TIMES A1, Dec. 16, 2005, *available at* http://www.nytimes.com/2005/12/16/politics/16program.html?pagewanted=1.

a congressional statute enacted in the wake of Watergate era scandals that strictly limits wiretapping without a judicial warrant.[27] The Bush Administration did not seriously deny this violation, but nevertheless defended their actions on two grounds: first, that Congress authorized the NSA program by passing the Authorization for the Use of Military Force (AUMF) of September 18, 2001, initiating the War on Terror, thereby setting aside the earlier rule established by FISA; and second, that in any event FISA is unconstitutional to the extent that it impedes the president's powers as Commander in Chief to gather intelligence.[28] The first argument is very weak. Even defenders of the administration's policies in the War on Terror, such as Professor Gary Lawson, appear to acknowledge that reading the AUMF to authorize *domestic* intelligence gathering, in plain violation of another congressional statute, is a "stretch."[29] The second argument is therefore the crux of the matter. The NSA program is no longer a live controversy, both because the Bush Administration agreed, in the wake of the New York Times disclosure, to abide by FISA's rules,[30] and because Congress later amended FISA to permit (with restrictions) some of the NSA's surveillance (in particular, Congress authorized warrantless surveillance of noncitizens located outside the United States, even if the effect was to intercept communications to or from the United States).[31] The constitutionality of the NSA program remains of abiding interest, however, both intrinsically and because of the precedent it sets for future executive actions.

Analysis of the NSA program poses great difficulties both because it represents a close question regarding the scope of presidential power *and* because of the fact that unlike many other policies in the War on Terror, this program had a direct effect on persons, including presumably citizens, within the United States, thereby raising serious questions under the Bill of Rights. Starting with the question of presidential authority, the reason why the NSA wiretapping program poses such a difficult question is because the core purpose of the program, which is to collect intelligence regarding potential attacks on the United States by foreign elements and their domestic allies, groups it might be added against

---

27. *See* Lee, *supra*, 12 Tex. J. Civ. Lib. & Civ. Rts. at 3–5.

28. Press Briefing by Attorney General Alberto Gonzales and General Michael Hayden, Principal Deputy Director for National Intelligence (Dec. 19, 2005), *available at* http://www.whitehouse.gov/news/releases/2005/12/20051219-1.html.

29. Gary Lawson, *What Lurks Beneath: NSA Surveillance and Executive Power*, 99 Boston L. Rev. 375, 379 (2008); *see also* Lee, *supra*, 12 Tex. J. Civ. Lib. & Civ. Rts. at 5–11.

30. *Id.* at 1 & n.5.

31. *See* FISA Amendments Act of 2008, Pub. L. 110-261, 122 Stat. 2436 (July 10, 2008), *available at* http://frwebgate.access.gpo.gov/cgi-bin/getdoc.cgi?dbname=110_cong_public_laws&docid=f:pub1261.110.pdf; Protect America Act of 2007, Pub. L. 110-55, 121 Stat. 552 (Aug. 5, 2007), *available at* http://frwebgate.access.gpo.gov/cgi-bin/getdoc.cgi?dbname=110_cong_public_laws&docid=f:pub1055.110.pdf.

whom Congress has authorized military attacks (in the September 18 AUMF), surely lies at the core of the president's powers as Commander in Chief. As Professor Evan Lee has explained, it is merely a matter of "common sense . . . that the Commander-in-Chief clause must imbue the President with the power to order electronic surveillance in support of a war."[32]

Of course, the fact that the president inherently possesses such power still leaves the problem of FISA, as well as the problem of the Bill of Rights. Does the president have the power to order "electronic surveillance in support of a war," even in the face of a congressional statute forbidding such surveillance (at least without a warrant)? That is a far more difficult and complex question and may well turn on the type and location of the surveillance at issue. Consider, for example, if the president orders the military to engage in certain electronic intelligence gathering purely abroad, as part of a congressionally authorized military operation. In that situation, attempts by Congress to micromanage such activities by statute might impinge on the president's clear, textual power as Commander in Chief to direct the nation's military, just as would a congressional statute trying to micromanage the tactics used in a particular battle. Given the lack of direct impact on the American People, there is a decent argument that such foreign military operations are one of the narrow powers that have been granted unilaterally to one branch of government, the president, free of interference by the other branches—though it should be acknowledged that there is also substantial historical evidence to the contrary, suggesting that even on tactical matters abroad, the president is subject to congressional control.[33] Regardless of the correct resolution of this dispute (which remains vigorously disputed), purely domestic intelligence gathering surely must be subject to congressional control. Any other approach places the American People at the mercy of a single government official, the very thing that the Constitution works so hard to avoid—as Justice Robert Jackson famously put it in condemning another aggressive assertion of presidential power, "the Constitution did not contemplate that the title Commander in Chief *of the Army and Navy* will constitute [the President] also Commander in Chief of the country."[34] The NSA program is troubling because it lies at the interface, the border as it were, between these two extreme possibilities. The communications the NSA was intercepting all had a foreign component, but also a domestic component, since they were between one person abroad and one within the country (according to the NSA, it did not intercept purely domestic communications). How is such intelligence gathering to be classified? There are decent arguments to be made on both sides on this

---

32. Lee, *supra*, 12 Tex. J. Civ. Lib. & Civ. Rts. at 18.

33. *See generally* Saikrishna Bangalore Prakash, *The Separation and Overlap of War and Military Powers*, 87 Tex. L. Rev. 299 (2009).

34. Youngstown Sheet & Tube Co. v. Sawyer, 343 U.S. 579, 643–644 (1952) (Jackson, J., concurring).

question, but on balance, the better conclusion seems to be that Congress should have power to regulate these sorts of presidential activities, for two reasons. The first is simply the strong presumption against unilateral, unchecked governmental authority—in case of doubt, one should assume that the constitutional system of checks and balances remains in place. The second is that cross-border surveillance of the sort engaged in by the NSA does directly affect U.S. residents, including citizens, and indeed provides a tool for potential intimidation or blackmail of such persons. In this respect, the fact that the other end of the communication is outside the United States is irrelevant. For this reason as well, granting the president unilateral, unchecked powers of this sort seems contrary to the spirit of the Constitution.

It must be acknowledged, however, that the question of presidential power to authorize the NSA wiretapping despite FISA is a close one. Even if we posit that presidential power in this area exists, however, that still leaves the problem of the Bill of Rights, and in particular, the Fourth Amendment, which imposes an independent limit on the power of the federal government. The Fourth Amendment states that "[t]he right of the people to be secure in their persons, houses, papers, and effects, against unreasonable searches and seizures, shall not be violated, and no Warrants shall issue, but upon probable cause. . . ."[35] In the modern era, the Supreme Court has interpreted this language to require that absent special circumstances recognized by the Supreme Court, the government may not engage in a search or a seizure of a person or property without first obtaining a judicial warrant.[36] There is no dispute that the NSA wiretapping program was conducted without proper warrants (indeed, that was the whole point of the program, to avoid the allegedly time-consuming delays imposed by a warrant requirement). So, a violation of the Fourth Amendment appears to have been established.

As Evan Lee points out, however, the matter is not so simple.[37] First of all, as noted earlier, with respect to purely foreign wiretapping, the Fourth Amendment does not apply. Of course, the NSA program had a significant, domestic component; and on the flip side, the Supreme Court has explicitly held that there is no general "national security" exception to the Fourth Amendment's warrant requirement, in a case involving a *domestic* security threat.[38] On the other hand,

---

35. U.S. Const., Amend. IV.

36. *See, e.g.*, Groh v. Ramirez, 540 U.S. 551, 559 (2004); Flippo v. West Virginia, 528 U.S. 11 (1999) (*per curiam*). Akhil Amar has demonstrated convincingly that this reading of the Fourth Amendment is almost certainly historically incorrect. See Amar, *supra*, THE BILL OF RIGHTS at 68–70. It is, nonetheless, the accepted modern reading of the Amendment, and I will presume its validity for the purposes of this discussion.

37. Lee, *supra*, 12 TEX. J. CIV. LIB. & CIV. RTS. at 40–41.

38. *Id.* at 40 & n.146 (*citing* United States v. U.S. District Court (*Keith*), 407 U.S. 297 (1972)).

what about communications involving at least one foreign party—might there be an exception to the warrant requirement with respect to such communications, when the president is engaging in collecting foreign intelligence? The Supreme Court has never considered this question, but according to Lee, most federal courts of appeals to consider the question *have* recognized a "foreign intelligence" exception, which would presumably cover the NSA program.[39] The argument in favor of such an exception is that when the president is acting to prevent foreign espionage or attacks, he is acting at the core of his powers as Commander in Chief and as the chief instigator of U.S. foreign policy, and that such activities are sufficiently unrelated to the general, domestic activities of the People of the United States that the Bill of Rights (or at least the warrant requirement of the Fourth Amendment) should not apply. The argument on the other side, of course, is that such intelligence gathering nonetheless directly impinges upon persons, including citizens, within the United States. As such, a foreign intelligence exception creates a potentially significant gap in the general rule that the executive branch's search and seizure powers should be subject to a judicial check. Professor Lee's ultimate conclusion is that the resolution of the Fourth Amendment issue may well be related to the resolution of the issue of congressional power. It is important that *some* check exist on the executive in this area; but it may well also be that Congress, with its greater access to classified information and its greater involvement in foreign affairs and national security matters, is in a better position to check the president than are federal courts, which lack all expertise in such matters. As such, so long as Congress retains regulatory power (i.e., so long as statutes like FISA are upheld against presidential claims of invalidity), a further judicial check may be unnecessary and unwise.[40] That conclusion seems both reasonable as a matter of constitutional design and a fair resolution of an indeterminate problem. Of course, it is critical that any "foreign intelligence" exception to the Fourth Amendment be strictly limited to situations where there is a strong foreign link to the intelligence gathering and only a peripheral domestic connection. But even under this narrow definition, the NSA program, at least as publicly disclosed and now authorized by Congress, would appear to qualify for a Fourth Amendment exception.

ENEMY COMBATANTS—YASER HAMDI, JOSE PADILLA, AND ALI AL-MARRI

We turn finally to the most enduring, and most vexing, constitutional problem posed by the War on Terror: the past and continuing detention without charges or trial of so-called "enemy combatants," accused terrorists, in military facilities

---

39. *Id.* at 40 & n.147.
40. *Id.* at 40–41.

both inside the United States and at the U.S. naval base in Guantanamo Bay, Cuba. We begin with enemy combatants held within the United States.

Yaser Esam Hamdi was born in Baton Rouge, Louisiana, in 1980, and as such was a natural born citizen of the United States. Hamdi's parents are Saudi Arabian, and as a young child he and his family returned to Saudi Arabia, where he was raised. In the wake of the September 11, 2001, attacks, the United States and a group of Afghan forces opposed to the ruling Taliban movement, the Northern Alliance, invaded Afghanistan in order to displace the Taliban, which had supported and was harboring Al Qaeda. During the invasion, Hamdi was captured by Northern Alliance forces and soon thereafter turned over to U.S. custody (the U.S. government claims that Hamdi was captured while fighting with Taliban forces, while Hamdi claims that he was in Afghanistan doing relief work). Hamdi was originally imprisoned in the detention facility at Guantanamo Bay, but when his U.S. citizenship was confirmed, he was transferred to a naval brig in Norfolk, Virginia, and then Charleston, South Carolina, where he was held without trial and without access to lawyers. Eventually, Hamdi's father filed on Hamdi's behalf a petition for a writ of habeas corpus—a legal action designed to require the release of a person held by the executive branch. After extensive litigation, the case eventually reached the Supreme Court.[41] The Court splintered sharply in the case (i.e., no five Justices could agree on a single opinion or line of reasoning). However, a majority appeared to agree that the president potentially did have authority, pursuant to the AUMF of September 18, 2001, to hold Hamdi as an "enemy combatant" during the duration of hostilities in Afghanistan, because capturing and holding enemy soldiers is "a fundamental incident of waging war," and that the fact that Hamdi was a citizen was no bar to holding him (in support of this result, the Court cited a case from World War II involving a U.S. citizen who was an alleged Nazi saboteur).[42] However, the Court also held that the Due Process Clause entitled Hamdi to a hearing (though not necessarily a formal trial) before a federal judge, at which he would have an opportunity to prove that he was not in fact an enemy combatant and so was entitled to be released. In so holding, the Court rejected an argument by the Bush Administration that the separation of powers forbade the courts from interfering with the president's power as Commander in Chief to detain enemy combatants—i.e., it held that the president's powers in this regard *were* subject to checks by the other branches, at least with respect to U.S. citizens.[43] It is noteworthy that four of the nine Justices, including Justice Antonin Scalia, a traditional conservative, would have even gone beyond this holding and held that the president simply lacked the power to hold a citizen as an enemy combatant, at least

---

41. Hamdi v. Rumsfeld, 542 U.S. 507, 510–516 (2004).
42. *Id.* at 519 (*citing Ex Parte Quirin*, 317 U.S. 1, 28, 30 (1942)).
43. *Id.* at 524–529.

without specific authorization from Congress.[44] In the wake of the Supreme Court's decision, the government, instead of granting Hamdi his hearing, instead reached an agreement with him whereby Hamdi was released and returned to Saudi Arabia, in exchange for his agreement to renounce his U.S. citizenship.[45]

Jose Padilla was born in Brooklyn, New York, in 1970 and was raised in Chicago. He apparently became involved with gangs at a fairly young age and was in and out of prison for many years. Eventually, he converted to Islam and moved to the Middle East to further his religious studies.[46] According to the U.S. government, Padilla was recruited by Al Qaeda, and received terrorist training. He fought against U.S. forces in Afghanistan and eventually escaped to Pakistan, where he was connected with senior Al Qaeda leaders. In May 2002, Padilla returned to Chicago. He was detained by FBI agents at O'Hare Airport in Chicago and was held on a material witness warrant because the FBI believed that Padilla was involved in an Al Qaeda plot to blow up buildings, perhaps using radioactive materials (hence Padilla's designation as the "dirty bomber"). In June, President Bush ordered Padilla to be designated an "enemy combatant," and he was transferred to military custody, at a brig in Charleston, South Carolina, where he was held without charge, trial, or access to counsel for several years.[47] Padilla's lawyer filed a petition for a writ of habeas corpus on his behalf, but his original claim was dismissed on technical grounds by the Supreme Court in June 2004 (on the same day that the Court decided the *Hamdi* case).[48] His lawyer then refilled the suit properly and was rewarded with a decision by a trial court that the government lacked the authority to hold Padilla as an enemy combatant because he had not been captured on the field of battle, as Hamdi had.[49] On appeal, however, the U.S. Court of Appeals for the Fourth Circuit reversed, holding that Padilla's case was indistinguishable from Hamdi's, since both had taken up arms against the United States and allied with its enemies.[50] Padilla sought to appeal this decision to the Supreme Court, but while his appeal was pending, the government issued a standard, criminal indictment against him and attempted to transfer him from military to civilian custody, thereby making his appeal (and lawsuit) moot (i.e., out of date). In an extraordinary decision, Judge J. Michael Luttig of the Fourth

---

44. *Id.* at 554–579 (Scalia, J., dissenting); *id.* at 539–554 (Souter, J., concurring in part, dissenting in part, and concurring in the judgment).

45. *See* Settlement Agreement, *Yaser Esam Hamdi v. Donald Rumsfeld, available at* http://news.findlaw.com/hdocs/docs/hamdi/91704stlagrmnt.html.

46. Deborah Sontag, *Terror Suspect's Path from Streets to Brig*, NEW YORK TIMES, April 25, 2004, *available at* http://query.nytimes.com/gst/fullpage.html?res= 9D04E6D8133AF936A15757C0A9629C8B63&sec=&spon=&pagewanted=1.

47. Padilla v. Hanft, 423 F.3d 386 (4th Cir. 2005).

48. Rumsfeld v. Padilla, 542 U.S. 426 (2004).

49. Padilla v. Hanft, 389 F. Supp.2d 678 (D.S.C. 2005).

50. Padilla v. Hanft, 423 F.3d 386 (4th Cir. 2005).

Circuit, a highly conservative judge on a conservative court, denied the government's request to transfer custody, hinting strongly that the government might have lied to the court of appeals about the security threat posed by Padilla.[51] The Supreme Court, however, granted the government's request, thereby eliminating Padilla's legal claim and removing him from military custody, after over three years of being held incognito.[52] Eventually, Padilla was convicted of several criminal charges—though, it should be noted, not on the most serious charges that the government had originally pressed—and sentenced to multiple years in prison.

Ali Al-Marri is a Qatari citizen, who legally entered the United States on September 10, 2001, with his wife and children, in order to attend graduate school. In December, Al-Marri was arrested in his home in Peoria, Illinois, and charged with various crimes, primarily financial in nature—the government's underlying claim being that Al-Marri had trained with Al Qaeda in Afghanistan and was a sleeper Al Qaeda agent. A year and a half of legal proceedings ensued. Then, in June 2003, President Bush signed an order designating Al-Marri an enemy combatant and transferring him to military custody in (yes) South Carolina. For the first sixteen months of his detention, Al-Marri was denied any outside access, to either his lawyers or his family (he continued, apparently, to be denied access to his family at least into 2008). Al-Marri's lawyer filed a petition for a writ of habeas corpus on his behalf in July 2003. After protracted legal proceedings, in July 2008 the U.S. Court of Appeals for the Fourth Circuit held, in a sharply divided opinion, that the president did have authority, pursuant to the AUMF of September 18, to hold Al-Marri as an enemy combatant, but that the Due Process Clause entitled Al-Marri to further hearings to rebut the charge that he is an enemy combatant.[53] On December 5, 2008, the U.S. Supreme Court agreed to hear Al-Marri's appeal from this decision,[54] but upon taking office President Barack Obama ordered that Al-Marri's status be reviewed.[55] Ultimately, President Obama ordered Al-Marri to be transferred to civilian custody,[56] and he pleaded guilty to terrorism-related criminal charges.[57]

---

51. Padilla v. Hanft, 432 F.3d 582 (4th Cir. 2005).

52. Hanft v. Padilla, 546 U.S. 1084 (2006).

53. Al-Marri v. Pucciarelli, 534 F.3d 213 (4th Cir. 2008) (en banc).

54. Al-Marri v. Pucciarelli, 2008 U.S. LEXIS 8886 (U.S. Dec. 5, 2008).

55. *See Review of Detention of Ali Saleh Kahlah al-Marri* (Presidential Memorandum), *available at*
http://www.whitehouse.gov/the_press_office/ReviewoftheDetentionofAliSalehKahlah/.

56. *See Transfer of Detainee to Control of the Attorney General* (Presidential Memorandum, signed February 27, 2009), *available at* http://www.whitehouse.gov/the_press_office/Transfer-of-Detainee-to-Control-of-the-Attorney-General/.

57. *See* John Schwartz, *Plea Deal Reached with Agent for Al Qaeda*, New York Times, April 30, 2009, *available at* http://www.nytimes.com/2009/05/01/us/01marri.html.

What do Yaser Hamdi, Jose Padilla, and Ali Al-Marri have in common? They are the only three individuals known to have been held as enemy combatants *within the United States* during the War on Terror. Each of their cases raises two distinct legal questions: first, did the president, as Commander in Chief, have the constitutional authority to detain them without trial, as enemy combatants; and second, did the Due Process Clause entitled them to a hearing to disprove the government's claims that they were enemy combatants? In each of these cases, the courts concluded that the president did have authority to detain the individual, but that due process entitled them to a hearing. Do these conclusions make sense?

Consider first the case of Yaser Hamdi. If Hamdi were not a U.S. citizen, the Supreme Court's conclusion that Hamdi could be held as an enemy combatant seems surely correct. After all, Hamdi was (allegedly) captured on the battlefield with a rifle in his hand. Capturing and holding enemy soldiers under those circumstances seems clearly within the core the president's Commander-in-Chief powers. Note that this would be true even if a captured soldier were detained within the United States, as POWs during World War II sometimes were (nor would such POWs normally be entitled to the protections of the Bill of Rights, given their lack of connection to this country). Hamdi, however, was a citizen, which complicates matters. A majority of the Court held his citizenship irrelevant, citing *Ex Parte Quirin*,[58] a World War II era case in which the Supreme Court upheld the detention, military trial, and eventual execution of several Nazi agents, including one U.S. citizen, who had landed on the East Coast to commit acts of sabotage. Justice Scalia, however, made a powerful argument that *Quirin* was incorrect in this regard and that the government lacked the authority to hold a citizen as an enemy combatant without trial unless Congress eliminated judicial power in the matter by suspending the writ of habeas corpus. Instead, the government must either charge a citizen with treason, or release him. The arguments on both sides on this question are frankly powerful. Justice Scalia marshals impressive historical evidence to support his view, but on the other hand, his view seems to lead to potentially absurd results, because it suggests that someone like Hamdi, who while born in the United States had been raised in, and considered himself a national of, Saudi Arabia, had to be either released or tried for treason if captured on a battlefield. Given these practicalities, the Court's decision is certainly defensible, and probably the correct one. On the other hand, once the president's power to detain citizens is acknowledged, it becomes absolutely vital that the Bill of Rights be read to place limits on the president's power. To read the Constitution otherwise, as the Bush Administration argued the Court should, would create a completely unchecked presidential power to hold U.S. citizens incommunicado, effectively indefinitely (given the indefinite nature

---

58. 317 U.S. 1 (1942).

of the War on Terror). There is surely no power more threatening to the freedom of the People than unrestricted executive detention authority—with such power, the executive could imprison its enemies, undermine political opponents, and consolidate its own power, all actions with historical antecedents that the framers were aware of. Indeed, it is the very point of the Due Process Clause to reject such power and prevent such an eventuality. The *Hamdi* Court's conclusions in this regard were, therefore, surely correct. Indeed, given the grave dangers posed by executive detention, the Due Process Clause should be read to protect citizens held by the executive even outside the United States.[59]

Compared to Yaser Hamdi, Jose Padilla poses a much more difficult issue regarding presidential detention authority, though a much easier due process question. Like Hamdi, Padilla appears to have associated himself with enemies of the United State—to wit, Al Qaeda—and taken up arms against this country; indeed, the evidence that Padilla had in fact associated himself with Al Qaeda appears to be significantly stronger than the evidence against Hamdi, who at most stood accused of joining the Taliban *before* it was at war with the United States. In addition, as we noted earlier, Padilla's U.S. citizenship probably should not be a bar to his designation as an enemy combatant. So far, then, the analogy to Hamdi seems strong. Crucially, however, Padilla, unlike Hamdi, was *not* captured on a traditional field of battle with arms in hand. Indeed, he was not captured abroad at all. Instead, he was arrested, obviously unarmed, at Chicago's O'Hare airport, after stepping off a plane, and the accusations against him essentially consist of charges that he planned to commit crimes within the United States. Absent the alleged link to Al Qaeda, clearly someone in Padilla's position could not be held without charges or trial—that is the very point of the Due Process Clause. But, of course, Padilla was allegedly associated with Al Qaeda, an organization with which the United States is, in a sense, in a state of war. If Padilla had been captured abroad, for example at an Al Qaeda training facility in Afghanistan or Pakistan, the argument that he could be held as an enemy combatant would become quite powerful. Padilla thus falls in a deeply gray area.

Indeed, the difficulty of properly classifying Padilla, as a simple criminal entitled to trial or as an enemy "soldier" to be held during the duration of hostilities, reveals the fundamental ambiguity regarding the nature of the War on Terror itself. Is it a sustained police investigation of a criminal organization, akin to, though vastly more dangerous than, the Mafia? Or is it a military operation against a non-national but nonetheless real foreign power? The answer is a little bit of both, making a clear characterization impossible. The implications of this

---

59. *See* Reid v. Covert, 354 U.S. 1 (1957) (holding that constitutional restrictions apply when the United States government criminally prosecutes civilian U.S. citizens abroad). The Supreme Court has also recently confirmed that federal courts have jurisdiction to hear habeas corpus claims by U.S. citizens held abroad by the U.S. military. Hanaf v. Geren, 128 S. Ct. 2207 (2008).

difficulty, however, are profound. As we began this chapter by noting, during wartime the Constitution inevitably permits the executive branch to claim expanded powers, both internationally and domestically, including (according to the Supreme Court in the *Quirin* and *Hamdi* cases) the detention of U.S. citizens as enemy combatants. In the criminal context, however, one of the key purposes of the Bill of Rights, indeed of the Constitution generally, is to prohibit executive detention without charges or trial. In addition to the Due Process Clause, the Sixth Amendment's guarantees of a speedy trial, the right of an accused to hear the charges against him, to confront witnesses, to call witnesses of his own, and to have the assistance of counsel, all further this policy,[60] as does the proscription in Article I that Congress can suspend the writ of habeas corpus only "when in Cases of Rebellion or Invasion the public Safety may require it."[61] On the proper treatment of Padilla, reasonable people can thus differ. Given the enormous political and constitutional risks posed by executive detention, however, and given the rather limited checks on such power afforded by the other branches (the hearing that the *Hamdi* Court held was required by the Due Process Clause falls far short of a proper trial), it seems essential to read the wartime detention power narrowly. Hamdi is an easy case for detention. Perhaps the war analogy can even be stretched so far as to cover the Nazi saboteurs in *Quirin*, who did land in the United States from German military vessels, wearing German uniforms, thereby arguably extending the "field of battle" to this country. But to extend this analogy to the circumstances of Jose Padilla is to unmoor it from its foundations. Padilla looks like a simple criminal, was originally treated as a criminal, and was ultimately tried and sentenced as a criminal. To treat him otherwise, because he was trained and directed by Al Qaeda, while not completely unreasonable it must be acknowledged, on balance grants the president simply too much unchecked power over citizens, the People, of the United States. It should also be noted that if we do assume the president had the power to detain Padilla, the conclusion that the Due Process Clause permits him to challenge his detention follows a fortiori from the conclusion that Hamdi was entitled to a hearing. Padilla was, after all, captured and detained within the United States; to permit the president to detain and hold citizens within the United States, with no external checks, simply on the president's say-so, would expand presidential power and pose a threat to the political independence of the People, which would turn the American constitutional tradition on its head.

We turn now to Ali Al-Marri. In most ways, Al-Marri's situation parallels Padilla's closely. He was, after all, arrested in the United States, while legally present, was originally charged in civilian, criminal proceedings, and was placed in military custody only later, because of his alleged link to Al Qaeda. Indeed, in

---

60. U.S. Const., Amend. VI.
61. U.S. Const., Art. I, Sec. 9, cl. 2.

one way Al-Marri's position appears stronger than Padilla's, because he was arrested in his home in the United States, not while stepping off a plane returning from meetings with Al Qaeda leaders. The key difference, of course, is citizenship—Padilla is a U.S. citizen, while Al-Marri is not. Is that distinction sufficient to distinguish their cases? That is a difficult question to answer. If the United States were at war with Al-Marri's native country, Qatar, the answer must be yes—the United States in general, and the president in particular, must possess authority to detain enemy aliens during wartime. Of course, the United States is not at war with Qatar. Is Al-Marri's alleged link to Al Qaeda sufficiently analogous to justify detention without trial? In the case of Jose Padilla, we concluded that it was not, and while Al-Marri's case is closer because he is not a citizen, and therefore his detention is not as clearly an assault on popular sovereignty as Padilla's, the same logic would seem to apply. Alleged "affiliation" with Al Qaeda through the course of an indefinite "War on Terror" is, unlike foreign citizenship during a traditional war, simply too nebulous a factor upon which to rest executive detention power. Therefore, if we were correct to conclude earlier that the Bill of Rights should be read to restrain government power over noncitizens present legally in the United States, then here too detention without trial should be held unconstitutional. Finally, as with the Padilla case, even if one concludes that the president's detention power over enemy combatants does extend to individuals such as Al-Marri, it remains imperative to require the government, pursuant to due process, to defend its designation of Al-Marri as an enemy combatant in a judicial hearing.

ENEMY COMBATANTS—GUANTANAMO BAY

In the previous section, we concluded that U.S. citizens captured abroad and held as enemy combatants by the U.S. government are entitled under the Due Process Clause to a hearing to demonstrate their innocence. Even with respect to noncitizens captured and held within the United States as enemy combatants, we concluded that some such procedure is necessary, if the executive branch is not to gain extremely troubling powers. Indeed, as we saw, it is doubtful if, at least in the context of the War on Terror, the president is authorized to hold individuals *captured within the United States*, either citizens or noncitizens, as enemy combatants. On the other hand, we noted earlier that the Constitution simply does not restrain the activities of the U.S. government completely outside of the United States vis-à-vis noncitizens, including indefinite detention of such individuals. We now turn to the most difficult borderline situation, the legal gray zone that is Gitmo, the detention facility for noncitizen enemy combatants operated by the U.S. military at the U.S. naval base in Guantanamo Bay, Cuba.

The U.S. naval base at Guantanamo Bay sits on forty-five square miles of land and water on the southeast coast of Cuba. The United States has occupied this land since 1903 pursuant to a lease agreement with the government of Cuba, which in 1934 was made permanent so long as the naval base remains in operation. Under this agreement, Cuba retains "ultimate sovereignty," but the United States exercises "complete jurisdiction and control over and within" the area of the base. The United States, of course, has not had diplomatic relations with Cuba since Fidel Castro came to power in 1959, and so any claim of Cuban sovereignty over Guantanamo Bay remains entirely hypothetical. Since October 2001, the United States has maintained a military detention center at Guantanamo Bay, colloquially known as "Gitmo," at which it detains non-U.S. citizen enemy combatants suspected of affiliation with either the Taliban or Al Qaeda.[62] All of these detainees were captured abroad, either by U.S. military forces in Afghanistan or by American and allied intelligence agents investigating Al Qaeda. Since 2001, hundreds of detainees have passed through Guantanamo Bay, and as of 2008 several hundred remained at the facility. A few of the Gitmo detainees have been tried before military commissions, but most continue to be held without charge or trial, subject only to extremely informal, abbreviated review by military panels called "Combatant Status Review Tribunals" (CSRTs).[63] Many allegations have been raised that detainees at Gitmo have been subject to mistreatment and extremely coercive interrogation techniques, perhaps rising to the level of torture. The continuing operation of Gitmo has also been widely criticized worldwide, including by most allies of the United States.

Since 2002, lawyers for a number of the Gitmo detainees have filed petitions for writs of habeas corpus, seeking their clients' release. On three different occasions, these lawsuits have reached the U.S. Supreme Court. First, in 2004 in *Rasul v. Bush*[64] the Court held that federal courts had jurisdiction, at least, to hear habeas corpus petitions filed by Gitmo detainees (reversing a lower court decision to the contrary), though the Court was silent as to what substantive rights the detainees might enjoy (*Rasul* was decided the same day as the *Hamdi* case and the first *Padilla* case). In response, Congress passed legislation sharply limiting the jurisdiction of federal courts to hear cases brought by Gitmo detainees. In 2006, in *Hamdan v. Rumsfeld*,[65] the Supreme Court interpreted this legislation extremely narrowly, concluding that it did not apply to lawsuits filed before the new legislation was passed. The *Hamdan* Court also held that the Bush Administration's attempts to try Gitmo detainees before military commissions established pursuant to an Executive Order issued by President Bush violated both a congressional statute, the Uniform Code of Military Justice, and the Geneva Conventions, treaties agreed to by the United States regarding the treatment of prisoners of war. Congress again passed legislation, the Military

---

62. Rasul v. Bush, 542 U.S. 466 (2004).

63. Boumediene v. Bush, 128 S. Ct. 2229 (2008).

64. 542 U.S. 466 (2004).

65. 548 U.S. 557 (2006).

Commissions Act of 2006, explicitly authorizing military commissions, and claiming to strip federal courts of jurisdiction over even pending lawsuits by detainees. In response, in 2008 the Supreme Court decided *Boumediene v. Bush*.[66] *Boumediene* has two critical holdings. First, the Court held that Congress's attempt to strip federal courts of jurisdiction over petitions for habeas corpus was unconstitutional under the Suspension Clause of Article I of the Constitution, mentioned earlier, which permits Congress to suspend the writ of habeas corpus only "when in Cases of Rebellion or Invasion the public Safety may require it"[67] (neither of which condition did Congress even claim had been satisfied). Crucial to the Court's holding on this point was its conclusion that "in every practical sense Guantanamo is not abroad; it is within the constant jurisdiction of the United States,"[68] and therefore, the historical writ of habeas corpus, protected by the Constitution, extended to Guantanamo Bay, even though earlier cases had held that the writ did not extend to the detention outside of the United States of foreign nationals by the U.S. government. Second, the Court held that because of its procedural limitations, the CSRT review process established by Congress was not an adequate substitute for judicial review pursuant to the writ of habeas corpus, and therefore the Gitmo detainees were constitutionally entitled to a judicial hearing in which they could challenge their designation as enemy combatants. Under *Boumediene*, therefore, noncitizen detainees at Guantanamo Bay are *constitutionally* entitled to a hearing before a federal judge to challenge their detention, though the case leaves open the question of exactly what legal standard would apply in such a hearing (i.e., it did not decide precisely what obligations the Due Process Clause imposed on the government, under these circumstances), and also did not resolve the constitutionality of using military tribunals, as opposed to civilian courts, to try detainees who *are* charged with crimes. Four Justices: Chief Justice John Roberts and Justices Antonin Scalia, Clarence Thomas, and Samuel Alito—dissented from these holdings, arguing vociferously that the CSRT procedures were adequate to protect any constitutional rights that the Gitmo detainees might enjoy, and more fundamentally,[69] that the historic writ of habeas corpus was strictly limited to the sovereign territory of the United States, thereby excluding Guantanamo Bay.[70]

The Guantanamo Bay detainees have thus had remarkable success in challenging their detention before the Supreme Court. In each of their three outings, they have won strong victories, albeit by closely divided votes, at the end of which they had secured an unambiguous entitlement to judicial hearings, in civilian, federal courts, to challenge their detention by the military without criminal charges.

---

66. 128 S. Ct. 2229 (2008).

67. U.S. Const., Art. I, Sec. 9, cl. 2.

68. Boumediene v. Bush, 128 S. Ct. 2229, 2261 (2008).

69. *Id.* at 2279–2293 (Roberts, C.J., dissenting).

70. *Id.* at 2293–2307 (Scalia, J., dissenting).

Do these results make sense? As a moral matter, and as a matter of public policy, certainly the Supreme Court's decision to accord legal protections to the Guantanamo Bay detainees is highly appealing. The legal black hole that the Bush Administration attempted to create in Guantanamo Bay, where no law applied and the executive branch could act free of any judicial oversight at all, flies in the face of fundamental rule-of-law values that underlie not just the American system of government, but Western democracy generally; this is, of course, precisely why Guantanamo Bay is so controversial and has become such a magnet for criticism. As a *constitutional* matter, however, it must be confessed that the Court's decision in *Boumediene* especially, is a stretch. Justice Scalia makes a powerful case in his dissent in that case that historically, and under the Supreme Court's own overwhelming precedent, the writ of habeas corpus had never extended outside of sovereign territory (originally, of England, and then after the American Revolution, of the United States). More fundamentally, he points out that "[t]here is simply no support for the Court's assertion that constitutional rights extend to aliens held outside U.S. sovereign territory,"[71] and that the right to habeas corpus is simply one of those inapplicable constitutional rights. Of course, the Court has a clear response to that argument—it concludes that for all practical purposes, Guantanamo Bay *is* "U.S. sovereign territory." But is it? More fundamentally, does it make sense, as a matter of first principles, to extend constitutional limitations to the actions of the U.S. military in Guantanamo Bay, Cuba?

The ultimate difficulty with the Court's decisions in *Boumediene* and its predecessor cases, extending constitutional protection to the detainees at Guantanamo Bay, can be illuminated by this question: Can it fairly be said that executive detention by the U.S. military, outside of the United States proper, of noncitizens captured in combat or related circumstances entirely outside the United States, poses the sorts of threat to American democracy, or to the balance of power between the sovereign People and the U.S. government, that the Bill of Rights and related provisions such as the Suspension Clause were designed to ward off? Posed in this way, the answer cannot be yes so long as this detention power is clearly delineated and limited. It is critical in this regard that the detention facility at Guantanamo Bay is strictly limited to noncitizens, captured outside the United States (in sharp contrast to the earlier enemy combatant cases we discussed). As a consequence, it is hard to see how the continuing existence of the Gitmo facility in any way threatens fundamental principles of popular sovereignty, or grants the government coercive power over the People of the United States. Moreover, as long as the Gitmo detentions are clearly distinguished from detention of citizens, or of noncitizens captured within the United States, the existence of this sort of executive detention does not appear to create any powers

---

71. *Id.* at 2302 (Scalia, J., dissenting).

or precedents that might in the future be used domestically against the People. In short, morally and politically troubling as the existence of the Guantanamo Bay detention facility is, the use of executive power represented by Gitmo simply does not raise the sorts of concerns about power and political sovereignty that drive our constitutional structure. As such, the Supreme Court's decisions extending the shield of the Constitution to detainees at Guantanamo Bay appear to be based on a flawed understanding of our constitutional structure.

The broader lesson from the Guantanamo Bay saga is that the Constitution and the courts do not provide a solution to every political and moral dilemma in American life. As noted earlier, the Constitution is an enabling document as well as a restricting one, and in particular, the Constitution is designed to enable popular control over the People's government. With the election of Barack Obama as president in November 2008, the problem of Guantanamo Bay might finally have found a political solution, given that during the presidential campaign President Obama publicly committed to closing the Gitmo facility[72] and soon after taking office issued an Executive Order requiring the closure of Gitmo within one year.[73] On the other hand, President Obama has subsequently suggested that he intends to continue to hold some of the Guantanamo detainees without trial, albeit not at Gitmo—a suggestion that has triggered sharp criticism of the administration by civil libertarians—and as of mid-2011, Gitmo continues to be open.[74] However this political dispute is resolved, the truth is that for the Guantanamo detainees, constitutional rights are probably a myth—it should be noted that despite their judicial victories, as of the end of 2008 not a single Gitmo detainee had been released by judicial order—but the American political process may well turn out to be their best hope of freedom. And so it might be for the rest of us as well.

---

72. Peter Finn, *Guantanamo Closure Called Obama Priority*, Washington Post A01, Nov. 12, 2008, *available at* http://www.washingtonpost.com/wp-dyn/content/story/2008/11/12/ST2008111200035.html.

73. *See Executive Order—Review and Disposition of Individuals Detained at the Guantanamo Bay Naval Base and Closure of Detention Facilities* (June 22, 2009), *available at* http://www.whitehouse.gov/the_press_office/ClosureOfGuantanamoDetentionFacilities/.

74. Warren Richey, *Obama: Bring Guantanamo Detainees to U.S., Detain Some Indefinitely*, Christian Science Monitor (May 21, 2009), *available at* http://www.csmonitor.com/2009/0521/p02s07-usgn.html.

INDEX

CPSIA information can be obtained
at www.ICGtesting.com
Printed in the USA
BVOW03s0318141216

470756BV00002B/10/P